Al-Suyūṭī, a Polymath of the Mamlūk Period

Islamic History and Civilization

STUDIES AND TEXT

VOLUME 138

The titles published in this series are listed at *brill.com/ihc*

Al-Suyūṭī, a Polymath of the Mamlūk Period

Proceedings of the themed day of the First Conference of the School of Mamlūk Studies (Ca' Foscari University, Venice, June 23, 2014)

Edited by

Antonella Ghersetti

BRILL

LEIDEN | BOSTON

Cover illustration: Interior of the Mosque of Shakhoun (Shaikhun), Cairo. From: David Samuel Margoliouth, *Cairo, Jerusalem, & Damascus: three chief cities of the Egyptian Sultans. With illus. in colour by W.S.S. Tyrwhitt, and additional plates by Reginald Barratt*, Chatto and Windus: London, 1907, p. 98.

Library of Congress Cataloging-in-Publication Data

Names: Conference of the School of Mamlūk Studies (1st : 2014 : Venice, Italy) | Ghersetti, Antonella, editor.
Title: Al-Suyūṭī, a polymath of the Mamlūk period : proceedings of the themed day of the First Conference of the School of Mamlūk Studies (Ca' Foscari University, Venice, June 23, 2014) / edited by Antonella Ghersetti.
Other titles: Islamic history and civilization ; v. 138.
Description: Leiden ; Boston : Brill, 2016. | Series: Islamic history and civilization, volume 138 | Includes index.
Identifiers: LCCN 2016036887 (print) | LCCN 2016042120 (ebook) | ISBN 9789004334502 (hardback : alk. paper) | ISBN 9789004334526 (E-book)
Subjects: LCSH: Suyūṭī, 1445–1505. | Mamelukes—History. | Egypt—History—1250–1517.
Classification: LCC PJ7760.S89 Z59 2016 (print) | LCC PJ7760.S89 (ebook) | DDC 892.7/84—dc23
LC record available at https://lccn.loc.gov/2016036887

Typeface for the Latin, Greek, and Cyrillic scripts: "Brill". See and download: brill.com/brill-typeface.

ISSN 0929-2403
ISBN 978-90-04-33450-2 (hardback)
ISBN 978-90-04-33452-6 (e-book)

This book is printed on acid-free paper and produced in a sustainable manner.

Contents

Notes on Contributors VII

Introduction 1
Antonella Ghersetti

1 Al-Suyūṭī as a Sufi 8
Éric Geoffroy

2 Al-Suyūṭī, the Intolerant Ecumenist: Law and Theology in *Taʾyīd al-ḥaqīqa al-ʿaliyya wa-tashyīd al-ṭarīqah al-Shādhiliyya* 15
Aaron Spevack

3 Al-Suyūṭī and Problems of the *waqf* 47
Takao Ito

4 *Bidʿa* or *sunna*: The *ṭaylasān* as a Contested Garment in the Mamlūk Period (Discussions between al-Suyūṭī and Others) 64
Judith Kindinger

5 Al-Suyūṭī's Stance Toward Worldly Power: A Reexamination Based on Unpublished and Understudied Sources 81
Christian Mauder

6 Casting the Caliph in a Cosmic Role: Examining al-Suyūṭī's Historical Vision 98
Mustafa Banister

7 Preservation through Elaboration: The Historicisation of the Abyssinians in al-Suyūṭī's *Rafʿ shaʾn al-Ḥubshān* 118
Christopher D. Bahl

8 Evidence of Self-editing in al-Suyūṭī's *Taḥbīr* and *Itqān*: A Comparison of his Chapters on *Asbāb al-nuzūl* 143
S.R. Burge

9 "Usefulness without Toil": Al-Suyūṭī and the Art of Concise *ḥadīth* Commentary 182
Joel Blecher

10 History, Comparativism, and Morphology: Al-Suyūṭī and Modern Historical Linguistics 201
Francesco Grande

11 Al-Suyūṭī and Erotic Literature 227
Jaakko Hämeen-Anttila

12 Revisiting Love and Coquetry in Medieval Arabic Islam: Al-Suyūṭī's Perspective 241
Daniela Rodica Firanescu

Index of Names 261
Index of Titles 268

Notes on Contributors

Christopher D. Bahl
is a PhD candidate in the History Department of the School of Oriental and African Studies (SOAS), University of London. He has MAs from the University of Heidelberg and from SOAS.

Mustafa Banister
Ph.D. (Toronto, 2015) is a research fellow at the Annemarie Schimmel Kolleg (University of Bonn). He has published articles on Mamlūk Cairo and is preparing a monograph on the ʿAbbasid Caliphate of Cairo.

Joel Blecher
Ph.D. (Princeton, 2013) is Assistant Professor of History at the George Washington University. He has published in *JNES*, *Oriens*, and is completing a book titled *In the Shade of the Hadith: Islam and the Politics of Interpretation across a Millennium*.

S.R. Burge
Ph.D. (Edinburgh, 2009) is Senior Research Associate at the Institute of Ismaili Studies, London. He has published articles on al-Suyūṭī and his works, including a monograph, *Angels in Islam: Jalāl al-Dīn al-Suyūṭī's* al-Habāʾik fī akhbār al-malāʾik (Routledge, 2012).

Daniela Rodica Firanescu
Ph.D. (Bucharest, 1997) is Assistant Professor of Arabic Studies at Dalhousie University (Halifax, Canada). She has published articles on Arabic linguistics, literature and cultural studies, including *Exclamation in Modern Literary Arabic—a Pragmatic Perspective* (Bucharest, 2003).

Éric Geoffroy
Ph.D. (1993) is an Expert in Islam and Professor in Islamic Studies in the Department of Arabic and Islamic studies at the University of Strasbourg. His last book is entitled *Un éblouissement sans fin – la poésie dans le soufisme* (Seuil, 2014).

Francesco Grande
Ph.D. (Pisa, 2011) is a Researcher in Arabic Language and Literature at Università Ca' Foscari of Venice. He has published articles on Arab(ic) linguistics and *Copulae in Arabic Noun Phrase: A Unified Analysis of Arabic Adnominal Markers* (Brill, 2013).

Jaakko Hämeen-Anttila
Ph.D. (Helsinki, 1994) is Iraq Professor of Arabic and Islamic Studies at the University of Edinburgh. He has published extensively on Classical Arabic literature.

Takao Ito
Ph.D. (Munich, 2007) is Associate Professor in the Graduate School of Humanities at Kobe University, Japan. His recent publications include "Al-Maqrīzī's Biography of Tīmūr", *Arabica* 62 (2015).

Judith Kindinger
Ph.D. candidate (Vrije Universiteit Amsterdam); Master in Political Studies and Near and Middle Eastern Studies (Heidelberg). She made contributions to the Conflict Barometer (2006, 2007, 2008, 2009, Heidelberg Institute for International Conflict Research), focussing on Sub-Sahara Africa.

Christian Mauder
is a PhD student at the Institute of Arabic and Islamic Studies of the University of Göttingen. He has published several studies on the intellectual, cultural and religious history of Mamlūk and Ottoman Egypt, including the monograph *Gelehrte Krieger* (Hildesheim, 2012).

Aaron Spevack
Ph.D. (Boston, 2008) is Assistant Professor of Religion (Islam) at Colgate University. He has published monographs and articles on Islamic Law, Theology, Logic, and Sufism, including *The Archetypal Sunni Scholar: Law, Theology, and Mysticism in the Synthesis of al-Bajuri* (SUNY, 2014).

Introduction

Antonella Ghersetti

This volume is a collection of several of the papers presented during the first themed day of the First Conference of the School of Mamlūk Studies (held at Ca' Foscari University, Venice, from June 23 to June 25, 2014), devoted to Jalāl al-Dīn al-Suyūṭī (d. 911/1505). The organizers of this First Conference—Marlis Saleh, Frédéric Bauden, and myself—thought it appropriate to devote the themed day of the conference to this Egyptian polymath who is probably the best representative of encyclopaedism, a genre that was practiced extensively in his time. The wide gamut of disciplines he dealt with was the ideal nucleus around which to gather specialists in different fields who could contribute to a better knowledge of his intellectual profile and, more generally, to a deeper understanding of the cultural and academic life of the last period of the Mamlūk empire.

Jalāl al-Dīn al-Suyūṭī, the most productive author of the pre-modern Islamic world and no doubt "the most controversial figure of his time,"[1] had a complex personality: arrogant, presumptuous, and polemic, he was involved in controversies of various kinds with his colleagues and with the political authorities of his time as well. His enemies were numerous, and a large number of his contemporaries displayed a remarkable and overt hostility against him. The most caustic among them, al-Sakhāwī, did not refrain from contesting his eminence as a scholar and from denigrating him and accusing him of plagiarism. Yet these tense relations with his colleagues, his overt criticism of the political authorities and, generally speaking, his unpleasant character conflicted not only with the affection showed by his pupils but also with "the aura of godliness"[2] that he enjoyed during his life; this makes his personality still more intriguing. The most visible feature of his scholarly profile is perhaps his eclecticism; indeed, he was a multifaceted intellectual and, though he declared *fiqh, ḥadīth*, and grammar to be his preferred sciences, the titles of his bibliography range from law to theology, from linguistics to history, including medicine and geography. His wide-ranging scholarly output is no doubt a result of his belief that the level of scholarship had declined, even decayed. He felt that it was his mission to preserve the rich cultural heritage of the past, and knowledge in general, from widespread ignorance and from the decline in the learning

1 Sartain, *Biography* 72.

2 Geoffroy, al-Suyūṭī 914.

 | DOI 10.1163/9789004334526_002

standards of his time. But this belief did not cause him to retreat into the works of earlier scholars. He was first and foremost a man of the times. As such, he responded to his opponents—many of his works were written as a response to them, thus testifying to his deep involvement in debates and disputes of a political or scientific character. He was also able to recognize public demand, both that of his colleagues, the *ʿulamāʾ*, and that of readers at large, and was ready to respond to it by producing rigorous but handy commentaries, treatises, or reference works.

Considered for a long time an author devoid of any originality and a "simple" compiler (an accusation which the bitter remarks of al-Sakhāwī played a part in), he was in fact an excellent teacher and a rigorous scholar. He had a meticulous and accurate working method, which manifested itself in the methodical and faithful citation of his sources and also resulted, as some essays in this volume demonstrate, in a careful and well thought out process of self-editing.

Six decades ago E.M. Sartain called for a reassessment of al-Suyūṭī's production by specialists in the disciplines he dealt with, and for a more nuanced position on the issue of his lack of originality.[3] In recent times and in a certain sense in response to her invitation, scholars have progressively changed their attitudes and started to appreciate al-Suyūṭī's scrupulousness, honesty, and also originality. E.M. Sartain's book, along with more recent contributions by Éric Geoffroy, Marlis Saleh, and Aaron Spevack are more than sufficient to introduce al-Suyūṭī's life and bibliography;[4] the themed day of the conference devoted to al-Suyūṭī was thus specially conceived to throw new light on specific aspects of his scholarly output, to stimulate a careful reassessment of his polymorphic, intriguing (perhaps provoking) intellectual profile, and to formulate a fresh appraisal of his scholarly achievements and his contribution to the intellectual life of the Mamlūk period. Readers will find in the present volume fresh insights into aspects already investigated, like his stance towards power, as well as original remarks and new insights into issues until now poorly investigated or overlooked in scholarly literature, like al-Suyūṭī's contribution to the genre of *ḥadīth* commentary or erotica. Commonly held opinions on al-Suyūṭī's intellectual profile and working method are also questioned; some studies in this volume call for a more nuanced evaluation of al-Suyūṭī's scholarly production, including his methods of quoting previous works (or even his own works) and his original and personal approach to linguistic questions. Last but not least, al-Suyūṭī's impact on modern religious discourse is also

3 Sartain, *Biography* 114–5.
4 See the bibliography at the end of this introduction.

represented in this volume, thus introducing new perspectives on the impact of historical heritage on contemporaneity.

Éric Geoffroy and Aaron Spevack's essays delve into aspects of al-Suyūṭī's thought that are, in different degrees, relevant to his reception and impact on modern and contemporary Islam and offer thought-provoking remarks on this. Geoffroy, taking al-Suyūṭī as the most prominent example of a trend of ninth/fifteenth-century Muslim scholars, deals with the multifaceted concept of his Sufi affiliation, including his strong defense of *taṣawwuf*, and carefully investigates al-Suyūṭī's approach to Sufism including the central and most challenging question of whether al-Suyūṭī tasted mystical experiences. Still on the topic of Sufism, *Taʾyīd al-ḥaqīqa al-ʿaliyya wa-tashyīd al-ṭarīqa al-Shādhiliyya* constitutes the core of Spevack's study. The backbone of this essay addresses the assumption that al-Suyūṭī's intellectual profile challenges affiliations and definitions and further examines his "unique perspective" on many issues. *Taʾyīd al-ḥaqīqa*, "a personal manifesto on Sufism," is first put into the context of other works of al-Suyūṭī. Spevack then thoroughly investigates al-Suyūṭī's controversial positions, notably the necessity of independent legal reasoning and the interconnections between Sufism and legal reasoning. Spevack's essay demonstrates al-Suyūṭī's original stand in bridging the gap between Sufis' and jurists' fields of action, in order to reconcile traditionist tendencies with rational theology and logic.

Takao Ito and Judith Kindinger address al-Suyūṭī's approach to legal matters involving practical aspects. Ito investigates al-Suyūṭī's approach to problems of *waqf* (endowment), a matter until now not fully investigated. His essay, which takes into account al-Suyūṭī's polemical attitude towards his colleagues and the relevant disputes concerning endowments, is based on al-Suyūṭī's theoretical positions and practical acquaintance with these matters, which derive from his positions as *shaykh* at a *turba* and a *khānqāh* and as a teacher of law. Three groups of questions are examined through the lens of his collection of *fatwā*s (entitled *al-Ḥāwī lil-fatāwī*): administration, beneficiary rights, and miscellaneous questions. Theory and practice are the two pillars of this careful investigation into al-Suyūṭī's pragmatic approach to *waqf*s. Ito demonstrates that al-Suyūṭī, although consistent in his ideas, did not deny the complexity of reality; he achieved a good balance between theory and practice. Kindinger's study tackles the symbolic value of dress through the lens of a legal debate, notably the opposition between innovation (*bidʿa*) and customary practice (*sunna*). The use of the *ṭaylasān* aroused hot debates, as attested by al-Suyūṭī's apologia, *al-Aḥadīth al-ḥisān fī faḍl al-ṭaylasān*, which Kindinger thoroughly scrutinized. Her investigation of the *ṭaylasān* explores its meanings as a marker of knowledge and a site for transcendence, but also as a garment that encroaches on gender boundaries and religious limitations. Kindinger demonstrates the value of clothing as a producer of communal identities; she thus emphasizes that the treatment of specific garments can become an arena to debate more sensitive matters.

Al-Suyūṭī's opinions on politics and history are at the core of the studies of Christian Mauder and Mustafa Banister. Mauder offers an in-depth analysis of some works concerning the relative positions of the sultan and the caliph: *Mā rawāhu l-asāṭīn fī ʿadam al-majīʾ ilā l-salāṭīn, al-Risāla al-sulṭāniyya*, and *al-Aḥādīth al-munīfa fī faḍl al-salṭana al-sharīfa*. Mauder investigates the treatises' attribution, their inter-relationship and the reasons driving their composition, in order to gain a better insight into al-Suyūṭī's political thought and into the relationship between his personal experiences with the rulers and his writings. Mauder's careful reading of the three works shows that, by means of an attentive selection of *ḥadīth*s, al-Suyūṭī critiques the rulers' wrongdoings and gives voice to his difficult relationships with the Mamlūk rulers. Banister focuses on al-Suyūṭī's views on history, and also hints at the existence of hot debates on the balance of power and the relationship between the sultanate and caliphate. He thoroughly explored *Ḥusn al-muḥāḍara* and *Taʾrīkh al-khulafāʾ* in order to investigate al-Suyūṭī's position on the caliphate and the way he depicts its superiority. His perusal of the texts shows that al-Suyūṭī's argument is based on the pivotal notion that ʿAbbasid caliphs of Cairo influenced the corporeal world and were thus essential to the functioning of the natural world. The autobiographical grounds of such a powerful vision of the caliphate are also examined and identified not only with careerism and opportunism, but also in terms of the expression of the mood of the people of that time.

Through literary analysis, Christopher Bahl concentrates on the historical thought of al-Suyūṭī, thus emphasizing the significance of literary texts for historical research. The article, focused on *Rafʿ shaʾn al-Ḥubshān*, delves into the tension between two perhaps divergent, but in practice combined, approaches to received texts: preservation and elaboration. By means of a thorough textual analysis dealing with the diverse techniques of compilation (e.g., segmentation, repetition, contrastive succession) operating in the treatise, Bahl presents some features of al-Suyūṭī's working method. Contrasting al-Suyūṭī's work with those of his predecessors on the same subject, the investigation shows how al-Suyūṭī creates a true historicisation of the Abyssinians by means of a historically rooted, subaltern Abyssinian identity through his techniques of textual compilation. The following study by Stephen Burge, an in-depth exploration of the principle of compilation, is a valuable contribution to our understanding of al-Suyūṭī's working method. *Al-Itqān fī ʿulūm al-Qurʾān*, at the core of Burge's essay, engages with other works al-Suyūṭī incorporated into it and is compared with *al-Taḥbīr fī ʿilm al-tafsīr*, an earlier treatise on the same subject. This inquiry calls for a more nuanced evaluation of the accusations of plagiarism against al-Suyūṭī by his contemporaries and modern scholars. The meticulous comparison of some passages from the works highlights al-Suyūṭī's method of reworking, rewriting, and revising his own (and others') materials; it thus assesses the extent to which al-Suyūṭī reworked his first treatise in order to improve and deepen it. This research, revolving around the process of self-editing, also follows the path of recent works that aim at investigating and elucidating the working methods of scholars of the pre-modern Muslim world.

Joel Blecher also chooses a textual approach to deal with a relatively overlooked topic: the practice of *ḥadīth* commentary. The genre of concise *ḥadīth* commentary is in fact taken as a case study of knowledge as a social practice, in the vein of Michael Chamberlain's seminal work,[5] thus taking into account the way authors work along with their audiences' expectations and habits. The essay explores al-Suyūṭī's approach to concise commentary in relation to his antecedents and models, like al-Zarkashī, and analyzes the way he preserves and curtails the tradition he inherited. Blecher comments on the techniques of the art of *ḥadīth* commentary during al-Suyūṭī's time and offers insights into al-Suyūṭī's contribution to it and his impact on the following generations as well. He demonstrates that, by also practicing what is called "strategic omissions," al-Suyūṭī sought a balance between practical value and exegetical succinctness. The results of this investigation hint that al-Suyūṭī's success was not determined by originality or the encyclopedic excess extensively practiced in his time, but by his balance of usefulness and conciseness conceived for an audience seeking "user-friendly" *ḥadīth* commentaries.

A variety of al-Suyūṭī's wide-ranging scholarly output are explored in the following essays, which examine fields of study not immediately associated to his renown as a scholar: linguistics and erotology. Francesco Grande's essay focuses on al-Suyūṭī's linguistic thought as expressed in his linguistic encyclopedia, *al-Muzhir fī ʿulūm al-lugha wa-anwāʿihā*. Grande's is a fortunate choice given that al-Suyūṭī declared himself especially fond of philology and grammar and that many of what he considered his most original works are in these fields. Concentrating on a case study of a morphological nature, Grande uses three conceptual elements (history, comparativism, and morphology) to demonstrate that al-Suyūṭī adopted a method of linguistic analysis similar to that of modern historical linguistics, thus Grande questions the generally held conviction that Arab grammarians have an ahistorical attitude. Through the

5 Chamberlain, *Knowledge*.

re-appraisal of al-Suyūṭī's diachronic and comparative perspective on language his critical approach is thus better recognized.

The essays of Firanescu and Hämeen-Anttila, both revolving around al-Suyūṭī's erotica books, nicely complement each other. Jaakko Hämeen-Anttila surveys the somehow indefinite boundaries of the notion of "erotica" and gives an overview of the titles pertaining to this genre that al-Suyūṭī himself lists in his autobiography. An overall presentation of these works, including their mutual relationship and relative chronology, precedes the more detailed presentation of three titles (*al-Wishāḥ fī fawāʾid al-nikāḥ, Nawādir al-ayk fī maʿrifat al-nayk*, and *Shaqāʾiq al-utrunj fī raqāʾiq al-ghunj*) which are probably a series of short treatises originating from a larger work he drafted as a comprehensive encyclopedia, but did not finalize. Questioning the reasons driving al-Suyūṭī to compose erotica, Hämeen-Anttila's essay stresses that, although he was a polymath and a religious scholar, al-Suyūṭī wrote freely on erotic topics, without any censure of obscene contents. The same absence of censure and freedom of approach is also evident in the following essay, by Daniela Rodica Firanescu, which focuses especially on *Shaqāʾiq al-utrunj*, described as an "example of transgression of the religious, ethical, and legal treatment of *nikāḥ*." The work in fact privileges a "worldly" approach to sexuality instead of the usual, more traditional, treatments. Taking as a case study the treatment of erotic vocalization (*ghunj*) in all its varieties, Firanescu's essay offers an in-depth study of the concept of marriage etiquette (*adab al-nikāḥ*). The author's sensitive understanding of the semantic implications of the texts constitutes a valuable tool for comprehending meanings and the intents of the work. Her contribution effectively investigates the way literary discourse creates models of ideal feminine behavior and demonstrates how such authoritative texts contribute to our understanding of the "culture of gender" in the Mamlūk period.

Our hope, as organizers of the First Conference of the School of Mamlūk Studies, and my personal hope as editor of this volume, is that the essays published herein constitute a meaningful contribution to a reassessment of the scholarly profile of this controversial but fascinating polymath and intellectual who uniquely interpreted and represented the cultural trends and political tensions of the last stage of the Mamlūk period.

As the local organizer of the First Conference of the School of Mamlūk Studies, I wish to thank all those who took part in what was the first of a—hopefully long—series of conferences; in particular I express my warmest gratitude to all the colleagues who accepted the invitation to animate the themed day on al-Suyūṭī. Their enthusiastic response made this first day a vivid, thought provoking, and stimulating opportunity for discussion and scientific enrichment, of which this volume will be a worthy testimony. My appreciation is also due to those who sent their papers for publication and patiently answered my many queries concerning translations, transliterations, or bibliographical details.

Bibliography

Chamberlain, M., *Knowledge and social practice in medieval Damascus 1190–1350*, Cambridge 1994.

Geoffroy, É., al-Suyūṭī, in *EI*², ix, 913–6.

Irwin, R., al-Suyūṭī (849–911/1445–1505), in J.S. Meisami and P. Starkey (eds.), *EAL*, ii, London 1998.

Saleh, M.J., Al-Suyūṭī and his works: Their place in Islamic scholarship from Mamluk times to the present, in *MSR* 5 (2001), 73–89.

Sartain, E.M., *Jalāl al-dīn al-Suyūṭī*. i: *Biography and background*, University of Cambridge Oriental Publications 23, Cambridge 1975.

Spevack, A., Jalāl al-Dīn al-Suyūṭī, in J.E. Lowry and D.J. Stewart (eds.), *Essays in Arabic literary biography*, ii (Mîzân. Studien zur Literatur in der islamischen Welt 17: Essays in Arabic literary biography), Wiesbaden 2009, 386–409.

CHAPTER 1

Al-Suyūṭī as a Sufi

Éric Geoffroy

In al-Suyūṭī's times, in the 9th/15th century, the Muslim scholar steeped in Sufism had become a somewhat familiar figure. Drawing from the great tradition of al-Junayd and al-Ghazālī, he merged within himself exoteric and esoteric sciences, argumentative approach (*al-istidlāl wa-l-burhān*), and intuitive discipline (*al-kashf wa-l-ʿiyān*). The path had already been prepared by a large number of *ʿulamāʾ* mostly following the Ashʿarī creed and belonging to the Shāfiʿī school of law. They constantly used the scholarly status they earned in various Islamic sciences in order to stress the superiority of spiritual knowledge and Sufism.[1]

Jalāl al-Dīn al-Suyūṭī[2] was undoubtedly the most prominent scholar involved in *taṣawwuf* of the Mamlūk era, and he acted as a pioneer in this field. Suyūṭī was so in the sense that he was famous as a *ʿālim* and a *muftī* in his lifetime, from India to Takrūr (West Africa), which was not the case of Ibn Ḥajar or Ibn Taymiyya for instance, and he was the first scholar to assume so clearly the defense of Sufism. However, inasmuch as is possible, we need to consider whether al-Suyūṭī did in fact taste mystical experiences or whether he merely claimed to have done so, for we know that he claimed his superiority in many disciplines.

1 The Nature of the Commitment of al-Suyūṭī to Sufism

To al-Suyūṭī, the discipline of *ḥadīth* represents "the noblest of sciences,"[3] because it is related to the prophetic model, which for him is the only way to reach God. Although he worked and wrote extensively in the formal field of *ʿilm al-ḥadīth*, he stressed the fact that this knowledge should not be confined to books but rather that it should be experienced with presence of heart and brought to life from the inside. Little wonder, then, that he should have claimed to have seen the Prophet more than seventy times whilst in a waking state

1 See Geoffroy, *Soufisme* 89–98.
2 On him, see Geoffroy, al-Suyūṭī and Spevack, *al-Suyūṭī*.
3 Al-Suyūṭī, *Ḥusn* i, 155.

 | DOI 10.1163/9789004334526_003

(*fī l-yaqaẓa*).[4] Such visions (*ru'yā*) of the Prophet lend great charisma in Sufism. In one of those visions the Prophet came to visit him in his house and called him "*shaykh al-sunna*."[5] Subsequently al-Suyūṭī explained that, during a vision, one may be directly informed by the Prophet about the validity of a *ḥadīth*.[6] Thus al-Suyūṭī succeeded in gaining a personal and mystical relation with the spiritual entity of the Prophet. It is not surprising, then, that he should have attached importance to the complementarity between the esoteric and exoteric aspects of the Prophet, as he did in a work with an explicit title: *al-Bāhir fī ḥukm al-nabī bi-l-bāṭin wa-l-ẓāhir* (The Brilliance of the Prophet's Judgment on Exoteric and Esoteric Matters). So, as in other fields of his scientific involvement, al-Suyūṭī was a profoundly traditionalist Sunni scholar: he was following the prophetic model not only outwardly, but also at a deep inward level.

2 His Initiatory Affiliations

At the time of al-Suyūṭī several modalities of initiatory affiliation were accepted in the Sufi path. The most common and less demanding was that of *tabarruk*, in which the seeker was given the Sufi "mantle" (*khirqa*) through which he received a spiritual impulse (*baraka*) from a *shaykh*. This impulse was transmitted through a chain of *shaykh*s (the *silsila*) leading back to the Prophet, who is held to be the originator of all mystic teaching. Al-Suyūṭī informs us that he was clothed in the *khirqa* by Ibn Imām al-Kāmiliyya in 869/1465 who gave him a licence (*ijāza*) to bestow the *khirqa* on whomever he wished.[7] The chains of authority (*isnād*) of this investiture come mainly from the Aḥmadiyya, Qādiriyya, and Suhrawardiyya branches.[8]

These multiple affiliations, as common as they were, could have variable impact from an initiatory perspective, and as such never replaced the personal relationship between a Sufi master and his disciple.[9] So one might have received a number of *khirqa* (sometimes over thirty) but could only have a *shaykh* of *tarbiya* at a single time. This was the case for al-Suyūṭī: his *shaykh* was Muḥammad al-Maghribī (d. 910/1504), a prominent Shādhilī master in

4 Al-Shaʿrānī, *Ṭabaqāt* 29.

5 Ibid. 28–29.

6 Al-Suyūṭī, *Taḥdhīr* 50.

7 Al-Suyūṭī, *Khiraq*.

8 Sartain, *Biography* 34; Geoffroy, *Soufisme* 516.

9 For the case of al-Suyūṭī see Geoffroy, *Soufisme* 202.

Cairo at the time.[10] This *shaykh* did not leave any writings but he is reported to have given genuine spiritual teaching, influenced by Ibn al-ʿArabī's *waḥdat al-wujūd* ("Unity of Being"). The choice of the Shādhilī path did obviously not come by chance. In this *ṭarīqa*, which claims to inherit the spiritual method of *imām* al-Junayd of Baghdad, al-Suyūṭī found a balance between the external Law and the inner Way. He extolled the virtues of the Shādhilī way in an important work: *Taʾyīd al-ḥaqīqa al-ʿaliyya wa-tashyīd al-ṭarīqa al-Shādhiliyya* (The upholding of the lofty Reality and the buttressing of the Shādhilī path).[11] Al-Suyūṭī himself acted as a Sufi master with several followers.[12] His main disciple, who served him for forty years, was called ʿAbd al-Qādir al-Shādhilī.

3 Al-Suyūṭī as a Saint?

The question arises as to whether a Sufi scholar (*al-ʿālim al-ṣūfī*) could claim sanctity (*walāya*) in the same way as "professional" Sufi masters, who were appointed by a former master and were given the task of guiding people to spiritual realization (*al-taḥqīq*). According to the standards of sanctity in those times, we have no reason to doubt the sanctity of al-Suyūṭī. One of the major manifestations of sanctity was of course the gift of miracles (*karāmāt*). Several instances are related in sources about al-Suyūṭī.[13] For instance, he was granted a supernatural favor not granted other scholars: "folding the earth" (*ṭayy al-arḍ*). This was the ability of crossing large distances in a very short space of time. His servant ʿAbd al-Qādir al-Shādhilī related in detail to the well-known Sufi ʿAbd al-Wahhāb al-Shaʿrānī how al-Suyūṭī took him once from Cairo to Mecca to pray the afternoon prayer in such a miraculous manner.[14] Among the supernatural favors attributed to al-Suyūṭī, one may also quote his predictions on the first Ottoman period.[15]

10 On him ibid., index.

11 Two editions: Cairo 1934, and Beyrut 2006.

12 Geoffroy, *Soufisme* 202.

13 Sartain, *Biography* 98–100; Geoffroy, *Soufisme* 171.

14 Al-Shaʿrānī, *Ṭabaqāt* 30–1; Geoffroy, *Soufisme* 296.

15 For instance, he would have predicted one year before his death (in 910 H.) the conquest of Egypt by Selim the Ottoman in the right year: 923/1517. Some other predictions are not very clear, as some "destructions" (earthquakes?) of Cairo in 933 at first, then in 957, and a stronger one, in 967. The commentators who have lived the first two events confirm them. Ibn Iyās, *Badāʾiʿ* v, 218; al-Shaʿrānī, *Ṭabaqāt* 30–2.

4 A Pioneer in the Defense of Sufism

Al-Suyūṭī is of course especially famous for presenting a strong and well-articulated defense for *taṣawwuf.* His personal commitment to the case led him to take advantage of his fame as a great *ʿālim* to spearhead a clear-sighted defense of Sufism and its masters, and to promote an enlightened Sunnism, experiencing the inner dimension of Muḥammad.

In his aforementioned *Taʾyīd al-ḥaqīqa al-ʿaliyya wa-tashyīd al-ṭarīqa al-Shādhiliyya*, he praises the orthodoxy of this Sufi path, which he ascribes to the sober method of al-Junayd.[16] In this book, he shows his profoundly deep grounding in Islamic scholarship, which allows him to juggle with Islamic and Sufi doctrines. Through a careful process of integration and exclusion, he manages to present a consistent and homogeneous image of *taṣawwuf.* He always justifies his statements with scriptural sources (Quran, *ḥadīth qudsī, ḥadīth nabawī*) in order to decisively counter attacks from critics of Sufism. For instance, he justifies Ibn al-ʿArabī's personality and doctrine of *waḥdat al-wujūd*, but in the same time lets someone else whom he quotes disapprove of the "absolute Unicity" (*al-waḥda al-muṭlaqa*) of Ibn Sabʿīn (who is, in al-Suyūṭī's eyes, a philosopher much more than a Sufi). Moreover, he uses evidence to distance genuine Sufism from any link with substantial union with God (*ittiḥād*) and incarnationism (*ḥulūl*). Al-Suyūṭī also gives credit to the gnostics (*ʿulamāʾ al-bāṭin*) and regards exoteric scholars (*ʿulamāʾ al-ẓāhir*) as generally being deficient.[17]

The scholar Burhān al-Dīn al-Biqāʿī was involved in a *fitna* in 864/1459 when he attacked Ibn al-ʿArabī in a tract entitled *Tanbīh al-ghabī ilā takfīr Ibn ʿArabī* (Warning to the Dolt that Ibn al-ʿArabī is an Apostate). Scholars opposed him in a variety of ways, but due to his eminence, only al-Suyūṭī managed to counter him in a tract entitled *Tanbīh al-ghabī bi tabriʾat Ibn ʿArabī* (Warning to the Dolt that Ibn ʿArabī is innocent [of these accusations]). In this reply al-Suyūṭī adopts a very nuanced position: he considers Ibn al-ʿArabī to be a very great saint, but he states that the reading of his writings should be forbidden to incompetent people and disciples ignorant of Sufi terminology.[18]

For posterity, however, it is above all in his legal pronouncements or advice (*fatwā*) that al-Suyūṭī appears as an advocate of Sufism: he was the first Muslim

16 Al-Suyūṭī, *Taʾyīd* 68–9. [Editor's note] On this work see Aaron Spevack, Al-Suyūṭī, the intolerant ecumenist, (15–46).

17 Ibid. 23.

18 See also Geoffroy, *Soufisme* 461.

scholar to have given formal consideration to the discipline of *taṣawwuf* within the field of *fatwā* formulation.[19] In his collection *al-Ḥāwī lil-fatāwī*, he delivers a great variety of statements on spiritual matters. For instance, he gives preeminence to mystical science over legal science, bestows inspiration (*ilhām*) and spiritual unveiling (*kashf*) a legal status: both have to be considered as "juridical proofs" as long as they do not run counter to a recognized point of law. He links unveiling and spiritual vision (*ruʾyā*) to the process of Revelation (*waḥī*) and asserts the possibility of seeing the Prophet and angels, stating that many of his contemporaries denied the reality of vision because they neglected Revelation and the Muḥammadian model (the *sunna*) and preferred to focus on rational and philosophical sciences. He sees the highest form of worship in the invocation of God (*dhikr*) and shows that one must interpret the sayings of the Sufis and not stop at their superficial meaning: *taʾwīl* applies to Sufi words as well as to Quranic verses. He maintains also that saints have the gift of ubiquity, gives scriptural grounds for the initiatory hierarchy of the saints, and so on.

He indeed opened the way for later *ʿulamāʾ* to write Sufi *fatwā*s, up to our times. Ibn Ḥajar al-Haytamī (d. 974/1567) explicitly acknowledged his influence, and he still stressed the position dedicated to Sufism in his own *fatwa*s.[20] The same may be said about Shihāb al-Dīn al-Ramlī (d. 957/1550) and Najm al-Dīn al-Ghayṭī (d. 983/1575). Some Sufi scholars of the 20th century followed in the wake of al-Suyūṭī. Shaykh al-Azhar ʿAbd al-Ḥalīm Maḥmūd (d. 1978), for instance, issued 43 *fatwa*s shedding some light on the most important aspects of Sufism.[21] More recently, ʿAlī Jumuʿa, a previous grand *muftī* of Egypt, published a collection of one hundred *fatwa*s,[22] many of them dealing with spiritual issues.

Following in the footsteps of *imām* al-Ghazālī, al-Suyūṭī seems to have foreseen the legalistic and literalist sclerosis that was to take hold of the Islamic world, and to lead to modern wahhabism and salafism. This degeneration was already present and nascent in al-Suyūṭī's age and was to give birth to the modern fanaticisms of our times. His *fatwa*s and his writings are astonishingly relevant to us since they defend celebrating the Prophet's birthday (*mawlid*),

19 A Sufi *ʿālim* from Bejaya (current Algeria), al-Wansharīsī (d. 914/1508), did the same in his own collection, but this scholar is much less known than al-Suyūṭī.

20 See his *Fatāwā ḥadīthiyya*.

21 *Fatāwā ʿAbd al-Ḥalīm Maḥmūd* ii, 327–408.

22 *Al-Bayān li-mā yashghal al-adhhān* (The clarification about the questions which worry the mind).

using a rosary (*sibḥa*), or performing invocation aloud (*al-dhikr al-jahr*). Not to mention those who justify the doctrine of the "unity of Being,"[23] or those who state the superiority of inspiration and esoteric knowledge over any formal science, be it profane or religious science.

To al-Suyūṭī, love will always prevail over law, and that is precisely what makes him a Sufi. Someone once asked him whether a believer who does not observe the Law (*ʿāṣī*) could enter Paradise for the sake of his love for the Prophet. His answer was "yes."[24]

Bibliography

Primary Sources

Ibn Iyās, *Badāʾiʿ al-zuhūr wa-waqāʾiʿ al-duhūr*, ed. M. Muṣṭafā, 5 vols. (BI 5a–e), Wiesbaden 1960–75.

al-Shaʿrānī, ʿAbd al-Wahhāb b. Aḥmad, *al-Ṭabaqāt al-ṣughrā*, ed. ʿA. al-Q. A. ʿAṭā, Cairo 1970.

al-Suyūṭī, *Ḥusn al-muḥāḍara fī akhbār Miṣr wa-l-Qāhira*, ed. M.A. al-F. Ibrāhīm, Cairo 1968.

al-Suyūṭī, *al-Ḥāwī lil-fatāwī*, 2 vols., Dār al-Kutub al-ʿIlmiyya 1984.

al-Suyūṭī, *Taʾyīd al-ḥaqīqa al-ʿaliyya wa-tashyīd al-ṭarīqa al-Shādhiliyya*, ed. ʿA.b.M.b. al-Ṣiddīq al-Ghumārī l-Ḥasanī, Cairo 1934, repr. Beyrut 2006.

al-Suyūṭī, *Taḥdhīr al-khawwāṣ min akādhib al-quṣṣāṣ*, ed. M. al-Ṣabbāgh, Beirut [1972].

al-Suyūṭī, *al-Bāhir fī ḥukm al-nabī bi-l-bāṭin wa-l-ẓāhir*, ed. M.Kh. Qīrbāshūghlū wa-qirāʾat ʿA. al-F. Abū Ghuddah, Cairo 1987.

al-Suyūṭī, *Tanbīh al-ghabī bi-takhṭiʾat Ibn ʿArabī*, Cairo 1990.

al-Suyūṭī, *Khiraq al-Suyūṭī*, ms. Damascus 6916.

Secondary Sources

Geoffroy, É., al-Suyūṭī, in *EI*², ix, 913–6.

Geoffroy, É., *Le Soufisme en Égypte et en Syrie sous les derniers Mamelouks et les premiers Ottomans: Orientations spirituelles et enjeux culturels*, Damascus 1995.

Jumuʿa, A., *al-Bayān li-mā yashghal al-adhhān*, Cairo 2005.

Maḥmūd, A., *Fatāwā ʿAbd al-Ḥalīm Maḥmūd*, Cairo 1981, repr. Cairo 2002.

23 Ibn al-ʿArabī is nowadays much better understood and much more extensively studied in the West than in Muslim countries.

24 Al-Suyūṭī, *Ḥāwī* i, 388.

Sartain, E.M., *Jalāl al-dīn al-Suyūṭī*. i: *Biography and background* (University of Cambridge Oriental Publications 23), Cambridge 1975.

Spevack, A., Jalāl al-Dīn al-Suyūṭī, in J.E. Lowry and D.J. Stewart (eds.), *Essays in Arabic literary biography 1350–1850* (Mîzân. Studien zur Literatur in der islamischen Welt 17: Essays in Arabic literary biography), Wiesbaden 2009, 386–409.

CHAPTER 2

Al-Suyūṭī, the Intolerant Ecumenist: Law and Theology in *Ta'yīd al-ḥaqīqa al-ʿaliyya wa-tashyīd al-ṭarīqa al-Shādhiliyya*

Aaron Spevack

1 Introduction

Al-Suyūṭī is an *independent yet affiliated*[1] scholar in the core sciences of law, theology and Sufism, as well as the other sciences of religion, such as Quran, *ḥadīth*, and the linguistic arts, necessary for the study and understanding of the sacred sciences. He also wrote a number of works in more mundane sciences such as belles-lettres and history. His many hundreds of works on a vast variety of different topics—ranging from shorter treatises to multi-volume compendiums[2]—and his sometimes outspoken or controversial views on various subjects establish him as an independent thinker with unique perspectives on a variety of issues.[3]

A broad examination of his works and discussions of various topics have given us a portrayal of al-Suyūṭī as a jurist of the Shāfiʿī school who had reached the highest level possible for a scholar affiliated with the legal school (*madhhab*). Like teachers and contemporaries, he was counted among the followers of the Ashʿarī school of theology, with reservations about rational theology (*kalām*) as it was commonly approached in his time, especially considering what had become a necessary connection between rational theology (*kalām*) and syllogistic logic (*manṭiq*). His Sufism, though rooted in a number of orders, was primarily of the Shādhilī order, in that his spiritual training (*tarbiya*) had been under a Shādhilī master.[4] Al-Suyūṭī was a master of prophetic narrations (*ḥadīth*) who claimed to have memorized all *ḥadīth*s in

1 Shāfiʿī, Ashʿarī, Shādhilī.

2 For a partial, yet lengthy list in English, see Spevack, al-Suyūṭī. For a complete list in Arabic, see Shaybānī and al-Khāzindār, *Dalīl*.

3 I discuss many of these issues related to law, theology, Sufism, and other sciences in several of my previous works. See Spevack, al-Suyūṭī; also Spevack, *Archetypal* and Spevack, Apples.

4 On this see Geoffroy, Al-Suyūṭī as a Sufi, (8–14).

 | DOI 10.1163/9789004334526_004

existence,[5] and an expert in the numerous Quranic sciences, knowledge of which was a condition of independent legal reasoning (*ijtihād*), a rank which al-Suyūṭī claimed for himself.

Centuries after his death, his works and opinions remain standard and oft-quoted in books of Islamic law, theology, Sufism, *ḥadīth*, and Quranic studies, to name a few. While his reception by later scholars was not uncritical and his relationship with many of his contemporaries was heated and often in disagreement, he remained an important and prominent authority for so many, especially within his native Egypt.

Al-Suyūṭī occupies an interesting space in Islamic intellectual history, especially with regard to how contemporary scholars of Islam—whether in the western academy or in Muslim religious scholarly circles—view the boundaries between various groups such as "rationalist" and "traditionalist," Ashʿarī and Atharī, early and later jurisprudential independence (i.e. rank of *ijtihād*), and a host of other issues. Al-Suyūṭī, the Intolerant Ecumenist, challenges the boundaries of our definitions and our assessment of pre-modern Islamic intellectual history. His many ironies (such as his apparent intolerance and ecumenism) problematize our all-too-quaint boundaries, definitions, and affiliational possibilities (i.e. the necessary positions that ascribe one to a particular school or method).

For example, while writing in the tradition of the Ashʿarī-affiliated Shādhilīs in the work to be discussed in what follows—whose luminaries were often vocal critics of the Ḥanbalī-Atharī-Qādirī jurist-theologian-Sufi Ibn Taymiyya—al-Suyūṭī nonetheless embraces Ibn Taymiyya and other Atharīs in certain legal and theological matters. In matters related to independent legal reasoning (*ijtihād*) and the rational sciences, al-Suyūṭī embraced the likes of Ibn Taymiyya—a staunch opponent of song and dance in Sufi ceremonies, Ibn al-ʿArabī's metaphysics, and Ashʿarī-Māturīdī *kalām*—yet sang and danced in Sufi sessions of remembrance, warned the ignoramus who found fault in Ibn al-ʿArabī, and argued for a Ghazālian Ashʿarism that was tolerant of *kalām* so long as it was limited to those in dire need.

On the other hand, his apparently intolerant side manifested in his harsh critiques of his opponents,[6] even those who shared his affiliations, as well as in his view that the centrality of the Shāfiʿī school in Ṣalāḥ al-Dīn's Sunni revival of Egypt more than three centuries prior was sufficient reason to critique

5 Ibn al-ʿImād, *Shadharāt* x, 76.

6 See examples in Spevack, al-Suyūṭī and Sartain, *Biography*.

the Mamlūk sultan's appointment of judges/*muftī*s from each of the schools of law.[7]

Al-Suyūṭī saw the pre-modern roots of what would later become the contemporary Neo-Salafi and Neo-Traditionalist movements—whose differences can spill over into the volatile politics of many contemporary Muslim-majority countries and communities—to be part of the same pool of orthodox perspectives, despite the harshness with which al-Suyūṭī might attack those within his ecumenical framework with whom he disagrees in the particulars. He offers a way out of false-dichotomies and simplistic categorization found so commonly in earlier Orientalist works (which have, in some instances, carried over into contemporary western scholarship) as well as contemporary Sunni Muslim sectarian debates. He may not have gotten along with everybody around him,[8] but he was able to embrace as legitimate a broad range of differing perspectives and the scholars that held them, even if he bitterly criticized them in one instance yet endorsed them in another; this ecumenical embrace is worth considering for our understanding of Islamic intellectual history, and the nuances of his individual interpretations of his particular legal, theological, and Sufi affiliations help us better understand a particular chronological and geographical manifestation of the jurist-theologian-Sufi archetype.

2 The *Ta'yīd* in Conversation with al-Suyūṭī's Other Writings

Al-Suyūṭī does not write as a reporter on what the Shādhilīs believed, in the sense of an outsider cataloging the beliefs of others, but rather from the perspective of an insider, as he seems to be giving us a view into the Shādhilī order of 10th/16th Egypt, which may have differed in subtle ways from its manifestations in parts of North-West Africa concurrently, or during al-Shādhilī's time.[9] For this reason, I see his *Ta'yīd* as a personal manifesto on Sufism, from the perspective of the Shādhilī order in particular. Al-Suyūṭī explores the Shādhilī order's broader connection to Sufism more generally, and its connection to the Sunni schools of law—particularly the Shāfiʿī school—and to the two dominant

7 Spevack, *Archetypal* 99. Also see Berkey, Culture 402.

8 See Spevack, al-Suyūṭī and Sartain, *Biography* for a number of his controversies and disagreements, including his being attacked by a group of Sufis over monthly stipends.

9 The most apparent example to me is al-Suyūṭī's lengthy defense of *samāʿ* (listening to spiritual odes), wherein he informs us that al-Shādhilī had not incorporated it into his order. Rather, al-Suyūṭī reports the Shāfiʿī *madhhab*'s perspective on its permissibility (see al-Suyūṭī, *Ta'yīd* 90–9; also Spevack, *Archetypal* 99–100).

schools of Sunni theology, namely the Ashʿarī and the Māturīdī schools. Through an examination of this text, some of the nuances and contours of al-Suyūṭī's approach to a number of apparently opposing perspectives is better understood.

The *Taʾyīd* covers a number of topics related to Sufism, beginning with its roots in the *ḥadīth* literature, its connection to the Prophet's companion ʿAlī, and the topic of connecting the succeeding generations through the passing of the Sufi *shaykh*'s cloak (*khirqa*) to his student. He then moves on to a discussion of early scholars' relationship to Sufism, such as Ḥasan al-Baṣrī and al-Shāfiʿī, as well as later scholars such as the Shāfiʿī-Ashʿarī-Sufi scholar Tāj al-Dīn al-Subkī (d. 771/1370).

Controversial topics such as the miraculous wonders (*karāmāt*) of saints, the legality of establishing endowments for Sufis, and the superiority of Sufis to jurists and theologians are discussed, as well as explanations of important terms, concepts, and practices, such as the belief in the spiritual poles (*aqṭāb*), the use of music and dance in Sufi rituals, and important theological and terminological principles that need clarification.

What follows is an investigation into a few of al-Suyūṭī's views on law and theology and their relationship to Sufism, as outlined in the *Taʾyīd* and in conversation with some of his other works, in particular his critique of syllogistic logic *Ṣawn al-manṭiq wa-l-kalām ʿan fann al-manṭiq wa-l-kalām* (Preserving speech and discourse from the science of logic and theology) and his treatise on the necessity of independent legal reasoning in every age *al-Radd ʿalā man akhlada ilā l-arḍ wa-jahila anna l-ijtihād fī kull ʿasr farḍ* (Refutation of those who cling to the earth and ignore that independent juridical reasoning is a religious obligation in every age).[10] The topics discussed below primarily help us understand some of his more controversial legal and theological positions, namely the continued necessity and attainability of independent legal reasoning and his loyalty to the Ashʿarī school, despite his rejection of logic and the science of theology (*kalām*) to which it was necessarily attached by his day. In arguing for each of these positions, al-Suyūṭī often drew from scholars who were extremely critical of his own legal, theological, and Sufi affiliations and positions, which also put him in conflict with many of his contemporary colleagues who shared his legal, theological, and Sufi affiliations. How a man who so vociferously opposed his colleagues, often with recourse to scholars who were themselves deeply critical of his own views, could paradoxically balance these opposing camps to argue for his own perspective, and simultaneously embrace them as legitimate and orthodox, problematizes our often

10 Al-Suyūṭī, *Radd*.

excessively quaint boundaries and definitions of legal, theological, and Sufi affiliations.

3 Jurists, Sufis, and Independent Legal Reasoning in the *Taʾyīd*

In the *Taʾyīd*, al-Suyūṭī mentions issues of independent legal reasoning (*ijtihād*) on a number of occasions. A few references may help us better understand al-Suyūṭī's interesting position on the matter, and his impact on later Islamic intellectual history. This section will begin with al-Suyūṭī's discussion of preference for the gnostic (*ʿārif*) over the legal scholar, followed by a related discussion of the relationship between the high Sufi states of experiential knowledge of Allah (*maʿrifa*) and independent legal reasoning. This will be followed by a discussion of al-Suyūṭī's synchronic reading of the ranks of independent legal reasoning and their continued existence, in comparison to some of his contemporaries as well as later scholars whose writings have affected the western view of independent legal reasoning and its nature throughout post-9th century Islamic history.

3.1 *The Problem with Jurists*

Despite spending much of his life debating in matters of law and claiming the rank of independent legal reasoning (*ijtihād*) for himself, al-Suyūṭī makes a considerable effort to critique the legal scholars who do not also follow the path of Sufism. In doing so, he bases himself on the writings of al-ʿIzz b. ʿAbd al-Salām (d. 660/1261), a scholar of the Shāfiʿī school who is said to have achieved a rank of independent legal reasoning.[11]

In the *Taʾyīd*, the question is raised regarding the superiority of the Gnostic (*ʿārif*) to the jurist, to which al-Suyūṭī responds, relying on al-ʿIzz, that the Gnostic is superior to the jurist. That is, one who knows Allah experientially, having been blessed with the high rank of absolute certainty in Allah's existence, omnipotence, omniscience, and volition is far better than a jurist, even if the latter reached some level of independent legal reasoning.[12]

He contrasts the knower of Allah (*ʿārif Allāh*) with the knower of legal judgments (*ʿārif al-aḥkām*),[13] the former knowing what is necessary for Allah with

11 Jackson, *Islamic Law* 11.

12 Al-Suyūṭī, *Taʾyīd* 23.

13 The following two paragraphs are summary paragraphs, at times literally translating from the text, at others summarizing. For clarity, quotations have not been used, though occasional terms are inserted in parentheses.

regard to His mighty (*jalāl*) and perfect (*kamāl*) attributes, and what is impossible for Him regarding defects and deficiencies. Indeed, the knower of Allah is superior to both the scholar of derived legal rulings (*al-furūʿ*) as well as the scholar of legal and theological foundational principles (*al-uṣūl*), because the superiority of knowledge is according to the superiority of what is known, as well as the fruits it produces. The argument goes that the knowledge of Allah's attributes is greater than the knowledge of any other thing known, in that that which stems from it is greater than the fruits of any other knowledge. He continues by explaining that for each attribute known, there is a resultant spiritual state (*ḥāl*). Knowledge of Allah's mercy, for example, leads to the state of hope. These in turn lead logically to other meritorious states, which all lead to the realization of Allah's many blessings, which leads to love of Allah, which in turn leads to more and more increase in high spiritual states and pious actions.

The knowledge of legal judgments, the argument goes, does not lead to any of these meritorious spiritual states and illumined actions. Furthermore, impiety (*fisq*) is often found among jurists, al-Suyūṭī informs us, who often have nothing to do with piety and uprightness (*iqāma*), rather, he accuses many of them of busying themselves with the heretical views of the philosophers in matters pertaining to both theological discussions of prophecy and the Divine. Some apostatize or waver in their belief.

After a more lengthy discussion, he concludes in summary with the statement that all the meritorious states of love, certainty, reliance, and others, along with the manifesting of miraculous breaks in the links of causality (*karāmāt* and *khāriqat al-ʿādāt*), are never seen from the jurists, unless they also tread the path of the Sufis.

Such damning criticism of jurists from a master jurist himself is not to imply that the knowledge sought in law is without merit or benefit, but its study in and of itself is insufficient and cannot produce the spiritual fruits that Sufism produces, since Sufism is linked to law and theology in the sense that it is the perfection of the two.[14] That is, knowledge of the impermissibility of a thing in and of itself does not lead to right action, it must also be accompanied by the realization that Allah as ultimate judge and law-giver is perceiving one at all times, threatens punishment for sin, and so on. The knowledge of impermissibility must be accompanied by knowledge of mercy, cognizance, justice, wrath, etc.

Whether independent legal reasoning is alive or dead with al-Suyūṭī, despite his adamant insistence on its presence and attainability, is of far less

14 Spevack, *Archetypal* 17.

importance to him than the achievability of experiential knowledge of Allah (*maʿrifa*). Perhaps he might say that a Gnostic who merely follows the legal opinions of another without knowing their proofs (i.e. a *muqallid*) is likely far superior to an independent legal scholar who lacks the certainty that comes from experiential knowledge of Allah; however, as mentioned shortly, he would argue that it is not appropriate for a gnostic to rely on following the scholarship of another, once he had attained experiential knowledge of Allah. This point addresses another angle on the discussion of the continued vibrancy of Islamic legal and philosophical scholarship in the post-7th/13th centuries, indicating that the spiritual priorities of al-Suyūṭī and his likes were not seen as antithetical to independent legal scholarship. His biographers narrate that he spent the remainder of his life, after retiring from public scholarship, in the practice of Sufism.[15] That his preference for Sufism is rooted in the legal and other sacred sciences, helps resist the anti-intellectualism sometimes attributed to Sufism, as the following discussion indicates.

3.2 *If You Know, Don't Follow*

After outlining the problem with many jurists, discussed above, al-Suyūṭī summarizes the views of Abū Ṭālib al-Makkī (d. 386/996), author of the very influential Sufi tract *Qūt al-qulūb*, on whether or not one who knows Allah is required to follow the scholarship of his teachers. The discussion grows out of the claim explored above that the one who knows Allah (i.e. the Sufis) is superior to the jurist who only knows the legal rulings and has not attained the high ranks of the Sufis.

This is an interesting twist on a common subject, as it frames the discussion of restrictively following another's scholarly opinions (*taqlīd*) with spiritual rank, rather than having merely traversed the ranks of independent legal reasoning.

Summarizing al-Makkī, al-Suyūṭī says:

> Know that if one remembers Allah Most High with experiential knowledge (*maʿrifa*) and certain knowledge (*ʿilm al-yaqīn*), following (*taqlīd*) one of the scholars is not sufficient. Likewise, when the earlier scholars reached this station, they departed from those who had taught them, due to the increase in certainty and understanding.[16]

15 Sartain, *Biography* and Spevack, al-Suyūṭī 408.

16 Al-Suyūṭī, *Taʾyīd* 26–7. Al-Suyūṭī also cites this in his defense of the continued existence of independent legal reasoning in *Radd* 43.

He then mentions the Prophet's companion Ibn ʿAbbās who is reported to have said that no one other than the Prophet is excluded from having some of their opinions adopted and others rejected. Likewise, Ibn ʿAbbās learned law (*fiqh*) from the companion Zayd b. Thābit, and Quranic recitation from Ubayy b. Kaʿb, then disagreed with each in these respective sciences.

Al-Suyūṭī then mentions the saying attributed to the early generation of scholars (*al-salaf*) that they took absolutely whatever came from the Prophet. As for knowledge they took from the companions of the Prophet, some of it they took and some of it they left (i.e. disagreed). As for the generation following the companions (*al-tābiʿūn*), they made the famous claim regarding them, "We are men and they are men, they opine, and we opine."

Al-Suyūṭī, again summarizing from al-Makkī, moves on to many scholars' having discouraged restrictive following of another's opinion (*taqlīd*), which he clarifies is their saying that one must not rule on a matter (*yaftī*) without knowing the differing opinions of other scholars (*ikhtilāf*), so that he might choose "the most religiously precautionary and the strongest with regard to certainty."[17] Unlike many modern readings of these early discouragements of *taqlīd*, al-Suyūṭī is not claiming that this is a requirement for all Muslims at any level of knowledge, for as discussed below, he affirms the popular ranking of independent legal scholars, which necessitates varying levels of restrictive following (*taqlīd*).[18]

He then indicates that one will be asked in the afterlife about his actions as they relate to his knowledge, not according to another's knowledge.[19] He then discusses the Quranic passage "... Those that have been given knowledge and faith," which indicates that knowledge and faith are connected, this being one of the ways in which another Quranic passage can be interpreted, namely "He wrote faith upon their hearts, and strengthened it with a *rūḥ* from it." Al-Suyūṭī explains: "... That is to say, He empowers them with the knowledge of faith (*ʿilm al-īmān*), and knowledge of faith is the *rūḥ* (soul) of faith."

Furthermore, al-Suyūṭī argues that the scholar is "from those who deduce (*istinbāṭ*) and infer (*istidlāl*) from the Book and *sunna*, and (who possess) the knowledge of the application of the craft and the tools of the trade" and is thereby from those who "possess discernment (*tamyīz*) and insight (*baṣīra*), as well as those who ponder and take heed (*tadabbur* and *ʿibra*)."[20] Here he is further detailing that the nature of the scholars capable of independent legal

17 Al-Suyūṭī, *Taʾyīd* 27.

18 See al-Suyūṭī, *Radd* 38–41.

19 Al-Suyūṭī, *Radd* 44.

20 Al-Suyūṭī, *Taʾyīd* 27.

reasoning (at the highest level of the founders, as well as the second level who can do deduce and infer with their founder's methodology) are also linked with spiritually reflective knowledge, not merely the knowledge of legal rulings. He then ends the section with the nine stations of certainty (*maqāmāt al-yaqīn*), namely repentance, patience, gratitude, hope, fear, abstention, reliance, satisfaction, and love.

The previously discussed chapter on the superiority of the gnostic to the jurist, combined with al-Suyūṭī's acknowledgement of the ranks of independent legal reasoning, indicate that he would likely consider the experiential knowledge and certainty of even a low-level jurist or a mere restricted follower (*muqallid*) to elevate such a gnostic above the higher level jurist without gnosis. However, the present chapter under discussion draws what appears to be if not a necessary then at least a highly recommended and probable connection between a) the paired states of experiential knowledge of Allah and certainty and b) independent legal reasoning. That is, one who has achieved gnosis and certainty would likely have acquired sufficient knowledge of legal rulings that excludes him or her from the common ranks of restricted followers, and if not, such a gnostic would be expected to rise to some level of independent legal scholarship, based on al-Makkī's insistence that remaining a restricted follower is inappropriate for the gnostic.

3.3 *The Legacy of al-Suyūṭī's Synchronic Reading of the Ranks of Independent Legal Reasoning*

Since the doors to gnosis and certainty were never closed, and the station of one who had reached these lofty states necessitated that he or she strive to achieve some level of independent legal reasoning, al-Suyūṭī connects Sufi experience with law in his *Ta'yīd* in a manner not often found in contemporary discussions of the continued possibility of independent legal reasoning and intellectual dynamism in Islamic intellectual history. That is to say, he challenges the common orientalist generalizations about Sufis and jurists as being entirely separate camps, and rather combines the highest levels and ideals of both sciences in the Sufi.

This almost necessary connection between gnosis and independent legal reasoning, and the unquestionable continued attainability of the former being either a (near) condition or necessitator of the latter, brings us to another controversial claim of al-Suyūṭī, namely his having attained the level of independent jurist (*mujtahid*).

Al-Suyūṭī was no stranger to controversy regarding matters of law. In what might be one of his most controversial positions, he claimed to have reached the level of independent legal reasoning (*ijtihād*), within the legal school (*madhhab*) with which he was affiliated, that of the Shāfiʿīs.[21] He was not claiming the ability to found his own legal school, that is, produce a unique methodology. Rather, he was claiming to have inherited the method of al-Shāfiʿī, and to have reached a level of competence to use this method in deducing rulings directly from the Quran and *sunna*, without having to follow or refer back to past precedents from al-Shāfiʿī or other independent jurists at the level that al-Suyūṭī claimed for himself (such as al-Shāfiʿī's immediate students, as well as al-Ghazālī).

Many of his contemporaries, however, seem to have interpreted his claim to be that he reached the level of an independent jurist capable of producing his own methodology, such as the early founders of the legal schools. It may also be the case that they understood the level he had claimed, but were confused as to whether or not this was still possible, given the general agreement that the founder-level independent legal reasoning was no longer possible. Furthermore, Hallaq has suggested that the rejection of his claim to independent legal reasoning was tied to his personality, as he was often in conflict with many of his colleagues.[22]

Al-Suyūṭī wrote a treatise to refute his detractors entitled *al-Radd ʿalā man akhlada ilā l-arḍ wa-jahila anna l-ijtihād fī kull ʿasr farḍ*, to clarify that only the founder-level independence was no longer possible, to prove that the level of school-affiliated independent legal reasoning was still possible and in fact a communal obligation (*farḍ kifāya*), and to further claim that he had indeed attained it. In addition to the aforementioned treatise, his defense of his qualifications despite his rejection of logic, as mentioned above,[23] he also discusses the subject in his *Taʾyīd*, from the perspective of its connection to the high Sufi states of gnosis and certainty.

Given the popularity of the idea of "the closing of the doors of independent legal reasoning (*ijtihād*)" in nineteenth- and twentieth-century discussions of Islamic law in both the western academy and Muslim scholarship, the question arises whether or not al-Suyūṭī's claim was anomalous, or if it had merit.[24] If it had merit, were there others after him who made this claim or at least considered it possible? In other words, are the more restrictive readings of the typologies of jurists and their legal reasoning capabilities representative of

21 See Spevack, al-Suyūṭī 401; al-Suyūṭī, *Ṣawn* 5, and Sartain, *Biography* 63; cp. on the specifics of this claim and the reactions.

22 Hallaq, Gate 27.

23 See previous footnote.

24 Calder, Typology. Calder considers al-Suyūṭī's claim to have merit, at least in terms of the strength of his argument.

the intellectual climate in the centuries after al-Suyūṭī, or was his expansive reading of the typologies of jurists defensible and attainable in later generations?

3.4 *Three Stages in the Development of the Typologies of Jurists*

Having informed us that the jurist without Sufism does not amount to much, and the fully realized Sufi who does not abandon following the opinions of others without some measure of scholarly independence has fallen short, it is important to understand how al-Suyūṭī justifies his claim that mastery of both the inner realities of faith and the outer demands of legal deduction are in fact attainable; it is to the latter claim that we now turn our attention.

In order to determine whether or not independent legal reasoning (*ijtihād*) in particular continued to exist in al-Suyūṭī's time and afterwards, one usually turns to discussions of the varying ranks of jurists and their differing capacities with regard to independent legal reasoning, that is deducing legal rulings from the primary texts and/or previously derived precedents (legal rulings or maxims).[25]

There are three general typologies of jurists that should be understood in order to understand al-Suyūṭī's thought on the matter:

1) those typologies that were proposed before his time (Ibn al-Ṣalāḥ, al-Nawawī, al-Āmidī, etc.)
2) al-Suyūṭī's own typology
3) those proposed after his time, reflecting changes in function and practice of the Shāfiʿī school in the generations after al-Suyūṭī's death (i.e. those that include mention of Ibn Ḥajar and al-Ramlī's role in determining the relied upon opinion in the school).

Regarding the first category, Ibn al-Ṣalāḥ's (d. 643/1245) typology and later al-Nawawī's (d. 676/1277), which is derived from the former's typology, are crucial to the later Shāfiʿī school's understanding of independent legal reasoning.[26]

Al-Suyūṭī directly engages with these two scholars' typologies, as well as those of others, and argues for the validity of his own similar typology and its

25 As I argue later, it is also useful to study the actual compendiums of edicts as well as the commentary literature (*ḥawāshī*) to detect evidence of continued independent legal reasoning in various forms and under differing restrictions, rather than just relying on a few isolated statements of legal theory.

26 See Calder's Typology for Ibn al-Ṣalāḥ's and al-Nawawī's recension of it.

particular interpretation.[27] Since al-Suyūṭī's typology is based on those of previous scholars, though interpretively and with differing terminology, it is safer to count his as a separate, though connected, typology.

Later discussions of the typology of jurists—especially after the arrival of Ibn Ḥajar and al-Ramlī, whose efforts at redacting the sea of differing opinions in the Shāfiʿī school had a major impact on the practice of granting legal edicts (*iftāʾ*)—inform us of the legacy of al-Suyūṭī's views on the typologies and the continued existence of independent legal reasoning. These typologies differ in content as well as implication with regard to the continued existence of independent legal reasoning. Two in particular, that of al-Birmāwī (d. 1106/1694–5) and close to two centuries later the slightly expanded version of al-Bājūrī (d. 1276/1860), indicate that some of the subtleties of al-Suyūṭī's interpretation of the typologies were lost on some from the later generations, and his opinion and interpretation was challenged.

3.5 *A Synthesized and Summarized Typology*

Before addressing al-Suyūṭī's legacy, it is crucial to understand that differing readings of the typologies have impacted both our understanding of Islamic legal history, especially with regard to how Islamic law functioned during the 3rd/9th through 13th/19th centuries.

One important problem with the typologies of jurists is the existence of terminological confusion; often scholars use differing terms for the same level of scholarship, while in other instances some scholars might use the same term for differing levels of scholarship.[28] To avoid similar confusion, and in the absence of a close comparison of the various typologies (which is outside the scope of this paper, and perhaps still insufficiently studied), a simplified version is included below:

1) The <u>founder-level independent jurist</u>, who possesses all of the qualifications of independent legal reasoning *and* has the ability to produce his own method of legal derivation, thus enabling him to directly engage with the primary sources (Quran and *sunna*) and independently deduce therefrom legal rulings.
2) The <u>independent and affiliated jurist</u> who possesses all of the previously mentioned qualifications and abilities, but chooses to use the methodology of the founder-level independent jurist whose method he finds

27 See al-Suyūṭī, *Radd* 38 ff.
28 See Hallaq, Gate.

sufficient, and in doing so affiliates himself with the founder's school, without actually restrictively following (*taqlīd*) the founder's method or rulings.

3) The restricted jurist who is at a very similar level as the independent and affiliated jurist, yet, rather than being qualified though unwilling to create his own methodology, he is not capable of producing a new methodology, and thus restrictively follows (*taqlīd*) the founder's method. He may, however, directly engage with the primary texts and independently deduce therefrom legal rulings, using the method of the founder. This is a subtle distinction that is often lost in later typologies, and is therefore an important cause for confusion and disagreement among jurists.[29]
4) The further restricted jurist who has the ability to weigh and judge the rulings of the jurists of previous three categories, and prefer certain rulings over others.
5) The redacting jurist who restricts his weighing and judging of rulings primarily to those in the previous level.

This is an admittedly insufficient typology, in that it excludes some important categories mentioned by al-Nawawī and Ibn al-Ṣalāḥ that are outside the scope of the present inquiry, and it also includes a level that came to be identified after al-Nawawī's time (level 5). Furthermore, there are those who can achieve levels 2–5[30] (or perhaps only 3–5)[31] in individual issues (such as inheritance or laws of worship). This is therefore a synthesis of several typologies, which nonetheless do not contain any contradictions that would problematize the arguments or purposes of this study.

3.6 *Three Readings of the Typologies*

There are three interpretations of the various typologies produced before, during, and after al-Suyūṭī's time that concern the current inquiry that help us better understand both al-Suyūṭī's views and legacy, as well as post-15th century legal history. They are:

29 In my own assessment of al-Bājūrī's typology, I did not sufficiently address the subtle difference between level 2 and 3 above, since he himself appears to lump these two levels into the level of *mujtahid al-madhhab*, and in doing so, describes it similarly to level 3 above. See Spevack, *Archetypal* 106–10.

30 According to al-Suyūṭī's view.

31 According to many of his contemporaries' view.

1) The Orientalist caricature,[32] being an extreme form of the diachronic reading, which has been largely discredited by Wael Hallaq and others.[33]
2) The diachronic reading, which mirrors a devolutionary view of sacred history, informed by eschatological concerns and a sort of self-effacing piety by scholars who often portrayed themselves as the scraps that were left before the end of time.
3) The synchronic reading, which is that of al-Suyūṭī, who saw that the ranks of jurists were open to all, excluding only that of the founders of the legal schools (*madhhab*s).

3.6.1 The Caricature

The first interpretation,[34] the orientalist caricature of the eschatological diachronic reading, is summarized as follows: After a period of intellectual vibrancy and gradual crystallization into legal schools, it was agreed that all major questions had essentially been addressed, and one could resort to past precedent in all legal matters. While some orientalists casually acknowledged a gradual decline and rigidification in following centuries, it came to be a popular interpretation that the 9th century marked the end of *all* independent legal ruling—or the closing of the gates of *ijtihād*—followed by the uncritical endeavor to keep Islam static and unchanging for the following millennium, until western-looking modernists kicked open the doors of independent legal reasoning in the late 19th century. When this is combined with the also popularly held belief that al-Ghazālī in the 12th century dealt a death-blow to Islamic philosophy, and the view that anti-rationalist so-called traditionalists dominated Orthodoxy, the western view of Muslims after the Golden era is quite bleak, and frankly flawed. This interpretation has been effectively debunked by a number of scholars in recent years, and will therefore not occupy a prominent place in the current discussion.

3.6.2 The Diachronic Reading

A more fair and justified interpretation of the typology of jurists is the diachronic reading of the ranks of scholars mentioned in the typologies.[35] That is, these ranks reflect a slow chronological and qualitative descent, from early

32 El-Shamsy, Hashiya 292.

33 Hallaq, *Authority*. Also see Hallaq, Gate.

34 The following paragraphs regarding the three interpretations of the typologies include some revised content of a talk I delivered at Colgate University, entitled *The Myth of Islamic Decline*, on March 3, 2015.

35 See El-Shamsy, Hashiya.

masters to more limited redactors who, unable to reason at the level of their predecessors, nonetheless could assess and critique, or at least prefer varying opinions within the school.

This is in keeping with the early devolutionary and eschatological view, and it is indeed an interpretation that came to exist, especially after the 16th century. It is certainly clear that al-Bājūrī writing in the 19th century is influenced by this reading in the manner in which he presents a more limited version of the above typology, which is also found in the works of his predecessors, such as the 17th century Egyptian scholar al-Birmāwī. While one can see evidence of chronological and qualitative decline in some typologies from Ibn al-Ṣalāḥ, to al-Birmāwī, to al-Bājūrī, to al-Kurdī, there is no explicit denial of reaching other than the first level of independent legal reasoning.

It is worth mentioning that the apparently diachronic readings during al-Suyūṭī's time, which wrongly omit the second level jurist and which al-Suyūṭī laments in his *Radd*,[36] need to be closely compared with those after his time, especially once Ibn Ḥajar and al-Ramlī's redactory efforts become central to the work of granting legal edicts (*iftaʾ*), especially when a judge was often merely capable of narrating the legal school's relied upon (*muʿtamad*) rulings and applying them in uniform circumstances.[37]

3.6.2.1 *Challenges to the Diachronic Reading*

Before addressing the third interpretation, al-Suyūṭī's synchronic reading, there are a few important challenges to the diachronic reading which should be considered, both from al-Suyūṭī's vantage point in his era, as well as with regard to the post-15th century trends in Islamic law (such as the rise of Ibn Ḥajar and al-Ramlī's important role in determining the relied upon position in the Shāfiʿī school).

One proposed argument for the primacy of the diachronic reading, especially after the 15th century, is based on the writings of al-Birmāwī and al-Bājūrī mentioned above, who explicitly challenge al-Suyūṭī's reading (though with important ambiguities and inaccuracies) and also serve as the foundation for the orientalist caricature.[38]

---

36 Al-Suyūṭī, *Radd* 38.

37 This is arguably restricted to common cases such as matters related to worship or basic financial transactions, and seems indefensible when cases with more contextual nuance are brought to the judge.

38 I address the inaccuracy of the orientalist caricature being based on al-Bājūrī's text in my *Archetypal* (see 105 ff.) and Disconnection. An important ambiguity that was produced by my discussions of independent legal reasoning in these two texts is that it appears that

Al-Birmāwī, defining the term *mujtahid* (one capable of independent legal reasoning) as used in the text he is commenting upon writes:

> that is, unrestricted legal reasoning (*ijtihād muṭlaq*)...which has been lost since the third [i.e. ninth] century. Al-Suyūṭī claimed that it would remain until the end of time, basing himself on the Prophet's saying that Allah sends at the beginning of each century one who renews this community's religion. It is answered that the intended meaning of "renewal" is establishing the religious laws, rulings, and such.
>
> Excluded by it (i.e., the author's reference to founder-level independent legal reasoning) is the independent jurist within the school (*mujtahid al-madhhab*),[39] such as the companions of al-Shāfiʿī who were able to derive rulings from his (al-Shāfiʿī's) methodological principles, and the independent jurist who gives legal edicts (*mujtahid al-fatwā*), who is able to weigh and give preponderance to varying different opinions (*tarjīḥ*), such as al-Nawawī—Allah have mercy on him. The root (meaning) of *ijtihād* is "striving to reach the objective"...[40]

Al-Bājūrī, commenting nearly two centuries later on the same text and basing himself on al-Birmāwī's commentary, has a similar statement, wherein he fleshes out the discussion a bit by including some of the names of scholars, associated with these three categories in al-Birmāwī's truncated typology. He mentions al-Shāfiʿī's companion al-Muzanī (d. 264/878) for the independent jurist within the school, repeats al-Birmāwī's example of al-Nawawī for the one who gives legal edicts, and adds his crucial counterpart al-Rāfiʿī. Al-Bājūrī

I am arguing that al-Bājūrī held a synchronic view similar to al-Suyūṭī's, while that is not the case. Rather, as I discuss herein, al-Bājūrī's writings on independent legal reasoning are a) not sufficiently detailed to produce a general and encompassing assessment of the state of Islamic law from the ninth through nineteenth century, as Snouck Hurgronje, Schacht, and others, attempted; b) contain clear evidence of terminological confusion; c) admit the possibility of synchronic readings, even if these are not popularly held in the expansive form that al-Bājūrī presents them (i.e. allowing founder-level independence); and d) contain examples of later scholars going against the redactory efforts of earlier scholars, including those in the higher rungs of the hierarchies.

39 As indicated by al-Suyūṭī's quote above, and adjusting for contradictory terminology, this is actually the level he was claiming for himself, and thus al-Birmāwī had clearly misunderstood what level al-Suyūṭī was claiming to continue to exist until the end of time. Al-Birmāwī does not in any way reject the possibility of the continued existence of this second level.

40 Al-Birmāwī, *Ḥāshiya* 8.

further mentions Ibn Ḥajar and al-Ramlī, and declares that they did not achieve any rank of independent legal reasoning, though admits that some said they may have reached the level of weighing (*tarjīḥ*, presumably at al-Nawawī's level) in some issues.

We therefore get from al-Birmāwī and al-Bājūrī the names of scholars at three of the levels of the synthesized typology mentioned above, namely al-Shāfiʿī (along with the other founders)[41] at level 1, al-Shāfiʿī's student al-Muzanī at level 3 according to al-Birmāwī and al-Bājūrī's system and at level 2 according to al-Suyūṭī's,[42] and al-Nawawī and al-Rāfiʿī at level 4 in the 7th/13th century. Despite the important role of weighing and judging the opinions of previous scholars, especially those in the fourth level, Ibn Ḥajar, al-Ramlī, and other important scholars of their generation and following generations, such as al-Shirbīnī (d. 977/1570), al-Anṣārī (d. 926/1520), and al-Shabrāmallisī (d. 1086/1676–7), and others are not granted any form of independent legal reasoning by al-Bājūrī (though in the case of al-Shabrāmallisī, Ibn Ḥajar, and al-Ramlī, he mentions the possibility of level 4 or 5 weighing—*tarjīḥ*—in certain matters). Here we see both a correlation between chronological and qualitative decline, and therefore a strong argument for a diachronic reading of the typology of jurists.

This view, however, is too quaint and is incomplete and misleading when presented out of context. There are a number of methodological differences that need to be correlated and corrected, if al-Birmāwī and al-Bājūrī's typology, and those that resemble it, are to be taken as accurate assessments of the possibilities for independent legal reasoning as well as the reality on the ground, especially after the 15th century.

As mentioned previously, there is the issue of terminological confusion, where the same term is used for different levels of independent legal reasoning, or where multiple terms are used for the same level. It is also important to note that to one who is somewhat new to the study of Islamic law, the diachronic reading of typologies of jurists, when presented in short summary form, seems to imply that, especially in the Shāfiʿī school, there were very few scholars involved in this process. We see al-Nawawī and al-Rāfiʿī as sole

41 They are mentioned by al-Bājūrī, *Tuhfa* 247–8.

42 Elsewhere, he mentions that all but the founders had to do *taqlīd* of methods and rulings, including the *mujtahid al-madhhab*, whom al-Bājūrī associates with al-Muzanī (al-Bājūrī, *Tuhfa* 250). This is an important difference in typologies, as al-Suyūṭī, Ibn al-Ṣalāḥ, al-Nawawī, and many others would consider al-Muzanī to be at level 2, that is free of *taqlīd* in method or rulings, but affiliated to al-Shāfiʿī in that he willfully used al-Shāfiʿī's method despite being able to create his own, at least according to al-Suyūṭī's reading.

representatives of the first stage in the ever-narrowing process of producing the relied upon opinion (*muʿtamad*) in the school. We are told that they were followed by Ibn Ḥajar and al-Ramlī a few centuries later, who weighed and assessed the output of al-Nawawī and al-Rāfiʿī's disagreement, and are the only doorway to al-Nawawī and al-Rāfiʿī's thought.[43] The agreement of Ibn Ḥajar and al-Ramlī, we are told, constituted a further development in identifying a relied upon opinion, and furthermore that judges after the era of these two level 5 redactors, were required to follow Ibn Ḥajar and al-Ramlī when they agreed, and could choose between their views if they disagreed. It implies that the opinions of previous generations are not available to the judge, nor other scholars who were contemporaries or intellectual descendants of Ibn Ḥajar and al-Ramlī (i.e. al-Anṣārī, al-Shabrāmallisī, etc.), and especially not after their time.

This, however, is not at all the case, as demonstrated in the actual post-16th century commentary literature and collections of legal edicts, including al-Bājūrī's.[44] These works indicate that there is a much more vibrant process at work; scholars go against later redactory scholars and, at times, opt for the opinions of earlier scholars (or vice versa).[45] They also cite authoritative scholars outside the narrow Nawawī-Rāfiʿī or Ibn Ḥajar-Ramlī framework of relied upon positions.

Furthermore, new questions emerge that need legal judgments, as well as old questions with new variables.[46] We might call these gap-issues, those legal queries that arise outside the framework of the most commonly discussed topics, especially those not mentioned by al-Nawawī, al-Rāfiʿī, Ibn Ḥajar, or al-Ramlī. More extensive studies of the reasoning process used in deciding these many gap-issues, as well as the careful cataloging of such issues themselves, need to be undertaken.

---

43 That is, after Ibn Ḥajar and al-Ramlī's time, no one else could skip over their opinions and assess al-Nawawī and al-Rāfiʿī's disagreements.

44 I go into the details of post-fifteenth century vibrancy and diversity of scholarship throughout the following book: Spevack, *Archetypal*. The reader is referred to chapters 3 and 4 in particular.

45 Al-Bājūrī himself states his own opinion against al-Shabrāmallisī's (see al-Bājūrī, *Ḥāshiya* 565), and also disagrees with al-Ramlī in another instance, citing al-Nawawī against him (ibid. 556).

46 Hallaq, Gate 31.

3.6.2.2 *Chronological Gaps*

In addition to the many gap-issues that were not discussed by al-Nawawī and al-Rāfiʿī and/or Ibn Ḥajar and al-Ramlī,[47] there are also important chronological gaps that challenge a simplistic diachronic reading. These chronological gaps are of two types, vertical[48] and horizontal.[49]

The vertical gaps are those generations between al-Shāfiʿī and al-Nawawī, which included not just al-Shāfiʿī's contemporary students such as al-Muzanī, but also al-Shīrāzī, al-Juwaynī, and al-Ghazālī (to name but a few) who are said to have reached the second level of independent legal reasoning, as well as those that reached the third level, which allowed them to directly engage with the primary sources using the methodology of the founder. That this continued well past the 3rd/9th century is a clear proof against the orientalist caricature, as well as a strong challenge to the diachronic reading.

Regarding the scholars of the horizontal gaps in al-Nawawī and al-Rāfiʿī's time, that is, those scholars who were contemporaries of the major scholars mentioned in the typologies, there were scholars such as al-ʿIzz b. ʿAbd al-Salām and his student Ibn Daqīq al-ʿĪd, who are considered to have achieved the second level of legal reasoning and argued that that level would always be attainable,[50] at least until the end of time when society deteriorates. There are many others to mention, but these two scholars, who play such a prominent role in later Shāfiʿī legal texts in that they are often quoted as authoritative sources, are an important challenge to the diachronic reading.

Returning to the vertical gaps in al-Birmāwī and al-Bājūrī's truncated schema, as well as the fuller synthesized typology offered above, al-Bājūrī's denial or doubting of Ibn Ḥajar and al-Ramlī having reached any rank of independent

47 We need to better assess and understand the scope of subjects covered by these four aforementioned "relied-upon" scholars, in order to understand where else we might look for evidence of continued independent legal reasoning before the twentieth century.

48 Imagining a typology of jurists which place the early founders at the top, followed by the founder's students, then al-Nawawī and al-Rāfiʿī, and finally Ibn Ḥajar and al-Ramlī, a diachronic reading indicates that time is flowing from top to bottom of the list, as the possibilities for independent legal scholarship decrease as one descends vertically down the list.

49 Imagining a typology that is presented chronologically from top to bottom, the scholars of the same generation extend out horizontally.

50 Al-Bājūrī understood al-ʿĪd to have argued for a continuation of the first level of *ijtihād*. However, based on further study of al-Suyūṭī's *Radd*, as well as al-Āmidī's typology, I think it more probable that he argued for the continued existence of the 2nd level independent jurist, in line with al-Suyūṭī's view. See Spevack, *Archetypal* 109–10; also, Bājūrī, *Ḥāshiya* 616–7.

scholarship is not an explicit denial of anyone reaching even al-Nawawī's level 4 abilities. While he may echo al-Birmāwī's rejection of al-Suyūṭī's interpretation of the *ḥadīth* of the centennial renewer (*mujaddid*) as pertaining to the continuation of independent legal reasoning at level of the founders (level 1), he does not extend this denial to the possibility of achieving level 2 or 3 independence in this passage. He does however give voice to Ibn Daqīq al-ʿĪd several chapters later, who argued for the continued existence of independent legal scholars as being possible and communally obligatory, contrasting this opinion with that of al-Ghazālī who denied the existence of level 1 scholars, further indicating that he considered the controversy to be over whether or not level 1 independent legal reasoning still existed, and in no way explicitly denies the existence of the other levels. Indeed, he mentions several scholars from the fifth/eleventh century who denied being restrictive followers of al-Shāfiʿī, indicating that a synchronic reading of the typologies was indeed possible.[51]

3.6.3 Al-Suyūṭī's Synchronic Reading

In any case, al-Suyūṭī is an important interruption to the tendency to read diachronically the typologies produced by Ibn al-Ṣalāḥ and al-Nawawī, as he lived and wrote between al-Nawawī's and Ibn Ḥajar's time, and made a strong argument for his synchronic reading which only disallowed the existence of founder-level independent jurists after the third/ninth century. He reads Ibn al-Ṣalāḥ and al-Nawawī, as well as other theorists, as arguing for the communal obligation of level 2 independent legal reasoning, and is cited for generations after as an authoritative source in so many sciences (al-Bājūrī cites him in his *ḥadīth*, Sufi, logic, theological, and legal works prominently and frequently).

Al-Birmāwī and al-Bājūrī mistake al-Suyūṭī to be reviving an older argument for the continued existence of level 1 jurists who could found their own schools based on unique methodologies, this being the apparent opinion of those whom al-Āmidī refutes centuries before when he denies the *ḥadīth* of the centennial renewer as applying to the continued existence of the first level of independent legal reasoning.[52] Since al-Bājūrī's typology has had such an impact on the western study of Islamic intellectual history, it could be wrongly assumed that al-Suyūṭī's reading was deemed invalid and rejected. Rather, one continues to see typologies produced after al-Suyūṭī's time, such as that of Muḥammad b. Sulaymān al-Kurdī's (d. 1194/1780),[53] that include the often misunderstood level 2 jurist among the possible levels of independent

51 Ibid.

52 Al-Āmidī, *Iḥkām* iv, 347–8.

53 Saqqāf, *Mukhtaṣar* 53–4.

reasoning, with no explicit denial of its attainability, despite the correlation between chronological and qualitative decline of some of the scholars given as examples in each rung of the hierarchy.

Regardless of the theoretical claims of various scholars, the final principle to be considered here with regard to al-Suyūṭī's challenge of the diachronic reading is that actions speak louder than words. That is to say, a close study of the collections of legal edicts and commentary literature, especially but not limited to the gap-issues and scholars of the vertical and chronological gaps, indicate a number of areas wherein scholars exercised juridical independence of some form, even if they did not always refer to it as independent legal reasoning.[54]

Throughout this exploration of al-Suyūṭī's approach to law via the lens of his *Ta'yīd*, it has been shown that al-Suyūṭī's synchronic reading of the typologies of jurists has merit, both in terms of his own arguments for the validity of such a reading, as well as in relation to the status of scholars who lived in the chronological gaps between those scholars mentioned in the apparently diachronic typologies, as well as the quality of their scholarly output and engagement with newly arisen issues requiring legal judgment. Furthermore, due to the quality of his interpretation of al-Nawawī's and Ibn al-Ṣalāḥ's typologies, the existence of terminological confusion in his time and apparently in some of his later interpreters such as al-Birmāwī and al-Bājūrī, his synchronic reading should continue to inform our reading of post-fifteenth century typologies and theories of independent legal reasoning's existence, despite the move towards pietistic avoidance of the term *ijtihād* in some circles.

Since al-Suyūṭī was misunderstood in his time, but possibly understood and affirmed by others, the possibility of others who shared his interpretation of Ibn al-Ṣalāḥ's and al-Nawawī's typologies should not be excluded outright based on the reading of a few terse passages in the commentary literature after his time. Basing an assessment of the state of legal scholarship on a few passages, primarily in the introductory chapters to a book of legal rulings rather than the foundational principles of law (*uṣūl al-fiqh*) is arguably what produced the Orientalist caricature.[55] Such commentators, like al-Bājūrī, while leaning towards a diachronic presentation of the typologies, do not shut the door on synchronic readings in that they give ample voice to other perspectives, like Ibn Daqīq al-ʿĪd's and others. Furthermore, later legal commentaries and collections of edicts contain examples of later scholars disagreeing with earlier

54 See Spevack, *Archetypal*; Hallaq, Gate; Gerber, *Islamic Law*, for more examples of "gap issues".

55 See Spevack, *Archetypal* ch. four, and Spevack, Disconnection.

scholars, indicating a continued vibrancy in the discourse. Finally, al-Bājūrī and al-Birmāwī's brief words on independent legal reasoning suffer from other interpretive problems, such as terminological confusion as mentioned previously, even if they report a valid critique of al-Suyūṭī's use of the *ḥadīth* of the centennial renewer as evidence of any form of independent legal reasoning. For these reasons and more, it is arguably very important to consider the merits of al-Suyūṭī's synchronic reading for the study of Islamic intellectual history after the fifteenth century.

It has also been shown that al-Suyūṭī saw the attainability of experiential knowledge of Allah (*maʿrifa*) and certain knowledge of His existence (*yaqīn*) as tied to the attainability of some level of independent legal reasoning. From the angle of law, he believed independent legal reasoning to be a communal obligation, and from the angle of spiritual experience, an individual necessity or near-necessity, as discussed in his treatment of al-Makkī's position. In any case, the *Taʾyīd* indicates that no matter the accomplishments and rank of a jurist, it matters little if he has not attained experiential noetic certainty. It is this latter point that warrants greater study via comparison to other scholars, and that clearly expresses the primacy of al-Suyūṭī's Sufi orientation in his legal thought.

4 Al-Suyūṭī and the Ashʿarī School: The Creed of the Sufis

Turning now from his legal thought and its relation to his Sufi worldview, as expressed in his *Taʾyīd*, al-Suyūṭī's somewhat curious positions on theology and his affiliation with the Ashʿarī school also warrant an investigation that the *Taʾyīd* illuminates.

Al-Suyūṭī can be considered an Ashʿarī due to certain theological positions he adopted,[56] his defense of al-Ashʿarī and al-Rāzī against al-Dhahabī,[57] and the strong connection of the Shāfiʿī school to the Ashʿarī school in his time. In fact, many of his teachers were Ashʿarīs, well-versed in the later Ashʿarī school's turn towards philosophical discussions[58] and the marriage of syllogistic logic to *kalām* (after a stormy courting period in the early years of Ashʿarism).[59]

Al-Suyūṭī had a strong aversion to all things rationalistic, that is, those subjects or sciences that relied on or mingled with the rational as opposed to

56 Spevack, *Archetypal* 95–6.

57 Ibid.

58 See al-Taftāzānī, *Commentary* 9–10.

59 El-Rouayheb, Theology.

revealed sciences. He was opposed to the study of syllogistic logic, following al-Nawawī's prohibition of it and opposing al-Ghazālī's having made it near mandatory for scholarship (although al-Suyūṭī claims al-Ghazālī recanted from this position, a view that is not widely held).

He also claimed to study the science of the foundations of law (*uṣūl al-fiqh*) without any influence of the Persian rationalism that dominated its study in his time,[60] and furthermore condemns anyone who introduces syllogistic logic into *uṣūl al-fiqh*.[61] Since rational theology (*kalām*) was deemed a source of *uṣūl al-fiqh*, and some have even gone as far as considering it the foundation of all religious sciences, including the study of the Quran and *ḥadīth*,[62] al-Suyūṭī's Ashʿarism-without-*kalām* position is somewhat surprising, and confusing.

In his *Ṣawn al-manṭiq*, he sets out to prove that the study of logic is forbidden, and certainly not a condition of independent legal reasoning (*ijtihād*) as many who challenged his claim to *ijtihād* had asserted.[63] Acknowledging that rational theology (*kalām*) and logic had become inextricably linked—which was not the case in al-Ashʿarī's time, as mentioned above—al-Suyūṭī felt compelled to narrate from scholars who not only condemned logic, but also those who considered rational theology to be forbidden.

In doing so, he at times relies on Atharī scholars who were adamantly against the Ashʿarīs.[64] How then do we reconcile his apparent Atharī tendencies in the rational sciences, including *kalām*, with his clear defense and praise of al-Ashʿarī, al-Rāzī, and the Ashʿarīs of the Shādhilī order to which he belonged and whose teachings he explains and defends in his *Taʾyīd*?

To begin, in the section on those who condemn *kalām* in his *Ṣawn al-manṭiq*, he gives the last word to al-Ghazālī who recommend against it in most cases, but acknowledges that it is necessary in the case of one whose faith can only be saved by means of it. From this, it appears that he, like al-Ghazālī, considers it a bitter medicine, only to be given to those who are sick and in dire need, rather

60 El-Rouayheb, *Syllogisms* 268. Al-Suyuti distinguished between Persian and Arab schools of scholarship, the former relying on the rational sciences and the latter being free of them.

61 Al-Suyūṭī, *Ṣawn* 171.

62 Al-Bājūrī, *Ḥāshiya*.

63 See al-Suyūṭī, *Ṣawn* 5. He says: "I know the roots of its foundational principles as well as what is built upon them and what comes from them, with a knowledge that none of the scholars of logic today have reached, except our *shaykh*, al-ʿallāma Muhyī l-Dīn al-Kāfiyajī…" the latter did not oppose *kalām* or *manṭiq*, and commented on the works of al-Taftazānī and others.

64 Cp. al-Suyūṭī, *Ṣawn* 75 ff.

than the masses, in contradiction to al-Baqillānī and al-Suyūṭī's contemporary in North-west Africa, al-Sanūsī (895/1490).

What then is an anti-*kalām* Ashʿarī, and is his creed synonymous with the Atharīs he cites or does he remain an Ashʿarī? A study of the creedal portion of the *Taʾyīd* indicates that his creed, more in line with the likes of creeds without *kalām* such as al-Ṭahāwī's, is not in total harmony with the likes of Ibn Taymiyya and the other Atharīs on whose scholarship he relies in his condemnation of logic, as well as in his various works arguing for the continuation of independent legal reasoning.[65]

Al-Suyūṭī quotes from al-Ghazālī's *Iḥyāʾ ʿulūm al-dīn* on a number of occasions in *Ṣawn*, including a passage where al-Ghazālī recommends which *ʿaqīda* texts one should study and teach, namely his *al-Risāla al-Qudsiyya* for the beginner, and his more comprehensive *al-Iqtiṣād fī l-iʿtiqād* for one who may have been plagued by certain doubts and heresies.[66] These are Ashʿarī creeds which should be taught to children, memorized, understood, and believed, without recourse to proofs, unless needed; these creeds have approaches to defining and understanding God's attributes as taught by the Ashʿarīs, not like Ibn Taymiyya's approach to literal[67] interpretations of attributes and directionality.

In *Iḥyāʾ*, al-Ghazālī mentions which degree of *kalām*-proofs should be studied for the corresponding degree of doubt or need, and that when a person is a hopeless cause, one should rely on God to return the person.[68] Therein he also mentions that there should be one person in every town who studies and understands the rational proofs of theology to aid those in need, but that the rest should abstain from them. Three conditions of one who should study rational theology are mentioned (intelligence, piety and good disposition, and a passion for knowledge), and a person with a trade who doesn't have time to study their way out of doubts that rational theology can produce is excluded.[69] Al-Suyūṭī narrates a similar passage from al-Ghazālī's *Fayṣal al-tafriqa bayna al-īmān wa-l-zandaqa*, wherein he mentions the only two people who are permitted to study *kalām*, namely the one plagued by doubts who can only be cured thereby, and the person of sound intellect, firmly grounded in faith, whose faith is established by the lights of the soul, intending to cure doubts.[70]

65 Al-Suyūṭī, *Ḥāwī*.

66 Al-Suyūṭī, *Ṣawn* 162.

67 For Ibn Taymiyya's use of the technical term "literal", see Spevack, *Archetypal* 126–33.

68 Al-Ghazālī, *Foundations* 33.

69 Ibid.

70 Al-Suyūṭī, *Ṣawn* 161.

Al-Suyūṭī's discussion of creed in the *Ta'yīd* further emphasizes the Ghazālian nature of his approach to Ashʿarism, finding a statement of creed sufficient, with no reference to rational proofs. This emphasis on learned creed, which is made experiential and firm via traveling the Sufi path, rather than delving deeply into rational theology, further emphasizes the Sufi orientation of al-Suyūṭī's approach to theology.

4.1 *Two Chapters on Creed*

Al-Suyūṭī provides two short chapters on creed in his *Ta'yīd*, the first outlining the agreed-upon creed of all the Sufis, narrated to show the orthodoxy of their belief. The second chapter mentions an area of disagreement between the Sufis, namely on the eternality of God's attributes of actions. In what follows, a brief analysis of these chapters indicates that al-Suyūṭī not only affirms a creed (without *kalām* proofs) written by the Sufi Abū Bakr al-Kalābādhī (d. 395/995) which would be agreeable to an Ashʿarī, despite apparently quoting passages from a "Ḥanbali" creed,[71] but also reflects the trends of Mamlūk Egypt (and beyond) which made the Ashʿarī and Māturīdī schools synonymous with the *ahl al-sunna*, regardless of whether or not one studied and understood the proofs.[72]

Al-Suyūṭī's narration of al-Kalābādhī's creed, translated below, provides a sufficient window into the beliefs that he considers to be agreed-upon points of faith that are representative of the Sufis in particular and the Sunnis in general. Quoting directly from al-Kalābādhī's *al-Taʿarruf li-madhhab ahl al-taṣawwuf*, he informs the reader that the Sufis were in agreement over the following:

> Allah Most High is one (*wāḥid* and *aḥad*),[73] singular, eternally self-sufficient (*ṣamad*), beginninglessly eternal, omniscient, omnipotent, real, hearing, seeing, subsisting, all-mighty, magnificent, majestic, great, generous (*jawād*), kind (*ra'ūf*), supreme (*mutakabbir*), compelling, first, God (*ilāh*), master (*sayyid*), possessor (*mālik*), lord, compassionate, merciful, willing, wise, speaking, creator, provider, described by all that He has attributed to Himself, named with all that He has named Himself. He does not cease to be beginninglessly eternal in His names and attributes, and does not resemble His creation in any way. His entity does not resemble other entities, nor do His attributes resemble other attributes, nor do the attributes of creation pertain to Him. He does not cease to be prior to

71 Holt and Lambton, History 613.

72 See Spevack, *Archetypal*, 69 ff. and 126 ff.

73 Al-Suyūṭī, *Ta'yīd* 51–2.

(*sābiq*) or preceding created things, existent before all things. None other than He is beginninglessly pre-eternal. He is not a physical body (*jism*), a disembodied spirit (*shabḥ*), a being with shape and form, nor is He an atom (*jawhar*) or contingent attribute (*ʿaraḍ*). Combining and separation do not apply to Him, nor movement, stillness, increase, or decrease. He does not have sections or parts, nor limbs (*jawāriḥ*) or organs. He does not have directions, nor do tribulations befall him. Years (*sanāt*) do not overtake Him, nor do the cycles of moments pertain to Him. Signs do not specify Him, space does not contain Him, nor does time befall Him. Neither touching nor seclusion are possible with regard to Him,[74] nor does God indwell in anything. Thoughts do not contain Him, veils do not conceal Him, and eyes do not perceive Him.

"Before" does not precede Him, "after" does not cut Him off, "whomever" does not leave Him, "about" does not agree/approve/confirm, "to" does not connect to Him, and "in" does not indwell within Him, if (*idh*) does not confirm Him[75] and if (*in*) does not command Him. "Above" does not shade Him, and "under" does not contain Him.

Limit does not face Him, and "with/at" does not crowd Him out, "behind" does not overtake Him, and "in front" does not limit Him, "before" does not manifest Him, "after" does not end Him, "all" does not gather Him, and "was" does not existentiate Him, "not" does not cause Him to be lost, nor does "hidden" veil Him.

His beginningless eternality is what precedes origination (*ḥudūth*) and beginningless eternality is His existence. The utmost limit is His eternality.

If you said "when", He was before time. If you said "before", then before is after Him. If you said "*huwa* (it)", then the letter *hāʾ* and *wāw* are His creation, even if you said "how", two opposing attributes can not coexist for other than Him,[76] thereby preventing (created things) from resembling Him.

---

74 The pairing of touching (*mumāssa*) and seclusion (*ʿuzla*) imply that neither is it possible for God to be in a face-to-face relationship to another, nor to be secluded away from another. In this sense, it is a further elucidation of God being uncontained by space.

75 As in the next phrase, "if" as part of a conditional phrase does not affirm Him (i.e. if x, then y).

76 The two opposing attributes are "before" and "after", which cannot exist simultaneously for created beings, when viewed from only one angle (i.e. not relationally).

> His action is without physical cause,[77] and his causing to understand is not through encountering. His guidance is not by way of gesticulation. Aspirations do not dispute Him, and thoughts do not confuse Him. His entity is not specified with modality (*takyīf*), and His actions are not charged with a duty (*taklīf*).
>
> They (the Sufis) agreed that eyes do not perceive Him, and doubts do not assault Him.
>
> His attributes do not change, nor are His names exchanged; He is still as such, and will remain as such.
>
> He is the first, the last, the outer, and the inner. He knows all things, and there is nothing like Him; He is the seeing and hearing.

Reflecting on the above creed, one sees significant emphasis on the non-spatial and non-corporeal nature of Allah, as well as His transcendence of time. Albeit in brief, summary form, his treatment of spatiality and directionality might be consolidated with Ibn Taymiyya's perspective on Allah's "aboveness," if we understand the latter's insistence on the literal meaning (*ẓāhir*) of these terms being their real and non-metaphorical meanings as defined by context (i.e. the Quranic descriptions of Allah),[78] without similarity to created beings, but it is more likely that a number of the statements in the *Ta'yīd* are phrased in such a way to prefer the Ashʿarī insistence on either a metaphorical or a deferential (*tafwīḍ*) approach to Allah's attributes,[79] which is the approach that al-Suyūṭī prefers, as narrated in his *al-Itqān fī ʿulūm al-Qur'ān*.[80] When combined with his Ghazālian approach to creed, as outlined in the *Iḥyā'* and quoted in *Ṣawn al-manṭiq*, we see that despite his respect for Ibn Taymiyya and other Atharīs, his preference for a conservative form of Ashʿarism becomes clearer.

Just as al-Ghazālī before him could show continued respect for Ibn Ḥanbal, even though he disagreed with him, since he recommended Ibn Ḥanbal's approach for some,[81] al-Suyūṭī shows continued respect for the later Ḥanbalī/Atharīs like Ibn Taymiyya, while disagreeing with him on key creedal issues,[82]

---

77 *Fiʿluhu min ghayr mubāshara*, meaning that His actions are not physically connected to their affects (in the sense that fire is the apparent cause of burning when cotton and flame touch).

78 See Spevack, *Archetypal*, 95 ff. and 126 ff.

79 Ibn Taymiyya rejected both approaches. See ibid.

80 Ibid.

81 Al-Ghazālī, *Foundations* 52.

82 Directionality, *ta'wīl* and *tafwīḍ* (See Spevack, *Archetypal* 95 ff.).

legal rulings related to Sufism,[83] and the orthodoxy of certain controversial Sufis such as Ibn al-ʿArabī and Ibn al-Fāriḍ.

The Ashʿarī (and Māturīdī) nature of his treatment of creed is further emphasized by the following chapter wherein al-Suyūṭī discusses the main area of disagreement among the Sufis who were otherwise in agreement on most issues of creed, namely the issue of whether or not Allah's "attributes of action" were eternal. The Ashʿarīs held that Allah's attributes of action (such as creator) were contingent and emergent (*ḥadītha*), unlike the Māturīdīs who held that they were eternal.

In this section, al-Suyūṭī mentions only two possible schools, the Ashʿarīs and the Ḥanafīs, by whom he means the Māturīdīs. While other portions of this chapter include quotations, there is no indication that al-Suyūṭī is quoting anyone when he says:

> Disagreement occurred with regard to (God's) attributes of action, the Ashʿarīs held that they were emergent in time (*ḥadītha*) while the Ḥanafīs held that they were beginninglessly eternal (*qadīma*); many of the Sufis held the latter opinion.[84]

The pairing of these two schools as representative of the Sunnis has a long history in Egypt and is apparent in the writings of Egyptian scholars before and after al-Suyūṭī. Al-Suyūṭī is clearly aware of Ibn Taymiyya's thought, at least with regard to the relation between logic and rational theology (and perhaps less so on his theological positions outlined in his *Darʾ al-taʿāruḍ*), but the fact that al-Suyūṭī frames the discussion in the two perspectives that came to be the dominant representation of Sunni creed from North-west Africa to the Levant, from Istanbul to Jakarta, in conjunction with the Shāfiʿī- Ashʿarī environment from which al-Suyūṭī came, further emphasizes the Ashʿarī nature of his approach to the creed, despite his relying on Atharī scholars in his condemnation of logic and rational theology, as well as in his defense of the existence and necessity of level 2 independent legal reasoning.

After mentioning various arguments for and against the Ashʿarī and Māturīdī opinions, al-Suyūṭī closes by saying:

---

83 Al-Suyūṭī defended the use of *samāʿ*, that is singing and dancing in Sufi rituals as a form of remembrancing God (*dhikr*), and also wrote treatise on the permissibility of celebrating the Prophet's birthday. See Spevack, *Archetypal* 100.

84 Al-Suyūṭī, *Taʾyīd* 52.

> The upshot is that the Ashʿarīs said that the (name) "Creator" is in reality "the one from whom the creation comes," and if it were beginninglessly eternal then the creation would be beginninglessly eternal. It is however true that if it were intended by the name "Creator": "The one with power over the creation", then there would be no disagreement over it (the name creator) being eternal.

In summarizing the debate, mentioning the different opinions, and attempting to find a means of harmonizing the difference, and limiting his commentary on this issue to the Ashʿarī and Māturīdī schools, we see a clear indication of his functioning within the predominant Ashʿarī/Māturīdī intellectual environment of his day.

5 Conclusion

Of the many issues discussed in al-Suyūṭī's *Taʾyīd*, this article has focused primarily on his presentation of the Shādhilī order from a Shāfiʿī and Ashʿarī perspective. Its Shāfiʿī-centric qualities include the chapter on singing and dancing in Sufi rituals, which promotes the dominant opinion on music in the Shāfiʿī school that only allows drums and voice, saying: "As for *samāʿ*, if it is without musical instruments, then our *madhhab* is that it not forbidden."[85] While narrating the dominant opinion in his school—which contrasts with al-Ghazālī's permitting musical instruments—he further supports his claim by noting that *Imāms* of all the schools of law attended sessions of *samāʿ*, and goes on to cite examples from the Ḥanbalī and Mālikī schools. Despite this fact, he informs the reader that al-Shādhilī himself did not include *samāʿ* in his order in his time, despite it being popularly associated with it in many branches after his time.

Further emphasizing the Shāfiʿī-centric approach of the text, al-Suyūṭī cites praise for the Sufis from al-Shāfiʿī and the deeply influential Shāfiʿī scholar of Tāj al-Dīn al-Subkī. Despite the heavy emphasis on Shāfiʿī opinions throughout, he frequently cites supporting evidence from the opinions of scholars of other schools.

Despite al-Suyūṭī's many public controversies and debates surrounding his legal positions, including his claim to independent legal reasoning, it is apparent in both *Taʾyīd* and *Radd* that al-Suyūṭī saw both experiential knowledge of God (*maʿrifa*) and independent legal reasoning (*ijtihād*) as attainable and

---

85 Al-Suyūṭī, *Taʾyīd* 90.

connected. Even if it is unlikely that al-Suyūṭī would make the claim that *maʿrifa* was a condition of *ijtihād*, it is clear that, for al-Suyūṭī, one who reached experiential knowledge of God should seek the level of independent legal reasoning attainable to him or her, even if it meant using the methodology of a founder-level independent jurist without actually restrictively following (*taqlīd*) that scholar's rulings or methods (i.e. such a gnostic should seek to be an independent yet affiliated jurist—level 2–).

Al-Suyūṭī praises and cites key anti-Ashʿarī/Māturīdī scholars in his critiques of logic, including those critiquing al-Ashʿarī himself, yet he concludes the section on *kalām* in *Ṣawn* with al-Ghazālī's conservative approach to *kalām*, namely that it was only to be studied by scholars who met specific conditions and only to be dispensed as bitter medicine in the appropriate doses, to those in dire need. Furthermore, in *Taʾyīd*, al-Suyūṭī narrates al-Kalābādhī's creed, whose views on corporeality and direction are arguably in contrast to Ibn Taymiyya and other Atharīs' creeds. Combined with al-Suyūṭī's stance on metaphorical and deferential interpretation (*taʾwīl* and *tafwīḍ*) in *al-Itqān*, his creed is thus far more in line with a Ghazālian-Ashʿarī theology. Finally, that the main area of disagreement between the Sufis—who are superior to all other scholars due to the nobility of the object of their study (i.e Allah)—is, according al-Suyūṭī, between the Ashʿarī's and Māturīdī's views on God's attributes of action.

Al-Suyūṭī's *Taʾyīd* in conversation with some of his other works, allows us to better understand his often confusing and controversial relationship with the Shāfiʿī school of law and Ashʿarī school of theology. His controversial disagreements with some of his own Shāfiʿī-Ashʿarī colleagues, embracing of legal and theological positions of other schools, combined with his brave and confident support for controversial Sufis such as Ibn al-ʿArabī, present us with a unique scholar who problematizes our tendencies to restrict our categorizations to popular formulations of schools and affiliations, and shows an ecumenical approach that allows for harsh and outspoken disagreement.

Bibliography

Primary Sources

al-Āmidī, *al-Iḥkām fī uṣūl al-aḥkām*, 4 vols., Beirut 2003.

al-Bājūrī, *Ḥāshiya al-shaykh Ibrāhīm al-Bajūrī ʿalā Sharḥ al-ʿallāma Ibn al-Qāsim al-Ghazzī ʿalā Matn al-shaykh Abī Shujāʿ*, Beirut 1999.

al-Bājūrī, *Tuḥfat al-murīd ʿalā jawharat al-tawḥīd*, ed. ʿA.M. Jumʿa, Cairo 2006.

al-Bājūrī, *Ḥāshiya ʿalā Sharḥ al-ʿAqāʾid al-Nasafiyya*, ms al-Maktaba al-Markaziyya lil-Makhṭūṭāt al-Islāmiyya (Cairo), cat. no. 3739.

al-Birmāwī, *Ḥāshiya Ibrāhīm al-Birmāwī l-Shāfiʿī ʿalā Sharḥ al-Ghāya li-Ibn Qāsim al-Ghazzī*, Cairo 1287/1870.

al-Ghazālī, [*Iḥyāʾ ʿulūm al-dīn*] *The foundations of the articles of faith*, trans. N.A. Faris, Lahore 1999.

Ibn al-ʿImād, *Shadharāt al-dhahab fī akhbār man dhahab*, 10 vols. Damascus 1986–1995.

al-Suyūṭī, *al-Ḥāwī lil-fatāwī*, Beirut 1983.

al-Suyūṭī, *al-Radd ʿalā man akhlada ilā l-arḍ wa-jahila anna l-ijtihād fī kull ʿasr farḍ*, Cairo n.d.

al-Suyūṭī, *Ṣawn al-manṭiq wa-l-kalām ʿan fann al-manṭiq wa-l-kalām*, ed. A.F. al-Mizīrī, Beirut 2007.

al-Suyūṭī, *Taʾyīd al-ḥaqīqa al-ʿaliyya wa-tashyīd al-ṭarīqa al-Shādhiliyya*, ed. ʿA.b.M.b. al-Ṣiddīq al-Ghumārī l-Ḥasanī, Cairo 1934.

al-Taftāzānī, [*Sharḥ al-ʿAqāʾid al-Nasafiyya*] *A commentary on the creed of Islam: Saʿd al-Dīn al-Taftāzānī on the creed of Najm al-Dīn al-Nasafī*, trans. E.E. Elder, New York 1950.

Secondary Sources

Berkey, J.P., Culture and society during the late Middle Ages, in C.F. Petry (ed.), *The Cambridge History of Egypt. i: Islamic Egypt*, Cambridge 1998, 375–411.

Calder, N., Al-Nawawi's typology of muftis and its significance for a general theory of Islamic law, in *Islamic Law and Society* 3 (1996), 143–52.

El-Shamsy, A., The hashiya in Islamic law: A sketch of Shafiʿi literature, in *Oriens* 41 (2013), 289–315.

Gerber, H., *Islamic law and culture, 1600–1840*, Leiden and Boston 1999.

Hallaq, W.B., *Authority, continuity, and change in Islamic law*, Port Chester, NY 2001 (ProQuest ebrary site.ebrary.com Web., accessed 7 May 2015).

Hallaq, W.B., Was the gate of *ijtihād* closed?, in *IJMES* 16 (1984), 3–41.

Holt, P.M. and A.K.S. Lambton, *The Cambridge history of Islam*, 2 vols., Cambridge 1970.

Jackson, S.A., *Islamic Law and the state: The constitutional jurisprudence of Shihāb al-Dīn al-Qarāfī*, Leiden and New York 1996.

Rouayheb, K., *Relational syllogisms and the history of Arabic logic, 900–1900*, Leiden 2010.

Rouayheb, K., Theology and Logic, in S. Schmidtke (ed.), *Oxford handbook on Islamic theology*, Oxford 2014 (online version).

Saqqāf, ʿA.b.A., *Mukhtaṣar al-Fawāʾid al-Makkiya fī mā yahtājuhu ṭalabat al-Shāfʿiyya*, Beirut 2004.

Sartain, E.M., *Jalāl al-dīn al-Suyūṭī.* i: *Biography and background* (University of Cambridge Oriental Publications 23), Cambridge 1975.
al-Shaybānī, M.b.I. and A. al-Khāzindār (eds.), *Dalīl makhṭūṭāt al-Suyūṭī*, Kuwait 1995.
Spevack, A., Apples and oranges: The logic of the early and later logicians, in *Islamic Law and Society* 17 (2010), 159–84.
Spevack, A., *The archetypal Sunnī scholar: Law, theology, and mysticism in the synthesis of al-Bājūrī*, Albany, NY 2014.
Spevack, A., Disconnection and doubt, in *Journal of Islamic Philosophy* 8 (2012), 3–23.
Spevack, A., Jalāl al-Dīn al-Suyūṭī, in J.E. Lowry and D.J. Stewart (eds.), *Essays in Arabic literary biography 1350–1850* (Mîzân. Studien zur Literatur in der islamischen Welt 17: Essays in Arabic literary biography), Wiesbaden 2009, 386–409.

CHAPTER 3

Al-Suyūṭī and Problems of the *waqf*

Takao Ito

As a famous jurist, Jalāl al-Dīn ʿAbd al-Raḥmān al-Suyūṭī was consulted about various problems, including those of the *waqf* (endowment or charitable trust). Moreover, he held teaching posts in jurisprudence and *ḥadīth* at certain institutions, and was the *shaykh* at a *turba* and a *khānqāh*, where his duties were mainly administrative. Thus, he was well acquainted with the *waqf* both in theory and in practice. Although his claim that the endowments made by the Mamlūks belong to the state treasury is already known (see below), his overall attitudes toward the *waqf* have not so far been fully investigated.[1] This article examines the problems of the *waqf* and al-Suyūṭī's response to them, in the hope of attaining this jurist's *waqf* activities and the relationship between the theoretical and pragmatic aspects of his life.[2]

1 As Professor and *shaykh*

First, a cursory look will be taken at al-Suyūṭī's career as a professor and *shaykh*. In 867/1463, at the age of eighteen, he was allowed to teach Shāfiʿī *fiqh* at the mosque of Shaykhū in Cairo, succeeding to the position of his father, who had died twelve years earlier, from his deputy who had taken this position in the meantime. In 872/1467, he began to teach the *ḥadīth*—and later other subjects as well—at the mosque of Ibn Ṭūlūn, where his father had preached. According to Sartain, it appears that he held no official post at this mosque, although he occupied a room there until his death.[3] Five years later, in 877/1472, he assumed

1 Only after submitting the manuscript, I noticed the important article of Hernandez, Sultan, scholar, and sufi. Examining al-Suyūṭī's *Inṣāf* and *al-Risāla al-Baybarsiyya* (see below), she discusses struggles between ruler, scholar, and Sufis, while I focus more on the problems of the *waqf*. Thus, I have given up incorporating her arguments into this paper. It should be noted, however, that the distinction between "private" and "public" endowments in *Inṣāf* do not correspond to that between "family" *waqf* (*ahlī* or *dhurrī*) and "charitable" *waqf* (*khayrī*). See Ito, Aufsicht und Verwaltung; cp. Hernandez, Sultan, scholar, and sufi 351–2.

2 For the most part, this paper is based on Sartain, *Biography*. On al-Suyūṭī's life and works, I consulted also Geoffroy, al-Suyūṭī; Saleh, al-Suyūṭī; Spevack, al-Suyūṭī.

3 Sartain, *Biography* 42, 46, 99–100, 105, 111.

 | DOI 10.1163/9789004334526_005

the professorship of the *ḥadīth* at the Shaykhūniyya opposite the mosque of Shaykhū.[4] Al-Suyūṭī insists, on the one hand, that one of his teachers and the *shaykh* of this institution, Muḥyī l-Dīn Muḥammad b. Sulaymān al-Kāfiyajī (d. 879/1474),[5] appointed him to this post after the predecessor's death. On the other hand, al-Sakhāwī (d. 902/1497), one of al-Suyūṭī's opponents, says that this appointment was made by Īnāl al-Ashqar (d. 879/1475), who was probably the supervisor of the Shaykhūniyya.[6] Sartain suggests that in the absence of Īnāl, al-Kāfiyajī appointed al-Suyūṭī to the post, knowing of Īnāl's approval of this choice.[7]

In 875/1470, al-Suyūṭī, while retaining these posts, was appointed the *shaykh* at the tomb of Barqūq al-Nāṣirī al-Ẓāhirī (d. 877/1473)[8] in al-Qarāfa. Al-Sakhāwī mentions that an influential judicial scribe from the same province (Asyūṭ), Abū l-Ṭayyib al-Asyūṭī/al-Suyūṭī (d. 893/1488) recommended al-Suyūṭī to Barqūq.[9] Although al-Suyūṭī at first hesitatingly accepted the position, he retained it until 901/1495.[10] Furthermore, Sultan Qāytbāy (r. 872–901/1468–96) appointed him as *shaykh* of al-Khānqāh al-Baybarsiyya in 891/1486, despite their rather bitter relationship. The ʿAbbasid caliph was said to have acted as a go-between.[11] Subsequently, al-Suyūṭī began to retire from teaching and

4 Al-Malaṭī, *Nayl* vii, 56; Ibn Iyās, *Badāʾiʿ* iii, 82.

5 On al-Kāfiyajī/al-Kāfiyājī, see al-Sakhāwī, *Ḍawʾ* vii, 259–61. On al-Suyūṭī's claim, see al-Shādhilī, *Bahja* 76; al-Suyūṭī, *Taḥadduth* 244; Sartain, *Biography* 43–4.

6 On Īnāl al-Ashqar, see al-Sakhāwī, *Ḍawʾ* ii, 330. On al-Sakhāwī's account of al-Suyūṭī's appointment, see al-Sakhāwī, *Ḍawʾ* iv, 66–7.

7 Sartain, *Biography* 44.

8 On him, see al-Sakhāwī, *Ḍawʾ* iii, 12; Ibn al-Ṣayrafī, *Inbāʾ* iii, 21–2, 206; al-Malaṭī, *Nayl* vii, 59; Ibn Iyās, *Badāʾiʿ* iii, 83.

9 Al-Sakhāwī, *Ḍawʾ* iii, 12; iv, 67. On Abū l-Ṭayyib al-Asyūṭī, see al-Sakhāwī, *Ḍawʾ* xi, 118; al-Malaṭī, *Nayl* viii, 98–9; Ibn Iyās, *Badāʾiʿ* iii, 247–8.

10 Al-Shādhilī, *Bahja* 159–60, 163; Sartain, *Biography* 45, 89, also 81. As al-Suyūṭī said that he did not want to lodge in the special house that Barqūq had prepared for a *shaykh*, the emir revoked this condition. The endowment deeds dated 4, 15 Rabīʿ II and 10 Jumādā I 875/6, 17 Sep. and 12 Oct. 1470, which must be related to this mausoleum, are stored in Dār al-Wathāʾiq al-Qawmiyya, Cairo under the number 26/169 (Amīn, *Fihrist* 42).

11 Al-Sakhāwī, *Ḍawʾ* iv, 69; al-Malaṭī, *Nayl* viii, 26; Ibn Iyās, *Badāʾiʿ* iii, 228. Here, it is worth drawing attention to the stipulation of the endowment deed of this *khānqāh*. According to it, the *shaykh* should be selected only from among the Sufis of the monastery; thus, in 791/1389, Ibn Khaldūn (d. 808/1406) had to be first appointed as Sufi and then as *shaykh* (Fernandes, *Evolution* 48; Ibn al-Furāt, *Taʾrīkh* 65). Nevertheless, whether al-Suyūṭī satisfied this condition does not seem to have come into question. He may have gone through the same procedure as Ibn Khaldūn.

issuing *fatwās*.[12] In 906/1501 he was dismissed from the post of the *shaykh* at the Baybarsiyya, after troubles with its Sufis.[13] Thereafter, he withdrew from public life and devoted himself to writing and revising his works in his house on Rawḍa Island until his death in 911/1505.

2 Rivalry and Disputes with Colleagues

As is well known, al-Suyūṭī had a polemical personality; he was involved in a great number of disputes with his colleagues. Our attention will be focused here on those which were related to the *waqf*, and which led to al-Suyūṭī's resignation from the post of the *shaykh* at the tomb of Barqūq al-Nāṣirī al-Ẓāhirī.

Shams al-Dīn Muḥammad b. ʿAbd al-Raḥmān al-Sakhāwī[14] was born in Cairo in 831/1427–28, eighteen years before al-Suyūṭī. His biography of al-Suyūṭī is full of criticisms as is often the case with him.[15] One of them concerns plagiarism. He claims that al-Suyūṭī took a number of old writings unknown to many of his contemporaries from the Maḥmūdiyya[16] and other places, changed them a little, and made them his own.[17] The Maḥmūdiyya library was renowned for its fine collection of books, which could not be borrowed. Al-Suyūṭī admits that he borrowed some books from it.[18] Moreover, already in 867/1462–63, he wrote *Badhl al-majhūd fī khizānat Maḥmūd* in order to justify himself.[19] Al-Sakhāwī's criticism may be a response to this treatise. In any case, al-Suyūṭī states in it that his teachers, ʿAlam al-Dīn Ṣāliḥ b. ʿUmar al-Bulqīnī (d. 868/1464)[20] and Sharaf al-Dīn Yaḥyā b. Muḥammad al-Munāwī (d. 871/1467),[21] borrowed books from the Maḥmūdiyya, and that the stipulation of the founder that books not

12 It is not clear until when al-Suyūṭī taught at the mosque of Shaykhū and the Shaykhūniyya. Sartain guesses that he may have given up teaching there in about 891/1486 but retained the posts and appointed a deputy (Sartain, *Biography* 81–2).

13 Ibn Iyās, *Badāʾiʿ* iii, 388, 471.

14 On him, see al-Sakhāwī, *Ḍawʾ* viii, 2–32; Petry, al-Sakhāwī.

15 Al-Sakhāwī, *Ḍawʾ* iv, 65–70.

16 It refers to a library of al-Madrasa al-Maḥmūdiyya, founded by Jalāl al-Dīn Maḥmūd b. ʿAlī b. Aṣfar (d. 799/1396–97) (see al-Maqrīzī, *Khiṭaṭ* ii, 395–7; Sayyid, Naṣṣān 126–9). On its collection of books, see also Ibn Iyās, *Badāʾiʿ* v, 179. On the founder, see also Ibn Ḥajar, *Durar* iv, 329.

17 Al-Sakhāwī, *Ḍawʾ* iv, 66; Sartain, *Biography* 75.

18 Al-Suyūṭī, *Taḥadduth* 165.

19 Al-Suyūṭī, *Badhl*; Sartain, *Biography* 202.

20 On him, see al-Sakhāwī, *Ḍawʾ* iii, 312–4.

21 On him, see al-Sakhāwī, *Ḍawʾ* x, 254–7.

circulate could be circumvented in four ways. He explains then one of these ways, for the founder intended that books be available as well as preserved; if someone requires the use of books for his writings but cannot consult them in the *madrasa* and will protect them, then he is permitted to take them out; however, this exception applies only if the books in question are difficult to find in other places, and if the borrowing period is not too long.[22]

In the 880s/1475–84, particularly the last two years of the decade, al-Suyūṭī mostly debated with Shams al-Dīn Muḥammad b. ʿAbd al-Munʿim al-Jawjarī,[23] who was born in Jawjar, Lower Egypt in 821/1418, making him twenty-seven to twenty-eight years older than al-Suyūṭī. After his father's death, al-Jawjarī was brought at the age of seven by his paternal grandfather to Cairo to learn. There, he distinguished himself by his intelligence and was appointed to teaching posts in various institutions, such as the *madrasa* of Umm al-Sulṭān Shaʿbān, al-Quṭbiyya, al-Qijmāsiyya, and al-Muʾayyadiyya. Like al-Suyūṭī, he delivered many *fatwā*s and wrote numerous works, but he is said to have been hasty and careless. In his autobiography, al-Suyūṭī lists the issues on which they disagreed, and to which he devoted tractates.[24]

One of them, *al-Inṣāf fī tamyīz al-awqāf*, which circulated both separately and as a part of *al-Ḥāwī lil-fatāwī*, is a well-known work. In it, al-Suyūṭī principally answers two questions. The questions are based on the action of an emir, who founded a *khānqāh*, to which he appointed a *shaykh* and Sufis, and who provided that they were to receive salaries and rations; however, over time, the income of the institution diminished. First, should the *shaykh* be given priority over the Sufis or should the income be distributed among all persons in proportionate shares? Second, should some of the rations be cut off or all of them proportionately reduced? In answering these questions, al-Suyūṭī begins by dividing the endowments into two types: One is founded on private property; the other is created by caliphs or rulers from the property of the state treasury (*bayt al-māl*) or by the Mamlūk emirs, who are, according to al-Suyūṭī, slaves of the *bayt al-māl*. He notes that all the scholars and students are entitled to receive their stipends from the *bayt al-māl*; hence, they are eligible for the endowments of the second type, which originate in the public treasury.

---

22 The other three ways are as follows: First, to claim that the founder's stipulation is invalid, which is weak; second, it is also weak to interpret the stipulation as prohibiting the taking out of all the books at once; and third, that the books are borrowed for the public interest (*maṣlaḥa*), which is a good (*ḥasan*) explanation.

23 On him, see al-Sakhāwī, *Ḍawʾ* viii, 123–6; al-Suyūṭī, *Taḥadduth* 183–5; al-Malaṭī, *Nayl* vii, 383; Ibn Iyās, *Badāʾiʿ* iii, 208.

24 Al-Suyūṭī, *Taḥadduth* 186–201; Sartain, *Biography* 55–9.

Thus, these 'public' endowments, which increased in number in the eighth/fourteenth century, should be treated as *irṣād* (earmark). As for the questions themselves, he states that, in the case of these endowments, the *shaykh* should be given priority over the Sufis if he alone is engaged in the scholarly activities and thus entitled to the money of the *bayt al-māl* or if he is needier; if all are engaged in scholarly activities and equally needy, the income should be distributed among all in proportionate shares; cutting off some rations is permissible, although money should be preferably untouched. Moreover, the appointment of a deputy or the inheritance of a post is also permissible. However, in the case of 'private' endowments, i.e., those drawn from private property, the *wāqif*'s stipulations are to be observed.[25]

Al-Suyūṭī and al-Jawjarī also disputed about a *madrasa* of Sultan Qāytbāy in Medina. Qāytbāy paid great attention to Mecca and Medina.[26] In and around Mecca, he founded, renovated, and extended institutions, and he also presented a large *minbar* to al-Masjid al-Ḥarām; in 882/1477–78, he had a *madrasa* built, which was opened during his pilgrimage in 884/1480. In Medina, Qāytbay repaired the Prophet's mosque in 879/1474–75 and 881/1476–77; from 881/1476–77 to 884/1479–80, candlesticks were, one after another, sent to the Prophet's mausoleum (al-Ḥujra). Returning from his pilgrimage in 884/1479–80, the sultan decided to establish an endowment to provide bread and *dashīsha* (porridge) to the poor of Medina. In 886/1481, a fire caused by lightning damaged the Prophet's mosque. Qāytbāy soon ordered that it be renovated and a *madrasa* adjacent to it be built. A door and windows of this *madrasa* that were designed to open on to the Prophet's mosque provoked debates.[27] While the inhabitants of Medina and some jurists, including al-Suyūṭī, maintained that this proposal was not permissible, others, such as al-Jawjarī and the chief judges of Cairo, approved it. In his *Shadd al-athwāb fī sadd al-abwāb* in a section of *Ḥāwī* on problems relevant to the *ḥadīth*, al-Suyūṭī argues that the Prophet Muḥammad prohibited doors and windows opening on to his mosque, except

25 Al-Suyūṭī, *Ḥāwī* i, 155–8; al-Suyūṭī, *Taḥadduth* 123, 189; al-Suyūṭī, *Ḥusn* i, 159; Sartain, *Biography* 85–6, 207–8 fn. 66. On this treatise and al-Suyūṭī's opinion in it, see also Amīn, *Awqāf* 65, 330–2; Cuno, Ideology; Ito, Aufsicht und Verwaltung; Behrens-Abouseif, *Cairo* 12; Igarashi, *State* 215–33. Hernandez says "since the *fatwā* fits the events of the Baybarsiyya incident so well, one should not exclude the possibility that al-Suyūṭī included the treatise after the incident." (Hernandez, Sultan, scholar, and sufi 348–9). On the Baybarsiyya incident, see below. On the "waqfization" of state lands, see also Igarashi, *Land tenure*; Walker, *Jordan* 247–53.

26 On the patronage of Qāytbāy in Mecca and Medina, see al-Sakhāwī, *Ḍaw'* vi, 206–7; Newhall, *Patronage* 232–43.

27 Al-Malaṭī, *Nayl* vii, 321–2; Ibn Iyās, *Badā'i'* iii, 196.

for a door or a small window (*khawkha*) of Abū Bakr and a door of ʿAlī. He also refutes the opinion that since a wall shared by the Prophet's mosque and the *madrasa* was built with the sultan's money, he can do what he wants to this wall. To counter this claim, al-Suyūṭī states that everything in the hand of a sultan belongs to the *bayt al-māl*; thus, the wall is not his private property. Nevertheless, when eventually built, the *madrasa* had at least windows.[28]

After the death of al-Jawjarī (889/1484), Burhān al-Dīn Ibrāhīm b. ʿAbd al-Raḥmān b. al-Karakī (d. 922/1516)[29] was al-Suyūṭī's chief opponent. He was born in Cairo in 835/1432, thus he was fourteen (lunar) years older than al-Suyūṭī. He could speak Turkish (*al-lisān al-turkī*) and associated with great emirs, including Qāytbāy. When Qāytbāy ascended to the throne, he gave Ibn al-Karakī various teaching, religious and administrative posts. However, Ibn al-Karakī suddenly lost the sultan's favor in 886/1481 and went into hiding until Dhū l-qaʿda 891/Aug.–Sep. 1486. It is noteworthy that al-Suyūṭī was appointed the *shaykh* of the Baybarsiyya in Rabīʿ II of this year, about seven months before Ibn al-Karakī came out of hiding.[30] Ibn al-Karakī then gradually regained his former station, and not only debated with al-Suyūṭī but was behind his troubles with Sultan Qāytbāy.

As mentioned above, al-Suyūṭī was the *shaykh* at the mausoleum of Barqūq al-Nāṣirī al-Ẓāhirī. After Barqūq's death in 877/1473, the sultan became its supervisor, following the founder's stipulation. Qāytbāy required al-Suyūṭī to come up to the Citadel every month to greet him and collect his salary as the *shaykh* of Barqūq's tomb, but al-Suyūṭī refused. Al-Suyūṭī says that subsequently, "the sultan delegated the responsibility for meeting with him (*fawwaḍa al-takallum*) to the founder's eldest son, ʿAlī Bāy." This remark probably means that ʿAlī Bāy visited the sultan in place of al-Suyūṭī. ʿAlī Bāy died in 897/1492 and his brother Aḥmad a year later.[31] Hence, Qāytbāy summoned al-Suyūṭī again at the beginning of 899/1493. Al-Suyūṭī and the Sufis of Barqūq's tomb presented themselves to the sultan and received their stipends, but al-Suyūṭī's wearing of a *ṭaylasān* at this meeting brought about a dispute with Qāytbāy and

28 Al-Suyūṭī, *Ḥāwī* ii, 12–31; al-Suyūṭī, *Taḥadduth* 123, 189; al-Suyūṭī, *Ḥusn* i, 159; Sartain, *Biography* 206 n. 65. On the establishment of this *madrasa* and the *dashīsha waqf*s by Qāytbāy in Medina, see Behrens-Abouseif, Qāytbāy's foundation; eadem, Qāytbāy's investments; eadem, Qāytbāy's *madrasahs*; Ito, Waqf.

29 On him, see al-Sakhāwī, *Ḍawʾ* i, 59–64; Ibn Iyās, *Badāʾiʿ* v, 96. On his conflicts with al-Suyūṭī, see Sartain, *Biography* 77–80, 88–90.

30 Al-Sakhāwī, *Ḍawʾ* i, 63; al-Malaṭī, *Nayl* vii, 296; viii, 26, 46; Ibn Iyās, *Badāʾiʿ* iii, 187, 228, 234.

31 On ʿAlī Bāy, see al-Sakhāwī, *Ḍawʾ* v, 150; Ibn Iyās, *Badāʾiʿ* iii, 288–9. On Aḥmad, see Ibn Iyās, *Badāʾiʿ* iii, 295; he died Jumādā II 898/Mar.–Apr. 1493.

Ibn al-Karakī. Although al-Suyūṭī was called many other times, he refused obstinately to go up to the Citadel, and his salary stopped. Ibn al-Karakī took his refusal as a sign of disobedience to the sultan, whom he provoked against al-Suyūṭī. Thus, al-Suyūṭī resigned from the post of the *shaykh* at Barqūq's tomb in 901/1495 and composed tractates to justify himself by explaining that the *ʿulamāʾ* should not pay frequent visits to sovereigns.[32]

Sartain says, "[t]his conflict... sprang from his [al-Suyūṭī's] obstinate refusal to go up to the Citadel on the first of every month."[33] It is true that this caused al-Suyūṭī's troubles with Qāytbāy, but the role of Ibn al-Karakī in the affair must have been large. Al-Suyūṭī opposed the building of Qāytbāy's *madrasa* in Medina; nevertheless, the sultan appointed him the *shaykh* of the Baybarsiyya, while Ibn al-Karakī was hiding. Qāytbāy himself seems to have tried to win over al-Suyūṭī, a famous scholar—at least at first. Furthermore, Ibn al-Karakī was possibly also behind al-Suyūṭī's trouble with al-ʿĀdil Ṭumānbāy (r. 906/1501), as will be seen below.

3 Questions and Answers about the *waqf*

In al-Suyūṭī's *al-Ḥāwī lil-fatāwī*, a chapter (*bāb*) contains sixteen short questions and answers as well as four treatises about the *waqf*, including *al-Inṣāf fī tamyīz al-awqāf*. The questions can be roughly classified into three groups: The first concerns the administration of the endowments, and of the sixteen questions and answers, seven belong to this group; the second involves the distribution of or succession to beneficiary rights and takes up six questions and answers; the last group consists of three miscellaneous queries and responses.

32 On these events, see al-Shādhilī, *Bahja* 159–64; Sartain, *Biography* 86–90. Al-Shādhilī quotes an account of them, allegedly from 892/1486–7 by al-Suyūṭī himself, but the former or his copyist seems to have confused the year. Al-Suyūṭī's passage begins: "On Tuesday, 1st of the month Dhū l-qaʿda 871 (sic) occurred a matter (*amr*), the beginning (*muqaddima*) of which we will relate. It is as follows..." He then mentions his appointment to the post of the *shaykh* at Barqūq's mausoleum in 875, and describes the troubles with Sultan Qāytbāy until the latter's death in 901 (not until 871 or 891). While 1 Dhū l-qaʿda 871 was Thursday, 4 June 1467, the same date of 891 was Sunday, 29 Oct. 1486, and this day of 901 was Tuesday, 12 July 1496. Furthermore, al-Suyūṭī's refusal to go up to the Citadel on 1 Dhū l-qaʿda 901 angered the sultan, but Qāytbāy became ill soon and died in this month, which the "matter (*amr*)" seems to indicate. It is therefore likely that this account by al-Suyūṭī concerns the year 901, although it may have been referred to in the account of the year 902, but not 892 (or 891), as al-Shādhilī or his copyist writes.

33 Sartain, *Biography* 90.

Among the questions of the first group is one that appears in *Inṣāf*: Should the religious ceremonies (*sha'ā'ir*) and the *shaykh* be given priority in case of a deficit in an endowment? Al-Suyūṭī's answer is the same: He divides the endowments into 'public' ones and 'private' ones; he notes that in the case of the former, needier and poorer beneficiaries should be given preference, and in the case of the latter, the income should be distributed according to the stipulation of the founder.[34]

Another question concerned whether an employee of an endowment may appoint a deputy, when, for example, he is ill or he has another job. This problem is discussed by al-Suyūṭī in a treatise entitled *Kashf al-ḍabāba fī mas'alat al-istināba*[35] in *Ḥāwī*. Quoting many examples, al-Suyūṭī shows that deputing is generally permissible as long as the *wāqif* has not prohibited it. In the latter case, the stipulation of the founder should be followed. In the case of a 'public' endowment, a person entitled to money from the state treasury is allowed to appoint a deputy and receive the salary, but an unqualified person may not collect it even if he carries out the entrusted duty. A similar question and answer is also found in the first group.[36] Also in *al-Naql al-mastūr fī jawāz qabḍ al-ma'lūm min ghayr ḥuḍūr*, an abridgement of *Inṣāf*, al-Suyūṭī classifies the endowments into those considered as *irṣād* or *ifrāz* (setting apart)—i.e. 'public' ones founded from the property of the *bayt al-māl*—and the 'true' or 'sound' *waqf*s (*waqf ḥaqīqī*) created out of private property, and states that, in the case of *irṣād* or *ifrāz*, the scholars and students are permitted not only to receive their stipends without performing their tasks but to inherit the positions of their fathers.[37]

Further questions of the first group include the following: If an endowment has a shortage in revenues, should its supervisor incur debts to pay the salaries of its *imām* and others? Al-Suyūṭī's answer is that it is not necessary; if an *imām* died while a supervisor was on a journey, and the sultan appointed a new *imām*, can the supervisor dismiss him and appoint another after his return from the journey? Al-Suyūṭī's answer is that such action is not allowed.[38]

34 Al-Suyūṭī, *Ḥāwī* i, 154. Elsewhere, al-Suyūṭī also explains that a leader (*imām*), such as Ṣalāḥ al-Dīn (Saladin) (r. 564–589/1169–93), can endow treasury lands for specific people without buying them beforehand, and that these endowments are unalterable and not invalidated later (*Ḥāwī* i, 152–3).

35 Al-Suyūṭī, *Taḥadduth* 126; al-Suyūṭī, *Ḥāwī* i, 158–63.

36 Ibid. 154.

37 Al-Suyūṭī, *Naql*; Sartain, *Biography* 85–6.

38 Al-Suyūṭī, *Ḥāwī* i, 149, 155.

A typical question of the second group is whether someone can gain profits from an endowment, a matter that he treats in *al-Mabāḥith al-zakiyya fī l-masʾala al-Dawrakiyya*[39] in *Ḥāwī*. Al-Suyūṭī was specifically asked about the following case from Dawrakī in the north of Aleppo province: A man made a mill (*ṭāḥūn*) into a *waqf* and stipulated that it should be for his male children (*awlādihi al-dhukūr*) and their male children, apart from the female (*awlād awlādihim al-dhukūr dūn al-ināth*); however, if there were no male children, it should become a *waqf* of his female children and so on. Twenty-seven years later, it was claimed that the stipulation meant the female children of the founder's male children were to be excluded as beneficiaries of the *waqf* (—which indicates that there were no such male children at that time—), and that its income should go to a mosque in Dawrakī. To this claim, al-Suyūṭī answers that not the female children of the male children but their children should be excluded, since the children of the male children held, whether male or female, a (paternal) genealogical connection to the founder; on the contrary, the children of the female children were generally known by their fathers' pedigrees and had no connection to the founder.

A treatise entitled *al-Qawl al-mushayyad fī waqf al-Muʾayyad*[40] in *Ḥāwī* deals with a similar problem of a *waqf* of Sultan al-Muʾayyad Shaykh (r. 815–824/1412–21). The stipulation of the endowment deed was as follows: The surplus should be given to the founder's children, then his grandchildren, and so on; the former generation should prevent the later generation from enjoying the benefits; a child or a descendant of a dead beneficiary should inherit the latter's portion, even if the latter is not entitled to it during his or her lifetime; if the dead beneficiary has no child nor a descendant, the portion goes to his or her full brother, paternal cousin, and so on in order of the closeness to a (male) blood relation. Eventually, the sultan and his children, other than a daughter, died. This daughter then passed away and left behind a daughter and a son of a son. The question was whether the daughter alone should receive the portion of her mother or whether she should share it with her nephew. Al-Suyūṭī's answer is that the daughter alone should receive it. He notes two reasons: First, it is stipulated that the portion of a dead beneficiary should go to his or her child or closest relative; second, the former generation should prevent the later generation from enjoying the benefits. He then explains similar cases in detail,

39 Al-Suyūṭī, *Taḥadduth* 124; al-Suyūṭī, *Ḥāwī* i, 163–6.

40 Al-Suyūṭī, *Taḥadduth* 126; al-Suyūṭī, *Ḥāwī* i, 166–76.

quoting Taqī l-Dīn ʿAlī b. ʿAbd al-Kāfī al-Subkī (d. 756/1355)[41] and Walī l-Dīn Aḥmad b. ʿAbd al-Raḥīm b. al-ʿIrāqī (d. 826/1423).[42]

It thus appears that there were a great number of disputes about the distribution of or succession to the beneficiary rights of a *waqf* because the stipulations of *waqfiyyas* were often open to different interpretations. The case of al-Muʾayyad Shaykh's *waqf* must have occurred in 891/1486, when his last surviving child Āsiya died, although it is not clear how it was settled finally.[43] In 877/1472, Shaqrāʾ (d. 887/1482),[44] a daughter of Sultan al-Nāṣir Faraj (r. 801–808, 808–815/1399–1405, 1405–12), clashed with her niece Fāṭima over a *waqf* of Faraj's father, Sultan Barqūq (r. 784–791, 792–801/1382–89, 90–99). This case was discussed before Sultan Qāytbāy. Although its result is also unclear, Muḥibb al-Dīn Muḥammad b. Muḥammad b. al-Shiḥna (d. 890/1485),[45] who sided with Shaqrāʾ, was dismissed as Ḥanafī chief judge.[46]

Judging from the title *Tanbīh al-wāqif ʿalā sharṭ al-wāqif*,[47] which does not appear extant, al-Suyūṭī probably concerned himself with these thorny legal problems and advised founders to stipulate endowment deeds as clearly as possible.

4 Problems at the Khānqāh Baybarsiyya

As al-Suyūṭī indicates in *Inṣāf* and in *Ḥāwī*, it is likely that institutions lacked the income to cover their expenses. Such shortfalls were especially evident at this time, the last years of the Mamlūk sultanate, since the regime was suffering from fiscal difficulties and did not hesitate to confiscate assets, including the *awqāf*. In 872/1468, Qāytbāy collected the judges and jurists and asked them if he was permitted to take the surplus revenues of endowments to fund an army to fight against the Dhu l-Qadrid ruler Shāh Suwār (d. 877/1472). Because of the resistance of the Ḥanafī *shaykh* Amīn al-Dīn Yaḥyā b. Muḥammad al-Āqṣarāʾī (d. 880/1475),[48] this imposition was not implemented.[49] In 894/1489, the sultan

41 On him, see Brockelmann, *GAL* ii, 86–7; Kondo, Qāḍī l-quḍāt.

42 On him, see al-Sakhāwī, *Ḍawʾ* i, 336–44.

43 Al-Malaṭī, *Nayl* viii, 45; Ibn Iyās, *Badāʾiʿ* iii, 234. On her, see also al-Sakhāwī, *Ḍawʾ* xii, 2.

44 On her, see al-Malaṭī, *Nayl* vii, 320.

45 On him, see al-Sakhāwī, *Ḍawʾ* ix, 295–305.

46 Al-Malaṭī, *Nayl* vii, 46–7; Ibn Iyās, *Badāʾiʿ* iii, 79–80.

47 Al-Suyūṭī, *Taḥadduth* 124.

48 On him, see al-Sakhāwī, *Ḍawʾ* x, 240–3.

49 Ibn Taghrī Birdī, *Ḥawādith* 636–7; al-Malaṭī, *Nayl* vi, 328; Ibn Iyās, *Badāʾiʿ* iii, 13–5; Petry, *Protectors* 166–8.

obtained the approval of the chief judges and ordered the confiscation of two months of the rents of endowments and private properties in order to give bonuses to the soldiers sent against the Ottomans; two years later, five months of rents were seized for another expedition against them.[50] Under these circumstances, it seems rather natural that al-Suyūṭī confronted the financial troubles of al-Khānqāh al-Baybarsiyya as its *shaykh*.[51]

In his *al-Ṭalʿa al-shamsiyya fī tabyīn al-jinsiyya min sharṭ al-Baybarsiyya*[52] or *al-Risāla al-Baybarsiyya*, al-Suyūṭī addresses the members of this *khānqāh*, stating that he did not take notice of them at first because their opinions and desires varied. He affirms that if he had acted according to the law, many of them would have become vexed. If he had taken their wishes into account, he would have violated the law, which he never does. Since the members of the *khānqāh* then requested that he not neglect their affairs, he ordered the collection of the current year's income and found that the revenue from Egypt, to the exclusion of that from Syria, would suffice for only ten months.[53] He suggested that all the revenues collected in a year be divided among them, but deducted from the total that was to be paid in that year (*fa-kull māl taḥaṣṣala fī sana yuqsam ʿalaykum wa-yukhṣam bihi min tilka l-sana wa-hākadhā*), which probably means that their annual sum could be reduced during difficult financial times, as when al-Suyūṭī wrote this epistle. Some members, however, did not agree, and al-Suyūṭī decided to act in accordance with the stipulation of the founder and the law. The endowment deed had stipulations concerning preferences in such a case. In addition, the endowment originated with the

---

50 Ibn Iyās, *Badāʾiʿ* iii, 260–1, 278–80, 331; al-Malaṭı, *Nayl* viii, 141, 217. A truce between the Mamlūks and the Ottomans was concluded in this year (896/1491), but the confiscated monies were not refunded; they were instead distributed to the emirs and the Mamlūks as bonuses shortly before Qāytbāy's death in 901/1496 (Ibn Iyās, *Badāʾiʿ* iii, 319–21).

51 On this *khānqāh*, see al-Maqrīzī, *Khiṭaṭ* ii, 416–8; Fernandes, *Evolution* 25–9, 48, 49, 54, 61, 62, 69–70.

52 Al-Suyūṭī, *Taḥadduth* 121; al-Shādhilī, *Bahja* 222. Al-Suyūṭī wrote also a treatise titled *Ḥusn al-niyya wa-bulūgh al-umniyya fī l-Khānqāh al-Rukniyya* (al-Suyūṭī, *Taḥadduth* 121; see also Arazi, Risāla 337 fn. 23, where he mistakes, however, that there would be two separate treatises, *Bulūgh al-umniyya* and *Ḥusn al-niyya*). It was called *Juzʾ fī l-Khānqāh al-Baybarsiyya* by al-Shādhilī. He lists this and other similar titles about al-Zāwiya al-Khashshābiyya, al-Khānqāh al-Ṣalāḥiyya and al-Khānqāh al-Shaykhūniyya among al-Suyūṭī's works concerning the history (*fann al-taʾrīkh*) (al-Shādhilī, *Bahja* 251, 254; also al-Suyūṭī, *Taḥadduth* 277 n. 151). Hence, in this treatise he seems to have dealt with the history of the *khānqāh*.

53 Arazi believes that al-Suyūṭī ordered the scattered *waqf* properties to be gathered in a limited area for better management (Arazi, Risāla 339, 350). It seems, however, that he simply ordered the collection of the revenues.

public treasury, and so the most learned and the neediest had to be given priority. Al-Suyūṭī chose some Sufis, but the others complained and asked him, in delaying payment, to treat them all equally. He argues that as the *shaykh*, he has the right to receive monthly a salary equaling 50 *mithqāl*s (of) gold in *dirham nuqra*, along with bread, meat, and other goods,[54] and that he can take them in full, even if the income is insufficient, but he does not do this. If he acts more strictly, it would harm many because they are not qualified as Sufis. In this way, al-Suyūṭī requires the members of the *khānqāh* to accept his choice.[55]

Al-Suyūṭī's claim that many people of the Baybarsiyya could not qualify as Sufis is certainly true, as Sartain and Arazi point out: At the time of al-Maqrīzī (d. 845/1442), "the *khānqāh* [wa]s occupied by insignificant people, shoemakers, and other common people"; a number of members of the Baybarsiyya and other monasteries left their positions in exchange for money and pleaded with influential persons to enter a new institution; many posts in the institutions were hereditary.[56]

However, al-Suyūṭī's action may have been misleading, if not insincere. In his tractate *al-Wajh al-nāḍir fī mā yaqbiḍuhu al-nāẓir* or *al-Wajh al-nāẓir fī mā yaqtaḍīhi al-nāẓir*, al-Suyūṭī maintains that the supervisor of an endowment can take an amount equivalent to his annual stipend or less from the income of the *waqf* and keep it in his control, and that the *shaykh* of a *madrasa*, who is also its *nāẓir*, has the same right.[57] Thus, it seems probable that in reality al-Suyūṭī "exercised this right of putting aside a sum from the revenue of the endowment from which he could draw his stipend every month,"[58] although he was the *shaykh* but not, to be exact, the *nāẓir* of the Baybarsiyya.[59]

In any case, his administration of the endowment provoked the Sufis' discontent. In 903/1498, "the Sufis who were at al-Khānqāh al-Baybarsiyya rebelled against their *shaykh* Jalāl al-Dīn al-Asyūṭī and nearly killed him, then

54 According to Fernandes, the *shaykh* should receive 100 *dirham nuqra*, 3 (or 6?) *raṭl*s bread and 2/3 *raṭl*s meat every month (Fernandes, *Evolution* 69–70). Thus, al-Suyūṭī seems to have greatly exaggerated the amount of his salary, unless he did not mistake it.

55 Al-Suyūṭī, *Risāla*; Sartain, *Biography* 94–6.

56 Sartain, *Biography* 102; al-Maqrīzī, *Khiṭaṭ* ii, 417 (the translation is Sartain's); Arazi, Risāla 340–1; al-Maqrīzī, *Sulūk* iv, 661–2.

57 Al-Suyūṭī, *al-Wajh al-nāḍir*; al-Suyūṭī, *al-Wajh al-nāẓir*; Sartain, *Biography* 101.

58 Sartain, *Biography* 101.

59 The endowment deed stipulated that the *wāqif*, then the vice-sultan (*nā'ib al-salṭana*) should assume the post of the *nāẓir* (Fernandes, *Evolution* 28–9, 62). As a sultan, such as Qāytbāy, appointed the *shaykh* of this *khānqāh*, it appears that a sultan was in reality the *nāẓir*, if only nominally.

they caught him by his clothes and threw him into the fountain (*fasqiyya*)."[60] The conflict worsened. When Ṭumānbāy, who disparaged al-Suyūṭī, became sultan in 906/1501, he wanted to kill him. Al-Suyūṭī went into hiding and was dismissed as *shaykh* at the Baybarsiyya.[61] According to one of his disciples, al-Shādhilī, the members of the Baybarsiyya caused a conflict between al-Suyūṭī and Ṭumānbāy; a man named ʿAbd al-Khāliq al-Mīqātī (b. 853/1449–50)[62] instigated it, and the *kātib al-sirr* Badr al-Dīn Muḥammad b. Abī Bakr b. Muzhir (d. 910/1504)[63] helped them.[64] In this case, perhaps Ibn al-Karakī can be added to al-Suyūṭī's enemies. Shortly before al-Suyūṭī went into hiding and was dismissed, Ibn al-Karakī was appointed, after a bribe, as Ḥanafī chief judge by Ṭumānbāy; after the latter was deposed and al-Suyūṭī came out of hiding, the governor (*wālī*) of Cairo searched Ibn al-Karakī's house for Ṭumānbāy in vain; it was then alleged that Ibn al-Karakī had taken charge of Ṭumānbāy's money.[65] Thus, the efforts of al-Suyūṭī's enemies rather than his 'mismanagement' of the endowment seem to have been the main reason for his dismissal from the Baybarsiyya, as the case with his resignation from the *turba* of Barqūq al-Nāṣirī.

5 Theory and Practice

As Sartain deduces,[66] al-Suyūṭī may have already resigned in about 891/1486 from his teaching posts in the Shaykhūniyya and Shaykhū's mosque, but following his beliefs (e.g., in *Kashf al-ḍabāba*), he may have appointed someone and continued to receive the stipends. Subsequently, after his dismissal from the Baybarsiyya, he secluded himself completely from public life. Nevertheless, he could afford to leave some property. According to al-Shādhilī, Sultan Qānṣawh al-Ghawrī (r. 906–922/1501–16) did not confiscate what al-Suyūṭī left after his death, saying that the latter had not received anything from him. The sultan charged al-Suyūṭī's mother with the care of his books, which he had made into a *waqf*. She left them in the mosque of Ibn Ṭūlūn, where they had been

60 Ibn Iyās, *Badāʾiʿ* iii, 388; Sartain, *Biography* 97–8.

61 Ibn Iyās, *Badāʾiʿ* iii, 471; Sartain, *Biography* 98.

62 ʿAbd al-Khāliq b. Muḥammad b. al-ʿUqāb is meant (al-Sakhāwī, *Ḍaw'* iv, 41; Sartain, *Biography* 97).

63 On him, see al-Sakhāwī, *Ḍaw'* vii, 197–8; Ibn Iyās, *Badāʾiʿ* iv, 71; Martel-Thoumian, *Civils* 273–4, *passim*.

64 Al-Shādhilī, *Bahja* 167, 169–70; Sartain, *Biography* 105–6, 99–100.

65 Ibn Iyās, *Badāʾiʿ* iii, 471; iv, 6, 8; see also Frenkel, *Ḍaw'* 13.

66 Sartain, *Biography* 86.

housed. Shaykh Sharmant(?), whom al-Suyūṭī had appointed as trustee of his books, heritage, and endowment, made the books available to any user. After al-Suyūṭī's mother died and was buried in the tomb she had built for her son, Shaykh Sharmant(?) took the books to his house. After the Ottoman conquest of Egypt, they were transferred to the Azhar mosque.[67] In addition, ʿAlī Pasha Mubārak (d. 1311/1893) reports on Zāwiyat al-Suyūṭī near Bāb al-Qarāfa, the place of al-Suyūṭī's tomb, as follows: It is still active, and the revenues from a mill (*ṭāḥūn*) and two houses (*manzil*) go to it under the supervision of a *dīwān*; a gate to its dome has the date 1211/1796–97, so it was newly built or renovated at that time; a feast (*mawlid*) for al-Suyūṭī takes place in Shaʿbān there.[68]

6 Conclusions

To sum up, al-Suyūṭī's life generally conformed to his ideas. He did not, however, ignore reality and simply put his theory into practice. Moreover, his attitudes towards the *waqf* were generally according to the religious norms of his time, and his troubles were mainly caused by the antipathy of his older colleagues. His claim that the endowments made by the Mamlūks belong to the *bayt al-māl* appears at first sight quite radical, but no evidence exists that it offended the Mamlūks or provoked a heated debate. It was based on the concept of *irṣād*, which had been presented by some earlier scholars. In *Inṣāf* and *Kashf al-ḍabāba*, al-Suyūṭī refers to Badr al-Dīn Muḥammad b. Bahādur al-Zarkashī (d. 794/1392)[69] and Kamāl al-Dīn Muḥammad b. Mūsā al-Damīrī (d. 808/1405)[70] as his sources for *irṣād*. Although in his *al-Faḍl al-ʿamīm fī iqṭāʿ Tamīm*[71] he does not discuss the legal issues of the concession given to Tamīm al-Dārī by the Prophet Muḥammad, his predecessors Ibn Ḥajar al-ʿAsqalānī (d. 852/1449) and al-Maqrīzī note in their treatises on the same theme that it should be treated as *irṣād*;[72] hence, there is no doubt that he knew their arguments. Al-Suyūṭī's contribution lies in his application of the concept of *irṣād*

67 Al-Shādhilī, *Bahja* 261–2; Sartain, *Biography* 23, 110–1.

68 ʿAlī Pasha Mubārak, *Khiṭaṭ* vi, 32. The *mawlid* used to be held also in Asyūṭ on 27 Shaʿbān (ʿAlī Mubārak, *Khiṭaṭ* xii, 106; Sartain, *Biography* 112).

69 On him, see Ibn Ḥajar, *Durar* iii, 397–8; Brockelmann, *GAL* ii, 91–2.

70 On him, see al-Sakhāwī, *Ḍawʾ* x, 59–62; Brockelmann, *GAL* ii, 138; s ii, 170–1.

71 Al-Shādhilī, *Bahja* 210; al-Suyūṭī, *Faḍl*.

72 Ibn Ḥajar, *Jawāb* 294, 295; al-Maqrīzī, *Ḍawʾ*, 238, 239.

(or *ifrāz*) to the endowments founded by the Mamlūks from treasury lands[73] and his justification of them in plain terms, while distinguishing them from the 'true' or 'sound' *waqf* created out of private property. His view was widely accepted in the Ottoman era.[74] This approval is also explained by the clarity and comprehensibility of his writings. Compared with the work of Taqī l-Dīn al-Subkī, one of his authorities, which contains more than one hundred *fatwā*s concerning the *waqf* and comes to 280 pages, the concision of al-Suyūṭī's *Ḥāwī*, with sixteen questions and answers, four treatises and twenty-seven pages, is evident.[75] Overall, al-Suyūṭī thus observed a good balance between theory and practice with regard to the *waqf*.

Bibliography

Primary Sources

'Alī Pasha Mubārak, *al-Khiṭaṭ al-Tawfīqiyya al-jadīda li-Miṣr al-Qāhira*, 20 vols., Cairo 1888–9.

Ibn al-Furāt, *Ta'rīkh Ibn al-Furāt*, ix, ed. C.K. Zurayk and N. Izzedin, Beirut 1936–8.

Ibn Ḥajar al-'Asqalānī, *al-Durar al-kāmina fī a'yān al-mi'a al-thāmina*, 4 vols., Hyderabad 1929–31.

Ibn Ḥajar al-'Asqalānī, *al-Jawāb al-jalīl 'an ḥukm balad al-Khalīl*, in Y. Frenkel, *Ḍaw' al-sārī li-ma'rifat khabar Tamīm al-Dārī*, 249–309.

Ibn Iyās, *Badā'i' al-zuhūr wa-waqā'i' al-duhūr*, ed. M. Muṣṭafā, 5 vols. (BI 5a–e), Wiesbaden 1960–75.

Ibn al-Ṣayrafī, *Inbā' al-haṣr bi-abnā' al-'aṣr*, ed. Ḥ. Ḥabashī, Cairo 1970.

Ibn Taghrī Birdī, *Ḥawādith al-duhūr fī madā al-ayyām wa-l-shuhūr*, ed. William Popper, Berkley 1930–42.

al-Malaṭī, 'Abd al-Bāsiṭ b. Khalīl, *Nayl al-amal fī dhayl al-duwal*, ed. 'U. 'A. al-S. Tadmurī, 9 vols., Sayda and Beirut 2002.

---

73 Some endowment deeds of the later Mamlūk period list the treasury land explicitly as *waqf* property. See Amīn, *Awqāf* 302; Behrens-Abouseif, Qāytbāy's foundation; eadem, Qāytbāy's investments; Reinfandt, *Mamlūkische Sultansstiftungen* 35; Igarashi, *State* 82–3; Ito, Waqf.

74 See Cuno, Ideology. This is also attested by the fact that many manuscript copies of *Inṣāf* are extant.

75 Cp. Taqī l-Dīn al-Subkī, *Fatāwā*. Al-Suyūṭī's *Shadd al-athwāb* is relatively long but takes up only about twenty pages. It thus hardly affects the result, if we also take this treatise into account.

al-Maqrīzī, *Kitāb al-Mawāʿiẓ wa-l-iʿtibār bi-dhikr al-khiṭaṭ wa-l-āthār* (=*Khiṭaṭ*), 2 vols., Bulaq 1853–4.
al-Maqrīzī, *Kitāb al-Sulūk li-maʿrifat duwal al-mulūk*, ed. M.M. Ziyāda and S.A. ʿĀshūr, 4 vols., Cairo 1934–72.
al-Maqrīzī, *Ḍawʾ al-sārī li-maʿrifat khabar Tamīm al-Dārī*, in Y. Frenkel, *Ḍawʾ al-sārī li-maʿrifat khabar Tamīm al-Dārī*, 107–247.
al-Sakhāwī, *al-Ḍawʾ al-lāmiʿ li-ahl al-qarn al-tāsiʿ*, 12 vols., Beirut n.d.
al-Shādhilī, *Bahjat al-ʿābidīn bi-tarjamat Ḥāfiẓ al-ʿAṣr Jalāl al-Dīn al-Suyūṭī*, ed. ʿA. Nabhān, Damascus 1998.
al-Subkī, Taqī l-Dīn, *Fatāwā*, 2 vols., Beirut n.d.
al-Suyūṭī, *Badhl al-majhūd fī khizānat Maḥmūd*, in F. Sayyid, Naṣṣān, 134–6.
al-Suyūṭī, *al-Faḍl al-ʿamīm fī iqṭāʿ Tamīm*, in Y. Frenkel, *Ḍawʾ al-sārī li-maʿrifat khabar Tamīm al-Dārī*, 321–43.
al-Suyūṭī, *al-Ḥāwī lil-fatāwī*, 2 vols., Beirut 1975.
al-Suyūṭī, *Ḥusn al-muḥāḍara fī akhbār Miṣr wa-l-Qāhira*, 2 vols., Cairo 1904.
al-Suyūṭī, *al-Naql al-mastūr fī jawāz qabḍ al-maʿlūm min ghayr ḥuḍūr*, Chester Beatty Library, Mr. 5500, 9b–11b.
al-Suyūṭī, *al-Risāla al-Baybarsiyya*, in A. Arazi, al-Risāla al-Baybarsiyya d'al-Suyūṭī.
al-Suyūṭī, *al-Taḥadduth bi-niʿmat Allāh*, in E.M. Sartain (ed.), *Jalāl al-dīn al-Suyūṭī.* ii: *al-Taḥadduth bi-niʿmat Allāh* (University of Cambridge Oriental Publications 24), Cambridge 1975.
al-Suyūṭī, *al-Wajh al-nāḍir fī mā yaqbiḍuhu al-nāẓir*, ed. M.S.b.I. Makkī, *Rasāʾil ḥawla al-waqf*, Riyadh 1999, 283–5.
al-Suyūṭī, *al-Wajh al-nāẓir fī mā yaqtaḍīhi al-nāẓir*, BNF, MS Ar. 4588, 89b–90a.

Secondary Sources

Amīn, M.M., *al-Awqāf wa-l-ḥayāt al-ijtimāʿiyya fī Miṣr*, Cairo 1980.
Amīn, M.M., *Fihrist wathāʾiq al-Qāhira*, Cairo 1981.
Arazi, A., al-Risāla al-Baybarsiyya d'al-Suyūṭī, in *IOS* 9 (1979), 329–54.
Behrens-Abouseif, D., Qāytbāy's foundation in Medina, the *Madrasah*, the *Ribāṭ* and the *Dashīshah*, in *MSR* 2 (1998), 61–71.
Behrens-Abouseif, D., Qāytbāy's investments in the city of Cairo: Waqf and power, in *AI* 32 (1998), 29–40.
Behrens-Abouseif, D., Qāytbāy's *Madrasahs* in the holy cities and the evolution of Ḥaram architecture, in *MSR* 3 (1999), 129–47.
Behrens-Abouseif, D., *Cairo of the Mamlūks*, London and New York 2007.
Brockelmann, C., *Geschichte der arabischen Literatur* [*GAL*], 2 vols. and *Supplementbände* [*GAL S*], 3 vols., Leiden 1937–49.
Cuno, K.M., Ideology and juridical discourses in Ottoman Egypt: The uses of the concept of *irṣād*, in *Islamic Law and Society* 6 (1999), 136–63.

Fernandes, L., *The evolution of a Sufi institution in Mamlūk Egypt: The khanqah*, Berlin 1988.
Frenkel, Y. (ed., trans. and comp.), *Ḍawʾ al-sārī li-maʿrifat khabar Tamīm al-Dārī*, (Bibliotheca Maqriziana 2), Leiden and Boston 2014.
Geoffroy É., al-Suyūṭī, in *EI*², ix, 913–6.
Hernandez, R.S., Sultan, scholar, and sufi: Authority and power relations in al-Suyūṭī's *Fatwā* on *Waqf*, in *Islamic Law and Society* 20 (2013), 333–70.
Igarashi, D., *State, fiscal administration, and religious endowments in medieval Islam: Studies on the Circassian Mamlūk sultanate* [in Japanese], Tokyo 2011.
Igarashi, D., *Land tenure and Mamlūk* waqfs, Berlin 2014.
Ito, T., Aufsicht und Verwaltung der Stiftungen im mamlukischen Ägypten, in *Der Islam* 80 (2003), 46–66.
Ito, T., *Waqf al-dashīsha* of Mamlūk sultan Qāytbāy [in Japanese], in *Asia Africa Gengo Bunka Kenkyū* (*Journal of Asian and African Studies*) 82 (2011), 31–60.
Kondo, M., *Qāḍī l-quḍāt* Taqī l-Dīn al-Subkī: His life and one of his judicial activities [in Japanese], in *Seinan Asia Kenkyū* (*Bulletin of the Society for Western and Southern Asiatic Studies*) 42 (1995), 59–73.
Martel-Thoumian, B., *Les Civils et l'administration dans l'état militaire mamlūk* (*IX*^e^*/XV*^e^ *siècle*), Damascus 1992.
Newhall, A.W., The patronage of the Mamlūk sultan Qā'it Bay, 872–901/1468–1496, PhD diss., Harvard University 1987.
Petry, C.F., *Protectors or praetorians*, Albany 1994.
Petry, C.F., al-Sakhāwī, in *EI*², viii, 881–2.
Reinfandt, L., *Mamlūkische Sultansstiftungen des 9./15. Jahrhunderts*, Berlin 2003.
Saleh, M.J., al-Suyūṭī and his works: Their place in Islamic scholarship from Mamlūk times to the present, in *MSR* 5 (2001), 73–89.
Sartain, E.M., *Jalāl al-dīn al-Suyūṭī.* i: *Biography and Background* (University of Cambridge Oriental Publications 23), Cambridge 1975.
Sayyid, F., Naṣṣān qadīmān fī iʿārat al-kutub, in *Majallat Maʿhad al-makhṭūṭāt al-ʿarabiyya* 4 (1958), 125–36.
Spevack, A., Jalāl al-Dīn al-Suyūṭī, in J.E. Lowry and D.J. Stewart (eds.), *Essays in Arabic literary biography 1350–1850* (Mîzân. Studien zur Literatur in der islamischen Welt 17: Essays in Arabic literary biography), Wiesbaden 2009, 386–409.
Walker, B.J., *Jordan in the late middle ages: Transformation of the Mamlūk frontier*, Chicago 2009.

CHAPTER 4

Bidʿa or *sunna*: The *ṭaylasān* as a Contested Garment in the Mamlūk Period (Discussions between al-Suyūṭī and Others)

Judith Kindinger

In the Mamlūk Period of Egypt, Islamic authorities (*ʿulamāʾ*) were identifiable by the way they dressed. Preachers (*khuṭabāʾ*) and judges (*quḍāh*) made great use of the manifold head-covers, prevalent in the Islamic traditional vestimentary system. Head covers such as the loose outer garment (*ridāʾ*), the headband (*ʿidhaba*), the turban (*ʿimāma*) and the shawl (*ṭaylasān*), were at times considered the crown (*tāj*) of the Arabs.[1] As a visible marker of religious identity, dress played an essential role in the formation of a sense of community, which oftentimes was accompanied by the creation of sartorial boundaries. Discussions leading to vestimentary provisions not only limited the freedom of choice of non-Muslims but also led to debates on sartorial choices of Islamic authorities, such as the wearing of the *ṭaylasān*.

In his *Kitāb Adab al-khaṭīb* (The book of the craft of liturgical preacher), Ibn al-ʿAṭṭār (d. 724/1324) vents his anger against the *ṭaylasān*, a shawl-like head-cover, which he considered to be an innovation (*bidʿa*) and furthermore the attire of the Jews of Isfahan.[2] Al-Suyūṭī (d. 911/1505) in contrast, defended the custom as being in accordance to the *sunna* of the Prophet Muḥammad in his *al-Aḥadīth al-ḥisān fī faḍl al-ṭaylasān* (Beautiful merits in favour of the *ṭaylasān*). Nonetheless, matters pertaining to the contested *ṭaylasān*, such as its accordance with the *sunna* of the Prophet, its alleged Jewish origins and its symbolism in Mamlūk society, sparked lively debates among Musim scholars.

The aim of this article is to present an outline of these discussions on the *ṭaylasān* that took place in the Mamlūk period and in this way elucidate its considerations as being a heretical doctrine (*bidʿa*) or a rightful practice (*sunna*). Information on specific garments like the *ṭaylasān* is rare and scattered across

1 The *ridāʾ* was a cloak worn over the shoulder and probably also covered the head, see Stillman, *Arab Dress* 43–5; Dozy, *Dictionnaire*. For the crowns of the Arabs see al-Subkī, *Fatāwā* 403; al-Nawawī, *Tahdhīb* ii, 44.

2 For more information on the *ṭaylasān* and the turban (*ʿimāma*), see Ibn al ʿAṭṭār, *Adab* 99–100.

 DOI 10.1163/9789004334526_006

textual sources. Historical sources such as Taqī l-Dīn al-Subkī (d. 756/1355),[3] Ibn Ḥajar al-ʿAsqalānī (d. 852/1449)[4] and al-Turkumānī (d. 748/1348)[5] contain only brief accounts of the *ṭaylasān* and comparable garments, with the exception of al-Suyūṭī's apologia *al-Aḥādīṯ al-hisān fī faḍl al-ṭaylasān*, which was edited and annotated by Albert Arazi in 1983. It is because of Arazi's scholarly research, published as "Noms de vêtements et vêtements d'après *al-Aḥādīṯ al-hisān fī faḍl al-ṭaylasān* d'al-Suyūṭī," that we possess a detailed enumeration of garments.[6] For pre-modern dress sources, research like Yedida Stillman's *Arab Dress*,[7] Dozy's *Dictionnaire détaillé des noms de vêtements chez les Arabes*,[8] and Mayer's *Mamlūk costume* are of great importance.[9]

1 The Importance of Islamic Dress

Clothing has always been a highly controversial topic, as human kind has always felt the need to turn the inner world to the outside. In the Muslim pious tradition, the subject of dress and the act of clothing the body appears to be a crucial and conscious element in the creation of communal identity. In pre-modern as well as in modern times, the holy Quran is generally recognized as the starting point of the demand to vest and wrap the body according to divine prescription. In the interpretation movement (*tafsīr*) for the Quran as well as the *ḥadīth*, which started in the eighth century, sartorial regulations and vestimentary requirements became the subject of discussions among the four Sunni-law-schools: The Shāfiʿī school of law, which was founded by al-Shāfiʿī (d. 204/820), the Mālikī school of law, founded by Anas b. Mālik (d. 179/795), the Ḥanbalī school of law, founded by Ibn Ḥanbal (d. 241/855) and the Ḥanafī school founded by Abū Ḥanīfa (d. 150/767).[10] According to al-Suyūṭī it was the Shāfiʿī law school that argued that the prophetic traditions provide evidence for the wearing of the *ṭaylasān* by the companions of the Prophet Muḥammad.[11]

3 Al-Subkī, *Fatāwā*. See as well Tāj al-Dīn al-Subkī, *Tabaqāt*.
4 Ibn Ḥajar, *Inbāʾ*.
5 Al-Turkumānī, *Lumaʿ*.
6 Arazi, Noms 109–55.
7 Stillman, *Arab Dress*.
8 Dozy, *Dictionnaire*.
9 Mayer, *Mamlūk Costume*.
10 Goldziher, *Islamic Theology* 50.
11 Al-Suyūtī, *Aḥadīth* 37.

Nevertheless, dress and its power of visibility were well understood for reasons of distinction, which could be made based upon it. Three main prescriptions were recognized and described as heresies (*bidʿa*) by the aforementioned fourteenth century Ḥanafī jurist al-Turkumānī: (1) Muslims should not resemble the non-Muslim in their attire; (2) Muslims should not wear red and yellow dyed clothes; and (3) men should not resemble women, and women should not resemble men in dress and attire.[12] In reality, however, historical sources show that expected distinctions by color or type of clothing like, for example, the long and the wide sleeves, originally for men, also attracted the attention of women at the end of the fourteenth century.[13] These distinctions oftentimes touched upon the boundaries of gender, religion, and profession and triggered lively discussions among agitated Islamic scholars.[14]

What is perhaps most conspicuous about the debates on Islamic dress and divine prescriptions is the vestimentary significance of the Prophet. The habits of the Prophet Muḥammad were the subject of close examination in terms of his vesture, gesture, and attire.[15] Hence, *ḥadīth* collections such as al-Bukhārī's (d. 256/870) *Ṣaḥīḥ*, Abū Dāʾūd's (d. 275/888) *Sunan*, and Ibn Ḥajar al-ʿAsqalānī's *Fatḥ al-barī*,[16] as well as juridical texts from the four law-schools all engage in vestimentary discussions and stress the importance of Islamic apparel as a sign of group cohesion.[17]

Most certainly, being visibly Muslim required the knowing of the divine vestimentary rules, which were oftentimes distilled to their visible characteristics. Here, special attention was granted to distinguishing marks such as color, fabric, and size. Differentiations are well described by eleventh century Shāfiʿī scholar al-Thaʿālibī (d. 429/1039), who named the turbans (*ʿamāʾim*) the crowns (*tījān*) of the Arabs and considered the hierarchy of garments placed on the body as highly significant. Cited by al-Suyūṭī, al-Thaʿālibī has the following to say about dressing the body with clothes of belief:[18]

---

12 Al-Turkumānī, *Lumaʿ* 336.

13 The spreading trend of the long and wide sleeves for women, which originated in the Levant and that spilled over to Egypt, was condemned by Islamic authorities because it touched upon gender boundaries; see Ibn Sabāṭ, *Taʾrīkh* ii, 696; Ibn Taghrī Birdī, *Nujūm* v, 541.

14 Al-Bukhārī, *Ṣaḥīḥ. Maghāzī*, v 59.

15 Bourdieu, Sozialraum 171–210; al-Dhahabī, *Kabāʾir*; see as well al-Suyūṭī, *Aḥadīth* 21–30.

16 Ibn Ḥajar, *Fatḥ* iii, 383, 384.

17 For discussions on the *ṭaylasān* as part of the dress-code of the ancestors, see al-Shāfiʿī, *Umm* ii, 108; Mālik b. Anas, *Muwaṭṭaʾ* 693–700.

18 Al-Thaʿālibī, *Tamthīl* i, 283.

> The smallest garment with which one wraps the head is called *bukhnuq*. It is a piece of cloth with which you wrap the front part of the head as well as the back. Then the *ghifāra* is placed above the *bukhnuq*. Then the *khimār* is placed on the latter because the *khimār* is bigger than the *bukhnuq*. Then comes the *miqnaʿa*, then the veil [*naṣīf*], which is half of the size of the *ridāʾ* but bigger than the *miqnaʿa*. Then there comes the *mijār*, which is bigger than the *miqnaʿa* but smaller than the *ridāʾ*. Then finally come the *qināʿa* and then the *ridāʾ*.[19]

This detailed itemization of garments by al-Thaʿālibī suggests the existence of a dress code and the immanent wish to structure everyday life by ritualizing the way to dress. The same goes for the different headgear (*aghṭiyat al-rāʾs*), as the turban (*ʿimāma*) for example was considered to be the general foundation of religious belief.[20] Many Arabic verbs, designating physical movement of placing a cover on the head also had metaphorical connotations. The loose outer garment (*ridāʾ*) could be thrown (*taraḥa*) over the shoulders whilst the head could be veiled (*ghaṭā*); one could even, in order to separate one's mind from mundane reality, erase the head (*ṭalasa*).[21]

The latter verb *ṭalasa* might already allude to the *ṭaylasān*, a shawl-like head cover, placed on the head or the turban, falling down on the shoulders.[22] The eighth century Anas b. Mālik emphasizes the wearing of the *ṭaylasān* by the Prophet and the early Muslim community, whereas Ibn Qayyim al-Jawziyya (d. 750/1350) was not convinced that the Prophet wore it.[23] Despite the diverging opinions on the *ṭaylasān*, it was occasionally given an exclusive status, only to be worn by Muslims, thereby restricting the freedom of choice of the Jewish and Christian minorities. Therefore, sartorial provisions, which were based on the so called Pact of ʿUmar (*al-shurūṭ al-ʿUmariyya*), a document probably dating from later times than its name suggests as discovered by recent investigations of Tritton and Fattal,[24] oftentimes spilled through the Mamlūk Empire, prescribing for non-Muslims what not to wear.[25] In practice, sartorial boundaries proved to be negotiable and trends like the *ṭaylasān* and Muslim

19 Al-Thaʿālibi in al-Suyūṭī, *Aḥadīth* 6.
20 Al-Suyūṭī, *Aḥadīth* 24.
21 Ibid. 5. See as well Ibn al Ḥājj, *Madkhal* 144.
22 Al-Suyūṭī, *Aḥadīth* 6. See as well Stillman, *Arab Dress* 18.
23 Al-Bukhārī, *Ṣaḥīḥ. Maghāzī* v, 59, 519. For other opinions on the wearing of the *ṭaylasān*, see al-Suyūṭī, *Aḥadīth* 50–6.
24 Levi-Rubin, *Non-Muslims* 60.
25 Al-Kalāʿī, *Iḥkām* 85. For the Pact of ʿUmar, see Levy-Rubin, *Non-Muslims* 113–4.

clothing of certain (dyed) colors had a strong appeal to the non-Muslim individual.[26]

2 Sartorial Trends under the Mamlūks

In addition to the wish to embellish the physical body aesthetically, a desire for status also prompted different sartorial trends. These included, for example, enlarging the turban (*ʿimāma*) and lengthening the sleeves (*al-akmām al-ṭawīla*), both of which were trends that touched upon the boundaries of gender and religion. Interestingly, it was especially the *ʿulamāʾ* that adorned themselves in clothes with wide sleeves (*tawsiʿat al-thiyāb wa-l-akmām*), turned the *ṭaylasān* around the neck, and wore the turban partially around the palate (*al-ʿamāʾim huwa al-taʿmīm duna ḥanak*).[27] Also, the *ṭaylasān* worn over the turban (*ʿimāma*), an act described by Ibn al-Ḥājj (d. 737/1336) as 'strangulation,' became the subject of discussions.[28] In this case, it was the practice of men using pins to keep the two in place—at the time considered a practice for women—that brought the trend close to gendered boundaries. Ibn al-Ḥājj puts it as follows:

> [...] The turban (*ʿimāma*) and the *ṭaylasān* met each other, until they choked themselves to death with it, which could be witnessed many times. It drew near the two sides of the cheek and was favorably disposed to one of the two sides. Then his face seemed to resemble that of women, who disappeared from sight (conceal) out of fear that their face became

---

26 Bourdieu, Sozialraum 171–210. See also Elias, Prozess and Ibn Sīrīn, *Tafsīr* 170. Other scholars underline the Prophets aversion to silk (*ḥarīr*) or dyed (*muʿaṣfar*) textiles. Believing Muslims, however, also avoided wearing certain colors. For example, a color such as red should not be worn as it was loved by the devil as well as by the *kuffār*. The wish for elegance in dress and manners for non-Muslims and Muslims became especially apparent at the end of the 'Abbasid caliphate and is described in Abū l-Ṭayyib al-Washshā''s book *al-Ẓarf wa-l-ẓurafāʾ* (see al-Washshāʾ, *Muwashshā* 199–210). For forbidden textiles like silk (*ḥarīr*) see as well Ibn Ḥajar, *Fatḥ* x, 287.

27 Al-Suyūṭī, *Aḥadīth* 27. Al-Kutubī gives the example of Abū l-Fatḥ al-Adīb, who used to wear a big turban (*ʿimāma kabīra*) and a lot of clothes during summer and who did not wear the *ṭaylasān* draped around his neck; see al-Kutubī, *Fawāt* ii, 40. The wearing of the *ṭaylasān* around the neck was later known as the *muḥannaka*, which was tied around the neck. See Stillman, *Arab Dress* plates, 47. Ibn al Hājj, *Madkhal* i, 148–9. See as well Fuess, Sultans with Horns 74; Ibn Sabāṭ, *Taʾrīkh* 696.

28 Ibn al-Hājj, *Madkhal* i, 144.

> visible to men. The latter even inserted needles in the *ṭaylasān* and the turban (*ʿimāma*) that the wind would not remove it from his head and face. In this manner the women proceeded with the head veil (*qināʿa*) and the face and head veil (*khimār*), indiscriminately sticking it together with needles and be mindful that the head veil (*qināʿa*) might be lifted from the head or that the face would become evident, which was forbidden. It is prohibited that men resemble women.[29]

The fear of men looking like women could also have been caused by the *ṭaylasān*'s resemblance to the round shawl (*miṭraf mudawwar*) that was worn by women.[30] In addition to gender boundaries, the *ṭaylasān* also encroached upon religious limitations, as Jews and Christians started wearing it. Sources such as Islamic regulations for the non-Muslims living in Muslim countries written by, for example, fourteenth century scholar Ibn Qayyim al-Jawziyya hint to the fact that non-Muslims over time wore the *ṭaylasān*.[31] These discussions are well preserved in al-Suyūṭī's apologia and that hint at the *ṭaylasān*'s popularity within the Muslim and non-Muslim community.[32] However, in scholarly circles the exclusiveness of the shawl for Muslims only was defended by some as being part of the *sunna* and dismissed by others, who saw in it an invention (*bidʿa*) of the first hour.

The expression "*Yā bn al-ṭaylasān*" (Oh, son of the *ṭaylasān*) became a common phrase to refer to someone of probable non-Muslim origin and was used by those who detested the head-cover and who challenged the authority of Islamic scholars.[33] In contrast, the phrase *arbāb al-ṭayālisa* was used to refer to the Muslim wearers of the *ṭaylasān*, such as judges (*quḍāh*), preachers (*khuṭubāʾ*), and employees of the sultan.[34] While these discussions were ongoing, to most Muslims its status remained unchanged. This is exemplified by an eyewitness account from fourteenth century Shāfiʿī scholar Taqī l-Dīn al-Subkī, written down in his *Fatāwā*, which tells the story of a Shāfiʿī employee

29 Ibid. The *ṭaylasān* could also only be placed on the head, without the turban, see Wheatley, *Places* 377.

30 Ibn Manẓūr, *Lisān* ii, 392.

31 Ibn al-ʿAṭṭār, *Adāb* 99–100. For discussions on the *ṭaylasān* and whether the non-Muslims were allowed to wear it or not, see Ibn Qayyim al-Jawziyya, *Aḥkām* ii, 176–8.

32 The *ṭaylasān* as well as the *ridāʾ* were well known garments in the non-Muslim community. However, the "round *ṭaylasān*" is presented as a sartorial marker of "the old Jews," which was also known by the Arabs, see al-Suyūṭī, *Aḥadīth* 47–8.

33 Yāqūt al-Ḥamawī, *Buldān* ii, 496; al-Maqqarī, *History* 407. See as well al-Turkumānī, *Lumaʿ* 337.

34 Al-Ghazalī, *Iḥyāʾ* i, 82. See as well Young, Review of *al-Aḥadīth al-Ḥisān* 102–3.

of the sultan and his predilection for the *ṭaylasān*. The servant, convinced of the *sunna*'s invocation of the *ṭaylasān*, used to wear the shawl at the time of the procession of the sultan. He was convinced that the *ṭaylasān* should be worn by all the Muslims as a marker of religious identity.[35] Similarly, in the year 703/1303, a man named ʿAbd al-Salām had his *ṭaylasān* thrown on the ground by an Islamic judge for misbehaving (felony unknown), as he was deemed unworthy of wearing such a marker of the Islamic religion.[36]

3 In a Private Box with God

The scholar al-Kalāʿī (d. 550/1156) stresses the importance of the *ṭaylasān* as a means for mediating between the mundane and divine world during the oratory (*khiṭāb*).[37] Al-Kalāʿī's notion resembles the "*khuluww al-ṣughrā*," the small hermitage, and the "*manām al-ḥayāt*," the dormitory of life, as the *ṭaylasān* was called by al-Suyūṭī[38] and later scholars such as Ibn Ḥajar al-Haytamī (d. 974/1567)[39] as well as al-Nābulusī (d. 1144/1731).[40] Therefore, the author of this article hypothesizes that besides religious identity, there is a more profound meaning to the *ṭaylasān*, namely as a site for transcendence. Humans perceive the world around them through their senses: sight, hearing, taste, smell, and touch. It is from these sensations that they evoke a sense of physical being. In this "sense" vesting the head by draping a piece of cloth over it blurs out the physical reality of the outside world: a practice that must stem from a deeper realization that Allah exists beyond the physical.[41] *Allāhu akbar* for he is mind over matter. Thus, the *ṭaylasān* was a private space for spiritual practice, to

35 Al-Subkī, *Ṭabaqāt* 207–8.

36 Abū Shāma, *Rawḍatayn* 57. For the *ṭaylasān* as a marker of knowledge, see Ibn Ḥajar, *Fatḥ* x, 287; al-Suyūṭī, *Aḥadīth*; al-Nābulusī, *Taʿṭīr*; Ibn Sīrin, *Tafsīr* 169.

37 Al-Kalāʿī, *Iḥkam* 89–95.

38 Al-Suyūṭī, *Aḥadīth* 23.

39 Al-Haytamī, *Darr* 36.

40 Al-Nābulusī, *Taʿṭīr* 72–3.

41 David J. Wasserstein hints at the increasing integration of Sufism in the everyday life of the Muslim community during the Mamlūk Period. The Sufi school of thought was acknowledged by *ʿulamāʾ* and political rulers. As such, scholars like al-Suyūṭī played an important role in the dissemination of Sufi ideas and Sufi scholarship, see Shoshan, Sufi Sermons, 106–12 and Geoffroy, *Soufisme*. See as well al-Haytamī, *Tuḥfa* and al-Haytamī, *Darr*.

devote oneself to the service of God, like a portable substitute for the site of worship (*muʿtakaf*).[42]

4 Vesting Mamlūk Bodies

It seems that clothes fulfill a double role for the wearer, as they not only cover the physical body but also allow the wearer to turn the inner and spiritual world to the outside. This idea is captured by al-Turkumānī, who distinguishes between clothes of the body (*libās al-abdān*) and clothes of belief (*libās al-īmān*), hereby illustrating that God (the Spirit) needs a physical mediator to become visible, which can only happen through the medium of clothes.[43] Hence, endowed with divine powers, clothes of belief, at times also the contested *ṭaylasān*, were favored by Islamic scholars such as preachers and jurists.[44]

5 The Preacher

As a religious authority, the preacher (*khaṭīb*) communicated the word of God and the proximate laws to the general public. Nonetheless, there were ongoing debates on the appropriate standard attire of the preacher in general and head-covers in particular. The widely used preacher manual of Ibn al-ʿAṭṭār alludes to the importance of the *khaṭīb* as a person that embodies the habits of the Prophet, also with regard to the vesting of the body:

> Concerning the wearing of the black garment (*al-thawb al-aswad*) it has to be mentioned that it is lawful if it is made of cotton, linen or wool. However, the color white is always more adequate, especially if it is silk and embellished with *ṭirāz* [...]. With regard to the black shoes, which are part of the attire (*zīna*), they can be luxurious and both of them can be black, but there is disagreement in the *sunna* about it.[45]

The black and white garments (*al-thawb al-aswad wa-l-abyaḍ*) as well as the black shoes (*al-khuff al-aswad*) were considered to be an integral part of

42 Al-Haytamī, *Tuḥfa*. For the usage of head-covers in the Christian tradition, see Watts, *In my own way* 77. For the *ṭaylasān* as the small hermitage, see al-Suyūṭī, *Aḥadīth* 23.

43 Al-Turkumānī, *Lumaʿ* 333.

44 Ibid.

45 Ibn al-ʿAṭṭār, *Adab* 89.

the vesture of a preacher. Even though Ibn al-ʿAṭṭār does not mention the *ṭaylasān* as being part of the attire of the preacher (*zīna*), manifold discussions show that this was the case nonetheless. For the Shāfiʿī *qāḍī* Ḥusayn, for example, the prayer outfit for men comprised of a blouse (*qamīṣ*), a long coat (*ridāʾ*), as well as the *ṭaylasān*.[46]

However, the Mamlūk scholar al-Qalqashandī (d. 821/1418) portends in his famous secretarial manual *Ṣubḥ al-aʿshā* that especially the black *ṭaylasān* belonged to the characteristics of the *khaṭīb*.[47] This is also apparent from the travelling account by Ibn Baṭṭūṭa (d. 771/1369), who witnessed preachers wearing a black *ṭaylasān* together with the black *ʿimāma* during their sermons (*khuṭba*):

> Their practice on Fridays is as follows. The blessed pulpit it set up against the wall of the illustrious Kaʿba in the space between the Black Stone and the ʿIrāqī angle, so that the preacher is facing the holy Station [of Ibrāhīm]. When the preacher comes out, he advances, dressed in a black robe and wearing a black turban and black hood [ṭailasān], all of which are the gift of al-Malik al-Nāṣir, with gravity and dignity, moving at a deliberate pace between two black standards, held by two muezzins, and preceded by one of the chief servitors carrying the *farqaʿa*.[48]

6 The Jurisprudent

The dress code of Egyptian jurisprudents (*fuqahāʾ*) was anything but profane. Its purpose was to visibly stand out from the general public at large, so people could recognize the learned people (*ʿulamāʾ*) by their clothes.[49] In many cases the clothes of the *fuqahāʾ* included a head cloth named *ṭarḥa*, which was often ceremonially bestowed on them by the sultan. According to the fifteenth century historian al-Maqrīzī, it was called the "round *ṭaylasān*" (*al-ṭaylasān al-muqawwar*) during the era of the Fatimids.[50] For the Muslim jurists, the

46 Al-Suyūṭī, *Aḥadīth* 39.

47 Al-Qalqashandī, *Ṣubḥ* i, 357.

48 Trans. Gibb, *Travels*, 231.

49 Ibn al-Ḥājj, *Madkhal* i, 139. Al-Suyūṭī mentions the Ḥanbalī master al-Shaykh ʿAbd al-Qādir al-Jīlānī (d. 561/1166), who dressed like the *ʿulamāʾ*. He put on the *ṭaylasān* and rode the mule (*baghla*); see al-Suyūṭī, *Aḥadīth* 72.

50 Al-Maqrīzī, *Khiṭaṭ* ii, 444.

ṭaylasān was oftentimes considered the “apparel of the jurisprudent” (*ziyy al-fuqahāʾ*).[51]

7 The Non-Muslims

Because the *ṭaylasān* was rooted in a system of values, such as honorable, perfect, and altruistic manhood (*murūʾa*), often worn by people of status and authority, it was desirable by many others too.[52]

Sartorial prohibitions (*taḍyīq*) that were implemented in the thirteenth century had to be enforced several times due to disobedience by the people. The Maronite Patriarch al-Duwayhī (d. 1116/1704) describes the legal requirements (*lizām*) for wearing the *ṭaylasān*, which were introduced in the year 754/1354, referring to the Pact of ʿUmar.[53] However, the non-Muslims were easily recognizable by their long coat (*jubba*) with long and wide sleeves and white wrappers (*izār*).[54] The Shāfiʿī-scholar Ibn Ḥajar al-ʿAsqalānī mentions the re-enforcement of a certain sartorial prohibition three times.[55] But even then, Christians, Jews and others kept enlarging their turbans (*ʿimāma*), neglecting sartorial enforcements. Similarly, Muslims from the lower social economic class wore the *ṭaylasān*, as exemplified in the case of a lamp carrier, who for this reason was mistaken for a figure of authority.[56] Perhaps the lamp carrier was a devout Muslim, wearing the *ṭaylasān* to symbolize his knowledge of the life of the Prophet Muḥammad and as a visible marker of his religious identity. One possible explanation for his wearing of the *ṭaylasān* could be a desire to practice his religion in a way according to what he subjectively thinks is right, what the interpreter of dreams Ibn Sīrīn (d. 110/728) calls “*qaḍāʾ al-dīn*.”[57]

---

51 Ibn Khallikān, *Wafayāt* ii, 159.

52 *Murūʾa* is “a quality of the mind by preserving, which a man is made to preserve in good manners and habits” (Lane, *Lexicon*, 2760). Al-Suyūṭī dedicated one chapter to the importance of *murūʾa* with regard to the *ṭaylasān* (al-Suyūṭī, *Aḥadīth* 41–5).

53 Al-Duwayhī, *Taʾrīkh* 318.

54 Ibn Ḥajar, *Inbāʾ* iii, 141.

55 Ibid.

56 Chamberlain, *Knowledge* 78.

57 Ibn Sīrīn, *Tafsīr* 169.

8 The Origin of the *ṭaylasān*

The origin of the *ṭaylasān* was a much-debated topic and to this day remains unknown. In his apologia, as-Suyūṭī provides evidence for the wearing of the *ṭaylasān* by the early Muslim community. However, a non-Muslim predecessor cannot be ruled out. Clues that it had a non-Muslim origin come from Iran and the Jewish community there. Abū Ḥilāl al-ʿAskarī (d. 396/1005) describes early in the eleventh century three types of *ṭaylasān* (-like) head-covers: the regular *ṭaylasān*, the round *ṭaylasān* (*al-ṭaylasān al-muqawwar*) or *sāja* (later called *ṭarḥa*),[58] which was often attributed to the old Jews, and the trapezoid shaped *sudūs*, for which etymological clues lead to Persia.[59] Astronomers[60] and geographers[61] from sixth to tenth century Iran used the word "*ṭaylasān*" to refer to a trapezoid shaped geometrical form, which could be the Arabized form of the Persian word *tālishān* according to the tenth century lexicographer Abū Manṣūr al-Azharī (d. 370/980).[62] Anecdotal evidence points to a Jewish origin. According to the writings of al-Bukhārī, the *ṭaylasān* belonged to the Jews of Khaybar, whilst Abū Muslim argues for the Jews of Isfahan in Persia—the story goes that the latter carried seven-thousand *ṭaylasān* with them into the Arab lands.[63] Based on this story, the Shāfiʿī scholar Ibn Ḥajar al-ʿAsqalānī points out that the early Muslim community wore the *ṭaylasān* abreast of the Jewish community, which alludes to the all-pervasiveness of the shawl at the time of the Prophet.[64] This idea of Jewish origin is well in accordance with Ḥanbalī scholar Ibn Abī Yaʿlā's (d. 459/1066) words:

> Don't forbid the non-Muslims the *ṭaylasān*, it is round and has two blind edges on both sides. This is not how the Arabs know it. This is the garment of the old Jews and barbarians, but the Arabs call it *sāja*.

Similar writings are known from the Ḥanbalī scholar Ibn Taymiyya (d. 728/1328) ("The *ṭaylasān*, the round one, is not rooted in the *sunna* and was not worn by the Prophet and his followers, but was the marker of the Jews")[65] and the Mālikī

58 Al-Suyūṭī, *Aḥadīth* 68.
59 Ibid., 68. See as well al-Nawawī, *Tahdhīb* ii, 187–8.
60 *Zig-i taylasān*, ff. 21a–27b.
61 Al-Muqaddasī, *Taqāsīm* i, 33.
62 Ibn Manẓūr, *Lisān* viii, 183. *Zig-i taylasān*, ff. 21a–27b.
63 Al-Suyūṭī, *Aḥadīth* 50; Sarshar, *Jews* 11.
64 Al-Suyūṭī, *Aḥadīth* 51.
65 Ibid. 53.

scholar Ibn al-Ḥājj ("[the *ṭaylasān*] was part of the non-Muslim authorities and was known at the time of our Prophet with the designation *ṭaylasān*").[66]

The difference of opinion on the origin of the *ṭaylasān* is nicely illustrated by the story of al-Suyūṭī and sultan Qāytbāy (d. 901/1496) taking place in the year 875/1470. According to the story, al-Suyūṭī, wearing the *ṭaylasān*, was received in audience of the sultan. Then the sultan's Ḥanafī *imām* drew the sultan's attention to the *ṭaylasān* and explained to him its possible Jewish origin, thereby challenging al-Suyūṭī's (and the Shāfiʿī law-school's) knowledge on the *sunna* of the Prophet.[67] This incident may have fuelled al-Suyūṭī's desire for the writing of *al-Aḥadīth al-ḥisān fī faḍl al-ṭaylasān*, his apologia on the *ṭaylasān*, twenty years later in the year 899/1492.[68]

Under the political circumstances of that time, however, the Shāfiʿī law-school was competing against the three other law-schools for religious authority and power. Therefore, the practice of wearing a specific head-cover like the *ṭaylasān* and the statement that went with it could place a school in the center of unwanted attention, a vulnerable position.[69] The situation had changed when al-Malik al-Ẓāhir Rukn al-Dīn Baybars I (r. 658–676/1260–1277) decided to delegate one representative chief judge (*qāḍī*) from every law-school. In 1265, sultan Baybars I declared a degree with the goal of reducing competition amongst the four law schools by delegating one representative chief judge (*qāḍī*) from each of the schools. Continuation of discussions on proper standard attire such as the *ṭaylasān* indicate that competition was still ongoing and that the law schools fought to enlarge their political influence also after the degree was declared. Even though the sultan's ruling eased the political tensions among the law-schools, written communication of Islamic scholars, however, hints at profound vestimentary discussions on the *ṭaylasān* after Baybars' decree.

9 The Quest for the *ṭaylasān*

Notable is the vast amount of Islamic scholars that are cited by al-Suyūṭī in his apologia, which is suggestive of the broader nature of the discussions

66 Ibid. 52.

67 Al-Suyūṭī describes the incident with the sultan in his *al-Fulk al-mashḥūn*, which has been lost. However, the happening is preserved in al-Shādhdilī's *Bahja*; see Sartain, *Biography* 86–94.

68 For the chapter on the liberation of the *ṭaylasān*, see al-Suyūṭī, *Aḥadīth* 56.

69 Stilt, *Islamic Law* 34–7.

centering on its being considered *sunna* or *bid'a* in the Fatimid, Ayyubid, and the Mamlūk period. Hence, in our author's vindication on the shawl, scholars in favor of the *ṭaylasān* such as al-Subkī and al-Sābūnī (d. 580/1184) are contrasted with scholars such as Ibn al-Ḥājj, Ibn Taymiyya, and Ibn Qayyim al-Jawziyya, known for their animosity towards it.[70]

Nevertheless, it seems that especially Shāfiʿī disciples such as the aforementioned al-Subkī but as well as al-Bayhaqī (d. 458/1066), al-Khaṭīb al-Baghdādī (d. 463/1071),[71] al-Māwardī (d. 449/1058), and al-Thaʿālibī were engaged in discussions on the *ṭaylasān* and are quoted as such by our author. Take for example the chapter dedicated to a specific form of the *ṭaylasān*, entitled *Taḥrīr al-ṭaylasān al-muqawwar*, in which al-Suyūṭī sets out to investigate the round shaped *ṭaylasān* as well as its alleged Jewish attributes.[72] By quoting Shāfiʿī scholars such as al-Nawawī (d. 676/1277), al-Isnāwī (d. 772/1370), and al-Ṣafādī (d. 763/1362) he demonstrates the all-pervasiveness and popularity of the *ṭaylasān* within the Muslim community since the lifetime of the Prophet Muḥammad.[73]

The frequent defending of the *ṭaylasān*, captured in the writings of the Shāfiʿī law-school, indicates that the wearing of the shawl is rooted in the Shāfiʿī tradition,[74] commemoration that did not stop after al-Suyūṭī and his apologia but that went on into the Ottoman Period. There, it was the Shāfiʿī scholar Ibn Ḥajar al-Haytamī who preserved the group memory of his Shāfiʿī forbearers and became the leading authority on the *ṭaylasān*. In his book *Darr al-ghamāma fī dharr al-ṭaylasān wa-l-ʿadhaba wa-l-ʿimāma*, written around the mid-sixteenth century (exact year of writing unknown), he explains how the *ṭaylasān* was still a heavily debated topic:

> The ancient *ʿulamāʾ*, the *ḥadīth* of the Shāfiʿī law-school and others have discussed the meaning of the *ṭaylasān*. Now, I feel the need to summarize the importance of the shawl (*ṭaylasān*) due to its increasing significance. The *ṭaylasān* is precious and important but as well implies questions.[75]

---

70 For al-Subkī's influence on the restrictions against the non-Muslims, see al-Duwayhī, *Taʾrīkh* 319.

71 For the *ṭaylasān* and its wearing by the early companions of the Prophet, see al-Khaṭīb al-Baghdādī, *Jāmiʿ* i, 607.

72 Steingass, *Arabic-English Dictionary* 269.

73 Al-Suyūṭī, *Aḥadīth* 50; al-Nawawī, *Tahdhīb* 187.

74 Assmann, *Memory* 38.

75 Al-Haytamī, *Darr* 28.

10 Conclusion

Head-covers such as the *ṭaylasān* are visible sartorial markers of religious membership. They are an essential element in the construction of group cohesion and communal identity. The present study shows that head-covers such as the *ṭaylasān* could as well be subject to lively debates among Islamic scholars. These controversies revolved around both its religious and gender boundaries. Those in favor of the *ṭaylasān* emphasized its accordance to the *sunna* of the Prophet, while others who regarded it as *bidʿa* stressed its deep rootedness in the Persian and Jewish origin. Nevertheless, ambiguity of the shawl did not do any harm to its attractiveness amongst the Muslim and non-Muslim community from wearing it. According to the findings of this study, the wearing of the *ṭaylasān* was passed down through generations of Shāfiʿī forbearers, and the ideology and history they attached to it is well preserved in their writings. From their point of view, the wearing of the *ṭaylasān* was in accordance with the *sunna* of the Prophet Muḥammad. According to al-Suyūṭī's apologia, the Shāfiʿī law school argued that the prophetic traditions provide anecdotal evidence for its wearing by the companions of the Prophet. The *ṭaylasān* made the members of the school stand out and became a visible sartorial marker of their identity. The many ways in which the *ṭaylasān* was worn, such as wrapping it around the neck, wearing it over the turban, and draping it over the head (possibly to create a site for transcendence), is indicative of its popularity, especially amongst the elite. Many primary sources describe how Islamic authorities (preachers) and other high officials such as jurisprudents identified with this particular head-cover. In order to maintain its exclusiveness, it was often forbidden for non-Muslim minority groups to wear it. But besides religious boundaries gender boundaries were also discussed because of its resemblance to female head-covers and the usage of pins that created concerns about men resembling women. It has become evident that the *ṭaylasān* and other types of head-covers can function as sartorial markers of religious identity, and that they can constitute an important element of group cohesion and communal identity. This study also shows that the attachment of identity to a head-cover can make it subject to lively debates with controversies revolving around boundaries of religion and gender.

Bibliography

Primary Sources

Abū Dāʾūd, *Sunan*, 3 vols., Beirut 1996.
Abū l-Fidāʾ, *al-Mukhtaṣar fī akhbār al-bashar*, 4 vols., Cairo 1998.

Abū Shāma, *Kitāb al-Rawḍatayn fī akhbār al-dawlatayn al-Nūriyya wa-l-Ṣalāḥiyya*, 5 vols., Beirut 1997.
al-Bayhaqī, *al-Sunan al-kubrā*, 10 vols., Hyderabad 1934.
al-Bukhārī, *Ṣaḥīḥ*, 9 vols., Beirut 1984.
al-Dhahabī, *Kitāb al-Kabāʾir*, Beirut 1985.
al-Duwayhī, *Taʾrīkh al-azmina*, Beirut 1980.
al-Ghazālī, *Kitāb Iḥyāʾ ʿulūm al-dīn*, 2 vols. Cairo 1885.
al-Haytamī, *Darr al-ghamāma fī dharr al-ṭaylasān wa-l-ʿadhaba wa-l-ʿimāma*, Cairo n.d.
al-Haytamī, *Tuḥfat al-muḥtāj bi-Sharḥ al-Minhāj*, maʿa ḥawāshī ʿAbd al-Ḥamīd al-Shirwānī wa-Aḥmad b. Qāsim al-ʿAbbādī, 10 vols., Bombay [197?–?].
Ibn al-ʿAṭṭār, *Kitāb Adab al-khaṭīb*, Beirut 1996.
Ibn Baṭṭūṭa, [Riḥla] The travels of Ibn Baṭṭūṭa, trans. H.A.R. Gibb, 5 vols., Cambridge 1958.
Ibn Ḥajar al-ʿAsqalānī, *Inbāʾ al-ghumr bi-anbāʾ al-ʿumr*, 3 vols., Cairo 1972.
Ibn Ḥajar al-ʿAsqalānī, *Fatḥ al-bārī bi-Sharḥ al-Bukhārī*, 17 vols., Cairo 1963.
Ibn al-Ḥājj, *al-Madkhal*, 2 vols., Alexandria 1876.
Ibn Khallikān, *Wafayāt al-aʿyān wa-anbāʾ abnāʾ al-zamān*, 7 vols., Beirut 1900.
Ibn Manẓūr, *Lisān al-ʿArab*, 3 vols., Beirut 1979.
Ibn Qayyim al-Jawziyya, *Aḥkām ahl al-dhimma*, Beirut 1995.
Ibn Sabāṭ, *Taʾrīkh: Ṣidq al-akhbār*, Beirut, 1993.
Ibn Sīrīn, *Tafsīr al-aḥlām al-kabīr*, Beirut 1988.
Ibn Taghrī Birdī, [*an-Nujūm az-zāhira*], *Abû ʾl-Maḥāsin ibn Taghrî Birdî's annals: entitled an-Nujûm az-Zâhirâ fî mulûk Miṣr wal-Ḳâhirā*, ed. W. Popper, (University of California Publications), Berkely 1960.
al-Kalāʿī, *Iḥkam ṣanʿat al-kalām*, Beirut 1966.
al-Khaṭīb al-Baghdādī, *al-Jamiʿ li-akhlāq al-rāwī wa-ādāb al-samiʿ*, 2 vols., Beirut 1994.
al-Kutubī, *Fawāt al-Wafayāt*, 2 vols., Cairo 1866.
al-Maqqarī, *The history of the Mohammedan dynasties in Spain*, ed. P. de Gayangos, 2 vols., London 1840.
al-Maqrīzī, *Kitāb al-Mawāʿiz wa-l-iʿtibār bi-dhikr al-khiṭaṭ wa-l-āthār*, 2 vols., Cairo 1853.
al-Muqaddasī, *Aḥsan al-taqāsīm fī maʿrifat al-aqālīm*, trans. from the Arabic and ed. G.S.A. Ranking and R.F. Azoo, 4 fasc., (Bibliotheca Indica: a collection of Oriental works, new series, no. 899, 952, 1001, 1258), Calcutta 1897–1910.
al-Nābulusī, *Taʿṭīr al-anām fī taʿbīr al-manām*, Cairo 1877.
al-Nawawī, *Tahdhīb al-asmāʾ wa-l-lughāt*, Cairo 1930.
al-Qalqashandī, *Ṣubḥ al-aʿshā fī ṣināʿ at al-inshāʾ*, 14 vols., Damascus 1987.
al-Shāfiʿī, *al-Umm*, 9 vols., Cairo 1987.
al-Subkī, Tāj al-Dīn, *Ṭabaqāt al-Shāfiʿiyya al-kubrā*, Cairo 1906.
al-Subkī, Taqī l-Dīn, *Fatāwā*, Beirut 1983.

al-Suyūṭī, *al-Aḥadīth al-ḥisān fī faḍl al-ṭaylasān*, ed. A. Arazi, (The Max Schloessinger memorial series 5), Jerusalem 1983.

al-Thaʿālibī, *al-Tamthīl wa-l-muḥāḍara*, Cairo 1981.

al-Turkumānī, *Kitāb al-Lumaʿ fī l-ḥawādith wa-l-bidaʿ*, 2 vols., Cairo 1986.

al-Washshāʾ, *al-Muwashshā aw al-ẓarf wa-l-ẓurafāʾ*, Beirut 1990.

Yāqūt al-Hamawī, *Muʿjam al-buldān*, 5 vols., Beirut, 1984.

Zig-i taylasan, Leiden Ms Or. 99:3 (*Catalogus Codicum*, 1175).

Secondary Sources

Arazi, A., Noms de vêtements et vêtements d'après *al-Aḥādīṯ al-ḥisān fī faḍl al-ṭaylasān* d'al-Suyūṭī, in *Arabica* 23 (1976), 109–55.

Assmann, J., *Cultural memory and early civilization: Writing, remembrance, and political imagination*, New York 2011.

Bourdieu, P., Der Sozialraum und seine Transformationen, in P. Bourdieu, *Die feinen Unterschiede. Kritik der gesellschaftlichen Urteilskraft*, Frankfurt am Main 1982 (*La distinction. Critique sociale du jugement*, Paris 1979).

Chamberlain, M., *Knowledge and social practice in medieval Damascus 1190–1350*, Cambridge 1994.

Dozy, R.P.A., *Dictionnaire détaillé des noms des vêtements chez les Arabes*, Amsterdam 1845.

Dozy, R.P.A., M.J. de Goeje and P. de Jong, *Catalogus codicum orientalium Bibliothecae Academiae Lugduno-Batavae*, 6 vols., Leiden 1851–77.

Elias, N., *Über den Prozess der Zivilisation*, 2 vols., Frankfurt am Main 1969.

Fattal, A., *Le statut légal des non-musulmans en pays d'Islam*, Beirut 1958.

Fuess, A., Sultans with horns: The political significance of headgear in the Mamlūk empire, in *MSR* 12 (2008), 71–94.

Geoffroy, É., *Le Soufisme en Egypte et en Syrie sous les derniers Mamelouks et les premiers Ottomans: Orientations spirituelles et enjeux culturels*, Damascus 1995.

Goldziher, D.I., *Introduction to Islamic theology and law*, trans. A. and R. Hamori; intr. and additional notes B. Lewis, Princeton 1981.

Lane, E.W., *Arabic-English lexicon*, 8 vols., London 1863–93; repr. Cambridge 1984 (2 vols.).

Levy-Rubin, M., *Non-Muslims in the early Islamic empire: From surrender to coexistence*, Cambridge 2011.

Mayer, L.A., *Mamlūk costume: A survey*, Geneva 1952.

Sarshar, H.M., *The Jews of Iran: The history, religion and culture of a community in the Islamic world*, New York 2014.

Sartain, E.M., *Jalāl al-Dīn al-Suyūṭī.* i: *Biography and background*, (University of Cambridge Oriental Publications 23), Cambridge 1975.

Shoshan, B., Popular Sufi Sermons in Mamluk Egypt, in D.J. Wasserstein and A. Ayalon (eds.), *Mamluks and Ottomans. Studies in honour of Michael Winter*, New York 2006, 106–13.

Steingass, F., *Arabic-English dictionary*, London 1882; repr. New Delhi 1978.

Stillman, Y., *Arab dress: A short history from the dawn of Islam to modern times*, Leiden 2003.

Stilt, K., *Islamic law in action: Authority, discretion, and everyday experiences in Mamlūk Egypt*, Oxford 2012.

Tritton, A.S., *The Caliphs and their non-muslim subjects: a critical study of the covenant of ʿUmar*, London 1930; repr., London: F. Cass 1970.

Wasserstein, D.J. and A. Ayalon, *Mamlūks and Ottomans: Studies in honour of Michael Winter*, New York 2006.

Watts, A., *In my own way: An autobiography, 1915–1965*, New York 1972.

Wheatley, P., *The places where men pray together: Cities in Islamic lands, seventh through the tenth centuries*, Chicago 2001.

Young, M.J.L., Review of *al-Aḥadīth al-ḥisān fī faḍl al-ṭaylasān*, in *JRAS* 118 (1986), 102–3.

CHAPTER 5

Al-Suyūṭī's Stance Toward Worldly Power: A Reexamination Based on Unpublished and Understudied Sources[1]

Christian Mauder

1 Introduction

> During it [viz. the month of *Rajab* of the year 906/early 1501], our *shakyh* Jalāl al-Dīn al-Suyūṭī went into hiding. The sultan had searched for him in order to slay him. There had been bad blood between the two since the time when al-ʿĀdil had been grand *dawādār*; and various things had happened between them that would take long to speak about.[2]

This short note in Ibn Iyās' chronicle sheds light on one of the most troublesome periods in Jalāl al-Dīn al-Suyūṭī's (d. 911/1505) life. In 906/1501, his old enemy, the Amīr Ṭūmānbāy (d. 906/1501), had become sultan by the name of al-Malik al-ʿĀdil. Alarmed by this development, al-Suyūṭī went into hiding for fear of his life. He reappeared only after Ṭūmānbāy's removal from the sultanate later the same year.[3]

While al-Suyūṭī's fear that sultan Ṭūmānbāy would kill him was a rather extreme aspect of his relations with the holders of worldly power, his contacts with other sultans were not particularly friendly either. Here, the towering figure of the long-ruling sultan Qāytbāy figures prominently. Al-Suyūṭī's

1 I would like to thank the participants of the First Conference of the School of Mamlūk Studies in general and Michele Petrone, Yehoshua Frenkel, and Konrad Hirschler in particular for their helpful advice. I am moreover grateful to Sebastian Günther as well as Jens Scheiner and the other members of the Area-III Research Meeting of the CRC EDRIS of the University of Göttingen, Germany, for their feedback on earlier versions of this study. Furthermore, I would like to thank the Directorate of Süleymaniye Library, Istanbul, Turkey, for the permission to use unpublished material from its collection in the context of the present study. Finally, a sincere word of thanks goes to the anonymous reviewer for his or her valuable comments.

2 Ibn Iyās, *Badāʾiʿ* iii, 471. All translations from the Arabic are mine unless otherwise indicated.

3 Sartain, *Biography* 97–102. See also Spevack, al-Suyūṭī' 407; Saleh, al-Suyūṭī 75; Garcin, Histoire 37; ʿAtlam, Muḥaddithan 299.

 | DOI 10.1163/9789004334526_007

contacts with this sultan were as long-lasting as they were problematic. Of special importance in this conflict was the quarrel between the polymath and sultan Qāytbāy as to whether or not al-Suyūṭī had to come to the Citadel and greet the ruler on the beginning of every month. In 875/1470, al-Suyūṭī had accepted the post of the *shaykh* at the tomb of Barqūq al-Nāṣirī. The latter had stipulated that, after his death, the ruling sultan would serve as the supervisor of the pious foundation attached to his mausoleum. In his position as supervisor of Barqūq's foundation, sultan Qāytbāy demanded that al-Suyūṭī as the *shaykh* of the tomb report to him on a monthly basis. Al-Suyūṭī's refusal to do so brought about a conflict that lasted for many years and ran through various stages of escalation, including the famous dispute between al-Suyūṭī and the sultan on whether it was permissible to wear a particular item of clothing known as *ṭaylāsan*. While Qāytbāy and his entourage considered the *ṭaylāsan* to be at best a garment particular to the Mālikī school of law, and at worst an uncanonical habit followed mainly by Jews, al-Suyūṭī argued that it was indeed a custom (*sunna*) recommended to all Muslims.[4] The series of disputes between the two men over these and similar points ended only with Qāytbāy's death in 901/1496.[5]

The various problems he experienced with the sultans of his day influenced al-Suyūṭī's decision to reduce and eventually abandon his public activities during the last years of his life.[6] He thus rejected posts and favors that Ṭūmānbāy's successor, sultan Qānṣawh al-Ghawrī (d. 922/1516), had wanted to bestow on him.[7] Nevertheless, al-Suyūṭī yielded considerable influence over the intellectual life of the sultan's court. This is attested to by the only partially edited descriptions of the latter's educated salons (*majālis*).[8] These texts report several of al-Suyūṭī's points of view regarding religious questions discussed in the sultan's *majālis*.[9] But although these and other sources show that members of the Mamlūk court recognized al-Suyūṭī as a prominent scholarly and religious person during the final years of his life, the fact remains that, in light of his

4 [Editor's note] On this see Judith Kindinger, *Bidʿa* or *sunna*, (64–80).

5 Sartain, *Biography* 77, 86–91. See also Saleh, al-Suyūṭī 74; Spevack, al-Suyūṭī 403; Garcin, Histoire 37.

6 His withdrawal from public life is discussed in Sartain, *Biography* 80–6, 102–6. See also ʿAtlam, Muḥaddithan 299–300; Saleh, al-Suyūṭī 75; Spevack, al-Suyūṭī 406–7, 409.

7 Cp. on al-Suyūṭī and al-Ghawrī Sartain, *Biography* 81, 98, 103–6, 110–1, 145; Spevack, al-Suyūṭī 407; Garcin, Histoire 37–8; al-Shādhilī, *Bahja* 164–5, 167, 261.

8 I am currently preparing an in-depth analysis of these sources.

9 Cp., e.g., al-Sharif, *Nafāʾis* 7, 160–1. See also ibid. 187.

previous experiences with worldly rulers, he did his best not to become too closely entangled with the Mamlūk power apparatus.[10]

The present study analyzes whether and how al-Suyūṭī's strained relations with the rulers of the Mamlūk Empire during the latter part of his life were expressed in his theoretical writings. To this end, light is first shed on his famous treatise *Mā rawāhu l-asāṭīn fī ʿadam al-majīʾ ilā l-salāṭīn* (What has been transmitted by the pillars [of faith] about not going to the sultans) and its less known (and still unpublished) condensed version *al-Risāla al-Sulṭāniyya* (The sultanic epistle). Thereafter, the focus is turned to his largely neglected work *al-Aḥādīth al-munīfa fī faḍl al-salṭana al-sharīfa* (The exalted traditions about the merit of the noble sultanate). Because all of these works consist largely of *ḥadīth*s, it should be pointed out here that the individual prophetic traditions—all of which are quoted by al-Suyūṭī with an abbreviated *isnād*—and their possible original meaning are not discussed here.[11] Rather, I concentrate on what their compilation tells us about al-Suyūṭī's political thought. Finally, the main findings of the analysis are summarized.

2 *Mā rawāhu l-asāṭīn fī ʿadam al-majīʾ ilā l-salāṭīn* and *al-Risāla al-Sulṭāniyya*

It is generally held that al-Suyūṭī's strained relationship with the sultans of his times found its way into his scholarly works as well. In his analysis of the polymath's historical works, Jean-Claude Garcin highlights that, while upholding the claims of the ʿAbbasid caliphate, al-Suyūṭī stood in opposition to what he understood as the "illegal character of [the Mamlūk sultans'] power."[12] Similarly, in Éric Geoffrey's entry on al-Suyūṭī in the second edition of the *Encyclopaedia of Islam* we read: "Al-Suyūṭī always rejected peremptorily the de facto power of the Mamlūk [...sultans]...Conversely, the Abbasid caliphs were for him the incarnation of legitimacy."[13] Even more pointedly, Amy W. Newhall calls

10 For information on al-Suyūṭī's relations with various holders of worldly power during his life, see also Sartain, *Biography* 42–5, 71, 89, 94, 196, 109.

11 Readers interested in the context and original meaning of the traditions in question might wish to consult Kister, Concepts.

12 Garcin, Histoire 66.

13 Geoffroy, al-Suyūṭī 914.

al-Suyūṭī's veneration of the caliph's authority "unparalleled" and speaks about his "special disdain for secular rulers."[14]

Among the prime evidence of the interpretation that al-Suyūṭī disdained sultanic power are his theoretical treatises *al-Ināfa fī rutbat al-khilāfa* (Exalting the rank of the caliphate),[15] in which he argues for the legitimacy and the canonical status of the 'Abbasid caliphate, and his *Mā rawāhu l-asāṭīn*, which is of key importance in the context of the present study. In this last-mentioned work, al-Suyūṭī collected a large amount of material that supported his standpoint in the conflict with sultan Qāytbāy, i.e., that a scholar neither had to nor indeed should visit worldly rulers.[16] Written in 901/1495, it is a direct product of al-Suyūṭī's struggle to free himself from the obligation to pay a courtesy visit to the sultan's palace every month. How he tries to accomplish this goal says much not only about his self-image as a scholar and pious Muslim, but also about his stance toward worldly power in general.

Mā rawāhu l-asāṭīn can be divided into five parts: The first part of the text consists of a carefully compiled list of sayings of the Prophet Muḥammad emphasizing that righteous scholars must avoid visiting rulers on all costs. The second part features reports about early Muslims upholding and buttressing the Prophet's warning, while the third one narrates pertinent examples from the life of pious scholars. The fourth section consists of a comprehensive quotation from al-Ghazālī (d. 505/1111) warning scholars from attending worldly rulers. The treatise concludes with a number of poems relevant to the topic.

While previous scholarship has often paid only superficial attention to what seemed to be a text written with a very straightforward and obvious agenda, a more detailed study of the prophetic traditions collected by al-Suyūṭī is indeed worthwhile. While all of these traditions have in common that they warn scholars against visiting rulers and their courts due to moral hazards, one may detect an interesting difference between the two types of *ḥadīth*s cited. The first category of traditions focuses exclusively on the behavior of the scholar himself and its possible consequences. A typical *ḥādīth* of this type reads: "The Messenger of God said: 'If you see a scholar who mingles (*yukhāliṭu*) often with

14 Newhall, *Patronage* 62 (both quotations). [Editor's note]. On al-Suyūṭī's attitude towards the caliphs see Mustafa Banister, Casting the caliph in a cosmic role, (98–117).

15 For an edition and study of this work, see Arazi and El'ad (eds.), Ināfa.

16 See on this work also e.g. Saleh, al-Suyūṭī 74; 'Abd al-Ra'uf, Mu'allafāt 116–7; 'Atlam, Muḥaddithan 325 and especially Sartain, *Biography* 89–90.

the sultan, know that he is a thief (*liṣṣ*).'"[17] Other, longer traditions belonging to this category are the following:

> The Messenger of God said: "[As for him] who reads the Quran and devotes himself to the religious law and then goes to someone in power (*ṣāḥib sulṭān*) avid for what the latter possesses, God makes a mark on his heart and he is punished every day with two kinds (*bi-lawnayn*) of punishments not afflicted before."[18]
>
> The Messenger of God said: "In hell, there is valley against which one should seek protection seventy times a day; God prepared it for the readers [of the Quran] who behave hypocritically in their actions (*al-murāʾīna fī aʿmālihim*), and verily, there is no creature more loathsome to God than a sultan's scholar (*ʿālim al-sulṭān*)."[19]

While these and similar traditions censure and warn only the scholar who associates himself with those in power, the second type of quoted traditions implies ethical judgments on the deeds of both the scholar and the ruler he visits. Here, the ruler's immoral acts are presented as the real danger to the righteous scholar, who has to keep himself apart from the powerful due to the presumed "contagiousness" of their misdeeds. Examples of *ḥadīth*s that fall into this second category are:

> The Prophet said: "After me, there will be sultans, and discord (*fitan*) is at their doors (*ʿalā abwābihim*) like resting places for camels, and they do not give anything to anybody unless they take away an equal share from his religiosity."[20]
>
> The Messenger of God said: "After me, there will be rulers (*umarāʾ*), and he who goes to them lends credibility to their lies (*ṣaddaqahum bi-kadhbihim*) and helps them, in their injustice (*ẓulm*) does not belong to me and I do not belong to him ..."[21]

By adducing examples of this second kind of tradition in his treatise, al-Suyūṭī does more than simply give moral advice to his fellow scholars; he is also criticizing the wrongdoings of those in power after the time of the Prophet

17 Al-Suyūṭī, *Mā rawāhu* 37.
18 Ibid. 51.
19 Ibid. 35. For other traditions of this kind, see also ibid. 31–8, 40–1, 44–7, 49–52.
20 Ibid. 49.
21 Ibid. 39. For similar traditions, see also ibid. 41–3, 45, 47–8.

Muḥammad—including thus implicitly also the rulers of his own days. Moreover, he links them to two the vilest acts known in Islamic political theory: First, when rulers are associated with the causing of *fitna*, i.e., a state of discord, trial, or even civil war that poses a threat to both the integrity of the Muslim polity and the purity of the faith of the individual believer;[22] and second, when those in power appear to be prone to abusing their position by practicing injustice and tyranny (*ẓulm*). By performing *ẓulm*, they act counter to the countless admonitions by Muslim political theorists that the upholding of justice (*ʿadl*) is among the prime duties of every ruler. Moreover, they also violate a key commandment of the Quran.[23] Viewed against this background, al-Suyūṭī's *Mā rawāhu l-asāṭīn* can be seen not only as a guide for the behavior of righteous scholars, but also as an expression of political critique, if not indeed outright opposition against those in power.

However, such a reading should keep in mind that *Mā rawāhu l-asāṭīn* was not addressed directly to the sultan, but rather to al-Suyūṭī's academic colleagues and rivals. The text actually sent to the sultan's court as part al-Suyūṭī's efforts to rid himself from the obligation of regular attendance bears the simple title *al-Risāla al-Sulṭāniyya*. While the existence of this short text has been noted by previous scholarship,[24] it has so far been neither edited nor studied.[25]

According to al-Suyūṭī's autobiography, studied by E.M. Sartain, the former dictated the treatise *al-Risāla al-Sulṭāniyya* to the envoys of a high-ranking *amīr* who was asked to mediate between him and sultan Qāytbāy. It was meant as an abridgment of *Mā rawāhu l-asāṭīn*, which had been written slightly earlier.[26] This information is confirmed by an introductory note at the beginning of *al-Risāla al-Sulṭāniyya*:

> He [sc. al-Suyūṭī] wrote it [sc. the treatise] when al-Ashraf Qāytbāy urged him to visit him frequently (*al-taraddud ilayhi*), but he refused to do so. Then, some of his [sc. al-Suyūṭī's] enemies came to him [sc. the sultan] and claimed that he had no reason to refuse to meet the sultan. Then he

22 Gardet, Fitna 930–1.

23 Badry, Ẓulm 567–9. On the connection of this term to *fitna*, see ibid. 568.

24 ʿAtlam, Muḥaddithan 321; Sartain, *Biography* 90.

25 In the present study, I use the manuscript Süleymaniye, Esad Efendi 3623. This manuscript can on paleographical grounds be dated to the sixteenth century and consists of a collection of smaller works by al-Suyūṭī. *Al-Risāla al-Sulṭāniyya* is included on fols. 114a–116b. On manuscripts of al-Suyūṭī's works in the Süleymaniye Library, see Iḥsān Oğlu, Makhṭūṭāt 151–2.

26 Sartain, *Biography* 89–90.

> [sc. al-Suyūṭī] sent it [sc. the treatise] to him. Thereupon, he [sc. the sultan] abstained from calling him in (*fa-taraka ṭalabahu*). It [sc. the treatise] is his selection from his large work (*min kitābihi l-kabīr*)[27] on that [topic] and what is similar to it.[28]

That the treatise made the sultan at least temporarily change his mind is also indicated in al-Suyūṭī's autobiography, where al-Suyūṭī stated that, at his request, *al-Risāla al-Sulṭāniyya* was read out to Qāytbāy, who—according al-Suyūṭī's report—did not voice any critique about its contents, but indeed declared: "If he [sc. al-Suyūṭī] took a stick and beat me with it after this, I would not say anything to him."[29]

As we have seen, *Mā rawāhu l-asāṭīn* included a number of prophetic traditions that could be understood as accusing those in power of severe misdeeds. It might thus be surprising to learn that Qāytbāy is said to have received its abridgment *al-Risāla al-Sulṭāniyya* in such a conciliatory manner—especially since, at first glance, its structure and content would appear to mirror exactly that of the longer work. However, a close reading of the section of *al-Risāla al-Sulṭāniyya* featuring prophetic traditions is quite revealing in this context: It consists almost entirely of *ḥadīths* belonging to the first category previously mentioned, that is, traditions that warn scholars from attending rulers without criticizing those in power directly. The only tradition from the second category included is a rather tame and restrained one, according to which a scholar attending a person in power shares with the latter his punishment in the afterlife.[30] Throughout *al-Risāla al-Sulṭāniyya*, no ruler is actually accused of committing *ẓulm* or causing *fitna*. Thus, al-Suyūṭī obviously avoided including in this text exactly those traditions that might have added fresh fuel to his quarrel with the sultan. Even such a headstrong person as al-Suyūṭī obviously considered it better not to be too outspoken when addressing the sultan nor to be too blatant in voicing political critique. Instead, he made a carefully considered decision on how to address what he perceived as the ills of his time. At the same time, he sought to legitimize his own behavior by demonstrating that he was merely following the Prophet's directives and emulating the pious ancestors' conduct.

---

27 This refers to *Mā rawāhu l-asāṭīn fī ʿadam al-majīʾ ilā l-salāṭīn*.

28 Al-Suyūṭī, *Risāla* fol. 114a.

29 Sartain, *Biography* 90 (Sartain's translation).

30 Al-Suyūṭī, *Risāla* fol. 115b, see also al-Suyūṭī, *Mā rawāhu* 45.

3 *Al-Aḥādīth al-munīfa fī faḍl al-salṭana al-sharīfa*

Such minor qualifications notwithstanding, the close reading of al-Suyūṭī's theoretical treatises so far supports common knowledge about his negative attitude toward worldly power. It is therefore most intriguing to note the existence of a third relevant text by al-Suyūṭī, which is decidedly different not only in tone, but also in content. So far, this work has been almost completely ignored by Western scholars focusing on the person of Jalāl al-Dīn al-Suyūṭī and his thoughts—despite its interesting and indeed revealing title: *al-Aḥādīth al-munīfa fī faḍl al-salṭana al-sharīfa* (The exalted traditions about the merit of the noble sultanate).

The most important reason for this neglect lies most probably in the difficult accessibility of this text. While there exists a small booklet that is meant to be a scholarly edition of *al-Aḥādīth al-munīfa*, this publication is fraught with so many problems that is seems to be usable only with caution, if at all. Based on the microfilm of a single incomplete manuscript of unknown age and value,[31] a major part of the introduction to the work is missing in this edition.[32] What is more, the editor thought the work to be much longer than it originally was and therefore included in his edition some material of unclear origin. Compared with other witnesses of the text, it turns out that only what the editor calls the first section (*bāb*) of the edited text[33] indeed belongs to al-Suyūṭī's original treatise, whereas the following, thematically clearly different sections[34] belong to one or several other works still to be identified. This situation is also reflected in the erroneous title of the edited text, which is given as *al-Aḥādīth al-munīfa fī faḍl al-salṭana al-sharīfa wa-anwāʿ al-khayrāt al-maʾlūfa*. All premodern and modern references to the work consulted, however, give its title (with very small variants) as *al-Aḥādīth al-munīfa fī faḍl al-salṭana al-sharīfa*.[35] None of them mentions the addition *wa-anwāʿ al-khayrāt al-maʾlūfa*, which may also be seen as interfering with the rhymed structure of the original title.

---

31 Al-Saʿdanī, Muqaddimat al-muḥaqqiq, in al-Suyūṭī, *Aḥādīth* 1 10–11 (*Aḥādīth* 1= al-Saʿdanī's ed.; *Aḥādīth* 2= MS Süleymaniye).

32 Al-Suyūṭī, *Aḥādīth* 1 13.

33 Ibid. 13–34.

34 Ibid. 35–120.

35 See, e.g., al-Khāzindār and al-Shaybānī, *Dalīl* 48 (no. 72); al-Baghdādī, *Hadiya* i, 535; ʿAtlam, Muḥaddithan 315.

According to available manuscript witnesses, which often offer a better text than the edition itself,[36] the work begins after the usual invocation of God and a prayer for the Prophet with a short introduction not found in the edition. It reads:

> I compiled this book on the merit (*faḍl*) of the discharge of the noble sultanate (*salṭana*) and collected in it what has been transmitted among the traditions and reports [about this topic] and what has been disposed about the reward for the discharge of this noble office (*al-manṣib al-sharīf*).[37]

Thereafter follows a compilation of 27 traditions, which can again be divided into two groups. The first type comprises *ḥadīth*s that include the keyword "*sulṭān*"[38] that is understood by al-Suyūṭī as not denoting an abstract concept such as "governmental power", but as meaning a particular office of political leadership—an interpretation already made explicit in the title and the introduction of the work.[39] Here, some examples of this first category of *ḥadīth*s:

> The Messenger of God said: "If you pass a locality without a sultan, do not enter it, for the sultan is the shadow and the lance of God on earth (*ẓill Allāh wa-rumḥuhu fī l-arḍ*)."[40]
>
> I heard the Messenger of God saying: "Do not insult (*lā tasubbū*) the sultan, for he is the shadow of God on earth."[41]
>
> The Messenger of God said: "The sultan is the shadow of God on earth. Who honors him (*akramahu*) is honored by God, and who disdains him (*ahānahu*) is disdained by God."[42]

36 For the reasons given above, all quotations from the edited version of the work have been checked against the text given in MS Süleymaniye, Reşid Effendi 988, fols. 502b–504a. On the reliability of this manuscript, see Arazi and Elʿad (eds.), Ināfa 244.

37 Al-Suyūṭī, *Aḥādīth* 2 fol. 502b.

38 On this term in the context of *ḥadīth* literature, see Kramers and Bosworth, Sulṭān 849, and on the shift in its meaning ibid. 849–51.

39 On al-Suyuti's understanding of the term as designating a particular office, see also Kramers and Bosworth, Sulṭān 850. For examples of a different understanding in earlier writers, see, e.g., Rosenthal, *Thought* 39.

40 Al-Suyūṭī, *Aḥādīth 1* 29; al-Suyūṭī, *Aḥādīth* 2 fol. 503a.

41 Al-Suyūṭī, *Aḥādīth 1* 23; al-Suyūṭī, *Aḥādīth* 2 fol. 503a.

42 Al-Suyūṭī, *Aḥādīth 1* 24; al-Suyūṭī, *Aḥādīth* 2 fol. 502b.

Although some of these traditions belonging to the first type emphasize the importance of justice on the part of the ruler,[43] his rank as the shadow of God on earth does not depend on it. In this capacity, he possesses a kind of particular religious quality earlier Muslim writers had accorded solely to the caliph. Moreover, the Prophet himself is presented as prescribing a sultan as a legally necessary element of an Islamic polity, as no Muslim may live in a place without a sultan. At any rate, the position of the sultan is here far removed from the negative image of those in power conveyed in al-Suyūṭī's other writings.

The significance of the second group of traditions is even greater. Here, not "*sulṭān*," but "*imām*" is the key term. Examples of this second group include the following:

> The Messenger of God said: "A day with a just (*ʿādil*) *imām* is better than sixty years of worship."[44]
>
> The Messenger of God said: "The person dearest (*aḥabb*) to God on the Day of Resurrection and the one who sits closest to him is a just *imām*."[45]
>
> The Messenger of God said: "He who dies without an *imām* dies a pagan death (*fa-mītatuhu jāhiliyya*)."[46]

As is well known, the word "*imām*" has not only religious meanings in Islamic thought.[47] In the political context, it was considered by Sunni thinkers as largely synonymous with the designation "*khalīfa*." To quote the late A.K.S. Lambton: "As used in the sources, the terms *khalīfa* and *imām* [...] are broadly interchangeable."[48] Going one step further, Michael Winter writes "[A]s is well known, the term *imām* in the Sunni legal terminology is the caliph, not the sultan."[49] This common usage that equates *imām* and *khalīfa* is also attested to in other works by al-Suyūṭī.[50]

It is thus intriguing to find traditions that speak about the office of the *imām* in a text by al-Suyūṭī dedicated to the topic of the "merit of the discharge of the

43 See, e.g., al-Suyūṭī, *Aḥādīth 1* 23; al-Suyūṭī, *Aḥādīth 2* fol. 503a.

44 Al-Suyūṭī, *Aḥādīth 1* 31; al-Suyūṭī, *Aḥādīth 2* fol. 503b.

45 Al-Suyūṭī, *Aḥādīth 1* 21; al-Suyūṭī, *Aḥādīth 2* fol. 502b.

46 Al-Suyūṭī, *Aḥādīth 1* 28. al-Suyūṭī, *Aḥādīth 2* fol. 503a, has a small textual variant at the end (*māta mīta jāhiliyya*).

47 See, e.g., Madelung, Imāma.

48 Lambton, Khalīfa 948. See also Rosenthal, *Thought* 36.

49 Winter, Judiciary 200. See on this question also Tezcan, Hanafism 71–2; Winter, Competition 197.

50 E.g., Arazi and Elʿad (eds.), Ināfa, 248–9, 252.

noble sultanate."[51] By including these traditions in his compilation, al-Suyūṭī implicitly acknowledges that the sultan can be identified with the *imām*. This stands in marked contrast to classical Sunni political theory, which sees the caliph as the *imām*. While al-Suyūṭī's departure from this older point of view is not without parallel in other Muslim thinkers from the Late Middle Period,[52] it is most surprising in his case for at least two reasons: First, it seems to contradict some of his other writings in which he emphasizes the exalted position of the caliphate, such as his *al-Ināfa fī rutbat al-khilāfa*. In this work, he lists a number of conditions a candidate must fulfill before he can be accepted as *imām*. Since descent not only from the tribe of Quraysh[53] but also from the ʿAbbasid family[54] figures prominently among these conditions, hardly any of the mainly Turkish, Circassian, and Mongol sultans of the Late Middle Period could, according to the stipulations cited by our author in this work, be considered rightful *imām*. Second, the identification of the sultan with the *imām* of the prophetic sayings is tantamount to a full-fledged recognition and highly positive evaluation of the office of the sultanate, now equated with the venerable and sublime Imamate. Al-Suyūṭī takes this step despite his problems with the holders of the sultanate. He thus legitimizes the power of those very men with whom he stood in a series of long-term conflicts, with one among them even allegedly making an attempt on his life.

But is *al-Aḥādīth al-munīfa* indeed an authentic work by al-Suyūṭī? According to present knowledge, there is nothing to suggest that the treatise was not penned by this author. The work appears in several lists of the polymath's authentic works,[55] including the one by his pupil ʿAbd al-Qādir b. Muḥammad al-Shādhilī (d. after 945/1538) in the latter's work *Bahjat al-ʿābidīn bi-tarjamat Jalāl al-Dīn* (Delight of the worshipers at the biography of Jalal al-Dīn).[56] However, the fact that it is not mentioned in al-Suyūṭī's autobiography, which the author seems to have largely abandoned in the 1490s[57] and which therefore lists his works only up until roughly 900/1495,[58] points to a rather late date of production during the last years of the author's lifetime.

51 Al-Suyūṭī, *Aḥādīth* 2 fol. 502b.
52 Cp. Lambton, *State* 139–43, 180–7; Madelung, Imāma 1168; Sourdel, K͟halīfa 945. See also Lambton, Khalīfa 949; Rosenthal, *Thought* 43–7.
53 Arazi and Elʿad (eds.), Ināfa 246–54.
54 Arazi and Elʿad (eds.), Ināfa 254–61.
55 E.g., al-Khāzindār and al-Shaybānī, *Dalīl* 48 (no. 72); al-Baghdādī, *Hadiya* i, 535; ʿAtlam, Muḥaddithan 315.
56 Al-Shādhilī, *Bahja* 202. On this work and its author, see Sartain, *Biography* 146–7.
57 Sartain, *Biography* 146.
58 Spevack, al-Suyūṭī 406.

Why then did al-Suyūṭī write this curious text? Unfortunately, the work itself contains no helpful information on this matter, and while we may assume that the treatise was dedicated to or written for a Muslim ruler holding the title of sultan,[59] it is hard to imagine al-Suyūṭī composing it for one of the Mamlūk sultans who ruled over Egypt and Syria during or after the last decade of the fifteenth century.

A possible answer to the problem of the original context of the work may lie in a short and largely neglected note by Africanist John Hunwick. While working at the Bibliothèque Générale et Archives in Rabat in 1967, Hunwick came across a manuscript of the work *al-Minaḥ al-ḥamīda fī Sharḥ al-Farīda* (The praiseworthy gifts regarding the commentary on *al-Farīda*) by Muḥammad Bābā b. Muḥammad al-Amīn al-Tinbuktī. This West African scholar died in d. 1014/1606 at the age of 82, thus being almost a contemporary of al-Suyūṭī. His *al-Minaḥ al-ḥamīda fī Sharḥ al-Farīda*, written as a commentary on al-Suyūṭī's *al-Farīda fī l-naḥw wa-l-taṣrīf wa-l-khaṭṭ* (The precious pearl in syntax, inflection and penmanship), contains a biographical note on the Egyptian scholar, which includes the following passage:

> When […] Askiya al-Ḥājj Muḥammad entered Egypt on his way to perform the pilgrimage, he met with him [sc. al-Suyūṭī] and frequented him and put questions to him on various matters. [Al-Suyūṭī] composed for him *al-Aḥādīth al-mutqana fī faḍl al-salṭana al-sharīfa*.[60]

This Askiya al-Ḥājj Muḥammad was an African Muslim ruler who had become sultan in 898/1493 and died in 944/1538. His realm, the Songhay Empire, was a West African polity that existed from the mid-fifteenth to the late sixteenth century and included the urban centers of Gao, Jenne, and Timbuktu in what is now the Republic of Mali. Askiya Muḥammad performed the *ḥajj* between 902/1496 and 903/1498.[61] On his way to Mecca, he spent considerable time in Cairo, where the ʿAbbasid caliph is said to have invested him with the rule of the lands of Takrūr, that is, the land of the West African Sahel.[62] This investi-

59 On al-Suyūṭī's habit of writing scholarly works "on demand," see Geoffroy, al-Suyūṭī 914.

60 Hunwick, Note 175–6 (Hunwick's translation, transliteration modified). Cp. also Saad, Timbuktu 47–8, who assumes that the work written for Askiya al-Ḥājj Muḥammad is no longer extant.

61 Hunwick, Muḥammad b. Abī Bakr. See for the broader context also Hunwick, Religion 296–9, 306–10; Hunwick, Power 181–2; Hunwick, Songhay 729.

62 Cp. al-Saʿdī, *Taʾrīkh* 120 (French text), 73 (Arabic text). See also Hunwick, Muḥammad b. Abī Bakr 394; Hunwick, Religion 307; Sartain, Relations 195–6; Saad, *Timbuktu* 47. On the

ture was allegedly made possible by the help of Jalāl al-Dīn al-Suyūṭī, who is known to have entertained particularly good relations with both the caliph in Cairo and the people of Takrūr.[63] Several sources emphasize the close contact between al-Suyūṭī and Askiya Muḥammad and show the ruler obtaining valuable instruction and advice from the scholar.[64]

Yet, according to present knowledge, Muḥammad Bābā al-Tinbuktī was the only scholar who explicitly stated that al-Suyūṭī wrote an independent work for Askiya Muḥammad. As to its title, there may be no doubt that *al-Aḥādīth al-mutqana* is a misreading or misspelling of the correct *al-Aḥādīth al-munīfa.*

To date, there is no way to confirm al-Tinbuktī's identification of Askiya Muḥammad as the dedicatee of al-Suyūṭī's treatise through an independent source of information.[65] But two points make it likely that the African scholar's statement is correct. First, one can perceive a certain hastiness in the compilation of the work: It contains numerous traditions that are weak by the standards of traditional Muslim scholarship, as must have been known to such a well-versed expert in *ḥadīth* studies as al-Suyūṭī.[66] Moreover, it is made up of only 27 instead of the more preferable 40 traditions usually included in *ḥadīth* collections on a specific topic. What is more, it places next to each other traditions that, from a legal point of view, might be thought to contradict one another, thus potentially leaving a reader interested in their juridical meaning confused. All of these facts, however, are easily explainable if *al-Aḥādīth al-munīfa fī faḍl al-salṭana al-sharīfa* was written within a short period of time for a ruler passing through. Second, according to the content of the treatise, al-Suyūṭī was on friendly terms with its dedicatee, who obviously held the

importance of this investiture, see also Hunwick, Piety 300; Hunwick, Successors 85–6, 88. For the term Takrūr, see also Hunwick, Takrūr 142–3; Hunwick, Successors 86. For a notably different account of Askiya Muḥammad's investiture, see Maḥmūd Kaʿti (attr.), *Taʾrīkh* 12.

63 On his relations with and influence on the people of Takrūr, see, e.g., Palmer, Conception; Hunwick, Notes; al-Shādhilī, *Bahja* 165, 279; Sartain, Relations; Saad, *Timbuktu* 47–8, 63, 66, 76, 79–81; Sartain, *Biography* 50–2, 70–1. On his role in an earlier similar investiture, see al-Suyūṭī, *Taḥadduth*, 158–9; Geoffroy, al-Suyūṭī 913; Saad, *Timbuktu* 47; Sartain, *Biography* 50–1.

64 See, e.g., Hunwick, Timbuktu 310–1; Hunwick, Successors 89; al-Saʿdī, *Taʾrīkh* (French text), 73 (Arabic text); Maḥmūd Kaʿti (attr.), *Taʾrīkh* 12–5, 68–9; Sartain, Relations 195–6; Sartain, *Biography* 51.

65 As Michele Petrone (University of Copenhagen) informed me, no manuscript of *al-Aḥādīth al-munīfa* is known to exist in West Africa libraries.

66 For al-Suyūṭī as an expert in the field of *ḥadīth*, see ʿAtlam, Muḥaddithan; Ṭaḥḥān, Muḥaddithan.

rank of a sultan. Since the work was apparently written during the last years of al-Suyūṭī's life, and given the strained relations between the scholar and the Mamlūk rulers of this period, its most plausible dedicatee was a foreign ruler, such as Askiya Muḥammad.[67] If this assumption is correct, the meeting with this ruler thus induced al-Suyūṭī to compile a work that bears witness to a much more positive evaluation of worldly power than previously known from his writings. Whereas his relations with many of the holders of the sultanate of his days were problematic, *al-Aḥādīth al-munīfa* suggests that al-Suyūṭī had a rather positive opinion of the office itself.

4 Conclusion

Let us now, by way of conclusion, sum up the main findings of our reexamination of al-Suyūṭī's stance toward worldly power. Without doubt, al-Suyūṭī's relations with the sultans of his time were mostly far from cordial. We know of several quarrels between him and sultan Qāytbāy. During the succession crisis that followed the death of the long-ruling sultan, our polymath even had to go into hiding for fear of his life. Later on, he refused to accept any office or favor from sultan al-Ghawrī. Nevertheless, he did wield considerable influence over the intellectual life of the sultan's court.

Al-Suyūṭī's strained relations with the rulers of his day found entry into at least some of his writings in the field of political theory. By means of a careful compilation of prophetic traditions, al-Suyūṭī not only explained in his *Mā rawāhu l-asāṭīn* why a scholar should not attend those in power, but also voiced a fundamental critique of their misdeeds. It is noteworthy, however, that this critique was almost completely missing in *al-Risāla al-Sulṭāniyya*, the condensed version of the aforementioned text that was actually sent to the sultan.

A totally different stance toward worldly power is however attested to in his *al-Aḥādīth al-munīfa*. Here, al-Suyūṭī did his best to compile traditions that praise the sultanate, which he considered to be officially sanctioned by the Prophet Muḥammad himself. Thereby, he was even willing to attribute to sultans prerogatives usually assigned to caliphs. An explanation for the curious character of this last studied treatise may be that it was most probably written for a foreign ruler. Nevertheless, its very existence shows that al-Suyūṭī's contribution to Islamic political theory is much more multifaceted than previously

67 For al-Suyūṭī's relations with other foreign rulers see, e.g., Sartain, *Biography* 49–50.

thought. We may therefore conclude that, also in this field of knowledge, al-Suyūṭī was a versatile and original author who deserves our full attention.

Bibliography

Primary Sources

al-Baghdādī, *Hadiyat al-ʿārifīn: Asmāʾ al-muʾallifīn wa-āthār al-muṣannifīn*, ed. R. Bilge, İ.M.K. İnal, A. Aktuç, 6 vols., Istanbul 1951–5.

Ibn Iyās, [*Badāʾiʿ al-zuhūr fī waqāʾiʿ al-duhūr*] *Die Chronik des Ibn-Ijās*, iii, AH 872–906/AD 1468–1501, ed. M. Muṣṭafā (BI 5c), Wiesbaden 1963.

Maḥmūd Kaʿti al-Tinbuktī, (attr.), *Taʾrīkh al-fattāsh fī akhbār al-buldān wa-l-juyūsh wa-akbār al-nās*, ed. O.V. Houdas and M. Delafosse, Paris 1913.

al-Saʿdī, *Taʾrīkh al-sūdān* (Documents arabes relatifs a l'histoire du Soudan 10), ed. and trans. O. Houdas, Paris 1900.

al-Shādhilī, *Bahjat al-ʿābidīn bi-tarjamat Ḥāfiẓ al-ʿAṣr Jalāl al-Dīn*, ed. ʿA. Nabhān, Damascus 1998.

al-Sharīf, *Nafāʾis majālis al-sulṭāniyya fī ḥaqāʾiq al-asrār al-Qurʾāniyya*, MS Topkapı Sarayı, Ahmet III 2680.

al-Suyūṭī, [*Aḥādīth 1*] *al-Aḥādīth al-munīfa fī faḍl al-salṭana al-sharīfa wa-anwāʿ al-khayrāt al-maʾlūfa*, ed. M.ʿA. al-Saʿdanī, Cairo 1992.

al-Suyūṭī, [*Aḥādīth 2*] *al-Aḥādīth al-munīfa fī faḍl al-salṭana al-sharīfa*, Süleymaniye, Raşid Effendi 988, fols. 502b–504a.

al-Suyūṭī, *Mā rawāhu l-asāṭīn fī ʿadam al-majīʾ ilā l-salāṭīn*, ed. A. Būsarīḥ, Beirut 1992.

al-Suyūṭī, *al-Risāla al-Sulṭāniyya*, MS Süleymaniye, Esad Efendi 3623, fols. 114a–116b.

al-Suyūṭī, *al-Taḥadduth bi-niʿmat Allah*, in Sartain, E.M., *Jalāl al-dīn al-Suyūṭī. ii: al-Taḥadduth bi-niʿmat Allāh* (University of Cambridge Oriental Publications 24), ed. E.M. Sartain, Cambridge 1975.

Secondary Sources

ʿAbd al-Raʾūf, ʿI., Muʿallafāt al-Suyūṭī, in al-Majlis al-Aʿlā li-Riʿāyat al-Funūn wa-l-Ādāb wa-l-ʿUlūm al-Ijtimāʿiyya (ed.), *Jalāl al-Dīn al-Suyūṭī: Buḥūth ulqiyat fī l-nadwa allatī aqāmahā al-Majlis al-Aʿlā li-Riʿāyat al-Funūn wa-l-Ādāb wa-l-ʿUlūm al-Ijtimāʿiyya bi-l-ishtirāk maʿa al-Jamʿiyya al-Miṣriyya lil-Dirāsāt al-Taʾrīkhiyya 6–10 mārs 1976*, Cairo 1978, 104–32.

Arazi, A. and A. Elʿad (eds.), al-Ināfa fī rutbat al-xilāfa de Ğalāl al-Dīn al-Suyūṭī, in *IOS* 8 (1978), 230–65.

ʿAtlam, ʿA., al-Suyūṭī muḥaddithan, in al-Majlis al-Aʿlā li-Riʿāyat al-Funūn wa-l-Ādāb wa-l-ʿUlūm al-Ijtimāʿiyya (ed.), *Jalāl al-Dīn al-Suyūṭī: Buḥūth ulqiyat fī l-nadwa allatī aqāmahā al-Majlis al-Aʿlā li-Riʿāyat al-Funūn wa-l-Ādāb wa-l-ʿUlūm al-Ijtimāʿiyya bi-l-ishtirāk maʿa al-Jamʿiyya al-Miṣriyya lil-Dirāsāt al-Taʾrīkhiyya 6–10 mārs 1976*, Cairo 1978, 292–374.

Badry, R., Ẓulm, in *EI*², xi, 567–9.

Garcin, J.C., Histoire, opposition politique et piétisme traditionaliste dans le *Ḥusn al-Muḥādarat* de Suyûti, in *AI* 7 (1967), 33–90.

Gardet, L., Fitna, in *EI*², ii, 930–1.

Geoffrey, É., al-Suyūṭī, in *EI*², ix, 913–6.

Hunwick, J.O., Askia al-Ḥājj Muḥammad and his successors: The account of al-Imām al-Takrūrī, in *Sudanic Africa* 1 (1990), 85–9.

Hunwick, J.O., Muḥammad b. Abī Bakr, in *EI*², vii, 393–4.

Hunwick, J.O., A note on Askiya al-Ḥājj Muḥammad's meeting with al-Suyūṭī, in *Sudanic Africa* 2 (1991), 175–6.

Hunwick, J.O., Notes on a late fifteenth-century document concerning 'al-Takrūr', in C. Allen and R.W. Johnson (eds.), *African perspectives: Papers in the history, politics and economics of Africa presented to Thomas Hodgkin*, Cambridge 1970, 7–33.

Hunwick, J.O., Piety and power: Relations between the religious estate and the ruling estate in Songhay under the Askiyas, in Maʿhad al-Dirāsāt al-Ifrīqiyya (ed.), *Le Maroc et l'Afrique subsaharienne aux débuts des temps modernes: Les Saʿadiens et l'empire Songhay* (Publications de l'Institut des études africaines. Série Colloques et séminaires 2), Rabat 1995, 283–303.

Hunwick, J.O., Religion and state in the Songhay Empire, 1464–1591, in I.M. Lewis (ed.), *Islam in tropical Africa: Studies presented and discussed at the fifth international African Seminar, Ahamdu Bello University, Zaria, January 1964*, Oxford 1966, 296–317.

Hunwick, J.O., Secular power and religious authority in Muslim society: The case of Songhay, in *Journal of African History* 37 (1996), 175–94.

Hunwick, J.O., Songhay, in *EI*², ix, 728–30.

Hunwick, J.O, Takrūr, in *EI*², x, 142–3.

Hunwick, J.O., *Timbuktu and the Songhay empire: Al-Saʿdī's* Taʾrīkh al-sūdān *down to 1613 and other contemporary documents* (IHC 27), Leiden, Boston and Köln 1999.

Iḥsān Oğlu, A., Makhṭūṭāt Jalāl al-Dīn al-Suyūṭī fī maktabāt Turkiyā, in M.T. Abū ʿAlī and Ṣ. Qashmar (eds.), *al-Imām Jalāl al-Dīn al-Suyūṭī faqīhan lughawiyyan wa-muḥaddithan wa-mujtahidan*, Beirut 2001, 149–52.

al-Khāzindār, A. and M.I. al-Shaybānī, *Dalīl makhṭūṭāt al-Suyūṭī wa-amākin wujūdihā*, Kuwait 1983.

Kister, M.J., Social and religious concepts of authority in Islam, in *JSAI* 18 (1994), 84–127.

Kramers, J.H. and C.E. Bosworth, Sulṭān, in *EI*², 849–51.

Lambton, A.K.S., Khalīfa. (ii) In political theory, in *EI*², iv, 947–50.

Lambton, A.K.S., *State and government in medieval Islam: An introduction to the study of Islamic political theory: The jurists* (London Oriental Series 26), Oxford 1981.

Newhall, A.W., "The patronage of the Mamlūk sultan Qā'it Bay, 872–901/1468–1496" PhD diss., Harvard University 1987.

Madelung, W., Imāma, in *EI*², iii, 1163–9.

Palmer, H.R., An early Fulani conception of Islam, 3 parts, in *Journal of the African Society* 13 (1914), 407–14; 14 (1914–15), 53–9, 185–92.

Rosenthal, E.I.J., *Political thought in medieval Islam: An introductory outline*, Cambridge 1958.

Saad, E.N., *Social history of Timbuktu: The role of Muslim scholars and notables 1400–1900* (Cambridge Studies in Islamic Civilization), Cambridge 1983.

Saleh, M.J., Al-Suyūṭī and his works: Their place in Islamic scholarship from Mamlūk times to the present, in *MSR* 5 (2001), 73–89.

Sartain, E.M., Jalal al-Din as-Suyuti's relations with the people of Takrur, in *JSS* 16 (1971), 193–8.

Sartain, E.M., *Jalāl al-dīn al-Suyūṭī.* i: *Biography and background* (University of Cambridge Oriental Publications 23), Cambridge 1975.

Sourdel, D., Khalīfa. (i) The history of institution of the caliphate, in *EI*², iv, 937–47.

Spevack, A., Jalāl al-Dīn al-Suyūṭī, in J.E. Lowry and D.J. Stewart (eds.), *Essays in Arabic literary biography 1350–1850*, (Mîzân. Studien zur Literatur in der islamischen Welt 17: Essays in Arabic literary biography), Wiesbaden 2009, 386–409.

Ṭaḥḥān, M.A., al-Suyūṭī muḥaddithan, in M.T. Abū ʿAlī and Ṣ. Qashmar (eds.), *al-Imām Jalāl al-Dīn al-Suyūṭī faqīhan lughawiyyan wa-muḥaddithan wa-mujtahidan*, Beirut 2001, 317–34.

Tezcan, B., Hanafism and the Turks in al-Ṭarasūsī's Gift for the Turks (1352), in *MSR* 15 (2011), 67–86.

Winter, M., The judiciary of late Mamlūk and early Ottoman Damascus: The administrative, social and cultural transformation of the system, in S. Conermann (ed.), *History and society during the Mamlūk period (1250–1517)* (Mamlūk Studies 5), Göttingen 2014, 193–220.

Winter, M., Inter-madhhab competition in Mamlūk Damascus: Al-Ṭarsūsī's counsel for the Turkish sultans, in *JSAI* 25 (2001), 195–211.

CHAPTER 6

Casting the Caliph in a Cosmic Role: Examining al-Suyūṭī's Historical Vision

Mustafa Banister

Authors of history during the Mamlūk period at best paid marginal attention to the men of the 'Abbasid family who reigned, but did not rule, since the sultan Baybars installed the first caliph of Cairo in 659/1261. One noteworthy exception to this trend is the late-fifteenth/early sixteenth century polymath and religious scholar Jalāl al-Dīn al-Suyūṭī (d. 911/1505).

As late samplings of Mamlūk historiography, some of the historical works of al-Suyūṭī deliver hindsight and nostalgia as well as more nuanced insights spanning nearly two and a half centuries of an evolving 'Abbasid ceremonial tradition that would become unique to Cairo.[1] Indeed, the detailed information provided in al-Suyūṭī's retrospective biographies of the Cairo caliphs, found both in his history of Egypt (*Ḥusn al-muḥāḍara fī taʾrīkh Miṣr wa-l-Qāhira*) and his caliphal history (*Taʾrīkh al-khulafāʾ*), comprise an indispensible backbone for any study of the subject.[2]

1 Al-Suyūṭī's "Cosmic Vision" of the Caliphate

The powerful though somewhat ill-defined relationship between God, the ruler, and politics are well-trodden territory in the context of Islamic studies, and of course, in studies of Mamlūk historiography. The reign of the Umayyad caliph 'Abd al-Malik (65–86/685–705) marks a change in the caliphal office as it assumed an increasingly formal, regal air and caliphs ceased to be regarded

1 For a recent study of the significance of the sanctity attained through the caliph's presence in the early Mamlūk period, see Mona Hassan, Loss of caliphate, which is the foundation of her forthcoming book *Longing for the lost caliphate: A transregional history* (Princeton University Press, 2017).

2 Important earlier studies of the 'Abbasid caliphate of Cairo by G. Weil, V. Barthold, T. Arnold, and J.-C. Garcin have benefited from a close reading of al-Suyūṭī's biographical entries of the caliphs. For examples of al-Suyūṭī's biographical entries of contemporary 'Abbasid family members in other works, see *Naẓm* 107–8; idem, *Rafʿ* 28–9, 127.

 | DOI 10.1163/9789004334526_008

as *primus inter pares* in the style of the bedouin tribal *shaykh*.[3] Among the early ʿAbbasid caliphs of Baghdad, caliphal dignity assumed numinous characteristics emphasized by the pomp and ceremony of the office influenced by the influx of Persian bureaucrats from the former Sasanian administration harboring their own notions of what rulership ought to look like. The caliph became venerated; the man himself hidden behind guarded doors, and petitioners who gained access often kissed the hem of his garment or the ground at his feet as an armed headsman looked on. The courtly reputation which prevailed under the ʿAbbasid caliphs of the tenth century and onward had been

> kingship of a universal type: half brutal power and half theatre. The theatre owed something to the fact that rulers had come to be credited with a cosmic role, in the sense that they were believed to influence the regularities of nature. Natural disasters would ensue if caliphs were killed, it was held [...] Both caliphs and kings were seen as having special access to the sources of life, health, energy and well-being, in short, of all the pagan desiderata which the great salvation religions had reduced to secondary importance. The basic assumption behind these ideas is that the regularities of nature depended on a moral order which it was the duty of the king to maintain. "When rulers act wrongly, the heavens dry up," a saying ascribed to the Prophet had it. The assumption was pagan, not only in the sense that it pre-dated the rise of monotheism and placed a high premium on well-being in this world, but also in the sense that it idolized a single human being in a manner that Sunnis were normally quick to disown.[4]

That the caliph and his office were supernaturally linked to balance in the corporeal world was not an uncommon proposition for scribes in the Mamlūk chancery.[5] Mamlūk caliphal investiture deeds (which al-Suyūṭī often reproduced in his historical works) frequently reiterate that the ʿAbbasid caliphate enjoyed such a mystical influence that, were it ever disturbed or outraged, serious repercussions would result in the physical universe.[6]

3 Watt, *Political thought* 40.

4 Crone, *God's rule* 163–4.

5 See Hassan's remarks on the collective public mood of Mamlūk Egypt which interpreted the presence of the caliph as a perpetuation of order and unbroken continuity: Loss of caliphate 143–53, 240–6.

6 See al-Qalqashandī, *Ṣubḥ* ix, 369–77; idem, *Maʾāthir* iii, 340–53; al-Suyūṭī, *Ḥusn* ii, 63–7; idem, *Taʾrīkh* 392–9.

In many ways al-Suyūṭī drew from pre-existing conventions of loyalty towards the caliphate apparent in some scholarly circles and sectors of society at large.[7] Relevant sections of both the *Taʾrīkh al-khulafāʾ* and the *Ḥusn al-muḥāḍara* closely follow the careers of the ʿAbbasid caliphs of Cairo and their interaction with the Mamlūk sultans, supplemented with fitting documents and panegyrics, some of which were carefully selected because of their emphasis on the cosmic link between the caliphate, the *bayʿa* or pledge of allegiance (to the caliph or sultan), and order in the natural world.[8] For al-Suyūṭī, the caliphate occupied a central interest, and as Garcin's work has demonstrated, his personal loyalty to it informed the *Weltanschauung* of his historiography. Much has been written on the outlook of al-Suyūṭī in regard to the religion and politics of his own time. Regarding the former, al-Suyūṭī has been characterized as a consistent advocate of Sunni piety in opposition against the Mamlūk usurpation of classical caliphal rights.[9]

In his discussion of the ʿAbbasid caliphs that reigned in mid-fourteenth century Cairo, we find that al-Suyūṭī's presentation was strongly influenced by reports and documents composed by the Syrian scribe Ibn Faḍl Allāh al-ʿUmarī (d. 749/1349).[10] One example was the narration of the sultan al-Nāṣir Muḥammad's (d. 741/1341) expulsion of the caliph al-Mustakfī bi-llāh (d. 740/1340) to the Upper Egyptian outpost of Qūṣ in 737/1337 following three decades of deteriorating relations.[11] When the caliph died in exile three years later, al-Nāṣir Muḥammad attempted to seal his revenge by blocking the investiture of the decedent's choice to the succession, his son Aḥmad al-Ḥākim bi-amr Allāh II, despite the witness of the top *ʿulamāʾ* of Qūṣ. Instead, the sultan offered his own candidate, the morally reprehensible ʿAbbasid prince

7 On these conventions see Hassan, Loss of caliphate 127, 132.

8 Al-Suyūṭī, *Ḥusn* ii, 45–94; idem, *Taʾrīkh* 381–413.

9 Using a variety of later Mamlūk sources, Garcin explored al-Suyūṭī's caliphate-centric worldview and described the political value of individual caliphs to the Mamlūk sultans. See Histoire 33–88. Jonathan P. Berkey also identified al-Suyūṭī's rather late advocacy for caliphal authority as an illustration of the complex hold the idea of the caliphate maintained upon Muslims living under Mamlūk rule in the early sixteenth century. See Mamlūk religious policy 12.

10 Al-Suyūṭī, *Ḥusn* ii, 67–8, 112–4; idem, *Taʾrīkh* 387–92.

11 Al-Shujāʿī, *Taʾrīkh* i, 14; al-Ṣafadī, *Wāfī* xv, 350; idem, *Aʿyān* ii, 420; Ibn Kathīr, *Bidāya* xiv, 178, 180, 187; Ibn Duqmāq, *Jawhar* 189; al-Qalqashandī, *Ṣubḥ* iii, 261; al-Maqrīzī, *Sulūk* ii, 417; idem, *Khiṭaṭ* iii, 784; idem, *Durar* ii, 209–10; al-Suyūṭī, *Taʾrīkh* 389; al-Qaramānī, *Akhbār* ii, 209. Several historians suggest this event occurred a year later in 738/1337–8: Ibn al-Wardī, *Taʾrīkh* ii, 469; Ibn Ḥabīb, *Tadhkira* ii, 297; Ibn Khaldūn, *Taʾrīkh* v, 947; Ibn Taghrī Birdī, *Manhal* vi, 21; Ibn Iyās, *Badāʾiʿ* i/i, 474 (12 Dhū l-Ḥijja 738/1 July 1338).

Ibrāhīm, and secretly installed him as al-Wāthiq bi-llāh.[12] This blatant defiance of the old caliph's wishes became a sore point for al-Suyūṭī, who took pains to recapitulate al-ʿUmarī's particularly harsh assessment of the incident.[13] The latter, after waging a lengthy public relations campaign in favor of the "rightful" caliph al-Ḥākim II, composed a caliphal document affirming that God had chosen the caliph's father al-Mustakfī as an honored servant, and that if that caliph had not been allowed to name his own successor (i.e. al-Ḥākim II), the earth would have grown narrow and unable to withstand the immensity of events unfolding upon its surface. The text went on to warn the Mamlūk court of dire consequences resulting from its irresponsible treatment of al-Ḥākim II, whose claim to the caliphate had been rebuffed by al-Nāṣir Muḥammad after a falling out with his father. For al-ʿUmarī, both *minbar* and *sarīr* (religious and military infrastructures, respectively) would be jeopardized if the deathbed wishes of al-Mustakfī were not honored.[14]

If indeed the Mamlūk intelligentsia formally (and theoretically) considered the classical caliphate as the next most important spiritual authority under God,[15] the alleged investiture document for the Cairo caliph al-Mustakfī, preserved by al-Suyūṭī, establishes a special relationship between God and the caliphate while also alluding to the institution's distinctive link to health and order in the physical world:

> Verily, God, since the prostration of His noble angels to Adam in bygone ages, has made obedience to the caliphs in His lands an imposition upon the rest of His slaves. Why should it not be thus when it is through [these caliphs] that creation prospers, limits (*ḥudūd*) are upheld, and the pillars of disbelief soundly destroyed!? So long as they live, the lands are secured (*taʾmanu l-bilād*), but as [the caliphs] near death, the moon dons a shroud of mourning and the celestial body (*jirm* or *jurum*) hides itself away.[16]

Although he was not primarily the author of historical works, al-Suyūṭī often used the writing of history as a venue to express his views of an ideal society.[17] Indeed, the scholar's "cosmic reading" linked the wellbeing of the caliphate

12 Ibn Taghrī Birdī, *Mawrid* i, 243. Cp. Garcin's coverage of these events in Histoire 55–8.

13 Al-Suyūṭī, *Taʾrīkh* 391.

14 Al-Qalqashandī, *Ṣubḥ* ix, 323; al-Suyūṭī, *Taʾrīkh* 394.

15 For a discussion of the position of the caliph in post-1258 Islamic legal theory, see Hassan, Loss of caliphate 154–70.

16 Al-Suyūṭī, *Ḥusn* ii, 63.

17 Garcin, Histoire 33.

to political continuity, natural order, and above all, spiritual harmony in the world at large.[18] Thus, al-Suyūṭī's conception of the caliphate and its role in society resembles the Shakespearean leitmotif expressed in dramas such as *Julius Caesar, Macbeth,* and *Hamlet* that posit an unbreakable bond between the political order and the natural realm: wrong rule in the political world will reflect itself in disruption within the natural world, in which "prodigies," ghosts, or violent storms are the result of uncomely political developments.

2 Al-Suyūṭī on the Position of the Contemporary Caliphate

Several scholars, medieval and modern, have taken pains to point out the relationship between al-Suyūṭī's loyalty to the caliphate and his close familial and patronage ties to the ʿAbbasid family.[19] For his companion, the caliph ʿAbd al-ʿAzīz al-Mutawakkil II (r. 884–903/1479–97), who also happened to be a former pupil of his father, al-Suyūṭī compiled at least two works on ʿAbbasid virtues and lineage: *al-Asās fī faḍl Banī l-ʿAbbās* and *Rafʿ al-bās ʿan Banī l-ʿAbbās*,[20] and named a treatise on foreign words in the Quran in his honor: *al-Mutawakkilī fī mā warada fī l-Qurʾān bi-l-lugha al-Ḥabashiyya wa-l-Rūmiyya wa-l-Hindiyya wa-l-Suryāniyya wa-l-ʿIbrāniyya wa-l-Nabaṭiyya wa-l-Qibṭiyya wa-l-Turkiyya wa-l-Zanjiyya wa-l-Barbariyya*.[21] But it is the *Ḥusn al-muḥāḍara* and *Taʾrīkh al-khulafāʾ* that showcase a unique image of the ʿAbbasid caliphate in late

18 On caliphal continuity in the Mamlūk period, see Hassan, Loss of caliphate 143–53.

19 Indeed, al-Suyūṭī's loyalty to the ʿAbbasid cause appears partially linked to the court favor and appointments offered to his family by virtue of ʿAbbasid patronage. Al-Suyūṭī's father Abū Bakr Kamāl al-Dīn (d. 885/1480) had been the "*imām*" of the caliph al-Mustakfī II (845–55/1441–51) and tutor to other ʿAbbasid family members in Cairo. The elder al-Suyūṭī later received the honor of composing the caliph's investiture deed (*Taʾrīkh* 409–10). The younger al-Suyūṭī, on the recommendation of al-Mustakfī's nephew, al-Mutawakkil II, was later named head of the mosque complex of Baybars II in 891/1486. Ten years later, al-Suyūṭī again used his relationship with al-Mutawakkil II to be briefly named "*qāḍī kabīr*" by caliphal delegation (see below). On the close relations between the Suyūṭī and ʿAbbasid families, see al-Sakhāwī, *Ḍawʾ* iv, 69, and xi, 72–3; al-Suyūṭī, *Taʾrīkh* 410; idem, *Taḥadduth* 8–10; al-Shādhilī, *Bahja* 57–8. See also Garcin, Histoire 34–7, 65–6; Sartain, *Biography* 22, 81–2. For al-Suyūṭī's justification and defense of ʿAbbasid prerogatives, see *Taʾrīkh* 11–4.

20 Al-Suyūṭī, *Ḥusn* ii, 92. Of his contemporary companion al-Mutawakkil II, al-Suyūṭī wrote that "the people never cease in their love for him." See *Ḥusn* ii, 72; idem, *Taʾrīkh* 412; Becker, Barthold's Studien 372.

21 Al-Suyūṭī, *Mutawakkilī* 32–3.

Mamlūk politics and society. In the latter work, a chronologically arranged history of every caliph since Abū Bakr al-Ṣiddīq down to his own time, al-Suyūṭī deals with the lacunae permeating the narrative history of the Cairo ʿAbbasids (many of whom were isolated from events by the Mamlūks) by including documents and notable events such as battles or natural disasters that occurred during a caliph's time in office.[22] The *Ḥusn al-muḥāḍara*, on the other hand, was a localized history of Egypt that drew attention to the relationship of its rulers with the caliphate. Al-Suyūṭī's presentation adopted the popular convention that held that in the years since Baybars's resurrection of the caliphal office, Egypt had emerged as a pious Islamic capital.[23] The closing passage of the *Ḥusn al-muḥāḍara*'s section concerning the Cairo caliphs appears to be a reworking of earlier observations attributed to the Damascene scholar ʿAbd al-Raḥmān Abū Shāma (d. 665/1268) after the Cairene investiture of the caliph al-Mustanṣir in 659/1261:

> Know that Egypt, since the time it became seat of the caliphate, aggrandized itself and increased the rituals of Islam practiced within it. It raised the *sunna* and erased innovation, and has been a place of residence for the *ʿulamāʾ* and a wayfaring stop for virtuous scholars (*maḥaṭṭu riḥāl al-fuḍalāʾ*). This is one of the divine mysteries of God; that wherever He deposits the prophetic caliphate, belief (*īmān*) accompanies it [...] Belief and knowledge (*ʿilm*) both accompany the caliphate, wherever it is [...] Think not that this can be attributed to the kings (i.e., the Mamlūk sultans), for the Ayyubids were superior in standing and greater in significance than their numerous successors; nevertheless, Egypt in their time

22 Described as a brooding and "superstitious" scholar, al-Suyūṭī frequently noted natural disasters and calamities in his histories and their prevailing effect upon the caliphate. See Garcin, Histoire 39, 54; Sartain, *Biography* 114.

23 Hassan, Loss of caliphate 119–20, 143–70, 246–7. The theme of Mamlūk Egypt as a legitimate Islamic capital alongside Medina, Damascus, and Baghdad was well known by al-Suyūṭī's time. Ibn Faḍl Allāh al-ʿUmarī identified Cairo, because of the presence of the caliph and the righteous scholars, with such epithets as "*umm al-mamālik*," "*ḥāḍirat al-bilād*," and "*dār al-khilāfa*." See *Taʿrīf* 247. Scholars and bureaucrats of the early fifteenth century such as al-Qalqashandī (d. 821/1418) trumpeted the importance of Cairo because of the caliphal presence. See *Ṣubḥ* iii, 263–5; idem, *Maʾāthir* i, 1. Abū Ḥāmid al-Qudsī (d. 888/1483) and the Iranian historian Faḍl Allāh b. Rūzbihān Khunjī-Iṣfahānī (d. 928/1521) both identified Egypt, thanks to the presence of the ʿAbbasid caliph, as the heartland of Islam (*bayḍat al-Islām*). See Haarmann, Injustice 63–4; idem, Al-Maqrīzī 149–65; Khunjī, *Taʾrīkh* 191. See also: Becker, Barthold's Studien 372; Broadbridge, Diplomatic Conventions 101.

> was unlike Baghdad. In the present regions of the earth, among kings, there are those who are steadfast in fortitude and militarily superior to the kings of Egypt [...] yet religion (*dīn*) is not established in their lands as it is in Egypt. The rituals of Islam do not appear manifest in their regions as they do in Egypt.[24]

Al-Suyūṭī's narrative presentation, like the caliphal documents he presents, stresses the presence of the caliph as a perpetuation of order in both the material and spiritual worlds. As Garcin's work suggests, divine punishment is meted out to historical actors who offend Islam and the prophetic legacy by harming their appointed representative, the incumbent ʿAbbasid caliph. Thus al-Suyūṭī's opinion of a given sultan correlates directly with their conduct towards the holders of the caliphate.[25]

In the Mamlūk period, al-Suyūṭī portrayed Baybars heroically and bestowed appreciation for that sultan's great act of restoring the caliphate.[26] On the other hand, the sultan Qalāwūn, having been convicted of ignoring, even suppressing the caliphate for the majority of his rule, is quickly brushed aside with scarcely a mention, despite his actual status as an influential figure in Mamlūk culture and society well after his death in 689/1290.[27] Instead, for al-Suyūṭī, the passing of Qalāwūn allowed the more propitious reign of his son al-Ashraf Khalīl, who "made manifest the authority of the caliph which had languished

24 Al-Suyūṭī, *Ḥusn* ii, 94. Earlier comments ascribed to Abū Shāma vary somewhat: "When the caliphate moved from Baghdad to Egypt, the significance of the latter dwarfed that of other lands. The sultan of Egypt became the most valuable of people and Egypt transformed into a land for the *ʿulamāʾ*, virtuous scholars (*al-fuḍalāʾ*) and ascetics to dwell while the sunna grew in importance and power in the land of innovation. This was the mystery of the ʿAbbasids—that wherever they should go, they would be honored and celebrated [...] Did you not see [evidence of] the mystery during their residence in Baghdad? They then went to Egypt which became akin to the City of Peace (*Dār al-Salām*, i.e. Baghdad). This is one of the divine mysteries of God—that wherever the ʿAbbasids reside, so too does the caliphate." Quoted in Ibn Iyās, *Badāʾiʿ* i/i, 321.

25 For coverage of this correlation in al-Suyūṭī's writing as it concerned earlier Islamic dynasties, see Garcin, Histoire 40–53.

26 Al-Suyūṭī, *Ḥusn* ii, 52–61, 95–7; Garcin, Histoire 47. Al-Suyūṭī describes Baybars as a creator of conditions in which the *ʿulamāʾ* were able to flourish. For the author, Baybars had been on good terms with many of the important religious scholars of his time and exchanged correspondence with them. See *Ḥusn*, ii, 96–101.

27 Al-Suyūṭī, *Taʾrīkh* 385. In the *Ḥusn* however, al-Suyūṭī acknowledges that Qalāwūn received delegation from the caliph and includes a copy of his investiture document: *Ḥusn* ii, 106–10. See Garcin, Histoire 48.

in the days of his father, to the point that his father had not even requested a document of investiture for his rule from [the caliph]."[28]

Al-Suyūṭī's interpretation of Cairene-'Abbasid history turns bitter concerning that sultan's younger brother and successor, al-Nāṣir Muḥammad, who banished the caliph al-Mustakfī to Qūṣ.[29] Al-Suyūṭī condemns that figure as an illegitimate sultan guilty of sidelining the caliphate and worse still, ignoring the rights of a caliph's recognized heir.[30] Not one to shrink from offering moral pronouncements, al-Suyūṭī reckoned that the failure of a worthy king to arise from al-Nāṣir Muḥammad's descendants was divine retribution for his betrayal of the Prophet's successor.[31] The offspring of al-Nāṣir Muḥammad likewise did not escape harsh words:

> The sultan al-Manṣūr [Abū Bakr] was deposed in the same year of his investiture (753/1352) due to his corruption and wine-drinking to the extent that he was even said to have copulated with his father's wives. He was banished to Qūṣ and there assassinated. That was retribution from God for what his father [al-Nāṣir Muḥammad] had done with the caliph [al-Mustakfī]. This is the way in which God deals with those who harmfully interfere with members of the 'Abbasid family.[32]

It is no secret that al-Suyūṭī, in his total acceptance of al-ʿUmarī's portrayal of al-Wāthiq as a notorious gambler and scoundrel, saw only the descendants of al-Mustakfī as legitimate candidates for the caliphate. Al-Suyūṭī judges al-Wāthiq as having acted so disgracefully that even his descendants were necessarily polluted as well, making the caliphate of anyone born outside the direct line of al-Mustakfī a perilous error.[33] Most other historians, perhaps unaware

28 Al-Suyūṭī, *Taʾrīkh* 385; idem, *Ḥusn* ii, 111. Cp. al-Dhahabī, *Taʾrīkh* li, 56.

29 Al-Shujāʿī, *Taʾrīkh* i, 14; al-Ṣafadī, *Wāfī* xv, 350; idem, *Aʿyān* ii, 420; Ibn Kathīr, *Bidāya* xiv, 178, 180, 187; Ibn Duqmāq, *Jawhar* 189; al-Qalqashandī, *Ṣubḥ* iii, 261; al-Maqrīzī, *Sulūk* ii, 417; idem, *Khiṭaṭ* iii, 784; idem, *Durar* ii, 209–10; al-Suyūṭī, *Taʾrīkh* 389; idem, *Ḥusn* ii, 67–8; al-Qaramānī, *Akhbār* ii, 209. Several historians suggest this event occurred a year later in 738/1337–8: Ibn al-Wardī, *Taʾrīkh* ii, 469; Ibn Ḥabīb, *Tadhkira* ii, 297; Ibn Khaldūn, *Taʾrīkh* v, 947; Ibn Taghrī Birdī, *Manhal* vi, 21; Ibn Iyās, *Badāʾiʿ* i/i, 474 (12 Dhū l-Ḥijja 738/1 July 1338).

30 The author judged al-Nāṣir Muḥammad illegitimate after forcing out Baybars al-Jāshnikīr who had the support of the caliph. See Garcin, Histoire 57.

31 Al-Suyūṭī, *Ḥusn* ii, 68. In his motifs of divine punishment meted out for interference with the 'Abbasid caliphate, al-Suyūṭī channeled similar sentiments expressed by al-Maqrīzī (*Sulūk* ii, 570), Ibn Ḥajar (*Durar* ii, 280), and Ibn Qāḍī Shuhba (*Taʾrīkh* ii, 206).

32 Al-Suyūṭī, *Taʾrīkh* 399. See also Ibn Iyās, *Badāʾiʿ* i/ii, 489.

33 Garcin, Histoire 57.

of al-ʿUmarī's report, judged al-Wāthiq and his branch far less harshly, allowing these descendants to serve the Mamlūk sultans as a convenient source for alternative ʿAbbasid caliphs.[34] It is worth mentioning, however, that al-Suyūṭī took some steps to rehabilitate the image of al-Nāṣir Muḥammad by writing that on his deathbed, the sultan chose to rectify the caliphal question by acknowledging the "true heir," al-Ḥākim II. Nevertheless, this was likely done more so to emphasize the importance and legitimacy of divinely-sanctioned caliphal succession rather than as an attempt to cleanse the career of a controversial sultan from wrong-doing.

Further confirmation that al-Suyūṭī favored the ʿAbbasid line of al-Ḥākim and al-Mustakfī's descendants against all others can be found in his mention of the first ʿAbbasid of Cairo, al-Mustanṣir bi-llāh, an ʿAbbasid candidate with a distant relation to al-Ḥākim, who "was put in office [by Baybars in 659/1261] but did not actually assume the caliphate (*fa-lam yuqim fī l-khilāfa*), for he received *bayʿa* in Egypt before advancing against the Mongols in Iraq, where he was killed, leaving the caliphate vacant for one year, until it was re-restored in Egypt, the first of [the caliphs being] al-Ḥākim."[35] This judgment seems to imply that for the author, selecting a candidate then having the people pledge allegiance was insufficient to make that person a true caliph. Instead, al-Suyūṭī specifically limits caliphal legitimacy to the line of al-Ḥākim and the subsequent caliphs descended from him.

The sultan Qāytbāy (r. 872–901/1468–96) proves a figure of interest, who, despite his renown as a pious Muslim sovereign who allegedly threatened to behead defamers of the ʿAbbasid caliph in his presence,[36] did not always find kind words in the pages (or personal attitudes) of Mamlūk period historians. As a *shaykh* appointed to the tomb of Barqūq (the endowment of which was overseen by Qāytbāy personally), the sultan expected al-Suyūṭī to leave his

---

34 See, for example, the somewhat less controversial coverage of al-Wāthiq bi-llāh recorded by: al-Qalqashandī, *Maʾāthir* ii, 148–9; al-Maqrīzī, *Sulūk* ii, 503; Ibn Iyās, *Badāʾiʿ* i/i, 474–5. Ibn Taghrī Birdī acknowledged that al-Wāthiq was indeed a controversial figure among historians and went as far as to say that the observer is at liberty, "when he learns of this matter, to either affirm [al-Wāthiq's status as a caliph] or reject it if he wishes." See *Mawrid* i, 244.

35 Al-Suyūṭī, *Taʾrīkh* 16. ʿAbd al-Bāsiṭ echoes the sentiment that al-Ḥākim was the first ʿAbbasid caliph of Egypt (*Nayl* i, 234) and al-Sakhāwī likewise numbered al-Ḥākim II the third caliph of Egypt, perhaps forgetting or omitting al-Wāthiq from the list (*Wajīz* i, 5). On the installation of the first two Abbasid caliphs in Cairo, refer to Holt, Some Observations 501–3; Heidemann, *Kalifat* 91–107; Hassan, Loss of caliphate 119–42, 256–90.

36 Al-Ḥusaynī, *Nafāʾis* 111.

teaching and writing activities each month to ceremoniously pay respects at the Citadel and receive his stipend in person. Perhaps irritated by the inconvenience, al-Suyūṭī reminded his patron of the ideal detachment that should exist between rulers and *ʿulamāʾ*. Thus, at the end of the ninth Islamic century began an escalating situation that antagonized the sultan, and threatened al-Suyūṭī with the prospect of imprisonment or worse. At roughly the same time, a severe fire ravaged the sultan's storehouse and burnt many of Qāytbāy's prized and costly war tents. Al-Suyūṭī would subsequently claim in his autobiography that the conflagration was divine retribution for the Mamlūk sultan's misdeeds.[37] It is noteworthy that Qāytbāy himself allegedly blamed al-Suyūṭī's ally, the resident caliph al-Mutawakkil II for the fire, which was rumored to have started in the kitchen near the caliphal residence in the Citadel. As a direct result, the sultan expelled the caliph and his family to another residential living space (*qāʿa*) near the shrine of Sayyida Nafīsa.[38]

3 The Caliphate in Late Fifteenth/Early Sixteenth Century Historiography

The historical presentation of al-Suyūṭī (and also his student Muḥammad b. Iyās, d. 930/1524) suggests that even by late Mamlūk times, debate persisted as to what the caliphate should be and which powers it should have, questions indeed as old as the office itself.[39] In the introduction to *Taʾrīkh al-khulafāʾ*, al-Suyūṭī refers to all of the caliphs down to his own time as men who "stood in authority over the *umma*."[40] The notion is at the very least his argument for symbolic continuity between the Rāshidūn caliphs and the figurehead ʿAbbasids of Cairo.[41]

While it appears likely that al-Suyūṭī used his proximity to the caliphate to bolster his own importance, his point of view is evidence that the ʿAbbasids maintained influence in Egyptian circles throughout the fifteenth century

37 Sartain, *Biography* 88–91. When Qāytbāy fell sick shortly after the fire and ultimately died of a throat-related affliction, al-Suyūṭī again linked it to the hand of God as a punishment for his own ill treatment.

38 Ibn Iyās insisted on the innocence of the caliph and claimed that rumors started by al-Mutawakkil's enemies (possibly within the ʿAbbasid family) had swayed the sultan against him. See *Badāʾiʿ* iii, 300–1. On the relationship between the ʿAbbasids of Cairo, the Nafīsī shrine and its environs, see al-Maqrīzī, *Khiṭaṭ* iii, 785; Rāgib, *Al-Sayyidah Nafīsa* 38–41.

39 Sourdel, Khalīfa 937.

40 Al-Suyūṭī, *Taʾrīkh* 3.

41 See Hassan, Loss of caliphate 143–53.

down to the end of the Mamluk sultanate in 923/1517. Al-Suyūṭī believed not only in the legitimizing force of the 'Abbasid family for a regime of former slave-soldiers and usurpers, but championed the caliph's privilege to recognize whomever he wished.

In his historical works, al-Suyūṭī forces a distinction between caliphs and sultans and his choice of engaging with Islamic history in the medium of a caliphal history rather than an annalistic chronicle appears to speak to his understanding that the caliph was central to the organization and efficiency of the natural world and that history incessantly unfolded within the reign of the caliph of the age. For that reason, whereas other *'ulamā'* historians recognized the demoted status of the caliphate for what it was, al-Suyūṭī insisted on the continuity between the current line of 'Abbasids at Cairo and the great caliphs of history who wielded incomparable power. He bemoaned the realities of their weakened position but saw no difference in their symbolic status compared with iconic caliphs such as 'Abd al-Malik b. Marwān (65–86/685–705) or Hārūn al-Rashīd (170–93/786–809).[42]

The histories of al-Suyūṭī exude the indignation of a staunch traditionalist who frequently bristled at what he perceived as the insults of the Mamlūk regime aimed at the contemporary caliphs, as well as their wrongfully diminished station in society.[43] In his own time, al-Suyūṭī points out that the sultan married a daughter of the caliph to one of his *amīr*s, implying that the Mamlūk sultan snubbed the caliph by not availing himself of the opportunity to wed an 'Abbasid princess.[44]

Elsewhere al-Suyūṭī observed that the caliph sometimes appeared "as if he were merely an *amīr* in the sultan's service," and it was perhaps not without a hint of antipathy that he composed a brief description of the caliph's monthly visits to the Mamlūk sultan:

42 It is a point of interest that in his own study of the historical caliphate, al-Suyūṭī did not consider the powerless 'Abbasid caliphs of his own time to be the nadir of the caliphate. Rather, he believed that the caliphs of Cairo had some degree of authority and were not comparable to the piteous state of relations between the 'Abbasid caliph al-Ṭā'i' (363–81/974–91) and the Buyid 'Aḍud al-Dawla (367–72/977–83) during whose reign, according to the author, the caliphate sank to its lowest point while the proto-sultanate was at its apex. See *Ta'rīkh* 327.

43 See al-Suyūṭī's brief discussion of the differences between the classical caliphate, mulk, and sultanate: *Ḥusn* ii, 125.

44 Al-Suyūṭī, *Ta'rīkh* 335–6. It was also common for 'Abbasid princesses to wed low-ranking Mamlūk amīrs. See al-Qalqashandī, *Ṣubḥ* xiv, 319–21; al-Sakhāwī, *Wajīz* ii, 874; idem, *Ḍaw'* xii, 54–5; Ibn Iyās, *Badā'i'* iii, 240–1 and iv, 82; Schimmel, *Glimpses* 354.

> Affairs have arrived at such a state in our own age that the caliph comes to the sultan to congratulate him at the start of each month, and the most that the sultan grants to the caliph of his right is to descend from his dais (*martabatihi*) and the two then sit together beyond it. Finally, the caliph stands and departs as if he were merely one of the people (*al-nās*), and the sultan again sits atop the throne of his kingdom (*fī dasti mamlakatihi*).[45]

It remains difficult to speak of the author's aspirations for the caliphate beyond general terms, though some clues emerge from his historical works and the writings of Ibn Iyās. At the outset, it seems clear that the 'Abbasid caliphate, as traditional guarantor of the *sharīʿa*, must underwrite the legitimacy of government *per se*. For al-Suyūṭī, Mamlūk sultans appeared to be only as good as their treatment of the Commander of the Faithful.[46] Failure to treat the caliphate with respect had the potential to corrode a sultan's legacy or unleash other supernatural consequences.

In Ṣafar 902/October 1496 amidst the atmosphere of chaos and confusion following the death of Qāytbāy and the succession of his adolescent son as al-Nāṣir Muḥammad IV, al-Suyūṭī, whose own position had grown precarious,[47] schemed to advance the political power of al-Mutawakkil II and create an opportunity for himself to be named as a kind of "executive *qāḍī*" (*qāḍī kabīr*). The incident provides further insight into the author's conception of the contemporary caliphate.[48] Aware as he was of the limitations that the Mamlūks and their *ʿulamāʾ* had placed on the caliphate, al-Suyūṭī nevertheless cited historical example and, according to Ibn Iyās, wished to be named as the *qāḍī kabīr* on the precedent that previous caliphs had appointed meritorious men as they saw fit. Al-Suyūṭī, a critic of the four grand *qāḍī* positions established by Baybars, put forward the idea of the *qāḍī kabīr* position and persuaded the caliph to name him to the office with his caliphal sanction and sign a document to that effect. In theory, the post would have granted al-Suyūṭī power to appoint and dismiss magistrates all over Islamdom.[49] Predictably, the guardians of the

45 Al-Suyūṭī, *Taʾrīkh* 327.

46 Garcin, Histoire 55.

47 Sartain, *Biography* 91.

48 On this episode, see Ibn Iyās, *Badāʾiʿ* iii, 339; Margoliouth, Caliphate 335; Schimmel, Kalif 31–2; eadem, Glimpses 357; Garcin, Histoire 37, 64–5; Sartain, *Biography* 91–3; Saleh, al-Suyūṭī 78.

49 Al-Suyūṭī's student and biographer al-Shādhilī includes a portion of the 9 Ṣafar 902/17 October 1496 document supposedly composed by al-Mutawakkil II. See *Bahja* 172–4; Ibn Iyās, *Badāʾiʿ* iii, 339.

status quo were scandalized, the caliph was rebuked by the incumbent chief *qāḍī*s, and the plan failed. Al-Suyūṭī, who offers little comment on the episode (largely because his autobiography ends in 900/1495), does, however, comment briefly in his *al-Wajh al-nāḍir fī mā yaqbiḍuhu al-nāẓir* on "the stupidity of people who say nowadays that the 'Abbāsid caliph is not permitted to appoint a *qāḍī*."[50]

Al-Suyūṭī thought little of the *qāḍī*s and religious scholars with close ties to the Mamlūk rulers.[51] A public falling out with Qāytbāy had also strained al-Suyūṭī's relations with many members of the formal Mamlūk religious establishment, who did their part to nurture the sultan's growing hostility towards the dissident scholar. In addition, al-Suyūṭī's own claims that he was a uniquely capable *mujtahid* as well as the *mujaddid*, or "religious reviver" of the tenth Islamic century had already made him a *persona non grata* in numerous Cairo circles.[52] By no means shy, al-Suyūṭī viewed himself as the most able and knowledgeable Islamic thinker of a time that for him was an age mired in corruption, ignorance, and relative scholastic decline, for much of which he blamed scholars close to the regime. It was his task alone to set things right, to preserve tradition and transmit it to posterity.[53]

Annemarie Schimmel suggested that by naming himself *qāḍī kabīr*, in addition to reigning supreme over all other *qāḍī*s and appointing offices as he saw fit, al-Suyūṭī might also deprive the Mamlūk sultan of profiting from the sale of lucrative appointments.[54] Marlis Saleh connected the attempt to al-Suyūṭī's desire to achieve prestige and wider scholarly recognition amongst his contemporaries.[55] As Garcin puts it, al-Suyūṭī may indeed have wished to "restore the natural order,"[56] as he longed to see at least *some* power restored to the caliphate, certainly more than it had enjoyed in previous decades. Al-Suyūṭī also wished to gather the authority of the four chief *qāḍī*s into the hands of one man, whether himself or at least an 'Abbasid caliph aided by a learned advisor.[57] It was not just a matter of al-Suyūṭī playing for more

50 Sartain, *Biography* 93.

51 Sartain, *Biography* 74, 85–6, 91.

52 For al-Suyūṭī's own remarks on these infamous claims, see *Taḥadduth* 215–27.

53 Sartain, *Biography* 24, 70–1, 115; Geoffroy, al-Suyūṭī 914; Saleh, al-Suyūṭī 76; Irwin, Mamlūk 169.

54 Schimmel, Kalif 31.

55 Saleh, al-Suyūṭī 78.

56 Garcin, Histoire 66.

57 Ibid. 64. Nūr al-Dīn Zengī had four chief judges in Syria during his reign and in Cairo the Fatimids had four chief judges: two Shiʿi judges (a Twelver and an Ismāʿīlī) and two Sunni (a Shāfiʿī and Mālikī). It was not until the Ayyubids came to power that the system

power; his suggestion was based on the Ayyubid precedent that Tāj al-Dīn b. Bint al-Aʿazz had appointed and dismissed all the magistrates of the empire.[58] Moreover, past history clearly demonstrated that a caliph also had the right to appoint whomever he saw fit to office.[59] Baybars's decision to create four chief *qāḍī* posts in the 660s/1260s had no history behind it, though it facilitated the efforts of Mamlūk sultans to control the religious establishment by divide and rule.[60] However, al-Suyūṭī also operated under the conviction that he himself, as the most qualified scholar, had a clear obligation to assume the office of *qāḍī kabīr* as a *farḍ kifāya*—an obligatory deed, which if performed by a few or even one, removes its burden from the rest of the Muslim community.[61] To some extent, al-Suyūṭī, with the aid of ʿAbbasid legitimacy, may have been setting out blueprints for a new version of "Caliphate" that he could serve.

At the end of it all, it appears that al-Suyūṭī could not accept the concept of the caliph as powerless figurehead, though paradoxically he may have been wary of a caliphate with too much power. Such a powerful image of the caliphate was likely focused on the religious sphere, seeking to maintain the caliph as the symbolic heart of Islam albeit with the power of selecting religious policies and making appointments in the world of the *ʿulamāʾ*, through informed counsel. This still differed from the classical caliph/*imām* capable of appointing governors, crafting political policies, and acting as the genuine commander-in-chief of the military. It is thus possible that al-Suyūṭī likewise adopted the popular convention of the ʿAbbasid caliph as *homme fétiche*—a figure too sacred to get involved in the mundane and undignified aspects of ruling.

Even if the ʿAbbasid caliphs of the later fifteenth century had been interested in acquiring more power (to be sure most were not), they were seldom presented with the opportunity to seize it and had no practical means of

changed into one with a single Shāfiʿī *qāḍī* before Baybars famously changed it to four in 663/1265. See Nielsen, *Justice* 23.

58 Al-Suyūṭī, *Taʾrīkh* 384; Ibn Iyās, *Badāʾiʿ* iii, 339. See also Escovitz, Establishment 529–31; Jackson, Primacy 61–5.

59 The example given by the document attributed to al-Mutawakkil II is Hārūn al-Rashīd's delegation of the imām al-Layth b. Saʿd (d. 175/791). See al-Shādhilī, *Bahja* 173. Meanwhile Ibn Iyās suggests that the Ayyubid investiture of Tāj al-Dīn b. Bint al-Aʿazz as a powerful "*qāḍī kabīr*" in his own right, was al-Suyūṭī's inspiration. See *Badāʾiʿ* iii, 339.

60 Arjomand, Legitimacy 252; Garcin, Histoire 64–5.

61 Al-Suyūṭī, as self-professed *mujtahid* and *mujaddid*, may well have seen himself as sanctioned by the ḥadīth attributed to the Prophet that "whoever is asked about knowledge and conceals it shall receive a bridle of hellfire (*lijām min nār*) on the Day of Judgment." See Ibn Taymiyya, *Muqaddima* 114–5. Cp. Geoffroy, al-Suyūṭī 914.

maintaining it.[62] On the surface, al-Suyūṭī did not appear to be seeking more political power for the caliph other than to name delegates in the religious sphere. While this posed no immediate threat to the Mamlūk ruling elite, it frightened prominent *ʿulamāʾ*, particularly the four chief *qāḍīs* who viewed it as an existential threat to their own positions. This, of course, had the potential to make trouble for the ruling Mamlūk regime. If the *ʿulamāʾ* were unhappy with the state of affairs, the sultan and his supporters would have the choice of either appeasing them or facing potentially embarrassing and scandalizing public displays of their displeasure.

4 Conclusion

Previous studies by Jean-Claude Garcin and Mona Hassan have demonstrated that the ʿAbbasid caliphate functioned as a symbol of prestige and religious authority in almost every stratum of Mamlūk society, including the sultan and his circle, the *ʿulamāʾ* and other civilian notables, and to some extent, the masses of Cairene Muslims. Al-Suyūṭī was a contemporary of the sultan Qāytbāy who emphasized his own nearness to the caliphate,[63] even though he did not scruple to deprive the ʿAbbasid caliph of revenues and properties if ever the need arose. After having alienated himself from Qāytbāy, shortly

62 This is in some ways contrary to the late fourteenth/early fifteenth century Mamlūk political climate in which the ʿAbbasid caliphs al-Mutawakkil I (1362–83, 1389–1406) and his son al-Mustaʿīn (1406–14) were occasionally drawn into politics and enticed with power, which ultimately ended in unhappiness and exile for the latter after having been briefly named interim sultan. For more on the possibilities of the caliph as a figurehead for revolt, see Wiederhold, Elite 203–35.

63 Qāytbāy tried to use an ʿAbbasid decree to appoint Ottoman sultan Bāyazīd II as a Mamlūk governor in 890/1485 (Ibn Iyās, *Badāʾiʿ* iii, 213). The Mamlūk sultan was also an enthusiastic participant in mawlid festivals celebrating the birth of the Prophet as well as saintly figures such as Sayyida Nafīsa. For his part, the caliph al-Mutawakkil II, at the behest of the sultan, participated in festive celebrations at the shrine in 889/1484 and 890/1485. The four chief *qāḍīs* and Cairene notables attended each year, and the Nafīsī mawlid had also been referred to as the "caliph's mawlid" (*mawlid al-khalīfa*) due to the presence of the Commander of the Faithful in his capacity as "cousin of the messenger of God," which proved useful at popular celebrations dedicated to the birth of members of the Prophet's family. See ʿAbd al-Bāsiṭ, *Nayl* vi, 372–3; Ibn Iyās, *Badāʾiʿ* iii, 206; Schimmel, Kalif 77–8; eadem, Glimpses 371. On the Nafīsī mawlid, see Kriss, *Volksglaube* i, 58. On the caliph as a link to the Prophet's family, see Hassan, Loss of caliphate 33, 44, 54, 64–5, 111, 142, 151.

before that sultan's death, some of al-Suyūṭī's intentions in closely associating with caliphal authority seem obvious.

Questions remain as to whether al-Suyūṭī actively promoted "popular" notions of caliphal loyalty that may have been woven into the fabric of Mamlūk society.[64] Based on the later chronicle of Ibn Iyās, 'Abbasid embarrassments in Istanbul helped accelerate the irrelevance of the family in the eyes of the Ottoman rulers, who had ideological precommitments to their own dynasty, and as the new rulers of former Mamlūk territory, failed to renew the 'Abbasid pageantry that had been at the heart of Egyptian political life for two and a half centuries.[65]

As a result, subsequent historians tended not to share al-Suyūṭī's view of 'Abbasid authority. The Meccan historian of Indian origin, Quṭb al-Dīn al-Nahrawālī (d. 990/1583),[66] who lived under Ottoman rule and claimed to have met the last 'Abbasid caliph of Cairo, al-Mutawakkil III, wrote that the Muslims had not had a caliph after 1258 and that the caliphs of Cairo were simply not on par with their antecedents in Baghdad and even lowlier than the caliphs under Buyid and later Seljuq tutelage from the tenth to the early thirteenth centuries.[67] On the other hand, later historians such as Aḥmad al-Qaramānī (d. 1019/1610) and Marʿī b. Yūsuf Karmī (d. 1033/1623–4) claimed that after the death of al-Mutawakkil III, the 'Abbasid caliphate "became extinct from the world."[68]

Al-Suyūṭī's reasons for transmitting an image of the caliph as a powerful symbol of authority can be traced, in part, to elements of political expediency, careerism, and opportunism, which certainly played some part, though he was a scholar who enjoyed a unique closeness to the people, thereby absorbing or perhaps even representing some of the contemporary *Zeitgeist*.[69] Al-Suyūṭī for his part alienated himself from the key players in the military and religious classes of Cairo, which may have contributed to his placing faith in the 'Abbasid caliphate and its fortunes.

How then, did the Mamlūks, their religious scholars, and historians of the late fifteenth century tend to view the caliphs of the age? Were they cosmic figures with power over supernatural events, or more like popular religious

64 Hassan, *Loss of caliphate* 143.

65 Tezcan, Hanafism 70–1.

66 On the life and career of Quṭb al-Dīn al-Nahrawālī, see Blackburn, *Journey* xi–xvi.

67 Becker, Barthold's Studien 372–3.

68 Al-Qaramānī, *Akhbār* ii, 226; Marʿī b. Yūsuf Karmī, *Nuzha* 67. See also Becker, Barthold's Studien 400.

69 Ḍāḥī, *Ra'y* 59–60.

leaders and revered holy men in line with the *bābā* or the *shaykh*? The answer lies somewhere in between. The caliphs were definitely understood by some contemporaries to be repositories of a special power that protected society and that should not be disturbed (although it occasionally was). At the same time, the caliphs were presented as holy men who inspired loyalty and wielded a unique (though conveniently undefined) religious authority.[70] Nowhere do these notions come across as clear as in the historical writings of al-Suyūṭī.

Bibliography

Primary Sources

ʿAbd al-Bāsiṭ [al-Malaṭī], *Nayl al-amal fī dhayl al-duwal*, ed. ʿU. Tadmurī, 9 vols., Beirut 2002.

al-Dhahabī, *Taʾrīkh al-Islām wa-wafayāt al-mashāhīr wa-l-aʿlām*, ed. ʿU. Tadmurī, 53 vols., Beirut 1990–2000.

al-Ḥusaynī, *Nafāʾis al-majālis al-sulṭānīya*, published as *Majālis al-Sulṭān al-Ghawrī: Ṣafaḥāt min taʾrīkh Miṣr fī l-qarn al-ʿāshir al-hijrī*, ed. ʿA. ʿAzzām, Cairo 1941.

Ibn Ḥabīb, *Tadhkirat al-nabīh fī ayyām al-Manṣūr wa-banīh*, ed. M. Amīn, 3 vols., Cairo 1976–7.

Ibn Iyās, *Badāʾiʿ al-zuhūr wa-waqāʾiʿ al-duhūr*, ed. M. Muṣṭafā, 5 vols. (BI 5a–e), Wiesbaden 1960–75.

Ibn Kathīr, *al-Bidāya wa-l-nihāya fī l-taʾrīkh*, 14 vols., Cairo 1932–9.

Ibn Khaldūn, *Taʾrīkh al-ʿallāma Ibn Khaldūn*, 8 vols., Beirut 1956.

Ibn Qāḍī Shuhbah, *Taʾrīkh Ibn Qāḍī Shuhba*, ed. ʿA. Darwīsh, 4 vols., Damascus 1977–94.

Ibn Taghrī Birdī, *al-Manhal al-ṣāfī wa-l-mustawfā baʿd al-wāfī*, ed. M. Amīn, 7 vols., Cairo 1984–93.

Ibn Taghrī Birdī, *Mawrid al-laṭāfa fī man waliya l-salṭana wa-l-khilāfa*, ed. N. Aḥmad, 2 vols., Cairo 1997.

Ibn Taymiyya, *Muqaddima fī uṣūl al-tafsīr*, ed. ʿA. Zarzūr, Kuwait 1971.

Khunjī, *Taʾrīkh-i ʿālam- ārā-yi amīnī*, ed. J. Woods (Oriental Translation Fund, n.s. 46), London 1992.

al-Maqrīzī, *Durar al-ʿuqūd al-farīda fī tarājim al-aʿyān al-mufīda*, ed. M. al-Jalīlī, 4 vols., Beirut 2002.

70 Hassan, *Loss of caliphate* 155–70.

al-Maqrīzī, *Kitāb al-Mawāʿiẓ wa-l-iʿtibār bi-dhikr al-khiṭaṭ wa-l-āthār*, ed. A. Sayyid, 4 vols., London 1995–2002.
al-Maqrīzī, *Kitāb al-Sulūk li-maʿrifat duwal al-mulūk*, ed. M. Amīn et al., 4 vols., Cairo 1956–73.
Marʿī b. Yūsuf Karmī, *Nuzhat al-nāẓirīn fī taʾrīkh man waliya Miṣr min al-khulafāʾ wa-l-salāṭīn*, ed. ʿA. al-Kandarī, Damascus 2012.
al-Qalqashandī, *Maʾāthir al-ināfa fī maʿālim al-khilāfa*, ed. ʿA. Farrāj, 3 vols., Kuwait 1964.
al-Qalqashandī, *Ṣubḥ al-aʿshā fī ṣināʿat al-inshāʾ*, 14 vols., Cairo 1963.
al-Qaramānī, *Akhbār al-duwal wa-athār al-uwal fī l-taʾrīkh*, ed. F. Saʿd and A. Ḥuṭayṭ, 3 vols., Beirut 1992.
al-Ṣafadī, *Aʿyān al-ʿaṣr wa-aʿwān al-naṣr*, ed. M. Shams al-Dīn, 6 vols., Beirut 1987.
al-Ṣafadī, [*al-Wāfī bi-l-wafayāt*] *Das Biographische Lexicon des Ṣalāḥaddīn Khalīl ibn Aibak aṣ-Ṣafadī*, ed. H. Ritter et al., 30 vols., Wiesbaden 1962–.
al-Sakhāwī, *al-Ḍawʾ al-lāmiʿ fī aʿyān al-qarn al-tāsiʿ*, 12 vols., Cairo 1934–6.
al-Sakhāwī, *Wajīz al-kalām fī l-dhayl ʿalā duwal al-Islām*, ed. B. Maʿrūf et al., 3 vols., Beirut 1995.
al-Shādhilī, *Bahjat al-ʿābidīn bi-tarjamat Ḥāfiẓ al-ʿAṣr Jalāl al-Dīn al-Suyūṭī*, ed. ʿA. Nabhān, Damascus 1998.
al-Shujāʿī, *Taʾrīkh al-Malik al-Nāṣir Muḥammad b. Qalāwūn al-Ṣāliḥī wa-awlādihi*, ed. B. Schäfer, 2 vols., Wiesbaden 1977.
al-Suyūṭī, *Ḥusn al-muḥāḍara fī taʾrīkh Miṣr wa-l-Qāhira*, ed. M.A. al-F. Ibrāhīm, 2 vols., Cairo 1967–8.
al-Suyūṭī, *The Mutawakkili of as-Suyuti: A translation of the Arabic text with introduction, notes and indices*, by W.Y. Bell, Cairo 1924.
al-Suyūṭī, *Naẓm al-ʿiqyān fī aʿyān al-aʿyān*, ed. P. Hitti, New York 1927.
al-Suyūṭī, *Rafʿ al-bās ʿan Banī l-ʿAbbās*, Tunis 2011.
al-Suyūṭī, *al-Taḥadduth bi-niʿmat Allāh*, in Sartain, E.M., *Jalāl al-dīn al-Suyūṭī*. ii: *al-Taḥadduth bi-niʿmat Allāh* (University of Cambridge Oriental Publications 24), ed. E.M. Sartain, Cambridge 1975.
al-Suyūṭī, *Taʾrīkh al-khulafāʾ*, Beirut n.d.
al-ʿUmarī, *al-Taʿrīf bi-l-muṣṭalaḥ al-sharīf*, ed. S. al-Droubi, Karak 1992.

Secondary Sources

Arjomand, S., Legitimacy and political organisation: Caliphs, kings and regimes, in R. Irwin (ed.), *The new Cambridge history of Islam*, iv, Cambridge 2010, 225–73.
Becker, C., Barthold's Studien über Khalif und Sultan, in *Der Islam* 4 (1916), 350–412.
Berkey, J., Mamlūk religious policy, in *MSR* 13 (2009), 7–22.
Berkey, J., Culture and society during the late Middle Ages, in C.F. Petry (ed.), *The Cambridge history of Egypt*, i, Cambridge 1998, 375–411.

Blackburn, R., *Journey to the Sublime Porte: Arabic memoir of a Sharifian agent's diplomatic mission to the Ottoman imperial court in the era of Suleyman the Magnificent*, Beirut 2005.

Broadbridge, A., Diplomatic conventions in the Mamlūk sultanate, in *AI* 41 (2007), 97–118.

Crone, P., *God's rule: Government and Islam*, New York 2004.

Ḍāḥī, F. and A. Mizbān, *al-Ra'y al-ʿāmm fī ʿaṣr al-Mamālīk*, Damascus 2011.

Escovitz, J., The establishment of four chief judgeships in the Mamlūk Empire, in *JAOS* 102 (1982), 529–31.

Garcin, J.-C., Histoire, opposition politique et piétisme traditionaliste dans le *Ḥusn al-muḥādarat* de Suyûti, in *AI* 7 (1967), 33–90.

Geoffroy, É., al-Suyūṭī, in EI^2, ix, 913–6.

Haarmann, U., Al-Maqrīzī, the master, and Abū Ḥāmid al-Qudsī, the disciple: Whose historical writing can claim more topicality and modernity?, in H. Kennedy (ed.), *The historiography of Islamic Egypt, c. 950–1800*, Leiden 2000, 149–65.

Haarmann, U., Rather the injustice of the Turks than the righteousness of the Arabs: Changing *ʿulamāʾ* attitudes towards Mamlūk rule in the late fifteenth century, in *SI* 68 (1988), 61–77.

Hassan, M., "Loss of caliphate: The trauma and aftermath of 1258 and 1924" PhD diss., Princeton University 2009.

Heidemann, S., *Das aleppiner Kalifat (A.D. 1261): vom Ende des Kalifates in Baghdad über Aleppo zu den Restaurationen in Cairo*, Leiden 1994.

Holt, P.M., Some observations on the ʿAbbāsid caliphate of Cairo, in *BSOAS* 67 (1984), 501–7.

Irwin, R., Mamlūk history and historians, in R. Allen and D.S. Richards (eds.), *The Cambridge history of Arabic literature*. vi: *Arabic literature in the post-classical period*, Cambridge 2006, 159–70.

Jackson, S., The primacy of domestic politics: Ibn Bint al-Aʿazz and the establishment of four chief judgeships in Mamlûk Egypt, in *JAOS* 115 (1995), 52–65.

Kriss, H., *Volksglaube im bereich des Islam*, 2 vols., Wiesbaden 1960.

Margoliouth, D., The caliphate historically considered, in *MW* 11 (1921), 332–43.

Nielsen, J., *Secular justice in an Islamic state:* Maẓālim *under the Baḥrī Mamlūks, 662/1264–789/1387*, Istanbul 1985.

Rāgib, Y., Al-Sayyidah Nafīsa, sa légende, son culte et son cimetière (suite et fin), in *SI* 45 (1977), 27–55.

Saleh, M.J., al-Suyūṭī and his works: Their place in Islamic scholarship from Mamlūk times to the present, in *MSR* 5 (2001), 73–89.

Sartain, E.M., *Jalāl al-dīn al-Suyūṭī.* i: *Biography and Background* (University of Cambridge Oriental Publications 23), Cambridge 1975.

Schimmel, A., Kalif und kadi im spätmittelalterlichen Ägypten, in *WI* 24 (1942), 1–128.
Schimmel, A., Some glimpses of the religious life in Egypt during the later Mamlūk period, in *Islamic Studies* 4 (1965), 353–92.
Sourdel, D., Khalīfa. (i) The history of institution of the caliphate, in *EI*², iv, 937–47.
Tezcan, B., Hanafism and the Turks in al-Ṭarasūsī's *Gift for the Turks* (1352), in *MSR* 15 (2011), 67–86.
Watt, W.M., *Islamic political thought: The basic concepts*, Edinburgh 1968.
Wiederhold, L., Legal-religious elite, temporal authority, and the caliphate in Mamlūk society: Conclusions drawn from the examination of a 'Zahiri revolt' in Damascus in 1386, in *IJMES* 31 (1999), 203–35.

CHAPTER 7

Preservation through Elaboration: The Historicisation of the Abyssinians in al-Suyūṭī's *Rafʿ shaʾn al-Ḥubshān*[1]

Christopher D. Bahl

1 Introduction

The text *Rafʿ shaʾn al-Ḥubshān* (lit. Raising the importance of the Abyssinians) is similar to other treatises from the late Mamlūk period in that it is a compilation entirely based on textual materials transmitted from the formative period (first/seventh to fourth/tenth centuries).[2] Al-Suyūṭī raised the importance of the Abyssinians in the form of a selection of prophetic traditions and historical reports.[3] According to G. Rotter the content of this work was invaluable for a literary-historical investigation into fifteenth century notions of racial prejudice in Arabic-Islamic societies.[4] He assigned the work to a corpus of *Verteidigungsschriften* (works written in defense of the blacks), but declined to embark on a source-critical exegesis of the text itself.[5] A. Muhammad continued where Rotter left off and analyzed the foreword as well as the table of

1 Acknowledgements. This article is based on parts of my M.A. dissertation "Das Werk Rafʿ šaʾn al-ḥubšān des Ǧalāl ad-Dīn as-Suyūṭī. Formale Ausgestaltung und semantische Aspekte eines spätmamlukischen Traktats," submitted at the University of Heidelberg in April 2013. I thank Professor Susanne Enderwitz and Professor Gita Dharampal-Frick for their support and critique. I would also like to thank Professor Konrad Hirschler for remarks and comments on an earlier draft of this paper. Several participants at the conference in Venice provided helpful questions and references. I thank Simon Leese for comments and suggestions. Errors and mistakes remain mine alone.

2 In the following the reference to the *Rafʿ shaʾn al-Ḥubshān* refers to the edition of Ṣ.ʿA. Dāwūdī [et al.]. For another edition cp. al-Khathlan, *Critical edition*. The latter also contains a detailed description of the surviving manuscripts of the *Rafʿ shaʾn al-Ḥubshān*, cp. ibid. 81–107.

3 The term *Ḥabash* (pl. *Ḥubshān*) literally means Abyssinian and *al-Ḥabasha* refers to the geographical region of Abyssinia with various usages in medieval geographical works. Cp. Beckingham, al-Ḥaba<u>sh</u> 6–7.

4 Cp. Rotter, *Stellung* 10.

5 Ibid. 10–7.

 | DOI 10.1163/9789004334526_009

contents and al-Suyūṭī's sources.[6] He considered the missing link to al-Suyūṭī's contemporary Abyssinian communities to be crucial.[7] It complicated or rather prevented any venture into reconstructing the socio-historical environments of Abyssinians during the late Mamlūk period.[8] The *Rafʿ* could not conform to "great expectations." Instead it was degraded to serve the purpose of "fact-mining" for earlier traditions or was left to gather dust on al-Suyūṭī's bookshelf of curiosities among his other works on the *Sūdān:* the *Nuzhat al-ʿumr fī tafḍīl bayna al-Bīḍ wa-l-Sūd wa-l-Sumr* (The enjoyment of life concerning the preference of the Whites, the Blacks and the Browns), a collection of poems written in "praise and satire of women,"[9] and the work *Azhār al-ʿurūsh fī akhbār al-Ḥubūsh* (The flowers of the thrones concerning the reports about the Abyssinians), an abridgement (*mukhtaṣar*) of the *Rafʿ* written towards the end of his life.[10] At best, the *Rafʿ* provided evidence for the wide-held notion of al-Suyūṭī's trivial reworking of existing marginal themes exhibited in numerous other works of his considerable oeuvre.[11]

B. Lewis further elaborated Rotter's designation of the text as a "work written in defense of the blacks" as part of his historical study *Race and slavery in the Middle East*. He argued that the close affinity of several treatises of defense in general could be read as an indicator for dominating hostilities towards people of black skin color throughout the Islamic medieval period.[12] Consequently, the text was defined according to literary criteria based on a general pattern of defense and subsumed under a tradition of similar texts. This corpus of *Verteidigungsschriften* presumably originated with the *Kitāb Fakhr al-Sūdān ʿalā l-Biḍān* by al-Jāḥiẓ (d. 255/868), a *mufākhara* within the field of *adab* advocating a hierarchical integration of black peoples in ʿAbbasid Iraq based on their ethnic and cultural qualities.[13] A few centuries later, the work *Tanwīr al-ghabash fī faḍl al-Sūdān wa-l-Ḥabash* (The enlightenment of the darkness concerning the merits of the Blacks and the Abyssinians) by

6 Cp. Muhammad, Image 57–9.

7 Cp. ibid. For the importance of "Abyssinian" eunuchs (*khuddām*) in general, cp. Ayalon, *Eunuchs* and as patrons of educational institutions in the Mamlūk period, cp. Petry, Slaves. A work by the historian al-Maqrīzī (d. 845/1442), *al-Ilmām bi-akhbār man bi-arḍ al-Ḥabasha min mulūk al-Islām*, deals with the Muslim rulers of Abyssinia. I would like to thank Yehoshua Frenkel for pointing this out to me.

8 Cp. Muhammad, Image 57–9.

9 Ibid. 58.

10 Cp. Rotter, *Stellung* 15–8.

11 Cp. Irwin, al-Suyuti 746.

12 Cp. Lewis, *Race* 28–33.

13 Cp. Enderwitz, *Gesellschaftlicher Rang* 45–9, 90.

Ibn al-Jawzī (d. 597/1200) established a new model.[14] It differed fundamentally from his predecessors, since it was based entirely on *ḥadīths* and *akhbārs*.[15] As Ibn al-Jawzī mentioned in the preface, he observed discriminatory attitudes towards contemporary Abyssinians and the *Sūdān* in Baghdad.[16] Therefore, he dedicated his treatise to them, refuting the biblical "curse of Ḥām" as the cause of blackness, denying the superiority of "white peoples" and stressing the importance of piety and good deeds.[17] Thus, according to Lewis, the main purpose of these works was to defend the *Sūdān* and positively acknowledge their qualities and peoples.[18] This interpretation was then cursorily conferred upon the *Rafʿ* assigning the text to a corpus of *Verteidigungsschriften* based on textual similarities.[19]

However, al-Suyūṭī never stated a particular social purpose similar to Ibn al-Jawzī. In the short foreword of the *Rafʿ* he expressed two intentions: firstly, he wanted to raise the importance of the Abyssinians, but he never mentioned a reason or an intended effect of his text.[20] Secondly, he claimed to surpass and complete the work of his predecessor Ibn al-Jawzī by treating the subject in the form of an abridgement (*talkhīṣ*) and a conclusion (*ikmāl*).[21] Although al-Suyūṭī based his work to a great extent on Ibn al-Jawzī's text, the compilatory emphasis differs considerably, a point that I will refer back to in the course of this paper. The *Rafʿ* comprises seven chapters of which three accumulatively list the appearance of Abyssinians in *ḥadīth, asbāb an-nuzūl* traditions, and Abyssinian words that occur in the Quran.[22] Then several narratives are quoted, referring to the migration of the Muslims to *bilād al-Ḥabasha* (land of Abyssinia) in the 5th year of the revelation (615 CE).[23] The longest chapter entails biographical entries of Abyssinian "excellencies,"[24] followed by the enumeration of special qualities and miscellanies.[25] The work is introduced by ethnographic and geographical details and concluded with prophetic traditions admonishing the believer to manumit his slave and marry his

14 Ibn al-Jawzī, *Tanwīr*.
15 Cp. Rotter, *Stellung* 12–4.
16 Cp. Muhammad, Image 52.
17 Ibid.
18 Lewis, *Race* 31–3.
19 Ibid. 33.
20 Cp. al-Suyūṭī, *Rafʿ* 31.
21 Ibid.
22 Cp. al-Suyūṭī, *Rafʿ* 37–68.
23 Ibid. 69–94.
24 Ibid. 95–202.
25 Ibid. 203–11.

concubine.[26] Apart from al-Suyūṭī's preliminary remarks, no further clues in terms of how to read the compiled materials can be retrieved from the text. All these aspects contributed to Rotter's dictum of historical and literary triviality.

Yet, new trends in the field of Mamlūk literature in general, and in the study of *ḥadīth* compilations in particular, run counter to such notions of triviality. The statement of historical and literary invalidity as expressed by scholars with respect to al-Suyūṭī's *Rafʿ* adhered to a broader notion of purported "decadence and stagnation," a paradigm of "cultural decline" that has long cast a shadow over the study of Mamlūk and Ottoman literature and was based on "Western prejudices that originated in the colonial climate of the nineteenth century."[27] T. Bauer formulates a general programmatic suggestion of approaching literary works with the consciousness of "relativity" as well as investigating "the social, aesthetic, and ideological circumstances of any period of Arabic literature and thus establish[ing] the values and standards that the members of the specific literary communities themselves applied to their own literature."[28] Following this line of approach is helpful in the study of the *Rafʿ* since it can contextualize the standards for interpreting this work in correspondence with al-Suyūṭī's academic and scholarly affinities.

More specifically, this fresh perspective can open up the interpretation of literary works deemed unworthy of consideration for historical research. An analysis that corresponds to the parameters of relative value and standard according to the respective literary community can reveal hitherto unacknowledged cultural significances of a text. Recent scholarship on the examination of *ḥadīth* compilations has advanced various concepts in order "to understand the motives behind the arrangements of *ḥadīth*s in a compilation" drawing on methodologies from literary theory and especially biblical studies such as "canonical criticism and redaction criticism."[29] In contrast to an earlier focus on *isnād* and the "authenticity" of the textual materials, the idea of "compilation criticism" now looks at ways of analyzing *ḥadīth* compilations by tracing an "authorial voice" embodied in the selection and arrangement of their

26 Ibid. 32–6, 212–5.

27 Cp. Bauer, Misunderstandings 105–7. For a general reformulation of the study of the wider "Nile-to-Oxus region" in terms of its multi-cephalous cultural, religious and intellectual landscape of the thirteenth to fifteenth century" cp. Pfeiffer, Introduction 1–3.

28 Bauer, Misunderstandings 107.

29 Cp. Burge, Reading 170–1. For further examples relating to the reading and interpretation of 40 *ḥadīth* compilations in their complex historical contexts cp. Mourad and Lindsay, *Intensification*.

textual units.[30] These methodological considerations can support an analysis of the *Rafʿ* by approaching the text based on commensurable notions of textual production.

Therefore, in contrast to the previous scholarship on al-Suyūṭī's *Rafʿ*, I will question the dicta of unoriginality and historical irrelevance. Instead of judging the literary contents of the work by their cursory similarity with other writings, a close reading of the *Rafʿ* can reveal its multiple layers of significance. My main argument is that al-Suyūṭī's work has to be read as a treatise that canonizes the historical legacy of the Abyssinians. Their share in Islamic culture is reflected in their social status as slaves, and in the symbolic role they performed in the early Islamic period. This cultural significance of the work is achieved through his scholarly methods that corresponded to the broader conventions in *ḥadīth* scholarship of his times. The presentation of his materials is based along the line of a preservationist method while an elaborative tendency is recognizable in his techniques of compilation. As a double-method of preservation and elaboration it generates the effect of a historicisation of the Abyssinians following the parameters of al-Suyūṭī's larger work.

In order to present this analysis, firstly, I will consider al-Suyūṭī's scholarly habitus as a point of departure to approach the text. Secondly, my analysis will follow "along the grains" of his methods of textual production. These generally build on a preservationist stance through the exact reproduction of historical reports. Thirdly, I will discuss his elaborative tendency through the specific selection and disposition of these materials. Finally, I will explicate the function of the list of biographical entries. This chapter has been constantly overlooked as simply an enumeration of worthy individuals. Instead I will argue that al-Suyūṭī structured this "biographical dictionary" in order to establish the Abyssinians as a diachronically evolving group within the Muslim community. In general, while the "morphology" (i.e. the textual materials) remains static, the "syntax" (i.e. the structure) of the *Rafʿ* is subject to an authorial voice. This elaborates on an argumentative space generating the historical significance of *al-Ḥabasha*.

2 Canonising Islamic Knowledge in an "Age of Decadence"—al-Suyūṭī's Academic Aspirations

Al-Suyūṭī's academic background will provide the crucial starting point for identifying a socio-cultural purpose of the work *Rafʿ sha'n al-Ḥubshān* during

30 Cp. Burge, Reading 177 and 196–7.

his time. Reconstructing a scholarly habitus, i.e. the framework, interests and methods that guided his erudite endeavors, can shed light on the intellectual environment in which the *Rafʿ* was composed. To this end, E.M. Sartain offers the most detailed analysis of al-Suyūṭī's education and scholarly self-image mainly based on his autobiographical writings *al-Taḥadduth bi-niʿmat Allāh* and a hagiographical account of his student ʿAbd al-Qādir al-Shādhilī, *Bahjat al-ʿābidīn bi-tarjamat Jalāl al-Dīn.*[31] A study of his academic career can discern significant traits which will then be brought into conversation with focal points in the fabric of his text. Following these significant traits will guide a reading of the *Rafʿ* that is in accordance with the parameters of his larger academic work.

The last decades of research on al-Suyūṭī have located his scholarly habitus squarely within an academic culture of the *ʿulamāʾ*, who stressed an educational conservatism with regard to religious knowledge (*ʿilm*), which in turn was widely considered as fixed and articulated by past scholars in an authoritative manner.[32] As a disparate professional group mainly concerned with such disciplines as *ḥadīth* (prophetic tradition) and *fiqh* (jurisprudence), the *ʿulamāʾ* derived their social importance and status through a self-proclaimed intermediary function among societal groups.[33] In general, they transmitted and interpreted the religious knowledge that in their self-conception constituted the normative regulatory principle in Mamlūk society.[34] This position was bolstered, for example, by the fact that the *ʿulamāʾ* represented the main group of recruitment for ranks in the higher educational echelons, holding posts at the *madrasas*, mosques, as well as Sufi *khānqahs* and thereby dominating the professional networks of scholarship in Mamlūk Egypt and Syria.[35]

While al Suyūṭī's autobiographical writings certainly followed the rationale of portraying excellent scholarly credentials, his educational upbringing nonetheless boasts of an extraordinarily broad range of disciplines. Corresponding to the customary curricula of his time al-Suyūṭī had memorized the Quran when he was still a child and devoted intensive studies to grammar (*naḥw*), jurisprudence (*fiqh*), belles-lettres (*adab*) and rhetoric (*ʿilm al-balāgha*), among others, in his subsequent schooling.[36] His autobiographical writings meticulously enumerate disciplines, teachers (*mashyakha*), and acquired teaching

31 Cp. Sartain, *Biography*. For a more recent biographical sketch cp. Spevak, al-Suyūṭī.
32 Cp. Hodgson, *Venture* ii, 437 ff.; Cp. Saleh, al-Suyuti 73–6.
33 Cp. Berkey, Culture 387; Berkey, *Transmission* 3–6; Gilliot, ʿUlamāʾ 802.
34 Ibid.
35 Berkey, *Transmission* 6–9.
36 Cp. Sartain, *Biography* 27–33.

certificates (*ijāzāt*), depicting himself as an erudite scholar while exhibiting a vast personal network of scholarly acquaintances across Cairo, Mamlūk Egypt, the Hijaz, and beyond.[37] This academic success is also reflected in the variety of institutional posts he held during his lifetime, for example teaching Shāfiʿī law at the Shaykhū-mosque, transmitting *ḥadīth* at the Shaykhūniyya madrasa, and pursuing administrative obligations at the Khānqāh Baybarsiyya and the mausoleum of Barqūq al-Nāṣirī, all in Cairo.[38]

In principle, al-Suyūṭī emphasized the importance of concentrating on a preservationist stance, conserving a corpus of authoritative knowledge transmitted from the prophetic age onwards by authoritative scholars. Amid his diverse studies and teaching duties this preoccupation with the field of *ḥadīth* and related sciences crystallized gradually. Such a proclivity towards legitimately transmitted prophetic knowledge was furthermore underscored by his full-fledged rejection of the so-called rational sciences (*al-ʿulūm al-ʿaqliyya*). Thus his pupil al-Shādhilī quoted him saying: "Know that, from the time I grew up, I have been inspired with a love of the *sunna* (exemplary practice of the Prophet) and of *ḥadīth*, and with a hate of *bidʿa* (heretical practices) and the sciences of the ancients, such as philosophy and logic. I wrote on the censure of logic when I was eighteen years old, and it was anathema to me."[39] In contrast, al-Suyūṭī considered *ḥadīth* as "the noblest branches of knowledge," but he disregarded the widely accepted and encouraged practice of *ṭalab al-ʿilm* (travelling in search of knowledge), instead preferring the study of related books with scholarly eminences of his immediate social environment.[40]

At the same time, this preservationist attitude was correlated with a strong tendency to distinguish himself from his colleagues and contemporaries. Again a quote can expound this notion:

> [...] I hoped, by the favour and grace of God, to be the *mujaddid* at the end of this ninth [fifteenth] century, just as Ghazālī had hoped for himself, because I alone have mastered all kinds of different disciplines, such as Qurʾānic exegesis and its principles, Prophetic tradition and its sciences, jurisprudence and its principles, language and its principles,

37 Ibid.

38 Cp. Geoffroy, al-Suyūṭī 913–4. Sartain, *Biography* 42–5.

39 Ibid. 32–3, quoted from al-Shādhilī, *Bahja* fol. 33b.

40 Cp. Sartain, *Biography* 30–1, quoted from al-Suyuti, *Taḥadduth* 247–8. Nevertheless, this didactic predilection did not prevent him from a series of personal studies with teachers he conducted while on the *ḥajj* and during travels to Alexandria and Damietta (868–869/1464–1465). Cp. Spevak, al-Suyūṭī 396.

> syntax and morphology and their principles, polemics, rhetoric and good style, and history. In addition to all this, there are my outstanding, excellent works, the like of which nobody has written before, and their number up till now is about 500. I have originated the science of principles of language (*uṣūl al-lugha*) and its study, and nobody has preceded me in this. It follows the same lines as prophetic traditions and principles of jurisprudence. My works and my knowledge have travelled to all countries, and have reached Syria, Rūm, Persia, the Hijaz, the Yemen, India, Ethiopia, North Africa, and Takrūr, and have spread from Takrūr to the ocean. In all that I have mentioned, I have no equal, nobody else living has mastered the number of disciplines which I have, and, as far as I know, nobody else has reached the rank of unrestricted *ijtihād* except for me.[41]

He clearly considered himself erudite in all the traditional subjects of his métier. Moreover, as an exceptional *ʿālim* his professional achievements also carried a responsibility with regard to the conservation of Islamic knowledge. The pretention of simultaneously exercising *ijtihād* (reaching independent legal decisions beyond the four *madhab*s based on the Quran and the *sunna*) and proclaiming himself as the renewer (*mujaddid*) of the age sparked public outcry and harsh criticism from other scholars.[42] According to K. Brustad these moves have to be understood as a mechanism by which he tried to differentiate himself from his colleagues in the scholarly community.[43] At the same time, it points to a deep-rooted incentive for interpretive duties and intellectual responsibilities on his behalf. In an age of decadence, as he understood it, he represented the last bulwark of Islamic guidance based on a transmitted authoritative Islamic corpus of knowledge that he had mastered to perfection. While especially the *mujaddid*-complex has to be viewed within the larger framework of an "Islamic premillenialism" and a transregional eschatological conjunction,[44] this academic posture makes an extraordinary claim with regard to scholarly autonomy and textual exegesis.

These exegetical rights that he exercised on a corpus of *ʿilm* represent an elaborative trend, a methodology that can be traced through the majority of his writings. Scholarship considered both the incipient explanation of his

41 Sartain, *Biography* 70–1, quoted from al-Suyūṭī, *Tanbiʾa* fol. 123a–b.

42 Cp. Sartain *Biography* 61–71. Especially the *ʿālim* al-Sakhāwī (d. 902/1497) vilified him in his writings. Cp. Saleh, al-Suyūṭī 79.

43 Brustad, Imposing order 329.

44 Cp. Poston, Islamic premillenialism 100–1.

academic approach and the accurate quotation and critique of existing materials as common traits of his writings.[45] Moreover, his intellectual endeavors featured an inclination towards the composition of specialized monographs.[46] As E. Geoffroy states, the wide range of the topics he dealt with in an encyclopedic manner were explained in terms of a self-proclaimed mission, "assembling and transmitting to coming generations the Islamic cultural patrimony before it might disappear as a result of the carelessness of his contemporaries."[47] Correspondingly, his *al-Taḥadduth bi-niʿmat Allāh* contains an enumeration of a great bulk of his works with the *Rafʿ* ranking among those that he regarded as particularly original and specific in their composition.[48] Thus, a close reading and analysis of the *Rafʿ* has to trace significances in the textual fabric along the lines of both a preservationist stance and an elaborative tendency, two criteria that dominated al-Suyūṭī's academic aspirations as a self-proclaimed savant extraordinaire.

3 Preservation as Authoritative Compilation

First of all, the application of a preservationist methodology has to be considered in al-Suyūṭī's *Rafʿ shaʾn al-Ḥubshān*. It builds on a bias towards canonical traditions and their correct transmission, two aspects that become clear when reading the *Rafʿ*. He gives priority to the exact citation of prophetic traditions and early Islamic historical anecdotes.[49] With respect to these *ḥadīth*s and *khabar*s S. Leder emphasized that in certain genres "transmission" was far more prevalent than the notion of "authorship."[50] The characteristics of *ḥadīth*s and *khabar*s as self-contained primary textual units comprising a chain of transmission (*isnād*) and the text (*matn*) of the utterance or anecdote made them suitable for constant de-contextualization from earlier works and re-contextualization within new compilations.[51] While the word *khabar* was generally used to refer to a historical event or anecdote, the term *ḥadīth* took on an exclusive religious connotation during the formative period, meaning sayings and deeds of the Prophet recorded by his followers (*al-ṣaḥāba*) and subsequent generations in order to provide guidance in all matters concerning

45 Cp. Geoffroy, al-Suyūṭī 914–5.
46 Cp. ibid.
47 Cp. ibid. 914.
48 Cp. al-Suyūṭī, *Tahadduth* 111–3.
49 Cp. especially the chapters 1–3 in al-Suyūṭī, *Rafʿ*.
50 Leder, Authorship 67 ff.
51 Ibid.

the Muslim community (*umma*).[52] Although over the course of time generations told stories in various ways and some were certainly made up to serve sectarian and political interests of one group or another,[53] editorial alterations due to changing narrative strategies and literary techniques produced different versions of the same *ḥadīth*, which could nonetheless denote the same thought and concept.[54] In several instances, al-Suyūṭī quotes similar or identical versions of a *khabar* or *ḥadīth* thereby expounding his breadth of knowledge and engaging with its history of transmission.

In the case of the *Rafʿ* both these *ḥadīth*s and *khabar*s constituted the building blocks of al-Suyūṭī's "*khabar*-history" with each of these textual units presenting an idea that had already been framed as a story to comply with established conventions of literary communication.[55] The link of the selected *ḥadīth*s and *khabar*s with Abyssinian figures represented the guideline for the composition. More specifically, it is the intersecting reference to Abyssinians in each *matn*, which provided for the common thematic ground of al-Suyūṭī's compilation. The succession of accumulatively arranged primary textual units displays a kaleidoscope of prophetic and early Islamic normative attitudes towards the *Ḥubshān*. A re-contextualization within this thematic configuration as addressed in the title, subtitles, and the foreword shifts the focus of the reader to the Abyssinians and their deeds, utterances, as well as related prophetic sanctions. At the same time, the majority of *ḥadīth*s in al-Suyūṭī's work enable a reader to view these sequences with a continued presence of the Prophet and his past. An idealized early Islamic age is implicit in the fabric of these primary textual units and thereby raises them to a supreme religious importance. This prophetic paradigm was never deleted, but, on the contrary, ensures the authoritative framework of the whole sequence a priori.

The full citation of the *isnād*, though commonplace, exhibits a significant technique of textual production. It provides for a scholarly framework legitimizing the statements on the Abyssinians according to generally acknowledged academic standards of al-Suyūṭī's times.[56] The extended version of the chain of transmission guarantees the soundness of a normative prophetic requirement. Furthermore, al-Suyūṭī sometimes adds commentaries for an assessment of the transmitters and for definitive purposes. Throughout the text, he strictly adheres to academic conventions of his profession enjoining a correct trans-generational dissemination of religious and historical knowledge

52 Cp. Conermann and Eisenbürger, Überlieferungen 155–8.

53 Donner, ʿUthmān 45–6.

54 Cp. Günther, Literary theory 171–6; Günther, Fictional narration 433–7.

55 For "*khabar* history" cp. Rosenthal, *History* 66; cp. Leder, Composite form 125–7.

56 Cp. Berkey, Transmission 30–2.

within the parameters of *taqlīd* (uncritical transfer). He thereby references earlier scholarly authorities such as al-Dhahabī, al-Ṭabarī, al-Ṭabarānī, and al-Tirmidhī, besides a variety of his teachers and contemporaries such as al-Bulqīnī and al-Shumunnī.[57] Thus his sources are situated across several disciplines ranging from *tafsīr* to *ḥadīth, taʾrīkh*, and *fiqh*, demonstrating the amplitude of his scholarship. In addition to this confirmation of erudition, the continuous use of the *isnād* displays his integration into various professional networks of his period.

Most importantly, though, the indication of his *ijāzāt* transcends a pure illustration of acquired knowledge and social networks. On the one hand, the chain of transmission in its person-centered configuration guarantees the authenticity of a report or prophetic tradition.[58] On the other hand, the chains of transmission also reveal the diverse trans-textual correlations of al-Suyūṭī's composition. G. Genette defined such intertexts as texts within a text maintaining secret and obvious connections with other texts.[59] Al-Suyūṭī displays these trans-textual relationships in the *Rafʿ* in a particularly explicit manner. Orally received prophetic traditions and numerous *ḥadīth*-compilations constituted his archive.[60] The additional use of standard works of Islamic scholarship indicates al-Suyūṭī's intention to collect a particularly broad spectrum of information on his subject. Through the *isnād*-based link with the "bygone authorities," these materials were defined per se as the knowledgeable corpus. Thus, the complementary, direct, and pervasive citation of the *isnād* with the diverse references to earlier authorities presents his work as a "multiple palimpsest." This form functioned as an authoritative framework for the statements made in the *matn*. Through this "multiple palimpsest" paradigm the argumentative pattern is evoked by external trans-textual references that award the historical and prophetic materials concerning the Abyssinians their normative quality.

4 Elaboration—Evoking Meaning through Techniques of Compilation

While the traits outlined above are generally acknowledged as common features of such compilations, an argumentative pattern is discernible that

57 Cp. al-Suyūṭī, *Rafʿ*. These scholars appear multiple times in the *isnād*s of the text.

58 Cp. Berkey, Transmission 30–2.

59 Cp. Genette, *Palimpseste* 9–10. For the semantic use of *ḥadīth* and other authoritative religious materials as intertexts in *adab* works cp. Malti-Douglas, Playing 59.

60 Cp. e.g. al-Suyūṭī, *Rafʿ* 44–5 and 183.

operates beyond a sanctioning of a linear sequential progression of *ḥadīth*s and *khabar*s. However, with this argumentative framework based on authoritative transmission, there remained no further exigency to expand on causality or lines of reasoning. The elaboration was intended in a different manner. The short foreword represents one of the very few parts of the *Rafʿ* in which the author does not quote transmitted knowledge, but exposes his subjective purpose in "his own words."[61] As mentioned previously, with his two objectives al-Suyūṭī wanted to set himself apart from Ibn al-Jawzī by composing an all-encompassing work focusing solely on the *Ḥubshān*, but not on the *Sūdān* in general.[62] However, the purpose of exalting the importance of the Abyssinians in the form of an abridgement and a completion indicates an additional reworking of his predecessor's book. Al-Suyūṭī used the argumentative space for his elaborative agency to create a historically rooted subaltern "Abyssinian identity."

In order to achieve this, al-Suyūṭī applied various procedures of textual compilation whereby a semantic calibration of a textual unit is evoked through a combination with other such units and their external approval or falsification, i.e. the assessment of the transmitters in the *isnād*. F. Donner explained in his analysis of Ibn ʿAsākir's *Taʾrīkh madīnat Dimashq* that techniques such as selection, repetition and placement could impart meaning in the compilation of transmitted texts.[63] As repositories of pre-existing materials these compilations reveal "a compiler's agenda" through the crafted order and structure of such works, even if they "almost never speak with one voice."[64] Through the analysis of al-Suyūṭī's elaborative techniques, the diverse semantic significances of the text can be probed in order to detect his appreciative characterization of the Abyssinians. In the following I will give major examples by concentrating on his techniques of segmentation, repetition, and contrastive succession.

Inducing meaning through the segmentation of textual materials was one of the standard methods of compilation. The division of al-Suyūṭī's work into chapters creates a variety of spheres of knowledge with respect to the Abyssinians' share in Islamic culture. Although all the textual materials consist of *ḥadīth*s and *khabar*s the first three chapters divide them with respect to Abyssinians' appearance in the prophetic traditions, the *asbāb al-nuzūl*,

61 Ibid. 31.
62 Ibid.
63 Donner, ʿUthmān 46–7.
64 Ibid. 46.

and their words in the Quranic terminology, respectively.[65] The *muqaddima* prefigures these sections by putting *al-Ḥabasha* on a definitive geographical and political map utilizing information from compendia.[66] Similarly, the fifth chapter contains a list of biographical entries of Abyssinians that resembles a biographical dictionary.[67] Thus, splitting up the corpus of *khabar*s and *ḥadīth*s into thematic sections provided a basic tool for structuring the compilation. The transmitted textual units were thereby ordered according to textual genres with each chapter accumulating a rearranged body of Islamic knowledge with respect to the Abyssinians.

As each chapter establishes the cultural and religious significance of the Abyssinians, a specific importance comes with a saying that introduces the *ḥadīth* section by laying down a prophetic position towards the *Ḥubshān*:

> Abū ʿAbdallāh al-Ḥalabī reported to me in written form (*mukātabatan*), based on the authority of [...], based on the authority of Ibn ʿAbbās, who said: "The Prophet of Allāh, peace be upon him, said: 'Take the *Sūdān*, because three of them belong to the masters of the people of paradise (*sādāt ahl al-janna*): Luqmān the Wise, the Najāshī and Bilāl the *muʾadhdhin*.' And al-Ṭabarānī said: The word *Sūdān* refers to *al-Ḥabash* [i.e. the Abyssinians]."[68]

This prophetic statement legitimizes the social integration of the Abyssinians into the *umma* by referring to the extraordinary status of three people that are characterized as the "masters of the people of paradise." Their fine example establishes the Abyssinians collectively as a respectable ethnic group within the Muslim community. However, a societal acceptance of the Abyssinians stipulates their social status as slaves.

Nonetheless, as an ethnic community, the Abyssinians played a crucial historical role during the lifetime of the Prophet Muḥammad. This aspect is epitomized in the fourth chapter through the strategy of repetition. It contains several much longer traditions that are concerned with the *hijra* of the early Muslim community to *al-Ḥabasha* in the fifth year of the beginning of the revelation (615 CE).[69] The central aspect of these narratives revolves around the confrontation of the Meccan Quraysh, who followed the Muslims to the

65 Cp. al-Suyūṭī, *Rafʿ* 37–68.

66 Ibid. 32–6.

67 Ibid. 95–202.

68 Ibid. 37.

69 Ibid. 69–94.

court of the Najāshī, the Abyssinian king. In the framework of a debate relating to the role of ʿĪsā in the Islamic revelation, the Najāshī accepts the strict monotheistic interpretation of the Muslim group. He is therefore considered to have converted to Islam, protecting the Muslims from the Meccan persecutors. Ibn al-Jawzī provides one narrative report of the migration.[70] However, in al-Suyūṭī's text the repetition of this report is based on multiple different chains of transmission.[71] This works as an emphasis within the overall structure of the narrative. The migration (*hijra*) to the land of *al-Ḥabasha* is highlighted as a critical event in the history of the early *umma*, providing a safe place for the adherents of the new prophetic revelation. Simultaneously, it accentuates the protective role of the Najāshī. It even goes so far as to regard him as a fellow Muslim, though in a rather patronizing manner. Since the Najāshī as the political sovereign can be viewed as the pars pro toto of the Abyssinians, the people of *al-Ḥabasha* are considered in the crucial role that they played in early Islamic history.

In another context, the mythological past of the Abyssinians is specified through the method of contrastive succession. This juxtaposition of contradictory reports demonstrates al-Suyūṭī's critical engagement with different traditions. He finalizes his own choice through the order of their arrangement. A case in point is the group of reports dealing with the fate of Ḥām the mythological ancestor of the *Sūdān* and the *Ḥubshān*.[72] Noah's curse was considered by several medieval scholars to explain the blackness of the African peoples.[73] In a further step, it provided a convenient ideological justification for their enslavement by the Arabs and Persians, the progeny of Ḥām's two brothers Shem and Japheth.[74] While al-Suyūṭī quotes traditions that support this position, he later engages with other opinions.[75] The latter explain the blackness in terms of an arbitrary divine intervention.[76] At this point, his argument conforms to Ibn al-Jawzī's, who rejects the curse as an explanation.[77] Then al-Suyūṭī presents a tradition according to which Noah had pity and transformed his dictum of slavery into a relationship of merciful servility for Ḥām

70 Cp. Ibn al-Jawzī, *Tanwīr* 62–9. Both al-Suyūṭī and Ibn al-Jawzī provide alphabetical lists of those Muslims who migrated to Abyssinia at that time. Cp. ibid. 57–60 and al-Suyūṭī, *Rafʿ* 90–4.

71 Cp. ibid. 69–94.

72 Cp. ibid. 32–5.

73 Cp. Enderwitz, *Gesellschaftlicher Rang* 26.

74 Cp. Lewis, Race 44–6.

75 Cp. al-Suyūṭī, *Rafʿ* 32–5 and 207–8.

76 Cp. ibid.

77 Al-Suyūṭī quotes Ibn al-Jawzī in this matter, cp. ibid. 207. Cp. Ibn al-Jawzī, *Tanwīr* 35.

towards his two brothers.[78] Thus, al-Suyūṭī reconfigures the servile position of the Abyssinians. His final position conforms to the overall benevolent attitude of the Prophet Muḥammad in his sayings and deeds, a religious guideline that could not be breached given his scholarly propositions.

A crucial qualification of the Abyssinians' historical role is detailed in the context of a disagreement between al-Suyūṭī and Ibn al-Jawzī relating to the assignment of the call to prayer (*adhān*). Here again, the technique of contrasting different traditions is used to construct a line of argument. Ibn al-Jawzī conceded this religious duty of the *adhān* to the Abyssinians by quoting a single tradition.[79] Accordingly, the caliphate belonged to the Quraysh, the judgeship to the Anṣār, and the Abyssinians were responsible for the call to prayer.[80] While al-Suyūṭī can cite two traditions in this respect, he finally refutes the Abyssinians as *mu'adhdhin*s of the *umma*, based on a commentary by the Meccan historian al-Fāsī.[81] Thus, Muḥammad's *mu'adhdhin* Bilāl was an exception and his role did not translate into a precedent that would honor the Abyssinians with this religious office.

In sum, the Abyssinians' historically rooted identity is elaborated on from various different perspectives exemplifying al-Suyūṭī's intensive engagement with his selected textual materials. A crucial element consists of a cursed mythological past as the progeny of Ḥām. They were condemned to serve as slaves based on the precedent established by a variety of traditions that developed the incident relating to Ḥām's discovery of Noah's nakedness, as it appears in the Book of Genesis. This past, however, was mitigated and upgraded symbolically by prophetic prescriptions, thus justifying their service as slaves and dependents in the *umma*. Such an integrative stance could again be based on their critical historical role as a refuge for the Muslim *umma*, with the Najāshī embracing the message of the prophet. Nonetheless, the difference of opinion between al-Suyūṭī and Ibn al-Jawzī with respect to the assignment of the call to prayer seems to emphasize a social status as slaves. In conclusion, the Abyssinians constituted an inherent and functional subaltern group within the *umma* during an ideal prophetic age and contributed positively to its evolution. All these aspects demonstrate al-Suyūṭī's dominant authorial voice that guides the reader along the effects of various structural techniques. The thread of his elaborative trend that runs through his work levels out a profile of significances that transcend the purely accumulative

78 Cp. al-Suyūṭī, *Raf'* 208.
79 Cp. Ibn al-Jawzī, *Tanwīr* 82.
80 Ibid.
81 Cp. al-Suyūṭī, *Raf'* 38–40.

features of a compilation. Al-Suyūṭī selects and revitalizes existing cultural knowledge about the Abyssinians in the early Islamic period. Through this rearrangement of authoritative reports he illuminates their crucial historical role by arguing within the parameters of prophetic attitudes and sanctions.

5 Historicisation—Constructing the Ideal Abyssinian Community

The historical significance of the Abyssinians is further embellished through a selection of worthy dramatis personae in the fifth chapter of the *Rafʿ*. This part can be understood as a biographical dictionary that lists biographical entries (*tarājim*) of altogether 35 individuals and of varying length.[82] The title of this chapter contains the phrase "a few of their noble ones" (*baʿḍ nujabāʾihim*) indicating that al-Suyūṭī focused this chapter on a particular group of Abyssinians.[83] These figures become even more exclusive through a short note that he placed after the penultimate biography emphasizing that, although there are numerous excellent ones among them, they cannot all be mentioned, especially because some of them do not fit the pattern.[84] Nonetheless, there are no more clues as to his criteria of inclusion and to the purpose of this miniature biographical dictionary within the entire composition. Therefore, as the compilatory characteristics of this chapter conform to the other sections of the *Rafʿ*, this chapter too, must be read accordingly. It has to be analyzed as a narrative text comprising religiously sanctioned materials that produce a specific meaning in their configuration as a biographical dictionary.

Scholarship has located this genre of "collective biography" within the parameters of historiographical texts. Conventionally, a collection of *tarājim* is delineated in contrast with "a single-subject and stand-alone biography" (*sīra*) that focuses on the prominent achievements of one individual.[85] The genre of collective biography was conceived as an intrinsic literary tradition of Arab-Islamic culture, with its origins residing in the formative Islamic period and the elaboration during the prolific ʿAbbasid era.[86] Sir H.A.R. Gibb stated that, "the conception that underlies the oldest biographical dictionaries is that the history of the Islamic Community is essentially the contribution of

82 Cp. ibid. 95–202.
83 Ibid. 95.
84 Ibid. 200.
85 Robinson, Historiography 61, 66.
86 Cp. Young, Arabic 168–73. On the historiographical and cultural significance of this genre cp. al-Qāḍī, Structure, and eadem, Biographical dictionaries.

individual men and women to the building up and transmission of its specific culture."[87] Correspondingly, M. Cooperson has argued for a close interrelation of biographical composition with the notion of genealogy and the collection of historical reports as practiced by the earliest historians (*akhbāriyyūn*).[88] Early writings from the formative period comprised lists (*tasmiyāt*) of personages with varying professional backgrounds, which runs counter to the idea that the collection of information on transmitters of *ḥadīth* stood out as the sole purpose.[89]

One possible point of entry for fathoming the narrative structure of such biographical dictionaries lies in the analysis of the contents and structure of its building blocks, i.e. the biographical entries (*tarājim*), within their overall arrangement in the composition. M. Cooperson advanced the concept of the *ṭāʾifa* (group) based on the "division-of-labor model" which, according to him, emerged as "the most productive paradigm for collective biography," with *ṭāʾifa* referring to a "group entrusted with an exclusive body of knowledge or characteristic activity."[90] These groups were usually furnished with a foundational figure, such as the *ḥadīth*-transmitters claiming the "heirship to the prophet," which played a pivotal role for the construction of their authoritative lineage in the transmission of *ʿilm*.[91] Similarly, other professions, for example musicians, grammarians and poets, articulated their group identity and traced the knowledge and skills of their occupation back to a point of origin, personified in the "exposition of the virtues of individual exemplars within the category" and framed in "self-defined fields of expertise."[92] Thus, the manner in which meaning is constituted through the disposition and linking of personages and their deeds offers an important line of inquiry.

A more specific literary-historical approach can highlight various aspects in this "act of constituting a community."[93] Especially in the case of biographical

87 Gibb, Islamic 54. Nevertheless, scholars have continuously debated the social function of biographical works. Cp. Auchterlonie, Historians 187.

88 Cp. Cooperson, Arabic biography 2.

89 Cp. ibid. 3. Nevertheless, "*rijāl*-works," which recorded the participants in the dissemination of knowledge and commented on the extent of their reliability in that matter, represent one of the major branches of the genre. Certainly, the exigencies of assuring an authoritative genealogical chain in the transmission of religious knowledge (*ʿilm*), and especially the sayings and deeds of the Prophet Muḥammad, provided a major impetus. Cp. ibid. 7–8.

90 Ibid. 14–5.

91 Cp. ibid. 13.

92 Ibid. 9–13.

93 Cp. Cooperson, Literary-historical 179.

dictionaries with a diachronic outline that follows the characters through the generations, their recording serves the preservation of a "mythologized version" of a group's authoritative historical account in the form of a "charter myth."[94] At this point authorial strategies feature prominently, since they determine the criteria for excluding or including figures in the *ṭāʾifa*.[95] On the whole, the narrative structure of the biographical works comprises an interrelation of "doctrinal necessity," "transmitted memory," and "compositional skills."[96] Thus, from this perspective, the ambivalent character of the biographical dictionaries is emphasized, combining the purpose of recording figures and their transactions with the framework of certain literary norms.[97]

For an analysis of al-Suyūṭī's Abyssinian biographical dictionary, the search for an authorial voice as it manifests itself in a group's "charter myth" and in the "transmitted memory" that preserves a "genealogy of authority" provides a crucial line of investigation.[98] In comparison, al-Suyūṭī's predecessor Ibn al-Jawzī divided his list of worthy *Sūdān* into nine chapters—one chapter for each group: prophets, kings, scholars and so forth.[99] Whereas Ibn al-Jawzī presents professional diversity and social omnipresence, al-Suyūṭī concentrates on a single community. Taken together his *tarājim* constitute the Abyssinians as one *ṭāʾifa* whose history evolves diachronically through the laudable deeds and lives of 35 individuals. However, while they equally appear as Abyssinians some of its members are considered more equal than others. It is the diachronic succession of these figures that reveals the internal structure and calibration of the biographical dictionary itself. Al-Suyūṭī's arrangement of his Abyssinian characters within the biographical dictionary creates a "semantic of disposition." In other words, the succession of characters combined with their function within the Abyssinian group at large produces a particular significance beyond the textual contents of the biographical entries.

More specifically, a "genealogy of authority" is established and a "transmitted memory" articulated through the sequential arrangement of three subgroups within the *ṭāʾifa*. The first consists of three figures that are quoted in the tradition on the "masters of the people of paradise" (*sādāt ahl al-janna*), three *Sūdān* who the prophet considered as particularly eminent.[100] First of

94 Cp. ibid. 179.
95 Cp. ibid.
96 Cp. ibid. 180.
97 Cp. ibid. 177.
98 Ibid. 179–80.
99 Cp. chapterisation in Ibn al-Jawzī, *Tanwīr* 31.
100 Cp. al-Suyūṭī, *Rafʿ* 37.

all, there is the extraordinary prophetic wisdom of the Quranic and mythical figure Luqmān that becomes evident from the various anecdotes displaying a pattern of moral behavior that in turn conforms to a normative set of Islamic guidance.[101] Secondly, the political role of the historical personality of the Najāshī in protecting the Muslim refugees during their *hijra* to Abyssinia is again emphasized in the context of a verbatim quoted correspondence between him and the Prophet Muḥammad.[102] At the same time, the Najāshī is invited to convert to Islam and follow the prophecy of Muḥammad, an act of submission that the Najāshī complies with in his response.[103] Finally, he is even characterized as a *tābiʿī* and thus obtains a crucial status within the Islamic hierarchy of approval and prestige.[104] Thirdly, the significance of Bilāl as Muḥammads *muʾadhdhin* is central to his very long biography, in addition to his participation in the battle of Badr.[105] Thus, all three biographies exhibit deeds and qualities that were conducive to the evolution and growth of the *umma* during the prophetic period. These exceptional personalities establish a triumvirate as foundational figures of the Abyssinian *ṭāʾifa*. With their exemplary lives they provide the "charter myth" that legitimizes the reference of the subsequent figures.

The following sub-group constitutes the great majority in al-Suyūṭī's biographical dictionary: slaves (*ʿabīd*) and freedmen (*mawālin*). Among them are, for example, Shuqrān al-Ḥabashī, who fought at Badr and transmitted *ḥadīth*;[106] the mutilated Yasār al-Ḥabashī, who used to clean and moisten the mosque;[107] as well as the prophet's nurse Umm Ayman, who was later manumitted by Muḥammad and participated in the *hijra* to both Abyssinia and Medina.[108] Besides their contribution to the transmission of prophetic traditions, their actions exhibit a variety of mainly symbolic values within the environment of Muḥammad. In this realm sanctioned by the prophet, they served as slaves in the early Muslim community and were integrated on the basis

101 Cp. ibid. 95–8. In this sequence of anecdotes his acquisition of prophetic wisdom is narrated. Then various maxims elaborate on the related moral codex. Cp. ibid. 95–109.

102 Cp. ibid. 115–6.

103 Cp. ibid.

104 Cp. ibid. 117.

105 Cp. ibid. 123–51.

106 Cp. ibid. 154–5.

107 Cp. ibid. 165.

108 Cp. ibid. 168–9.

of their laudable forebears to perform various functions. Nevertheless they retain their overall subaltern status throughout.

The last group of a few poets, scholars, and Sufis then demonstrates the possibility of professional careers. Figures such as the two poets Suḥaym and Abū Dulāma are praised for their literary qualities, underscored by excerpts from their poetry.[109] The ascetic Abū l-Khayr al-Tinānī's importance is demonstrated by his performance of miracles (*karāmāt*),[110] while the scholar ʿAṭāʾ b. Abī Rabāḥ is characterized in multiple ways as famous for his inexhaustible knowledge.[111] Altogether, the figures of this last sub-group excel in their fields of knowledge and are acknowledged by their contemporaries. Their professional careers point towards a certain degree of social mobility in the later centuries of the formative period. These achievements build on the individual effort of each personality, simultaneously defying restrictions of social ascent based on ethnic prejudice.

However, this selection of successful professional careers is then finally contrasted with the case of an insurmountable ethno-cultural barrier. A hierarchical subaltern status of the Abyssinians is epitomized by the historical example of Kāfūr al-Ikhshīdī, who is introduced as "one of their leaders" (*min ruʾasāʾihim*).[112] Bought as a slave under the Ikhshīdid dynasty of Egypt in the fourth/tenth century, he rose to the highest military ranks.[113] Later he declared himself sultan and reigned until his death a few years later. This *tarjama* is separated deliberately from the previous figures through al-Suyūṭī's remark on the exclusive provenance of his Abyssinians.[114] Al-Suyūṭī then concludes this biographical entry by quoting verses by the famous poet al-Mutanabbī (d. 354/955), who lived and worked at the court of Kāfūr for some time. The first verses praise him:

> I go to Kāfūr and abandon the others,
> For he, who approaches the sea, despises the little waters
> There comes a human who is an important man of his times
> He leaves the whites behind himself and even in the corner of his eyes[115]

109 Cp. ibid. 190–4.
110 Cp. ibid. 194–6.
111 Cp. ibid. 184–8.
112 Cp. ibid. 201–2.
113 Cp. ibid.
114 Ibid. 200.
115 Ibid. 202.

And the following lines ridicule him:

> Who taught the castrated black a noble deed?
> Are his people the whites or rather his ancestors the hunted ones?
> And when even strong white people are incapable of good deeds
> How then should a castrated black be capable of them.[116]

While the first section praises Kāfūr's unstoppable rise to political power, the verses that follow revile him as the progeny of "hunted" slaves. He is incapable of "good deeds" because of his blackness and thus condemned to serve and never to exert political power. His failure in the words of the poet functions as an admonishing historical example (*ʿibra*) at the end of the biographical dictionary, which retrospectively underscores the subaltern role of the Abyssinians. Their main historical and social value is restricted to their primary function as slaves within a normative Islamic societal framework sanctioned by the prophet.

6 Conclusion

In conclusion, one can link the different argumentative threads in order to identify possible social and cultural purposes of al-Suyūṭī's treatise and thus how it made sense in his academic and societal context. On the one side, Rotter saw the sole motivation in the final *ḥadīth*s that are concerned with the legitimate treatment of concubines and slaves.[117] According to him, this was justified associatively through the laudable depiction of the servile and subaltern Abyssinians. On the other side, al-Suyūṭī clearly stated in the preface his intention to supersede his predecessor Ibn al-Jawzī. However, a more comprehensive reading discloses al-Suyūṭī's work as part of his broader scholarly concerns. The two notions of preservation and elaboration connect authoritative scholarly methods with a diverse compilatory reworking of religious traditions to generate the historical significance of the Abyssinians. Al-Suyūṭī's authorial voice is guided by the strict adherence to a sound transmission of religious traditions. Nevertheless, his agency is visible in the revitalization and arrangement of existing textual materials, a process that creates knowledge through the recalibration of historical and religious significance within a specialized monograph on the Abyssinians.

116 Ibid.

117 Cp. Rotter, Die Stellung des Negers 16–7.

While a societal purpose that lauds them as worthy slaves might be read into the work, the full effect of al-Suyūṭī's work unfolds primarily on a normative academic level. The Abyssinians are treated as an aspect of a normative scholarly discourse and within al-Suyūṭī's oeuvre they are canonized as one essential element of the Islamic cultural heritage. Instead of Ibn al-Jawzī's rather straightforward positive religious dedication, al-Suyūṭī aimed at a meaningful historicization within the parameters of an Islamic religious culture. The praiseworthy historical legacy of the Abyssinians was elaborated as part of a broader process of canonization, through the construction of an "Abyssinian identity" that emerges as part of the memory of the early *umma* as well as their diachronic development as a discernible group within it. This differentiation of Islamic knowledge was meant to memorialize the intrinsic share of the Abyssinian community within the early Muslim community justifying their integration and paving the way for numerous individual contributions to its evolution. The Abyssinians are acknowledged in their symbolic performances and social role as slaves, but never transcend the predetermined normative prophetic framework.

Bibliography

Primary Sources

Ibn al-Jawzī, *Tanwīr al-ghabash fī faḍl al-Sūdān wa-l-Ḥabash*, ed. M.ʿA. Ibrāhīm, Riyadh 1998.

al-Shādhilī, *Bahjat al-ʿābidīn bi-tarjamat Jalāl al-dīn*, ms. Chester Beatty 4436.

al-Suyūṭī, *Rafʿ sha'n al-Ḥubshān*, ed. Ṣ.ʿA. Dāwūdī [et al.], Jeddah 1995.

al-Suyūṭī, [*Kitāb Rafʿ Shān al-Hubshān*] al-Khathlan, S.H., A critical edition of *Kitāb Rafʿ Shān al-Hubshān* by Jalāl al-Dīn al-Suyūtī, PhD diss., University of St. Andrews 1983.

al-Suyūṭī, *al-Taḥadduth bi-niʿmat Allāh*, in E.M. Sartain (ed.), *Jalāl al-dīn al-Suyūṭī.* ii: *al-Taḥadduth bi-niʿmat Allāh* (University of Cambridge Oriental Publications 24), Cambridge 1975.

al-Suyūṭī, *al-Tanbi'a bi-man yabʿathuhu Allāh ʿalā ra's kull mi'a*, ms. Dār al-kutub (Egyptian National Library), Majāmīʿ 98.

Secondary Sources

Auchterlonie, P., Historians and the Arabic biographical dictionary: Some new approaches, in R.G. Hoyland and P.F. Kennedy (eds.), *Islamic reflections, Arabic musings: Studies in honour of professor Alan Jones*, [Cambridge] 2004, 186–200.

Ayalon, D., *Eunuchs, caliphs and sultans: A study in power relationships*, Jerusalem 1999.

Bauer, T., Mamlūk literature: Misunderstandings and new approaches, in *MSR* 9 (2005), 105–32.

Beckingham, C.F., Ḥabash, Ḥabasha, (iii) al-Ḥabash in Muslim geographical works, in *EI*², iii, 6–7.

Berkey, J.B., *The transmission of knowledge: A social history of Islamic education*, Princeton 1992.

Berkey, J.B., Culture and society during the later Middle Ages, in C.F. Petry (ed.), *The Cambridge history of Egypt*, i: *Islamic Egypt, 640–1517*, Cambridge 1998, 375–411.

Brustad, K., Imposing order: Reading the conventions of representation in al-Suyūṭī's autobiography, in *Edebiyat* 7 (1997), 327–44.

Burge, S.R., Reading between the lines: The compilation of *ḥadīṯ* and the authorial voice, in *Arabica* 58 (2011), 168–97.

Conermann, S. and B. Eisenbürger, Die Überlieferungen vom Propheten und seinen Genossen (*aḥādīṯ*) als Gattung, in S. Conermann [et al.](eds.) *Was sind Genres? Nicht-abendländische Kategorisierungen von Gattungen*, Berlin 2011, 154–214.

Cooperson, M., *Classical Arabic biography: The heirs of the prophets in the age of al-Maʾmūn*, Cambridge 2000.

Cooperson, M., Classical Arabic biography: A literary-historical approach, in V. Klemm and B. Gruendler (eds.), *Understanding Near Eastern literatures: A spectrum of interdisciplinary approaches* (LiK 1), Wiesbaden 2000, 177–88.

Donner, F.M., ʿUthmān and the Rāshidūn caliphs in Ibn ʿAsākir's *Taʾrīkh madīnat Dimashq*: A study in strategies of compilation, in J.E. Lindsay (ed.), *Ibn ʿAsākir and early Islamic history*, Princeton 2001, 44–61.

Enderwitz, S., *Gesellschaftlicher Rang und ethnische Legitimation: Der arabische Schriftsteller Abū ʿUṯmān al-Ǧāḥiẓ (gest. 868) über die Afrikaner, Perser und Araber in der islamischen Gesellschaft* (IU 53), Freiburg 1979.

Genette, G., *Palimpseste: Die Literatur auf zweiter Stufe*, trans. W. Bayer and D. Honig, Frankfurt 1993.

Geoffroy, É., al-Suyūṭī, in *EI*², ix, 913–6.

Gibb, Sir H.A.R., Islamic biographical literature, in B. Lewis and P.M. Holt (eds.), *Historians of the Middle East*, London 1962, 54–8.

Gilliot, C., ʿUlamāʾ. (i) In the Arab world, in *EI*², x, 801–5.

Günther, S., Fictional narration and imagination within an authoritative framework: Towards a new understanding of *ḥadīth*, in S. Leder (ed.), *Story-telling in the framework of non-fictional Arabic literature*, Wiesbaden 1998, 433–71.

Günther, S., Modern literary theory applied to classical Arabic texts: *Ḥadīth* revisited, in V. Klemm and B. Gruendler (eds.), *Understanding Near Eastern literatures: A spectrum of interdisciplinary approaches* (LiK 1), Wiesbaden 2000, 171–6.

Hodgson, M.G.S., *The venture of Islam: Conscience and history in a world civilization*, ii: *The expansion of Islam in the Middle periods*, Chicago 1977.

Irwin, R., al-Suyūṭī (849–911/1445–1505), in J.S. Meisami and P. Starkey (eds.), *EAL*, ii, London and New York 1998, 746.

Leder, S., Authorship and transmission in unauthored literature: The *akhbār* attributed to al-Haytham ibn ʿAdī, in *Oriens* 31 (1988), 67–81.

Leder, S., The use of the composite form in the making of the Islamic historical tradition, in P.F. Kennedy (ed.), *On fiction and* adab *in medieval Arabic literature*, Wiesbaden 2005, 125–48.

Lewis, B., *Race and slavery in the Middle East*, New York 1990.

Malti-Douglas, F., Playing with the sacred: Religious intertext in *adab* discourse, in A. Afsaruddin and M. Zahniser (eds.), *Humanism, culture and language in the Near East: Studies in honor of Georg Krotkoff*, Winona Lake, Ind. 1997, 51–9.

Muhammad, A., The image of Africans in Arabic literature: Some unpublished manuscripts, in J.R. Willis (ed.), *Slaves and slavery in Muslim Africa: Islam and the ideology of enslavement*, i, London, 1985, 125–59.

Mourad, S.A. and J.E. Lindsay, *The intensification and reorientation of Sunni jihad ideology in the Crusader period: Ibn ʿAsākir of Damascus (1105–1176) and his age, with an edition and translation of Ibn ʿAsākir's* The forty hadiths for inciting jihad (IHC 99), Leiden 2013.

Petry, C.F., From slaves to benefactors: The Ḥabashīs of Mamlūk Cairo, in *Sudanic Africa* 5 (1994), 57–66.

Pfeiffer, J., Introduction: From Baghdad to Marāgha, Tabriz, and beyond: Tabriz and the multi-cephalous cultural, religious, and intellectual landscape of the 13th to 15th century Nile-to-Oxus Region, in J. Pfeiffer (ed.), *Politics, patronage and the transmission of knowledge in 13th–15th century Tabriz* (IS 8), Leiden and Boston 2014, 1–11.

Poston, L., The second coming of ʿIsa: An exploration of Islamic premillenialism, in *MW* 100 (2010), 100–16.

al-Qāḍī, W., Biographical dictionaries: Inner structure and cultural significance, in G.N. Atiyeh (ed.), *The book in the Islamic world: The written word and communication in the Middle East*, Albany 1995, 93–122.

al-Qāḍī, W., Biographical dictionaries as the scholars' alternative history of the Muslim community, in G. Endress (ed.), *Organizing knowledge: Encyclopaedic activities in the pre-eighteenth century Islamic world* (IPT 61), Leiden and Boston 2006, 23–75.

Robinson, C.F., *Islamic historiography*, Cambridge 2003.

Rosenthal, F., *A history of Muslim historiography*, Leiden 1952, ^{2}1968 (rev. ed.).

Rotter, G., *Die Stellung des Negers in der islamisch-arabischen Gesellschaft bis zum 16. Jahrhundert*, Bonn 1967.

Saleh, M.J., Al-Ṣuyūṭī and his works: Their place in Islamic scholarship from Mamlūk times to the present, in *MSR* 5 (2001), 73–89.

Sartain, E.M., *Jalāl al-dīn al-Suyūṭī.* i: *Biography and background* (University of Cambridge Oriental Publications 23), Cambridge 1975.

Spevack, A., Jalāl al-Dīn al-Suyūṭī, in J.E. Lowry and D.J. Stewart (eds.), *Essays in Arabic literary biography 1350–1850*, (Mîzân. Studien zur Literatur in der islamischen Welt 17: Essays in Arabic literary biography), Wiesbaden 2009, 386–409.

Young, M.J.L., Arabic biographical writing, in M.J.L. Young et al. (eds.), *The Cambridge history of Arabic literature*. iii: *Religion, learning and science in the 'Abbasid Period*, Cambridge 1990, 168–87.

CHAPTER 8

Evidence of Self-editing in al-Suyūṭī's *Taḥbīr* and *Itqān*: A Comparison of his Chapters on *Asbāb al-nuzūl*

S.R. Burge

Jalāl al-Din al-Suyūṭī (d. 911/1505) is most well-known for his work on the Quranic sciences (*ʿulūm al-Qurʾān*) entitled *Kitāb al-Itqān fī ʿulūm al-Qurʾān*.[1] This work has achieved something of "canonical" status in the field of Islamic Studies. It is a work that is highly regarded by Muslim and non-Muslim scholars alike, and it is seen as unparalleled in its exposition of the Quranic sciences; indeed Claude Gilliot has described it as being "the most complete handbook on the genre."[2] However, the *Itqān* does have a much smaller and less famous younger brother, the *Kitāb al-Taḥbīr fī ʿilm al-tafsīr*. This earlier work was edited by Zuhayr ʿUthmān ʿAlī Nūr as part of his Masters' programme at Umm al-Qura University and was subsequently published in 1988. The *Taḥbīr* was al-Suyūṭī's first offering on the Quranic Sciences, but, as is very well known, when he read al-Zarkashī's *Kitāb al-Burhān fī ʿulūm al-Qurʾān* he realized that his first attempt was much worse than the *Burhān*. Al-Suyūṭī consequently decided a re-write was needed and the *Itqān* was born. He says all of this openly in the introduction to the *Itqān*:

> I rejoiced to make the acquaintance of this book and I praised God greatly, being strengthened in my resolve to carry out my intention, I made firm my determination to compose the work I had in mind, and I therefore set down this book of exalted rank and manifest proof, full of benefit and firm of meaning. I arranged the subject matter in a way more suitable than that of the *Burhān*, combining certain topics with each other and separating those that deserved to remain distinct as well as adding to the useful and unique matters contained in the *Burhān*, its general principles

1 Al-Suyūṭī, *Itqān*. The work has been edited a number of times including those prepared by Maulavī Sadīd al-Dīn Khān (et al.), and Muḥammad Abū l-Faḍl Ibrāhīm, see the bibliography for further details. ʿAttār's 2003 edition is used throughout this paper.

2 Gilliot, Traditional disciplines 328.

© KONINKLIJKE BRILL NV, LEIDEN, 2017 | DOI 10.1163/9789004334526_010

> and the miscellaneous information, topics that will delight the ear of the reader.[3]

While al-Suyūṭī is quite happy to acknowledge the quality of al-Zarkashī's *Burhān*, he seeks to frame his praise within a critique and details how he hoped to improve it. To complicate matters further, the *Taḥbīr* is itself based on the *Mawāqiʿ al-ʿulūm fī mawāqiʿ al-nujūm* of Jalāl al-Dīn al-Bulqīnī (d. 824/1421),[4] which al-Suyūṭī revised, edited and "improved." Despite noting that the *Mawāqiʿ al-ʿulūm* was a "fine book, an elegant composition, well arranged and well written, with rich and varied contents,"[5] al-Suyūṭī also adds that al-Bulqīnī "goes on to discuss each topic in an extremely brief manner that calls for much significant elaboration, supplementation, and addition. It therefore occurred to me to include sections al-Bulqīnī had omitted and to add important matters he had not adequately treated."[6] The same could be said of al-Suyūṭī's *Taḥbīr*. Unfortunately, al-Bulqīnī's *Mawāqiʿ al-ʿulūm* does not appear to be extant,[7] which means that it is difficult to assess what al-Bulqīnī's original text looked like. Al-Suyūṭī does frequently refer to the fact that he is adding material throughout the *Taḥbīr*, but, nevertheless, it still remains extremely difficult to recover the *Mawāqiʿ al-ʿulūm*.

The *Itqān* is, therefore, the culmination of a chain of four works: al-Bulqīnī's *Mawāqiʿ al-ʿulūm*, al-Suyūṭī's *Taḥbīr*, al-Zarkashī's *Burhān* (although written before both the *Mawāqiʿ al-ʿulūm* and the *Taḥbīr*), and al-Suyūṭī's *Itqān*. Added to this already complicated textual history for the *Itqān*, al-Suyūṭī compiled other works such as his *Lubāb al-nuqūl fī asbāb al-nuzūl*,[8] the results of which were also fed into this new guide to the Quranic sciences. Al-Suyūṭī adds in his introduction to the *Itqān* that "[m]ost of the topics treated in each

---

3 Al-Suyūṭī, *Perfect guide* xxviii. The translations of the *Itqān* used in this article are taken from this volume; however, as this translation includes a number of errors in the transliteration of names, these have been corrected, where necessary. This translation has come in for some criticism, but most of criticisms centre on issues of transliteration and presentation; see Rippin, Review: Algar et al., Burge, Review: Algar et al., trs.

4 On ʿAbd al-Raḥmān b. ʿUmar b. Rustān b. Nuṣayr b. Ṣāliḥ al-Bulqīnī (Bulqaynī), Jalāl al-Dīn see Moore, al-Bulqīnī family.

5 Al-Suyūṭī, *Perfect guide* xxi; idem, *Itqān* 5. Al-Suyūṭī states that he was referred to al-Bulqīnī's *Mawāqiʿ al-ʿulūm* by al-Bulqīnī's brother, Ṣālīh b. ʿUmar ʿAlam al-Dīn al-Bulqīnī (d. 868/1464); see Moore, al-Bulqīnī family; and Petry, Civilian elite 232–40.

6 Al-Suyūṭī, *Perfect guide* xxii; idem, *Itqān* i, 5.

7 Cp. Brockelmann, *GAL* ii, 112 and *GAL S* ii, 139.

8 Al-Suyūṭī, *Lubāb*. These "supplementary" genres of *tafsīr* also had a great impact on al-Suyūṭī's *al-Durr al-manthūr*; see Burge, Muʿawwidhatān 295–300.

chapter have been made the subject of separate works, the majority of which have come to my notice."[9] Similarly Claude Gilliot has noted that al-Suyūṭī's *Muʿtarak al-aqrān fī iʿjāz al-Qurʾān* shares material in common with the *Itqān*, which suggests that al-Suyūṭī incorporated a number of works into the *Itqān*; however the chapters been analysed in this study do not show any use of this work, since his *al-Muʿtarak* focuses on the question of *iʿjāz* and rhetorical-stylistic analyses of the Quran.[10]

To be quite frank, the *Taḥbīr* has little to offer as a work on the Quranic Sciences, since it is very basic in its scholarly analysis and is of only marginal academic interest, save for an appreciation or "index" of different ways of approaching the Quranic text in exegesis. However, this study will use the work to analyse the development of al-Suyūṭī as a scholar and also to see the way he re-worked and revised older material (both his own and others') to produce new works. This study will illustrate the extent to which al-Suyūṭī made use of the *Taḥbīr* in the *Itqān* through a case study analysis of the chapters on *asbāb al-nuzūl* and its related topics. This goes somewhat counter to the perception of the *Itqān* that has been seen as being deeply influenced—including structurally—by the *Burhān*.[11] Indeed, in his analysis of the sources of the *Itqān*, Kenneth Nolin comments that "apparently al-Suyūṭī made very little use of the *Taḥbīr* in his new attempt."[12] Specific analysis of the *Taḥbīr* and the *Itqān* has not yet been made, which this chapter will try to begin to redress. This chapter will examine how the material differs in both works and will try to make some suggestions as to why al-Suyūṭī decided to make the changes that he made in the *Itqān*.

Before going into some case-study analysis, it will be helpful to provide a short overview to the *Taḥbīr*. According to the manuscript used by Zuhayr ʿUthmān ʿAlī Nūr, the work was completed on 7 Rajab 872/1 February 1468,[13] when al-Suyūṭī was just 23 years old; that is, shortly after moving to his first major posting at the mosque of Ibn Ṭūlūn.[14] It comprises 102 short chapters, each detailing one of the *ʿulūm al-Qurʾān*. The most striking aspect of the

---

9 Al-Suyūṭī, *Perfect guide* xxxi; idem, *Itqān* i, 7.

10 Gilliot, Traditional disciplines 328.

11 However, Rippin's article predates the publication of the *Taḥbīr* and he did not have access to the manuscripts, so was only able to base his comments on the relationship between the *Taḥbīr* and the *Itqān* on Nolin's work, see Rippin, al-Zarkashī 246 fns. 20, 21.

12 Nolin, *Sources* 30 fn. 89. Claude Gilliot recommends some caution in using Nolin's monograph since it contains a number of errors; see Gilliot, Traditional disciplines 330.

13 Al-Suyūṭī, *Taḥbīr* 219–20. The manuscript dates to 1016/1608.

14 See Sartain, *Biography* 41–2 and al-Suyūṭī *Taḥadduth* 86.

work is its extreme brevity (hence its name).[15] This seems to indicate that the work was a kind of "text-book" for those beginning to study *tafsīr*. Although al-Sakhāwī said that al-Suyūṭī "taught a crown of common people at the mosque of Ibn Ṭūlūn and began to dictate to some of those who are good at nothing…,"[16] it seems unlikely that the *Taḥbīr* was aimed at the masses; but its target audience was probably students, whom al-Sakhāwī held in equal disdain. The mosque of Ibn Ṭūlūn was one of the most important centres of learning in late Mamlūk Cairo, which had an endowment to provide for both an academic staff and stipends for students.[17] An "undergraduate" audience would seem to be the most appropriate for the *Taḥbīr*. However, the *Taḥbīr* lies in stark contrast to the *Itqān*, which is highly technical and comprehensive and, whilst still acting as a kind of textbook, is aimed at a much more learned reader and advanced student.

The most common assumption made about the *Itqān* is that it was heavily influenced by al-Zarkhashī's *Burhān*. While this may be true of the depth in which al-Suyūṭī wrote the chapters of the *Itqān*, the overall structure of the *Itqān* shows a remarkable similarity to the *Taḥbīr* and is notably dissimilar to the way in which al-Zarkashī arranged his own work (see appendix B). This is important to note, since it presents significant nuances to the way the *Itqān* is perceived. An analysis of the structures of the *Itqān*, the *Burhān*, and the *Taḥbīr* shows that although al-Suyūṭī took some ideas from al-Zarkashī's *Burhān* and incorporated it into what became the *Itqān*, the *Burhān* did not serve as the principal model of organization (appendix B), since it is ordered and arranged significantly differently. In contrast, although there are some differences in the structures of the *Taḥbīr* and the *Itqān* (appendix A), particularly in the last quarter or so of the two works, the *Taḥbīr* does seem to have acted as a model for the *Itqān*. This is crucial, since it means that the *Itqān* is really a revision of the *Taḥbīr*, and not simply a re-working of the *Burhān*. As will be seen in the case studies that follow, the revisions in the *Itqān* are, in some cases, extremely extensive, so the *Itqān* should really be considered a new work, rather than simply as a "revision" of either the *Taḥbīr* or the *Burhān*. It is the process of

15 *Taḥbīr* means "to beautify," but in the sense of beauty being something that is simple, clear and elegant (see Lane, *Lexicon*, 498). As is often the case in the titles that al-Suyūṭī gives his works, he appears to be playing with these senses of "beauty" and "simplicity": the *Taḥbīr* is beautiful in its simplicity.

16 Al-Sakhāwī, *Ḍaw'* iv, 66–7; Sartain, *Biography* 42.

17 Berkey, *Transmission* 52. Boaz Shoshan has also shown how "popular" literature was dominated by historical tales, folktales and anecdotes; see Shoshan, Popular literature 352–8.

revision that is the focus of this chapter and this will be explored through the analysis of specific "case studies" on the topic of *asbāb al-nuzūl* and the dating of the Suras. A comparative analysis of all three works is not feasible here, but the chapters discussing the contexts of the revelation provide examples of different ways in which al-Suyūṭī made use of the *Taḥbīr* in his *Itqān* that are replicated throughout the rest of the work.

1 Heavy Citation of the *Taḥbīr* in the *Itqān*: Summer and Winter Verses

The reasons why the distinction between the revelation of verses during the summer and the winter is important may seem a little arcane to modern readers, but this chapter details some obvious benefits. Kenneth Cragg has commented that the distinction between Meccan and Medinan is important because "these two locales are not only about *where*: there are also about *when*, seeing that the pre- and post-*hijra* conjoin a decisive history with a precise geography."[18] In a similar way, the distinction between summer and winter verses, although quite vague, is used exegetically to help interpret the Quran. In its more basic sense, the classification of summer and winter verses can help distinguish chronologies of the Quran, which has important ramifications in fields of law, as can be seen in the *asbāb* material on *kalāla* at the beginning of the chapter.[19] In the second instance, the distinction between summer and winter verses also places the verse in a specific milieu: it is not simply an "occasion" of revelation in which there is some kind of external cue that precipitates the revelation, but the designation of a verse as being revealed in the summer or the winter creates a deeper sense of *mise-en-scène* that heightens the emotional impact of the verse. For example, one verse (Q 9:81) is directly related to the heat of summer; and in another Muḥammad is said to have sweated during the sending down of the verses concerning ʿĀʾisha in Q 24:11–26 that were sent down in winter, so the sweat can only be attributed to his mental torment, rather than any heat. This is in line with contemporary understandings of *asbāb al-nuzūl* that argue that they function to place a verse of the Quran

18 Cragg, Historical geography 81.

19 For a more detailed discussion on the term *kalāla*, see Cilardo, Qurʾānic term; and Powers, Muḥammad.

in a specific ("aggadic" rather than "halakhic") context.[20] Therefore knowing whether a verse was revealed in the summer or the winter does have some bearing on the interpretation of the Quran.

The chapters on Summer and Winter verses are very similar in the *Taḥbīr* and the *Itqān*, so much so that it is possible to reproduce them side by side. The table below shows the two sources, where they deviate and where they reproduce material verbatim (marked in bold).

TABLE 8.1 *Parallel translation of the chapters on Summer and Winter verses*

Taḥbīr	*Itqān*
[§7] The first of these is akin to the second, but al-Bulqīnī did not mention anything other than this: the verse of *kalāla* (Q 4:12);	[§4] Al-Wāḥidī says: "God has revealed two verses concerning *kalāla*, one of them in winter, towards the being of *Sūrat al-Nisāʾ* [Q 4:12] and the other in summer, which was the last verse of the Sura [Q 4:176].

In the *Ṣaḥīḥ* Muslim [it is cited] on the authority of ʿUmar: "There is no subject on which I queried the Messenger of God as much as I did on the state of *kalāla*, and there is no subject on which he answered more firmly, to the point of thrusting his fingers against my chest and saying: "Umar, is not the verse at the end of *Sūrat al-Nisāʾ*, the verse revealed in the summer, enough for you?'."

And in [al-Ḥākim al-Nīsābūrī's] *al-Mustadrak* [it is cited] on the authority of Abū Hurayra: "Someone said: 'Messenger of God what is *kalāla*.' He replied, 'Have you not heard the verse that was revealed in the summer: 'They will ask thee for a pronouncement. Say: 'God pronounces to you concerning indirect heirs'..." [Q 4:172].

20 Cp. Rippin, Function 20. Using the Hebrew terms *haggadic* and *halakhic*, Wansbrough makes the distinction between interpretation that developed through legal reflections (cp. Jewish *halakhic* exegesis), and narrative expansions to explain scripture outside a legal context (cp. Jewish *aggadic* exegesis). See Wansbrough, *Qur'anic studies*, 119. (However, it should be noted that Wansbrough confuses the terms *haggadic* and *aggadic*; cp. Aggadah, *EJ* i, 354–66).

Taḥbīr	*Itqān*
Al-Ḥākim said: It is sound according to the method of Muslim (*ʿalā sharṭi Muslim*). I [al-Suyūṭī] say:	

As mentioned above this was revealed during the journey of the Farewell Pilgrimage.

The second, third and fourth [are]: Q 2:281;	Other verses which came down during the summer [include]

Q 5:1; 5:3;

Since that was what was revealed during the Farewell pilgrimage, and they [were revealed] at a point near in time to the verse of *kalāla*. Fifthly, the majority of the verses that were sent down …	Q 2:281; and Q 2:282 ("the verse of debt"/ *ayāt al-dayn*) and Q 110. The verses that were sent down …

… concerning the raid on Tabūk [in *Sūrat al-Barāʾa* (*Taḥbīr*)], which came at the height of the hot season.

Just as it is said in the tradition, when God designated in his book and said: "They said: 'Go not forth in the heat.'" Q 9:81].	

Al-Bayhaqī said [*Taḥbīr*] /reported [*Itqān*] **in his *Dalāʾil*, through the intermediary of Ibn Isḥāq, on the authority of ʿĀṣim b. ʿUmar b. Qatāda and ʿAbd Allāh b. Abī Bakr b. Ḥazm that the Messenger of God (ṣ) would never depart on an expedition without pretending that his destination was a place other than where he was heading. The raid on Tabūk was an exception; he said: "People, I am heading to Byzantium," thus informing the Muslims of his intentions. This was at a time (*zaman* [*T*] /*zamān al-baʾs* [*I*]) of hardship, extreme heat (*shiddatin min al-ḥarr* [*T*]/*shiddat al-ḥarr* [*I*]) and scarcity in the land. While the Messenger of God was busy making his preparations, he said to al-Jadd b. Qays: "Jadd, Do you like the women of the Byzantines?" He said: "Messenger of God, my people know that no one loves women more than I do. I fear that if I see the women of the Byzantines, they will tempt me, so permit me to stay behind." Then God sent down: "Some of them there are that say: 'Give me leave and do not tempt me' …" [Q 9:49].**

Similarly, when one of the hypocrites said: "Do not go out to war in this heat!" God sent down: "Say: 'Gehenna's fire is hotter' …" [Q 9:81].

TABLE 8.1 *Parallel translation of the chapters on Summer and Winter verses* (cont.)

Taḥbīr	*Itqān*
[§8] As for the second category, it is akin to the first, but al-Bulqīnī did not mention anything other than this [subject]: the ten verses concerning the repentance of ʿĀʾisha in *Sūrat al-Nūr* [i.e. Q 24:11–26] [belong to this category].	As for verses revealed in the winter, Q 24:11–26 belong to this category. In the *Ṣaḥīḥ*, on the authority of ʿĀʾisha, were sent down on a winter's day.
First: "Those who came with the slander…" [Q 24:11]. In al-Bukhārī, there is the *ḥadīth* of ʿĀʾisha: By God! The Messenger of God did not have concerns, and no one from amongst the house of the Prophet went out until [this verse] was sent down, and he experienced the distress that he used to experience, with sweat flowing down from him, like beads of water, and it was a winter's day, all because of the severity of the words that were sent down.	
Second: "Let not those of you who posses bounty and plenty…" [Q 24:22][A] It was sent down when Abū Bakr swore an oath that he would not provide any maintenance for Mistaḥ,[B] when he discussed the calumny, while the event was still recent.	
Third: al-Wāḥidī said: "God has revealed two verses concerning *kalāla*, one of them in winter, towards the beginning of *Sūrat al-Nisāʾ* [Q 4:12] and the other in summer, which was the last verse of the Sura [Q 4:176]. But I am astounded by how al-Bulqīnī paid no attention to this!	

Taḥbīr	*Itqān*
	Fourth: the verses in *Sūrat al-Aḥzāb* concerning the Battle of the Trench were sent down during the cold season. According to a tradition of Ḥudhayfa: The people had separated themselves from the Prophet on the night of Confederates, save for twelve men. The Prophet then came to me [Ḥudhayfa] and said: "Ibn al-Yamānī, arise and go to the camp of the confederates and see how they are." I said: "Messenger of God, by the One who sent you in truth, in this cold it is only my shame before you that compels me to rise." The *ḥadīth*: according to some versions (*ṭuruq*) he said after that: "Then God sent down ..." [Q 33:9] to the end. Al-Bayhaqī cited it in his *Dalā'il*.

A The full verse reads: "Let not those of you who possess bounty and plenty swear off giving kinsmen and the poor and those who emigrate in the way of God; but let them pardon and forgive, Do you not wish that God should forgive you? God is All-forgiving, All-compassionate." Trans. Arberry, *Koran* 354.

B Misṭaḥ b. Uthātha was a cousin of Abū Bakr, and Abū Bakr provided him with maintenance.

These two chapters produce some intriguing data: first, the *Taḥbīr*, which is typically much shorter, is longer in the case of this chapter; second, all of the material from the *Taḥbīr* has been incorporated into the version in the *Itqān*; third, there is evidence of self-editing, in that the citation from al-Wāḥidī has been moved; and lastly, there are some differences in the actual data that has been presented. It will be helpful to look at each of these in turn.

The change in actual information seen in the *Itqān* is the most significant difference and warrants particular attention. The following table lists the verses cited as summer and winter verses.

The move of the material cited from al-Wāḥidī regarding the verses on *kalāla* (Q 4:12 and 4:176) from the end to the beginning of the chapters illustrates the way in which al-Suyūṭī revised his material. The actual citations are verbatim, so it is just a question of how the text has been reordered. In the *Itqān*, with the verses of *kalāla* opening the discussion of summer and winter verses, there is a greater stress on the utility of knowing when the verses were revealed: the season helps to determine which verse was abrogated by the other. This moves the distinction away from just general trivia, which could be one way of reading the entry in the *Taḥbīr*. Given the extensive treatment of *asbāb al-nuzūl* in chapter nine of the *Itqān*, it is possible to read the opening chapters (§1–8) as building up towards the question of the occasions of revelation, since these opening chapters are all used to help construct a chronology of the Suras, which have a resultant impact on the use of the Quran in Islamic

TABLE 8.2 *Qur'anic citations in the chapters on Summer and Winter verses*

Taḥbīr	Both	*Itqān*
4:12 (Winter)		4:12 (Winter)
	4:176 (Summer)	
		4:172 (Summer)
2:281 (Summer)		
	5:1 (Summer)	
	5:3 (Summer)	
		2:281 (Summer)
		2:282 (Summer)
		110 (Summer)
	9:81 (Summer)	
	9:49 (Summer)	
	24:11–26 (Winter)	
4:12 (Winter)		
4:176 (Summer)		
	33:9 (Winter)	

law and in abrogation (*naskh*). The move of the al-Wāḥidī passage is also more aesthetically pleasing, since it creates clear sections of "winter" and "summer" verses, whereas in the *Taḥbīr* version there are more moves from one to the other. Overall this means that the citation of al-Wāḥidī is much more successful and more thoughtfully considered in the *Itqān* than it is in the *Taḥbīr*, and indicates that al-Suyūṭī was an active reviewer of his own work.

The most important difference between the two works is the addition and omission of material. From the opening statements of each of the chapters in the *Taḥbīr*, al-Suyūṭī makes it clear that the vast majority of the material is his, rather than al-Bulqīnī's, since he says: "al-Bulqīnī did not mention anything except for the verse of *kalāla* [§7]/the verses concerning the repentance of 'Ā'isha in *Sūrat al-Nūr* [§8]."[21] This is important, since it means that the changes made from the *Taḥbīr* to the *Itqān* are evidence of al-Suyūṭī reviewing and correcting his own work rather than someone else's text. While there is no removal of any of the data included in the *Taḥbīr* in the *Itqān*, al-Suyūṭī does add two other verses that were revealed in the summer. In the case of Q 2:282,

21 Mutatis mutandis; al-Suyūṭī, *Taḥbīr* 35.

al-Suyūṭī simply expands Q 2:281 (referred to in the *Taḥbīr*) to cover the following verse.

Second, there are some noteworthy differences. For example, why has the statement by al-Ḥākim al-Nīsābūrī on the soundness of the Abū Hurayra *ḥadīth* been removed in the *Itqān*? There are numerous examples of al-Suyūtī giving similar statements elsewhere in the *Itqān*, but it is very difficult to come to any firm conclusion about the reason why it has been excised from the text. The phrase "*ʿalā sharṭi Muslim*" to give an assessment of authenticity is not one that al-Suyūṭī uses often; in his *al-Durr al-manthūr* the vast majority of references to soundness are given on the authority of other scholars (usually al-Ḥākim al-Nīsābūrī), using the formula "*akhraja al-Ḥākim wa-ṣaḥḥaḥahu/-ḥassanahu/-ḍaʿʿafahū ʿan …*" ("the *ḥadīth* was cited by al-Ḥākim on the authority of and he deemed it to be sound/good/weak").[22] It may be that he is cutting someone else's comment in the *Itqān*, but this is conjecture; perhaps it just seemed redundant to give the strength of the *ḥadīth* in this situation.

The addition of Q 110 (*Sūrat al-Naṣr*) is the only completely new addition to al-Suyūṭī's catalogue of summer and winter verses. There is, however, some complication regarding *Sūrat al-Naṣr* as a summer verse. The Sura, with its references to victory, is frequently linked to the Battle of Ḥunayn and the Conquest of Mecca that occurred during the early part of Shawwāl 8 AH, which was in the winter (January–February 630) and not the summer.[23] For example, al-Wāḥidī states that "This was sent down when the Prophet left after the Battle of Ḥunayn. The Prophet only lived two years after this was sent down."[24] However, the Sura is also associated with the Prophet's death, as are Q 2:281–2; *Sūrat al-Naṣr* is also held to be the last Sura revealed to Muḥammad, shortly before his death, usually given as 12 Rabīʿ I/8 June 632. This was clearly a matter of debate as is discussed by Ibn al-Jawzī in the introduction to his *Tafsīr*.[25] Although the Sura is about an event that occurred in the winter, al-Suyūṭī places its revelation in the summer. This illustrates the complexity of the *asbāb* material and whether the material is responding to the question *why* and/or *when* a verse was revealed: these are two quite different questions. This is not the place to provide a detailed discussion of the function of the *asbāb al-nuzūl*

22 Burge, Scattered pearls 254–5.

23 Guillaume, *Life* 566–87. Mecca was captured on 20 Ramaḍān 8/11 January 630, and the Battle at Ḥunayn occurred soon after, and is usually dated to the early part of Shawwāl 8 (22 January–20 February 630); see al-Ṭabarī (trans. Poonawala), *Last years* 1–39; and Kamal and Lammens, Ḥunayn 578.

24 Al-Wāḥidī, *Asbāb* 240 (my own translation).

25 McAuliffe, Ibn al-Jawzī 109.

literature, but it is important to note that (i) the medieval Muslim analysis of *asbāb al-nuzūl* was extremely complex and scholars, such as al-Suyūṭī, detail a range of uses for the material; and (ii) that, following Andrew Rippin,[26] the *asbāb* material is not simply concerned about legal issues, but is focused on establishing a contextual framework for the interpretation of the verses of the Quran.[27]

Lastly, there is a substantial omission in the *Itqān* of material from the *Taḥbīr*: notably the passage about ʿĀʾisha and its relationship to Q 24:11–26, the so-called *ḥadīth* of calumny (*ḥadīth al-ifk*).[28] However, neither the *Taḥbīr* nor the *Itqān* give an account of the events themselves. In the *Taḥbīr* al-Suyūṭī merely states: "As for the second category, it is akin to the first, but al-Bulqīnī did not mention anything other than this: the ten verses concerning the repentance of ʿĀʾisha in *Sūrat al-Nūr* [i.e. Q 24:11–26] [belong to this category]."[29] The details of ʿĀʾisha's alleged affair with Ṣafwān b. al-Muʿaṭṭal al-Sulamī are not given here; and the following *ḥadīth* cited by al-Suyūṭī, taken from al-Bukhārī's *Ṣaḥīḥ*, describes Muḥammad's prophetic experience and emotional anguish.

First: "Those who came with the slander ..." [Q 24:11]. In al-Bukhārī, there is the *ḥadīth* of ʿĀʾisha: By God! The Messenger of God did not have concerns, and no one from amongst the house of the Prophet went out until [this verse] was sent down, and he experienced the distress that he used to experience, with sweat flowing down from him, like beads of water, and it was a winter's day, all because of the severity of the words that were sent down.[30]

The emphasis here is on Muḥammad's sweating, and although in this case it is used to create an emotional impact, there are other *ḥadīth* which describe the revelation in similar ways; indeed, biblical prophets are often described as experiencing physical pain during revelation or visions.[31] The same event is mentioned in the *Itqān* in chapter ten, but only in passing.[32] It is difficult to come to any firm conclusions as to why al-Suyūṭī cut this section about ʿĀʾisha in the *Itqān*, only reproducing a very short summary; but, given that the

26 Rippin, Function; and idem, al-Zarkashī; and, more recently, idem, Construction 184–90.

27 Rippin, al-Zarkashī 257–8.

28 See Asfarrudin, ʿĀʾisha; Walker and Sells, Wiles; Abbott, *ʿĀʾisha* 29–38; and Spellberg, *Politics* 61–99. Some scholars have highlighted similarity to Jewish attacks on Mary's virginity; cp. Robinson, Jesus 161–75; Spellberg makes the link between the narrative and the apocryphal text Suzanna, see Spellberg, *Politics* 74–90.

29 Al-Suyūṭī, *Taḥbīr* 36.

30 Ibid.

31 See Burge, Reading 183–4.

32 Al-Suyūṭī, *Itqān* i, 49; idem, *Perfect guide* 72.

episode was well-known, he may not have found it necessary to include detailed information about the event in this chapter.

The way in which al-Suyūṭī has edited this chapter can be seen in many of the other chapters in the *Itqān*, but importantly not all. Those chapters that principally consist of lists of verses, such as the chapter on "verses in residence and while travelling" (*Taḥbīr* §3–4; *Itqān* §2), are dealt with in a similar vein. In general, the lists in the *Itqān* tend to add verses, rather than remove them; so in the chapters on residence and travelling in the *Taḥbīr* al-Suyūṭī cites fourteen examples, but this is increased to thirty-six in the *Itqān*.[33] There is, then, evidence of a process of self-editing and redaction: the *Itqān* is not simply transposing material from the *Taḥbīr* to the *Itqān* without updating or improving it. This can be seen in the chapters on summer and winter verses, as well as other chapters with a similar, less discursive and more list-orientated focus.

2 Minimal Citation of the *Taḥbīr* in the *Itqān*

If the chapter on summer and winter verses shows a heavy dependence on the *Taḥbīr*, other chapters do not. This is seen most clearly, and most famously, in his chapter that deals with the topic of *asbāb al-nuzūl* specifically (*Taḥbīr* §11; *Itqān* §9). The chapter on *asbāb al-nuzūl* in the *Taḥbīr* is incredibly short, amounting to only 254 words; in comparison the corresponding chapter in the *Itqān* is more than ten times longer. Despite the *Taḥbīr* being dwarfed by the *Itqān* on this subject, there are five sections of text in the *Taḥbīr* that are reproduced in some way in the *Itqān*. Andrew Rippin made a comparison of al-Suyūṭī's and al-Zarkashī's chapters on *asbāb al-nuzūl* in 1985 that focused on the hermeneutic approaches of the two authors towards *asbāb al-nuzūl*;[34] however, this chapter is not interested in the intellectual substance of the material, but rather in the physical text and the way it has been (re)arranged and, in particular, the extent to which al-Suyūṭī used, or did not use, the *Taḥbīr*.

33 Al-Suyūṭī only lists those that were revealed when travelling, all others were revealed while in residence. He cites 14 examples in the *Taḥbīr*: Q 2:196, 281, 285; 3:144; 4:58;5:3; 8:9, 16; 9:113–14; 22:39; 28:86; 30:1–4; 63; 110; and he cites 36 examples in the *Itqān*: 2:125, 189, 196, 281, 285; 3:172; 4:43, 58, 102, 176; 5:1–11, 67; 8:9; 9:35, 42, 65, 113; 16:126; 17:76; 22:1–2, 19, 39; 25:45, 85; 30:1–4; 43:45; 47:13; 68; 68:13; 54:45; 56:13, 81, 82; 60:10; 77; and 96:1–2. See al-Suyūṭī, Taḥbīr 28–33; al-Suyūṭī, *Itqān* i, 25–8; idem, *Perfect guide* 25–30.

34 See Rippin, al-Zarkashī.

The opening of the chapter on *asbāb* in the *Taḥbīr* is found almost verbatim in the *Itqān* (see A in appendix C),[35] but it is expanded greatly. In the *Taḥbīr*, al-Bulqīnī/al-Suyūṭī write: "... people have written many books upon it, the best of them is the work (*kitāb*) of al-Wāḥidī, then that of the Shaykh of Islam, the Guardian of the Age (*ḥāfiẓ al-ʿaṣr*), Abū l-Faḍl b. Ḥajar."[36] In the *Itqān* this short summary becomes a detailed survey of the literature on *asbāb al-nuzūl*; al-Suyūṭī writes:

> A number of important scholars have written works on the subject, the most ancient of them being ʿAlī b. al-Midyānī, a teacher of al-Bukhārī. The most celebrated of the books they have written is that of al-Wāḥidī, despite its deficiencies. Al-Jabarī abridged it by deleting the chains of transmission for the traditions it contains and adding nothing new of his own. Shaykh al-Islam Abū l-Faḍl b. Ḥajar wrote a book on the subject, but it never progressed beyond draft form because of his death, and I have been unable to find a complete copy of it. I, too, have written a book on the subject, comprehensive yet brief and unrivalled; I entitled it, *Lubāb al-nuqūl fī asbāb al-nuzūl*.[37]

This extract is quite illuminating, since it does a number of things: (i) it reveals al-Suyūṭī's knowledge of scholarly material; (ii) he provides critique that is not present in the *Taḥbīr*, namely, he says that al-Wāḥidī's book is the best in the field, "despite its deficiencies"; (iii) there is an homage to Ibn Ḥajar, whom al-Suyūṭī claimed as a teacher[38]; (iv) it shows that in the *Taḥbīr* al-Suyūṭī did not check or corroborate al-Bulqīnī's original material, but when he came to write the *Itqān* he has evidently been unable to find Ibn Ḥajar's work; and (v) as always with al-Suyūṭī there is some self-promotion.[39] In a way, this

35 The full Arabic texts of these citations, both in the *Taḥbīr* and the *Itqān*, can be found in appendix C at the end of this article.

36 Al-Suyūṭī, *Taḥbīr* 39. *Ḥāfiẓ al-ʿaṣr* is more properly "the *Ḥāfiẓ* of his age"; a *ḥāfiẓ* is someone who has memorised the text of the Quran by heart.

37 Al-Suyūṭī, *Itqān* i, 40; idem, *Perfect guide* 55.

38 Al-Suyūṭī's father, Kamāl al-Dīn al-Asyūṭī, was a pupil of Ibn Ḥajar al-ʿAsqalānī, but al-Suyūṭī claims he received an *ijāza* from him when he was very young; see Sartain, *Biography* 26. In the late Mamlūk period it was common to try to shorten the chains of transmission, including transmission through children; see Davidson, *Carrying on*.

39 Al-Suyūṭī often gave his works to his students who were travelling, so that they could be published more broadly; he gives accounts of this in his autobiography. His fame stretched from North Africa to India, and his own attempts at self-promotion aided this; see Burge, *Angels* 19–21; see also Sartain, *Biography* 48–50 and 75–7; and eadem, Relations 193.

extract sums up al-Suyūṭī's project for the *Itqān*: he wants it to be the best work on the *ʿulūm al-Qurʾān* available—hence his criticisms of al-Wāḥidī and his comments on not being able to locate Ibn Ḥajar's work; but, perhaps more importantly, the *Itqān* is also a vehicle through which he can promote himself as a scholar.[40]

The second quotation (B) of the *Taḥbīr* in the *Itqān* appears after a very significant quantity of new material. This second quotation concerns the use of *ḥadīth* attributed to companions and successors. The *Taḥbīr* reads:

> Concerning what is found in it [regarding a *sabab* of a verse] given on the authority of a Companion, whose chain of authority is raised (*marfūʿ*):[41] If the statement of the Companion is being used, then intellectual reasoning (*ijtihād*) should not be used [when dealing with] a raised *ḥadīth*, or, in the case of a Follower, then it [intellectual reasoning] should not be used [when dealing with] a loose (*mursal*)[42] *ḥadīth*, [both] when it is the case that the chain of authorities preceding both of them is sound. The second [possibility] adds [a case] where the narration is raised but it is only related on the authority of the Companions, or when it [the *ḥadīth*] was related by a witness which is *mursal* or uninterrupted (*muttaṣil*), but not weak (*ḍaʿīf*). When two *ḥadīth* [concerning a *sabab*] are conflicting (*tāʿarraḍa*), it may be possible to harmonize the two, as is the case with the "verse of condemnation."[43]

In the *Itqān*, this is changed to:

> If what counts in the case of a Companion as a tradition going back to the Prophet is related by a Follower, it is treated as *marfūʿ* and *mursal*. If the chain of transmission of the Follower is sound; if, moreover, he is one of the authorities on the interpretation of the Quran who learned from the Companions—people like Mujāhid, ʿIkrima, and Saʿīd b. Jubayr; and finally, if his saying is reinforced by another *mursal* tradition—if all this is found, his statement is to be accepted.[44]

40 Al-Suyūṭī's efforts at self-promotion evidently worked, since, as John Voll has shown, he became one of the most highly cited transmitters of *ḥadīth*; see Voll, Hadith scholars 265.

41 A *marfūʿ ḥadīth* is one in which a companion gives details of what the Prophet said or did. See Ibn al-Ṣalāḥ al-Shahrazūrī, *Introduction* 31.

42 See ibid. 39–41.

43 Al-Suyūṭī, *Taḥbīr* 39.

44 Al-Suyūṭī, *Itqān* i, 45; idem, *Perfect guide* 63.

A long discussion on how to resolve conflicting *asbāb* material is then found and towards the end, the *Itqān* includes the statement:

> If it is not possible to reconcile different traditions concerning the occasion of revelation of a verse, this should be attributed to a multiple or repeated revelation of the verse. One example of such a case is furnished by the following three traditions [concerning Q 9:113] ...[45]

Although this certainly does not constitute a verbatim citation of the *Taḥbīr* in the *Itqān*, as can be seen in the first citation, the *Taḥbīr* does appear to have contributed something to the revisions of this material in the *Itqān*: there are similar turns of phrase and the material is covering the same ground. However, in the *Itqān* al-Suyūṭī expands the basic statements of the *Taḥbīr* into a highly technical discussion of the authenticity of *asbāb* material, involving a number of different scenarios. The *Taḥbīr* does not include much by the way of examples, but in the *Itqān* al-Suyūṭī adds a significant amount of source material, explaining how specific problems can be resolved: the *Itqān* becomes a much more helpful and didactic work since it provides ample case studies to explore the ways in which exegetes need to handle the *asbāb* literature. Citation D, a continuation of C, is not found in the *Itqān*; this seems to be largely because the more complex material on the *asbāb* seen in the *Itqān* mean that this paragraph is not needed: it has been superseded by the new material. Although it will not be particularly helpful to compare citations C and E in detail, these two quotations reveal a similar trend: the phrasing of the version in the *Itqān* has altered the text of the *Taḥbīr*, but is still clearly thematically related to it as they discuss similar ideas and problems, although in the case of E only the theme, the story, and the citation of Q 4:85 establishes a link between the *Itqān* and the *Taḥbīr*.[46]

To complicate matters further the material that is cited from the *Taḥbīr* appears in a different order in the *Itqān*. Unlike the change made in the chapter on Summer and Winter verses, in which one quotation from al-Wāḥidī has been moved from the end of the chapter to the beginning, this represents a wholesale revision of the material. It is also not an expansion of material: that is al-Suyūṭī has not taken the *Taḥbīr* as a model to which he added new material; a model of composition that al-Suyūṭī uses frequently elsewhere.[47] The changes witnessed in the *Itqān* constitute a completely new version of his

45 Al-Suyūṭī, *Itqān* i, 47; idem, *Perfect guide* 67.

46 Cp. al-Suyūṭī, *Itqān* i, 43–4; idem, *Perfect guide* 39; idem, *Taḥbīr* 39.

47 See Burge, *Angels* 21–5; and idem, Scattered pearls 256–62.

chapter on *asbāb al-nuzūl*, the impetus of which appears to have been his reading of al-Zarkashī's *Kitāb al-Burhān fī ʿulūm al-dīn*. In many respects, al-Suyūṭī went back to the drawing board, yet the material that is shared in common shows that al-Suyūṭī did have his *Taḥbīr* in mind, or even to hand, when he wrote the *Itqān* version, but he actively chose to rewrite the chapter. Added to the influence of the *Burhān* is al-Suyūṭī's own work on the *asbāb*, his *Lubāb al-nuqūl*, which he wrote in the intervening period. Al-Suyūṭī feels confident enough to state at the end of the chapter on *asbāb al-nuzūl* in the *Itqān*:

> Ponder well all that I have mentioned in this chapter and hold firmly to it, for I have written it not simply in accordance with my own thoughts but through gathering and examining all that the leading authorities have said in their diverse compositions. None has preceded me in such a venture.[48]

Looking beyond the hubris of this closing remark, it is possible to see the merits of the *asbāb* chapter in the *Itqān*, and it is certainly something that could not have been said of the corresponding chapter in the *Taḥbīr*. A comparison of these two works reveals the growth in al-Suyūṭī's own academic development, from a relatively young scholar to one working at the height of his intellectual ability. It is, however, worthy to note that despite the improvements made to the *Taḥbīr* in the *Itqān* in this chapter, there is still evidence to show that al-Suyūṭī did make use of his earlier work; although, its presence is clearly dwarfed by and lost in the sheer quantity of new information and the detailed case studies included in the *Itqān*.

3 "New" chapters in the *Itqān*

Within the broad group of chapters that discuss the context of the revelation of the Quran, the *Itqān* includes four additional chapters that are not found in the *Taḥbīr*. Interestingly, given the importance assigned by scholars, such as Nolin, to al-Zarkhashī's *Burhān* in the development of the *Itqān*, these chapters do not appear in the *Burhān* either. Consequently, they must be seen as ideas that, on reflection, al-Suyuṭī decided warranted more detailed discussion. These four chapters are:

48 Al-Suyūṭī, *Perfect guide* 70.

(i) verses revealed on earth and in heaven (*Itqān* §6)
(ii) verses revealed in conformity with the sayings of the companions (*Itqān* §10)
(iii) verses which anticipated the promulgation of an ordinance (*Itqān* §12)
(iv) verses accompanied by angels (*Itqān* §14).

Each of these chapters suggests that al-Suyūṭī had specific reasons for including them, and a short précis of each chapter and a brief analysis will follow.

The chapter on "verses revealed on earth and verses revealed in heaven"[49] is based almost entirely on a quotation from Abū Bakr b. al-ʿArabī (d. 543/1148). The quotation states that all the verses of the Quran were revealed in Mecca or Medina, except for six: "None of us is there, but has a known station; we are the rangers, we are they that give glory" (Q 37:164–66); "Ask those of Our Messengers We sent before thee: 'Have We appointed, apart from the All-merciful, gods to be served?'" (Q 43:45); and the long doxological prayer at the end of *Sūrat al-Baqara* (Q 2:285–286). The quotation of *Sūrat al-Ṣaffāt* (Q 37:164–66) is often seen by exegetes as the direct speech of the angels, hence their "revelation" in the heavens. Although the angels are given a voice in many other places within the Quran (e.g. Q 2:30–32),[50] this is usually within the context of a narrative frame; that is the angels' words are reported speech, albeit reported directly (i.e. it remains *oratio directa*). In *Sūrat al-Ṣaffāt* there is no such contextual frame and the verses stand as words said by the angels; creating something of a hermeneutic problem given the divine origin of the Quran. A similar problem is seen in the verse from *Sūrat al-Zukhruf* (Q 43:45), which is associated with the Prophet's *miʿrāj*/*isrāʾ* during which he met the prophets.

Al-Suyūṭī's is very dismissive of Ibn al-ʿArabī's position that some verses of the Quran were revealed in heaven; and the sources available show that Ibn al-ʿArabī did receive some criticism as a *ḥadīth* transmitter; indeed al-Suyūṭī's "teacher" Ibn Ḥajar al-ʿAsqalānī declared him to be weak (*ḍaʿīf*).[51] Al-Suyūṭī appears to have theological difficulty attributing a divine location to the revelation of these verses, although his main dispute with Ibn al-ʿArabī is that he can find no *ḥadīth* to substantiate the position. Al-Suyūṭī writes:

> As for these [verses], I am not aware of any proof for who has mentioned this, except for the final verses of [*Sūrat*] *al-Baqara*, for which it is possible to provide evidence: Muslim cited on the authority of Ibn Masʿūd:

49 Al-Suyūṭī, *Itqān* i, 32–3; idem, *Perfect guide* 39.
50 The use of angelic speech in Q 2:21–39 is discussed in Ourghi, Auch die Engel 368–77.
51 See Robson, Ibn al-ʿArabī, 707.

> When the Messenger of God was transported at night to the *Lote-Tree of the Boundary* [Q 53:14] … [and the rest of the] *ḥadīth*. Included in it is [the statement]: "The Messenger of God was given three things. He was given the five prayers; he was given the final two verses of *Sūrat al-Baqara*; and forgiveness of major sins (*muqḥimāt*) for those from amongst his community who do not associate anything with God.[52]

This section, with its sole focus on Ibn al-ʿArabī, seems to be a direct reaction to a comment that al-Suyūṭī had read that he felt needed rebutting, but one that he read after writing the *Taḥbīr*. By having its own chapter—i.e. a *bāb* rather than a *faṣl*—it suggests that al-Suyūṭī felt that it deserved some prominence and singling out as an erroneous position to take. It also stresses the importance of *ḥadīth* in al-Suyūṭī's study of the Quranic sciences.

The chapter on "verses which were sent down by angels" (§14)[53] is slightly different, in that it adds a much more detailed discussion of the topic. The chapter is related to the *faḍāʾil* literature, and similar material is related again in the chapter on the "merits of the Quran" (*faḍāʾil al-Qurʾān*; §72) in the *Itqān*,[54] but is not mentioned in the chapter on the *faḍāʾil* chapter in the *Taḥbīr*. This means that this material about angels coming down with verses is new in the *Itqān*, and something which al-Suyūṭī clearly thought needed adding. The use of *faḍāʾil* as a means of harnessing *baraka* became an important component of al-Suyūtī's worldview, and *faḍāʾil* material dominates certain passages within his exegetical work *al-Durr al-manthūr fī l-tafsīr bi-l-maʾthūr*, and pervades the work more generally.[55] Rather than being a critique of another scholar's opinion, as in the chapter on verses revealed in heaven and on earth, this chapter represents a development and a change in al-Suyūṭī's own sense of spirituality. Although the Shādhilī *ṭarīqa* dominated late Mamlūk Cairene society,[56] al-Suyūṭī does seem to have been an active defender of Sufism and a proponent of the Shādhilī way, both in formal written works such as his defences of Ibn al-Fāriḍ and Ibn al-ʿArabī,[57] but in his oeuvre more generally.[58]

A similar trend is also seen in the other two chapters added to the *Itqān* in this section, the chapters on "verses revealed in conformity with the

52 Al-Suyūṭī, *Itqān* i, 32–3; idem, *Perfect guide* 39.

53 Al-Suyūṭī, *Itqān* i, 53–5; idem, *Perfect guide* 83–5.

54 Al-Suyūṭī, *Itqān* ii, 512–20.

55 See Burge, Muʿawwidhatān 291–5; see also idem, Impurity 339–46.

56 Knysh, *Mysticism* 212–8, especially 214; Abun-Nasr, *Muslim communities* 96–112.

57 See Saleh, al-Suyūṭī 74; and Geoffroy, al-Suyūṭī 915.

58 See Burge, Search 70–2.

sayings of the companions" and "verses which anticipated the promulgation of an ordinance" (*Itqān* §10 & 12).[59] However, here the impetus for including these chapters seems to have arisen out of al-Suyūṭī's work in the field of *ḥadīth* and in *asbāb al-nuzūl*. As with the chapter on "verses which were sent down by angels," the chapter is not a rebuttal of another scholar's opinion or judgement; and the chapter can be viewed as a witness to al-Suyūṭī's deeper knowledge of the field when he came to write the *Itqān*.

The chapters in the *Itqān* which are not found in the *Taḥbīr* show that al-Suyūṭī added to the work freely. The material added is not necessarily systematic and it is not representative of a new approach to the *ʿulūm al-Qurʾān*, but, rather, these added chapters reflect both his personal development and his critiques of other scholars' work. The only programmatic element behind the inclusion of new material is to deepen and broaden the ways the Quran can be studied and approached. The aim that al-Suyūṭī had for the *Itqān* is to make it far more comprehensive, both in what the *ʿulūm al-Qurʾān*/Quranic sciences are, and the way in which they are described and presented. More broadly, this illustrates that al-Suyūṭī approached the *Itqān* with comprehensiveness in mind and that he was very willing to add further material to his earlier attempt at a presentation of the *ʿulūm al-Qurʾān*, filling in lacunae within the *Taḥbīr* that he uncovered at a later date. The immaturity of the *Taḥbīr* and the maturity of the *Itqān* become more evident when these additions and expansions are recognized as the product of a scholar who has learnt much in the period between the composition of both works.

4 Al-Suyūṭī, Self-editing, and the Creation of the *Itqān*

The principal aim of this article has not been to explore the function of the *asbāb* material within the *ʿulūm al-Qurʾān*, but rather to focus on the relationship between the *Taḥbīr* and the *Itqān*. That the *Taḥbīr* was used as a source for the *Itqān* now seems certain, especially in the chapters of the *Itqān* studied here. The remaining chapters of the *Itqān* may produce different results, but whatever results emerge from the study of other chapters the *Taḥbīr* clearly played a part in the production of the *Itqān*.

From other studies of al-Suyūtī's *oeuvre* it can be seen that al-Suyūṭī frequently wrote new works using a base text of some sort. The presence of an earlier work—either his own or someone else's text—is often found in his output: base texts can be seen readily in his *ḥadīth* collections, such as his *al-Ḥabāʾik*

59 Al-Suyūṭī, *Itqān* i, 49–50, 51–3; idem, *Perfect guide* 71–3 and 77–9.

fī akhbār al-malāʾik,[60] and his *al-Hayʾa al-saniyya fī l-hayʾa al-sunniyya*.[61] In his main exegetical work, *al-Durr al-manthūr*, al-Suyūṭī uses four different exegetical works as a base source; he then selects one of these four to generate his own text for his exegesis of each Sura.[62] In another example, Leon Nemoy comments that al-Suyūṭī's *Tuḥfat al-kirām fī khabar al-ahrām* "is really an enlarged redaction of the corresponding chapter in one of al-Suyūṭī's major works, his history of Egypt entitled *Kitāb Ḥusn al-muḥāḍara fī akhbār Miṣr wa-l-Qāhira*."[63] In a slightly different way, his linguistic work *al-Muzhir fī ʿulūm al-lugha* is a compendium of linguistic works, and "only a few of al-Suyūṭī's own opinions are found in this book."[64] Although it is greatly problematic to extend a general working principle from a relatively small sample of texts, the trend seems to occur more often than purely by chance, and consequently it does seem plausible to suggest a hypothesis that al-Suyūṭī's standard writing style is to utilise another source as a base text from which to build a new work—a hypothesis that can be tested over time as more of al-Suyūṭī's works are studied.

Al-Suyūṭī was famously accused of plagiarism during his lifetime, particularly by his main rival al-Sakhāwī, who said that "he would take … a lot of earlier works in various fields which were not well known to his contemporaries, change a little bit, and then present them attributed to himself, and make a great fuss in presenting them such that the ignorant would suppose them to be something unequalled."[65] Al-Suyūṭī has not escaped criticism from modern scholars either, particularly Robert Irwin who is strongly dismissive of him.[66] Ikhwan puts it rather more carefully, arguing that al-Suyūṭī's ability to synthesize other material made him "a very responsive and productive writer in various subjects."[67] However, although there are certainly many instances when such accusations of plagiarism could be substantive, in other cases it would seem to be unfair, since some of his works, particularly the *Itqān* and his *al-Durr al-manthūr*, are works of the highest sophistication and scholarship; the use of a base text should not detract from the quality of these works. The question of plagiarism was also raised against al-Maqrīzī, who has been

60 Burge, *Angels* 21–5.

61 Heinen, *Cosmology*. The work is dominated by the scholar Abū l-Shaykh (Abū Muḥammad ʿAbd Allāh b. Muḥammad b. Jaʿfar b. Ḥayyān, d. 371/981–2).

62 See Burge, Scattered pearls 256–62.

63 Nemoy, Treatise 17.

64 Ikhwan, Kitāb al-Muzhir 378.

65 Al-Sakhāwī, *Ḍawʾ* iv, 66; trans. Saleh, al-Suyūṭī 79. Al-Sakhāwī also accused others, including al-Maqrīzī, of plagiarism; see Bauden, Maqriziana IX 161–74.

66 Irwin, al-Suyūṭī; see also Nemoy, Treatise 18.

67 Ikhwan, Kitāb al-Muzhir 382.

described as "one of the most renowned scholars that Islamic civilization has produced."[68] The question of plagiarism in medieval Arabic literature has been widely discussed, and a detailed discussion here is not appropriate; but it is important to note that the modern concept of plagiarism "is understood with moral and aesthetic implications that were not necessarily valid in earlier times and different cultures."[69] The use of sources or a base text does not always constitute plagiarism and given the evident sophistication of the *Itqān* it would be difficult to accuse al-Suyūṭī of plagiarism in this work.

There is, however, one aspect of plagiarism in the *Itqān* that does require some discussion: al-Bulqīnī, the author of the work on which the *Taḥbīr* is based, is noticeably absent in the *Itqān*. Al-Bulqīnī does not appear in the list of al-Suyūṭī's sources at the beginning of the *Itqān*, and there appears to be only a smattering of references to him throughout the entire *Itqān*.[70] There seems, then, to have been an active attempt to remove the place and influence of al-Bulqīnī when the work was developed into the *Itqān*. Where al-Suyūṭī's additions to al-Bulqīnī's work are noted openly in the *Taḥbīr*,[71] there is little acknowledgement of al-Bulqīnī or the passages that al-Bulqīnī presumably wrote that are present in the *Itqān*. Al-Suyūṭī states that much of the material in the *Taḥbīr* comprises his own additions to al-Bulqīnī's text: of the 102 chapters al-Suyūṭī credits al-Bulqīnī with only 14 chapters (13.7%),[72] he uses the phrase "this chapter is my addition" in 47 chapters (46.1%),[73] and the remaining 41 chapters (40.2%) are unclear in their attribution or give a different source.[74] Kenneth Nolin has highlighted the fact that al-Suyūṭī cites passages of al-Zarkashī's *Burhān* in the *Itqān* with attribution, and in those cases where al-Zarkashī is citing another earlier scholar it is easy for a reader

68 Bauden, Maqriziana IX 159.

69 Bauden, Maqriziana IX 186. For a full discussion of plagiarism in medieval Islam, see ibid. 186–201.

70 E.g. al-Suyūṭī, *Itqān* i, 107 (§22) and ii, 569 (§80); there are likely to be a few more references, but not many.

71 For example, al-Suyūṭī begins some chapters with the statement "This chapter is my addition" (*hādhā al-nawʿ min ziyādatī*); al-Suyūṭī, *Taḥbīr* 171 (§95), 172 (§96); others begin "al-Bulqīnī said…" (*qāla al-Bulqīnī*), ibid. 175 (§97).

72 Al-Suyūṭī explicitly cites al-Bulqīnī as the source of the following chapters in the *Taḥbīr*: §3–10, 21–4, 97 and 100.

73 Al-Suyūṭī states that he added the following chapters: §14–20, 27–9, 36–8, 44–6, 51–2, 65, 69–70, 73–96, 101–2.

74 The chapters without any clear identification are: §1–2, 11–13, 25–6, 30–5, 39–43, 47–50, 53–64, 66–8, 71–2, 98–9.

to assume that the citation from the *Burhān* has ended and that it is al-Suyūṭī (rather than al-Zarkashī) citing the earlier source.[75] Given that the *Taḥbīr* is said by al-Suyūṭī himself to be an adaptation or emendation of al-Bulqīnī's *Mawāqiʿ al-ʿulūm fī mawāqiʿ al-nujūm*, it seems curious (if not suspicious) for al-Bulqīnī to be responsible for a mere fourteen chapters. It seems plausible that a number of the other chapters in the *Taḥbīr* are at least in some way dependent on the *Mawāqiʿ al-ʿulūm*, although this cannot be confirmed until manuscript evidence becomes available. Turning to the *Itqān*, for example, chapter twenty-two of the *Itqān* on the transmission of *mutawātir*, *mashhūr* and *āḥād* readings of the Quran cites al-Bulqīnī at the start of the chapter,[76] but much of the material in the *Taḥbīr* is found in the rest of the chapter of the *Itqān*, but al-Bulqīnī is not cited. The intriguing question then remains: how much of the *Itqān* is ultimately derived from al-Bulqīnī's original? What is clear is that al-Bulqīnī's influence is largely exorcised from the text of the *Itqān*, and he becomes a scholar simply mentioned in passing.

One of the interesting aspects of al-Suyūṭī's utilization of the *Taḥbīr* is that al-Suyūṭī incorporates the material from the *Taḥbīr* into the *Itqān* in a number of different ways. In some cases al-Suyūṭī "cuts and pastes" material from the *Taḥbīr*; other chapters, such as the specific chapter on *asbāb al-nuzūl*, adapt and reframe material from the *Burhān*. This specific chapter appears to have been a reaction on al-Suyūṭī's part to the quality and depth of the chapter on *asbāb al-nuzūl* in al-Zarkashī's *Burhān*. Of the fourteen chapters in the *Itqān* that form the focus of this survey: seven show direct citation of the *Taḥbīr* with some additional comments (§2–5, 11, 13 and 15); three show some use of the *Taḥbīr*, but with significant edits (§1, 7 and 8); four are completely new (§6, 10, 12 and 14); and only one shows little reference or no reference to the *Taḥbīr* (§9). This does contradict what Nolin has said about the role of the *Taḥbīr* in the evolution of the *Itqān*: the *Taḥbīr* does appear to have exerted a very strong influence on the *Itqān*—at least in the case of the chapters on the revelation of the Quran; the same may not be true in other cases. Claude Gilliot has highlighted al-Suyūṭī's use of his *Muʿtarak al-aqrān fī iʿjāz al-Qurʾān* in the *Itqān*:[77] given al-Suyūṭī's general working method, it is possible that al-Suyūṭī used a number of works he had written earlier as a basis from which to compile his *Itqān* of which the *Taḥbīr* is one of a large pool of sources.

75 Nolin, *Itqān* 53–9.
76 Al-Suyūṭī, *Itqān* i, 107; idem, *Perfect guide* 181.
77 Gilliot, Traditional disciplines 328.

By comparing the *Taḥbīr* and the *Itqān* it becomes possible to see the ways in which al-Suyūṭī developed earlier works to produce new ones: the content may be more sophisticated and developed, but he did not compose these works afresh, but developed and expanded works that he had already written. Not only that, but there is also evidence of a high level of editing and engagement with the earlier text: the move of the quotation from al-Wāḥidī in the chapter on summer and winter verses clearly shows a desire to improve the structure of his earlier attempt. In other cases, such as the quotations of the *Taḥbīr* in the chapter on *asbāb al-nuzūl*, al-Suyūtī chose to completely revise and rethink his approach to the subject; yet the *Taḥbīr* is still present, although in a very partial way.

Despite the physical changes to the *Taḥbīr*, there is no actual development, change or revision in al-Suyūṭī's approach to the *ʿulūm al-Qurʾān* from the *Taḥbīr* to the *Itqān*, but what can be seen is the development of much more sophisticated work. The problems that arose out of an emphasis on brevity, which are particularly apparent in the *Taḥbīr*'s chapter on *asbāb al-nuzūl* itself, show a complete rethink on al-Suyūṭī's part. In the *Itqān* it is possible to see both implicit and explicit acknowledgements of the *Taḥbīr*'s failings and as well as evidence of al-Suyūṭī striving to produce the best that he can offer. To be frank, the *Taḥbīr* is a poor work and it is not particularly helpful as a resource or a guide to the *ʿulūm al-Qurʾān*; but by comparing these two works it becomes possible to witness this development in al-Suyūṭī's scholarship. The *Itqān* is a work which reveals more confidence, authority, and knowledge: when he wrote the *Taḥbīr* al-Suyūṭī was a bright, but young, scholar, by the time he came to write the *Itqān* it is possible to see a scholar whose reputation, knowledge and ability have grown. In the *Itqān* al-Suyūṭī is the producer of a work that is regarded as "the most complete handbook on the genre"[78] and the most important work written on the *ʿulūm al-Qurʾān* in both the late-medieval and modern periods.

78 Ibid. 328.

Appendix A

TABLE 8.3 *Contents List of the* Taḥbīr *and the* Itqān

Taḥbīr		*Itqān*	
Topic	*§*	*§*	*Topic*
A. Issues of Chronology[C]			
Meccan Suras	1	1	Meccan and Medinan Suras
Medinan Suras	2		
Verses revealed while resident	3	2	Verses revealed while resident and travelling
Verses revealed while travelling	4		
Verses revealed during the daytime	5	3	Verses revealed at daytime and at night
Verses revealed at night	6		
Verses revealed during the summer	7	4	Verses revealed during summer and winter
Verses revealed during the winter	8		
Verses revealed in bed	9	5	Verses revealed in bed or sleeping
Verses revealed while sleeping	10		
		6	Verses revealed on Earth and in heaven
Occasions of Revelation	11		
The first verses to be revealed	12	7	The first verses to be revealed
The last verses to be revealed	13	8	The last verses to be revealed
		9	Occasions of Revelation
Knowledge of the month, day, and hour of revelation	14		
		10	Verses revealed in conformity with the sayings of the companions
		11	Verses revealed more than once
		12	Verses of anticipation
		13	Suras revealed in segments and as a whole
		14	Suras revealed with angels
Verses revealed only to the Prophet	15	15	Verses revealed only to the Prophet and verses revealed to previous prophets
Verses revealed to previous prophets	16		

TABLE 8.3 *Contents List of the* Taḥbīr *and the* Itqān (cont.)

Taḥbīr		*Itqān*	
Topic	§	§	*Topic*
What was revealed more than once	17		
Suras revealed in segments	18		
Suras revealed as a whole	19		
B. The Text of the Quran and Its Transmission			
The manner of the revelation	20	16	The manner of the revelation
		17	The names of the Suras and their divisions
		18	Collection and organization of the Suras
		19	Number of Suras, Ayas, words and letters
		20	Transmitters of the Quran
		21	*Isnāds* of Quranic transmission
Widespread *ḥadīth*	21	22	Widespread *ḥadīth*
		23	Well known *ḥadīth* (*mashhūr*)
Those *ḥadīth* with a single transmission (*āḥād*)	22	24	Those *ḥadīth* with a single transmission (*āḥād*)
The non-canonical (*shādhdh*)	23	25	The non-canonical (*shādhdh*)
		26	Forged *ḥadīth* (*mawḍūʿ*)
		27	Inserted *ḥadīth* (*mudraj*)
C. Recitation			
The readings of the Prophet	24		
Narrators	25		
Transmitters	26		
Method of learning (*taḥammul*) the Quran	27		
The exalted and lowly reciters	28		
Linked verses (*musalsal*)	29		
The ending of verses	30	28	The beginnings and ends of verses
The beginning of verses	31		

Taḥbīr		*Itqān*	
Topic	§	§	*Topic*
		29	Vocalization of the letters
Lengthening (*imāla*)	32	30	Lengthening (*imāla*)
Lengthening (*madd*)	33	31	Assimilation (*idghām*), the retention of phonetic value (*iẓhār*), suppression (*ikhfāʾ*) and metathesis (*alqāb*)
Reduction of *hamza* (*takhfīf*)	34	32	Lengthening (*madd*)
Assimilation (*idghām*)	35	33	Reduction of *hamza* (*takhfīf*)
Suppression (*ikhfāʾ*)	36		
Metathesis (*alqāb*)	37		
		34	Forms of learning the Quran
		35	Etiquette of reciting the Quran
Phonetics (*makhārij al-ḥurūf*)	38		
D. Linguistic, Lexicological and Stylistic Issues			
On knowing unusual words	39	36	On knowing unusual words
Arab words	40	37	Non-*ḥijāzī* words
		38	Non-Arab words
		39	Polyvalence (*wujūh*) and synonyms (*naẓāʾir*)
		40	The meanings of particles
		41	Vocalization
		42	Rules of exegesis
		43	Clear (*muḥkam*) and ambiguous (*mutashābih*) words
		44	Earlier and later parts of the Quran
		45	General and specific
		46	Summary verses and detailed verses
		47	Abrogating and abrogated verses
Allegory (*majāz*)	41		
Common words (*mushtarak*)	42		
Synonyms (*tarāduf*)	43		
Clear (*muḥkam*)	44		
Ambiguous (*mutashābih*)	45		

TABLE 8.3 *Contents List of the* Taḥbīr *and the* Itqān (cont.)

Taḥbīr			*Itqān*
Topic	*§*	*§*	*Topic*
Difficult (*mushkil*)	46	48	Difficult and disputed verses
Summary verses (*mujmal*)	47		
Specific verses (*mubīn*)	48		
		49	Absolute and restricted verses
		50	Words and meaning
		51	Different forms of address (*mukhāṭabāt*)
		52	Literal and allegorical
Metaphorical (*istiʿāra*)	49	53	Simile (*tashbīh*) and metaphors (*istiʿārāt*)
Simile (*tashbīh*)	50		
Metonymy (*kināya*)	51	54	Metonymy (*kināya*) and allusion (*taʿārīḍ*)
Allusion (*taʿārīḍ*)	52		
The universal and general	53		
Special verses (*makhṣūṣ*)	54		
Specific verses (*alladhī urīda bihi l-khuṣūṣ*)	55		
		55	Restriction (*ḥaṣr*) and specification (*ikhtiṣāṣ*)
		56	Conciseness (*ījāz*) and prolixity (*iṭnāb*)
		57	Informative (*khabar*) and performative (*inshāʾ*)
		58	On the wonders of the Quran
		59	On the division of the Ayas
What the book specifies concerning the *sunna*	56		
What the *sunna* specifies concerning the book	57		
Opening verses	58	60	The openings of the Suras
		61	The endings of the Suras
Understandable verses (*mafhūm*)	59		
E. From here on, the two works diverge in their organization			
Un restricted verses (*muṭlaq*)	60	62	The links between the Ayas and Suras

Taḥbīr		*Itqān*	
Topic	*§*	*§*	*Topic*
Restricted verses (*muqayyad*)	61	63	Verses similar to each other
Abrogating verses	62	64	The inimitability of the Quran
Abrogated verses	63	65	Sciences that can be deduced from the Quran
What was done for one person, then abrogated	64	66	Parables of the Quran
What is only obligatory for one person	65	67	Oaths (*aqsām*) in the Quran
Conciseness (*ījāz*)	66	68	Arguments in the Quran
Verbosity (*iṭnāb*)	67	69	Referents (*mubhamāt*)
Equivalence (*musāwāh*)	68	70	Names of people for whom verses were sent down
Similarity (*ashbāh*)	69	71	Names of people for whom verses were sent down
Separating (*faṣl*)	70	72	The merits (*faḍā'il*) of the Quran
Joining (*waṣl*)	71	73	The excellent and most excellent parts of the Quran
Shortening (*qaṣr*)	72	74	Simple words of the Quran (*mufradāt*)
Connections (*iḥtibāk*)	73	75	The properties (*khawāṣṣ*) of the Quran
Statements of injunction (*mawjūb*)	74	76	Orthography (*marsūm al-khaṭṭ*) and customs of writing
Congruous (*muṭābiq*)	75	77	Exegesis (*tafsīr*) observed by the exegete (*shurūṭ al-mufassīr*
Appropriateness (*munāsaba*)	76	78	Conditions and customs to be observed by the exegete (*shurūṭ al-mufassīr*)
Similarity (*mujānasa*)	77	80	Biographies of the exegetes (*ṭabaqāt al-mufassirīn*)
Ambiguity (*tawriya*)	78		
Utilization (*istikhdām*)	79		
Involution (*laff*)	80		
Evolution (*nashr*)	81		
Rhetorical pronominal shift (*iltifāt*)	82		
End-rhyme terminations (*fawāṣil*) and	83		

TABLE 8.3 *Contents List of the* Taḥbīr *and the* Itqān (cont.)

Taḥbīr		*Itqān*	
Topic	*§*	*§*	*Topic*
Sura endings (*ghāyāt*)			
The most excellent parts (*afḍal*) of the Quran	84		
The most excellent (*fāḍil*) and excellent parts (*mafḍūl*) of the Quran	85		
Simple words of the Quran (*mufradāt*)	86		
Parables	87		
Etiquette of the reader (*qāri'*)	88		
Etiquette of the reciter (*muqri'*)	89		
Etiquette of the exegetes	90		
Who has advocated *tafsīr* and who has attacked it	91		
Unusual interpretations	92		
Exegesis (*tafsīr*)	93		
The Writing of the Quran (*kitābat al-Qur'ān*)	94		
The names of the Suras	95		
The sequence (*tartīb*) of the Ayas and Suras	96		
Names	97		
Patronymics (*kunan*)	98		
Epithets (*alqāb*)	99		
Referents (*mubhamāt*)	100		
Names of people for whom verses were sent down	101		
History (*ta'rīkh*)	102		

C Different scholars have divided the chapters of the *Itqān* in various ways, and such divisions of the text are quite objective, although necessary to make the text more manageable. These divisions generally follow Gilliot's scheme, but with some variation in order to align the *Taḥbīr* and the *Itqān*. Gilliot divides the *Itqān* as follows: I: "Where and the How the Quran was sent down" (§1–16); II: Its edition (§17–19); III: Its Transmission (§20–27); IV: Its recitation (§28–35); V: Its linguistic aspects (§36–42); VI: Its normative (legal) aspect (§43–50); VII: Its rhetorical and stylistic aspects and its inimitability (§51–64); VIII: Various accepts (§65–76); and IX: Exegetes and exegeses (§77–80). See Gilliot, Traditional disciplines 331–5. Krawulsky divides the text into thirteen sections, and Wansbrough into five; Wansbrough, *Quranic studies*, 119–121; Krawulsky, *Einführung* 46–51; see also McAuliffe, Exegetical sciences.

Appendix B

TABLE 8.4 *Contents of the* Itqān *and the* Burhān

§	*Itqān*	§	*Burhān*
1	Meccan and Medinan Suras	1	Occasions of revelation
2	Verses revealed while resident and travelling	2	The mutual congruity of verses
3	Verses revealed at daytime and at night	3	Terminations of verses
4	Verses revealed during summer and winter	4	Words with multiple meanings and near-synonyms
5	Verses revealed in bed or sleeping	5	Verses of allegorical meaning
6	Verses revealed on earth and in heaven	6	Ambiguous meaning
7	The first verses to be revealed	7	The mysteries contained in certain opening verses
8	The last verses to be revealed	8	The conclusions of the Suras
9	Occasions of revelation	9	Meccan and Medinan verses
10	Verses revealed in conformity with the sayings of the companions	10	The first verses to be revealed
11	Verses revealed more than once	11	The dialects in which the Quran was revealed
12	Verses of anticipation	12	The manner of its revelation
13	Suras revealed in segments and as a whole	13	How it was collected and preserved by the companions
14	Suras revealed with angels	14	The division of the Quran
15	Verses revealed only to the Prophet and verses revealed to previous prophets	15	The names of the Quran
16	The manner of the revelation	16	Words in the Quran not belonging to the Hijazi dialect
17	The names of the Suras and their divisions	17	Non-Arabic words in the Quran
18	Collection and organization of the Suras	18	Unusual words in the Quran
19	Number of Suras, Ayas, words and letters	19	Declension
20	Transmitters of the Quran	20	Ordinances
21	*Isnāds* of Quranic transmission	21	Whether a simple word (*lafẓ*) or a compound word (*tarkīb*) is more eloquent
22	Widespread *ḥadīth*	22	The variation of words through augmentation and diminution
23	Well known *ḥadīth* (*mashhūr*)	23	Dialectics
24	Those *ḥadīth* with a single transmission (*āḥād*)	24	Pauses

TABLE 8.4 *Contents of the* Itqān *and the* Burhān (cont.)

§	*Itqān*	§	*Burhān*
25	The non-canonical (*shādhdh*)	25	Orthography
26	Forged *ḥadīth* (*mawḍūʿ*)	26	Virtues and properties of the Quran
27	Inserted *ḥadīth* (*mudraj*)	27	Properties of the Quran
28	The beginnings and ends of verses	28	Is one part of the Quran better than another
29	Vocalization of the letters	29	The arts of the recitation of the Quran
30	Lengthening (*imāla*)	30	Is it permissible to use verses of the Quran in compositions, letters and sermons
31	Assimilation (*idghām*), the retention of phonetic value (*iẓhār*), suppression (*ikhfāʾ*) and metathesis (*alqāb*)	31	The parables contained in the Quran
32	Lengthening (*madd*)	32	The ordinances contained in the Quran
33	Reduction of *hamza* (*takhfīf*)	33	The disputations contained in the Quran
34	Forms of learning the Quran	34	Abrogating and abrogated verses
35	Etiquette of reciting the Quran	35	Verses that give rise to disagreement
36	On knowing unusual words	36	How to distinguish clear, unambiguous verses
37	Non-*ḥijāzī* words	37	Allegorical verses containing the divine attributes
38	Non-Arab words	38	The inimitability of the Quran
39	Polyvalence (*wujūḥ*) and synonyms (*naẓāʾir*)	39	The unanimously accepted obligatory nature of unanimously accepted Quran
40	The meanings of particles	40	The reinforcement of the Quran by the *sunna*
41	Vocalization	41	The interpretation of the Quran
42	Rules of exegesis	42	The different forms of address contained in the Quran
43	Clear (*muḥkam*) and ambiguous (*mutashābih*) words	43	The literal and the allegorical
44	Earlier and later parts of the Quran	44	Metonymies and allusions
45	General and specific	45	Different types of meaning in the Quran
46	Summary verses and detailed verses	46	The styles of the Quran
47	Abrogating and abrogated verses	47	Particles
48	Difficult and disputed verses		

§	*Itqān*	§	*Burhān*
49	Absolute and restricted verses		
50	Words and meaning		
51	Different forms of address (*mukhāṭabāt*)		
52	Literal and allegorical		
53	Simile (*tashbīh*) and metaphors (*istiʿārāt*)		
54	Metonymy (*kināya*) and allusions (*taʿārīḍ*)		
55	Restriction (*ḥaṣr*) and specification (*ikhtiṣāṣ*)		
56	Conciseness (*ījāz*) and prolixity (*iṭnāb*)		
57	Informative (*khabar*) and performative (*inshāʾ*)		
58	On the wonders of the Quran		
59	On the division of the Ayas		
60	The openings of the Suras		
61	The endings of the Suras		
62	The links between the Ayas and Suras		
63	Verses similar to each other		
64	The inimitability of the Quran		
65	Sciences that can be deduced from the Quran		
66	Parables of the Quran		
67	Oaths (*aqsām*) in the Quran		
68	Arguments in the Quran		
69	Referents (*mubhamāt*)		
70	Names of people for whom verses were sent down		
71	Names of people for whom verses were sent down		
72	The Merits (*faḍāʾil*) of the Quran		
73	The excellent and most excellent parts of the Quran		
74	Simple words of the Quran (*mufradāt*)		
75	The properties (*khawāṣṣ*) of the Quran		
76	Orthography (*marsūm al-khaṭṭ*) and customs of writing		
77	Exegesis (*tafsīr*)		
78	Conditions and customs to be observed by the exegete (*shurūṭ al-mufassīr*)		
79	Unusual interpretations		
80	Biographies of the exegetes (*ṭabaqāt al-mufassirīn*)		

Appendix C

TABLE 8.5 *The complete Arabic text of the chapters on* Asbāb al-nuzūl *(§11, 39) in the* Taḥbīr, *with their counterparts in the* Itqān

---

A تحبير

وهو نوع مهم محتاج اليه وصنّف الناس فيه مصنفات، ومن احسنها كتب الواحدي، ثم شيخ الاسلام حافظ العصر أبي الفضل بن حجر،

إتقان

أفرده بالتصنيف جماعة أقدمهم علي بن المديني شيخ البخاري، ومن اشهرها كتاب الواحدي على ما فيه من إعواز، وقد اختصره الجعبري فحذف أسانيد ولم يزد عليه شيئاً، وألف فيه شيخ الاسلام أبي الفضل بن حجر كتابًا مات عنه مسودة فلم نقف عليه كاملاً، وقد ألفت كتابًا حافلاً موجزًا محررًا لم يؤلف مثله في هذا النوع سميته: لباب النقول في اسباب النزول.

(*Itqān*, i, 40; *Perfect Guide* 55)

B تحبير

وماكان منه عن صحابي فهو مسند مرفوع، إذ قول الصحابي فيما لا دخل فيه للاجتهاد مرفوع، او تابعي فمرسل، والشرط قبولهما صحة السند، ويزيد الثاني أن يكون راويه معروفًا بأن لا يروي إلا عن الصحابة، او ورد له شاهد مرسل او متّصل ولو ضعيفاً، وإذا تعارض فيه حديثان فإن أمكن الجمع بينهما فذاك كآية اللعان.

إتقان

تنبيه ما تقدم انه من قبيل المسند من الصحابي إذا وقع من تابعي فهو مرفوع ايضًا لكنه مرسل فقد يقبل إذا صح المسند اليه وكان من أئمة التفسير الآخذين عن الصحابة كمجاهدة وعكرمة وسعيد بن جبير أو واعتمد بمرسل آخر ونحو ذلك.

(*Itqān*, i, 45; *Perfect Guide* 63)

C تحبير ففي الصحيح عن سهل بن سعد الساعدي أنها نزلت في قصة عويمر العجلاني وفيه أيضاً انها نزلت في قصة هلال بن امية، فيمكن انها نزلت في حقهما أي بعد سؤال كل منهما فيجمع بهذا، وان لم يمكن قدّم ماكان سنده صحيحاً او له مرجح ككون راويه صاحب الواقعة التي نزلت فيها الآية ونحو ذلك، فإن استويا فهل يحمل على النزول مرتين او يكون مضطرباً يقتضي طرح كل منهما؟ عندي فيه احتمالان و في الحديث يشبهه . . .

إتقان واخرج الشيخان عن سهل بن سعد قال جاء عويمر الى عاصم بن عدي فقال اسأل رسول الله صلعم ارأيت رجلاً وجد مع امرأته رجلاً يقتله أيقتل به أم كيف يصنع؟ فسأل عاصم رسول الله صلعم فعاب السائل فأخبر عاصم عويمرًا فقال والله لآتين رسول الله صلعم فلأسألنه فأتاه فقال إنه قد أنزل فيك و في صاحبتك قرآن الحديث جمع بينهما بأن أول من وقع له ذلك هلال وصادف مجيء عويمر أيضًا فنزلت في شأنهما معًا، والى هذا جنح النووي وسبقه الخطيب فقال لعلهما اتفق لهما ذلك في وقت واحد.

(*Itqān* i, 47/*Perfect Guide* 66–7)

D تحبير وربما كان في إحدى القصتين (فتلا) فوهم الراوي فقال: (فنزل) كما تقدم في آية الزمر، البارع الناقد يفحّص عن ذلك، وأمثلة هذا النوع تُستقرأ من الكتب المصنفة فيه وذُكر منها كثير في هذا الكتاب في الانواع السابقة والتي ستأتي.

إتقان –

This paragraph is not found in the *Itqān*.

TABLE 8.5 *The complete Arabic text of the chapters on* Asbāb al-nuzūl (*§11, 39*) (cont.)

E	تحبير	ثم منها المشهور وهو قسمان: صحيح كقصة الإفك وآية السعي والتيمم والعرنيين وموافقات عمر، وضعيف كآية "إنّ الله يَأمُرُكُمْ أنْ تُؤَدّوا الأمَانَاتِ إلى أهْلِها . . ."، وقد اشتهر انها نزلت في شأن مفتاح الكعبة، وأسانيد ذلك بعضها ضعيف، وبعضها منقطع، ومنها الغريب وهو إيضاً قسمان: صحيح وضعيف، والله أعلم، وهذا الفصل مما حررته واستخرجته من قواعد الحديث ولم أسبق اليه وبالله التوفيق.
	إتقان	. . . "إنّ الله يَأمُرُكُمْ أنْ تُؤَدّوا الأمَانَاتِ إلى أهْلِها . . ."، فهذا عام في كل أمانة وذاك خاص بأمانة هي صفة النبي صلعم بالطريق السابق . . . This paragraph is not found directly in the *Itqān*. (*Itqān* i, 43–4/*Perfect Guide* 61)

Bibliography

Primary Sources

Ibn Isḥāq, [*Sīrat Rasūl Allāh*] *The life of Muhammad: A translation of Ibn Isḥāq's* Sirat Rasūl Allāh, trans. A. Guillaume, Karachi and New York 1967, repr. Karachi 2006.

al-Sakhāwī, *al-Ḍawʾ al-lāmiʿ li-ahl al-qarn al-tāsiʿ*, 12 vols., Cairo, 1353–5/1934–6.

al-Shahrazūrī, [*Kitāb Maʿrifat anwāʿ ʿilm al-ḥadīth*] *An introduction to the science of the* ḥadīth: Kitāb Maʿrifat anwāʿ ʿilm al-ḥadīth, trans. E. Dickinson, Reading 2006.

al-Suyūṭī, [*al-Hayʾa as-saniyya fī l-hayʾa al-sunniya*], *Islamic cosmology: A study of al-Suyūṭī's* al-Hayʾa as-sanīya fī l-hayʾa as-sunnīya, ed. A.M. Heinen, Beirut 1982.

al-Suyūṭī, *Kitāb al-Itqān fī ʿulūm al-Qurʾān*, ed. K. al-ʿAṭṭār, 2 vols., Beirut 2003.

al-Suyūṭī, [*Kitāb al-Itqān fī ʿulūm al-Qurʾān*] *Soyûty's Itqân on the exegetic sciences of the Qorân*, ed. Maulavī S.D. Khān, Maulavī B.D., A. Sprenger, Calcutta 1857, repr. Osnabrück 1980.

al-Suyūṭī, [*Kitāb*] *al-Itqān fī ʿulūm al-Qurʾān*, ed. M.A. al-F. Ibrāhīm, Cairo 1967, ^{2}1974–5.

al-Suyūṭī, [*Kitāb al-Itqān fī ʿulūm al-Qurʾān*] *The perfect guide to the sciences of the Qurʾān*: al-Itqān fī ʿulūm al-Qurʾān, trans. Ḥ. Algar, M. Schub and A. Abdel Haleem, Reading 2011.

al-Suyūṭī, *Lubāb al-nuqūl fī-asbāb al-nuzūl*, Tunis 1981.

al-Suyūṭī, *Muʿtarak al-aqrān fī iʿjāz al-Qurʾān*, ed. ʿA.M. al-Bijāwī, 3 vols., Cairo 1969–73.

al-Suyūṭī, *Kitāb al-Taḥbīr fī ʿilm al-tafsīr*, ed. Z.ʿU. ʿAlī Nūr, Beirut 1988, repr. Beirut 2013.

al-Suyūṭī, *al-Taḥadduth bi-niʿmat Allāh*, in E.M. Sartain (ed.), *Jalāl al-dīn al-Suyūṭī*. ii: *al-Taḥadduth bi-niʿmat Allāh* (University of Cambridge Oriental Publications 24), Cambridge 1975.

al-Ṭabarī, [*Taʾrīkh al-rusul wa-l-mulūk*] *The history of al-Ṭabarī*. ix: *The last Years of the prophet*, trans. I.K. Poonawala, Albany 1999.

al-Wāḥidī, *Asbāb al-nuzūl*, ed. M.ʿA.Q. Shāhīn, Beirut 1421/2000.

al-Zarkashī, *Kitāb al-Burhān fī ʿulūm al-Qurʾān*, ed. M.A. al-F. Ibrāhīm, 4 vols., Cairo 1957–8.

Secondary Sources

Abbott, N., *ʿĀʾisha, the beloved of Mohammed*, Chicago 1944, repr. London 1998.

Abun-Nasr, J.M., *Muslim communities of grace: The Sufi brotherhoods in Islamic religious life*, London 2007.

ʿAlī Nūr, Z.ʿU., *al-Taḥbīr fī ʿilm al-tafsīr lil-Imām Jalāl al-Dīn al-Suyūṭī: taḥqīq wa-dirāsa*, MA diss., Umm al-Qura University 1404/1983.

Arberry, A.J., *The Koran interpreted*, 2 vols., London and New York, 1955; repr. Oxford 1998.

Asfarrudin, A., ʿĀʾisha bt. Abī Bakr, in *EI*[3] [online version, http://referenceworks.brillonline.com/entries/encyclopaedia-of-islam-3/aisha-bt-abi-bakr-COM_23459?s.num=0&s.f.s2_parent=s.f.book.encyclopaedia-of-islam-3&s.q=a%27isha+bint+abi+bakr, last accessed 30 Jan 2015].

Bauden, F., Maqriziana IX: Should al-Maqrīzī be thrown out with the bath water? The question of his plagiarism of al-Awḥadī's *Khiṭaṭ* and the documentary evidence, in *MSR* 14 (2010), 159–232.

Berkey, J., *The transmission of knowledge in medieval Cairo: A social history of Islamic education*, Princeton 1992.

Brockelmann, C., *Geschichte der arabischen Literatur* [*GAL*], 2 vols. and *Supplementbände* [*GAL S*], 3 vols., Leiden 1937–49.

Burge, S.R., Impurity/Danger! in *Islamic Law and Society* 17 (2010), 320–49.

Burge, S.R., Reading between the lines: The compilation of *ḥadīṯ* and the authorial voice, in *Arabica* 58 (2011), 168–97.

Burge, S.R., *Angels in Islam: Jalāl al-Dīn al-Suyūṭī's* al-Ḥabāʾik fī akhbār al-malāʾik, London 2012.

Burge, S.R., Jalāl al-Dīn al-Suyūṭī, the *Muʿawwidhatān* and the modes of exegesis, in K. Bauer (ed.), *Aims, methods and contexts of Qurʾanic exegesis (2nd/8th–9th/15th centuries)*, Oxford 2013, 277–307.

Burge, S.R., Scattered pearls: Exploring al-Suyūṭī's hermeneutics and use of sources in *al-Durr al-manthūr fī l-tafsīr bi-l-ma'thūr*, in JRAS 24 (2014), 251–96.
Burge, S.R., Review: Ḥ. Algar et al., (trans.): *The perfect guide to the sciences of the Qur'ān*: al-Itqān fī 'ulūm al-Qur'ān, in JQS 18 (2016), 142–9.
Burge, S.R., The search for meaning: *Tafsīr*, hermeneutics and theories of reading, in *Arabica* 62 (2015), 53–73.
Cilardo, A., *The Qur'ānic term* kalāla: *Studies in the Arabic language and poetry,* ḥadīth, tafsīr, *and* fiqh. *Notes on the origin of the Islamic law,* Edinburgh 2005.
Cragg, K., The historical geography of the Qur'an: A study in *asbāb al-nuzūl*, in JQS 1 (1999), 81–92.
Davidson, G., Carrying on the tradition: An intellectual and social history of post-canonical *hadith* transmission, PhD diss., University of Chicago 2014.
Geoffroy, É. al-Suyūṭī, in EI^2, ix, 913–6.
Gilliot, C., The traditional disciplines of Quranic Studies, in EQ, v, 319–39.
Ikhwan, M., *Kitāb al-Muzhir* of Jalāl al-Dīn al-Suyūṭī: A critical edition and translation of section twenty on Islamic terms, in *Al-Jāmi'a* 47 (2009), 377–410.
Irwin, R., al-Suyūṭī (849–911/1445–1505), in J.S. Meisami and P. Starkey (eds.), EAL, ii, London and New York 1998, 746.
Kamal, 'A.H. and H. Lammens, Ḥunayn, in EI^2, iii, 578.
Knysh, A., *Islamic mysticism: A short history*, Leiden 2000.
Krawulsky, D., *Eine Einführung in die Koranwissenschaften: 'Ulūm al-Qur'ān*, Bern 2006.
Lane, E.W., *Arabic-English lexicon*, 8 vols., London 1863–93; repr. Cambridge 1984 (2 vols.).
McAuliffe, J.D., Ibn al-Jawzī's exegetical propaedeutic: Introduction and translation, in *Alif: Journal of Comparative Literature* 8 (1988), 101–13.
McAuliffe, J.D., Exegetical sciences, in A. Rippin (ed.), *The Blackwell companion to the Qur'ān*, London 2006, 403–19.
Moore, R., al-Bulqīnī family, in EI^3 [online version http://referenceworks.brillonline.com/entries/encyclopaedia-of-islam-3/al-bulqini-family-COM_24603?s.num=0&s.q=bulqini+family, last accessed, 30 Jan 2015].
Nemoy, L., The treatise on the Egyptian pyramids (*Tuḥfat al-kirām fī akhbar al-ahrām*), in *Isis* 30 (1939), 17–37.
Nolin, K.E., The *Itqān* and its sources: A study of *Al-Itqān fī 'ulūm al-Qur'ān* by Jalāl al-Dīn al-Suyūṭī with special reference to *al-Burhān fī 'ulūm al-Qur'ān* by Badr al-Dīn al-Zarkashī, PhD diss., Hartford Seminary Foundation 1968.
Ourghi, A., Auch die Engel sprachen mit Gott im Koran: Die *parrhesia* der Engel, in *Der Islam* 85 (2011), 360–97.
Petry, C.F., *The civilian elite of Cairo in the later Middle Ages*, Princeton 1981.
Powers, D.S., *Studies in* Qur'ān *and* ḥadīth*: The formation of the Islamic law of inheritance*, Berkeley 1986.

Powers, D.S., *Muḥammad is not the father of any of your men: The making of the last prophet*, Philadelphia 2009.

Rippin, A., Al-Zarkashī and al-Suyuti [sic] on the function of the "occasion of revelation" material, in *IC* 59 (1985), 243–58.

Rippin, A., The function of *asbāb al-nuzūl* in Quranic Exegesis, in *BSOAS* 51 (1988), 1–20.

Rippin, A., The construction of the Arabian historical context in Muslim interpretation of the Qur'ān, in K. Bauer (ed.), *Aims, methods and contexts of Qur'anic exegesis (2nd/8th–9th/15th centuries)*, Oxford 2013, 173–98.

Rippin, A., Review: Ḥ. Algar et al. (trans.): *The perfect guide to the sciences of the Qur'ān* (al-Itqān fī 'Ulūm al-Qur'ān), *by Imām Jalāl-al-Dīn 'Abd al-Raḥmān al-Suyūṭī*, i, in *JAOS* 133 (2013), 394–6.

Robinson, N., Jesus and Mary in the Quran: Some neglected affinities, *Religion* 20 (1990), 161–75.

Robson, J., Ibn al-ʿArabī, in *EI*², iii, 707.

Saleh, M.J., Al-Suyūṭī and his works: Their place in Islamic scholarship from Mamlūk times to the present, in *MSR* 5 (2001), 73–89.

Sartain, E.M., *Jalāl al-dīn al-Suyūṭī.* i: *Biography and background* (University of Cambridge Oriental Publications 23), Cambridge 1975.

Sartain, E.M., Jalāl al-Dīn al-Suyūṭī's relations with the people of Takrūr, in *JSS* 16 (1971), 193–8.

Shoshan, B., On popular literature in medieval Cairo, in *Poetics Today* 14 (1992), 349–65.

Spellberg, D.A., *Politics, gender and the Islamic past: The legacy of 'Ā'isha bint Abī Bakr*, New York 1994.

Voll, J.O., Hadith scholars and tariqas: An ulama group in the 18th century Haramayn and their impact in the Islamic world, in *Journal of Asian and African Studies* 15 (1980), 264–73.

Walker, A.M. and M.A. Sells, The wiles of women and performative intertextuality: 'Ā'isha, the *hadith* of the slander, and the Sura of Yusuf, in *JAL* 30 (1999), 55–77.

Wansbrough, J., *Quranic studies: Sources and methods of scriptural interpretation* (London Oriental Series 31) London 1977, Amherst 2004 (new ed. with forew., trans., and expanded notes by A. Rippin).

CHAPTER 9

"Usefulness without Toil": Al-Suyūṭī and the Art of Concise *ḥadīth* Commentary

Joel Blecher

Al-Suyūṭī grew up in the shadow of a generation in Cairo that produced some of the most elaborate multi-volume commentaries on *ḥadīth*. To suggest something of an analogy, one might say that the late Mamlūk period was for Cairene *ḥadīth* commentary what the late Baroque period was for Roman architecture. *Ḥadīth* commentary was not the only genre of Islamic literature of the era that flooded quires with ink, but it was an influential one.[1] During his childhood, al-Suyūṭī witnessed the passing of two great masters of commentarial excess, Ibn Ḥajar al-ʿAsqalānī (d. 852/1449) and Badr al-Dīn al-ʿAynī (d. 855/1453), both of whom produced competing commentaries on *Ṣaḥīḥ al-Bukhārī* that far surpassed any prior *ḥadīth* commentary in terms of volume and detail, and expanded the range of hermeneutic techniques and resources available to the *ḥadīth* commentator. As I have argued elsewhere, such works emerged in a culture in which live commentary on *ḥadīth* collections were spectacular and sometimes destructive contests in which rival commentators debated the finer points of law, terminology, and chains of transmission in the presence of students, patrons, and colleagues.[2] Persuading these diverse audiences of one's superior memory, world travels, and mastery over encyclopedic detail were symbolic not only of one's devotion to the Prophet's example, but were also signs of prestige in a context in which powerful teaching and judicial appointments could be won and lost. William Blake may have aphorized that "the road of excess leads to the palace of wisdom," but for the Mamlūk era *ḥadīth* commentators, the road of excess just as surely lead to the palace of the sultan.

And yet, al-Suyūṭī's *ḥadīth* commentaries turned away from this aesthetic of excess towards one of extraordinary breadth and concision. Nevertheless, al-Suyūṭī's commentary on *Ṣaḥīḥ al-Bukhārī*, called *al-Tawshīḥ* (The Adorned), was among his most popular works and was known to have circulated among

1 For a discussion of "the boom in encyclopaedic and otherwise compilatory literature in the 14th-century," see Muhanna, Encyclopaedism.

2 Blecher, *Ḥadith* Commentary.

 | DOI 10.1163/9789004334526_011

audiences in the Maghrib, the Hijaz, and West Africa throughout the 880s (late 1470s and early 1480s).[3] Likewise, his commentaries on the collections of Ibn Māja and al-Nasāʾī were among the first attempts ever to systematically comment on those works.[4] His commentary on *Sunan al-Nasāʾī* attracted a super-commentary by Muḥammad Ḥayāt al-Sindī (d. 1163/1750), an eminent and influential *ḥadīth* scholar who was active two and a half centuries after al-Suyūṭī's death.[5] These works have also enjoyed a vibrant afterlife in contemporary print.[6]

Despite their enduring success, al-Suyūṭī once described his commentaries on *Ṣaḥīḥ al-Bukhārī* and *Ṣaḥīḥ Muslim* as texts "for which comparable works have been composed, and a very learned person could produce its like," and his commentaries on Ibn Māja and al-Nasāʾī as works "which I started then lost interest in, having written only a little."[7] If not for their originality or virtuosic comprehensiveness, what explains their warm reception in their own time and beyond? The answer, I believe, lies in understanding an exegetical good al-Suyūṭī strived to achieve in his *ḥadīth* commentary: *al-nafʿ bilā taʿab*, "usefulness without toil."[8]

In this chapter, I will offer a few observations on al-Suyūṭī's practice as a *ḥadīth* commentator, which, like the *ḥadīth* commentary tradition more broadly, has been virtually overlooked in the current scholarly literature. Through a comparison of al-Suyūṭī's interpretive strategies in his commentary on *Ṣaḥīḥ al-Bukhārī* with his predecessors', I will explore how al-Suyūṭī worked within the freedom and constraints of his social historical context to both preserve and pare down the elaborate tradition of *ḥadīth* commentary he inherited. In concluding, I hope to offer a portrait of al-Suyūṭī's scholarly output that helps us rethink knowledge as a *social practice* in Mamlūk Cairo that includes competition over material and social goods *as well as* exegetical goods. After all, commentators like al-Suyūṭī not only competed for social capital within the day-to-day pressures and politics of the scholarly scene, but they were also

3 Sartain, *Biography* 48, 50; al-Suyūṭī, *Taḥadduth* 157–9.

4 Brown, *Hadith* 53.

5 Al-Nasāʾī, al-Suyūṭī, al-Sindī, *Sunan*.

6 Saudi presses have been especially active in printing these works, two of which have been used in the making of this essay: The latter work, *al-Dībāj*, was edited by Abū Isḥāq al-Ḥawaynī, an Egyptian student of al-Albānī and a celebrity *ḥadīth* scholar among Salafī audiences.

7 Saleh, al-Suyūṭī 87–8; al-Suyūṭī, *Taḥadduth* 107, 130.

8 Al-Suyūṭī, *Tawshīḥ* 42; Dihlawī, *Garden* 341.

motivated by exegetical goods that were defining of and defined by the commentarial tradition.

1 Shifting Reading Cultures and Slimmer Volumes

After the passing of Ibn Ḥajar and al-ʿAynī, the production of elaborate *ḥadīth* commentaries did not come to an immediate halt. Indeed, one of al-Suyūṭī's own competitors, Shihāb al-Dīn al-Qasṭallānī (d. 923/1517), produced an enduring commentary on *Ṣaḥīḥ al-Bukhārī* that not only combined the works of Ibn Ḥajar, al-ʿAynī, and their predecessors, but surpassed them in terms of its preservation of the multiple recitations of the *Ṣaḥīḥ*.[9] Indeed, al-Suyūṭī's first attempts at commentary on prophetic traditions conformed with the grander displays of encyclopedism modeled by Ibn Ḥajar. His early treatment of Ibn Mālik's *Muwaṭṭaʾ*, for instance, surpassed its predecessors in terms of detail and the preservation of the multiple recitations of the work.[10] But by the end of his life, al-Suyūṭī practically boasted of his ability to comment on Aḥmad b. Ḥanbal's tremendous *Musnad* in a single volume.[11]

Nevertheless, there were some indications of a countering trend among audiences that sought more abbreviated *ḥadīth* commentary, at least in Cairo. While recitations and live commentary of *Ṣaḥīḥ al-Bukhārī* in the Citadel in the presence of the sultan had customarily spanned two months during the days of al-Muʾayyad Shaykh (r. 814–824/1412–1421),[12] in al-Suyūṭī's adult life they had all but ceased. Only after an earthquake struck Egypt in 875/1472 were readings of *Ṣaḥīḥ al-Bukhārī* revived at the Citadel for the sultan, but even then they lasted no longer than the month of Ramadan.[13] Regular dictation of *ḥadīth* in other venues in Cairo vanished, and both al-Suyūṭī's and Ibn Ḥajar's student Shams al-Dīn al-Sakhāwī's (d. 902/1497) attempts to reestablish the practice fizzled.[14] It would be at least another generation until manuscript evidence and narrative sources suggest that live commentary on *Ṣaḥīḥ al-Bukhārī* had been revived at teaching sessions (*majālis*) in Ottoman Syria and Yemen.[15] Al-Suyūṭī tells us in his autobiography that his earliest *ḥadīth* commentar-

9 Al-Khaṭīb al-Qasṭallānī, *Irshād*.
10 Anas, al-Suyūṭī, *Muwaṭṭaʾ*.
11 Al-Suyūṭī, Ibn Ḥanbal, *ʿUqūd*.
12 Jaques, *Ibn Hajar* 94.
13 Al-Suyūṭī, *Ḥusn* ii, 304.
14 Sartain, *Biography* 41.
15 Al-ʿAydarūs, *al-Nūr al-sāfir* 413; al-Safīrī, *ʿIdda*.

ies, those on the *Musnads* of al-Shāfiʿī and Abū Ḥanīfa, emerged from a series of live lessons at the *madrasa* of the Shaykhūniyya and other venues for live gatherings.[16] However, there is little evidence that his serial commentaries on the six canonical *ḥadīth* collections emerged in concert with live dictations, so it may be safest to assume they did not.

Suyūṭī's own training reflects this trend, as he viewed live sessions in a far less glamorous light than the previous generation of *ḥadīth* experts. As al-Suyūṭī scholar E.M. Sartain pointed out, al-Suyūṭī famously preferred learning *ḥadīth* from books rather than audition, which had fallen, in his opinion, under the direction of "common people, rabble, women, and old men."[17] Although al-Suyūṭī studied some works of *ḥadīth* with Muḥyī l-Dīn al-Kāfiyajī (d. 879/1474), and much of *Ṣaḥīḥ Muslim* with Shams al-Dīn Muḥammad b. Mūsā al-Sīrāmī (d. 871/1466–7), it is difficult to determine what influence, if any, these studies had on al-Suyūṭī's commentarial practice.[18] ʿAlam al-Dīn Ṣāliḥ al-Bulqīnī (d. 868/1464), with whom al-Suyūṭī studied Shāfiʿī *fiqh*, could be added to this list of possible influences, as al-Suyūṭī was often referenced as an authority on the legal benefits of the *ḥadīth*.[19] Of course, al-Suyūṭī once attended a *ḥadīth* study session with Ibn Ḥajar but he was no more than a toddler at the time.[20]

One clear inspiration, however, was Badr al-Dīn al-Zarkashī (d. 794/1392). Al-Suyūṭī modeled his Quran commentary, *al-Itqān*, on al-Zarkashī's *Burhān*, so it may come as little surprise that al-Suyūṭī's *ḥadīth* commentary, *al-Tawshīḥ*, was modeled on al-Zarkashī's *al-Tanqīḥ*—the very titles echo one another.[21] Al-Zarkashī, in the introduction to *al-Tanqīḥ*, wrote that "excess invites boredom ... I hope that this dictation will spare the toil of checking, investigation and reading [...]."[22] This marked a departure from the commentarial encyclopedism articulated a century earlier by Muḥyī l-Dīn al-Nawawī who longed to write an "expansive work, a work stretching to more than a hundred volumes, without repetition or pointless expansion."[23] Al-Nawawī's choice to resign himself to a mere ten volumes represented "the weakness of aspirations, the

16 Al-Suyūṭī, *Taḥadduth* 130.

17 Sartain, *Biography* 31.

18 Ibid. 27.

19 Ibid. 26–8.

20 Ibid. 26. It was not unusual for children to attend auditions of *ḥadīth* and an elevated status was conferred on adults who had been fortunate to attend auditions with master *ḥadīth* transmitters as children. See Davidson, *Carrying on* 95–106, 174–8.

21 Rippin, al-Zarkashī.

22 Al-Zarkashī, *Tanqīḥ* i, 1–2; Dihlawī, *Garden* 313.

23 Al-Nawawī, *Ṣaḥīḥ* i, 4–5 (trans. Calder, *Islamic*, 107).

paucity of seekers, and fear that an even longer book would have no market, students being little inclined towards long books."[24] In this way, al-Zarkashī's gloss would have lacked the prestige of these more elaborate commentaries that conspicuously signaled to audiences the depth of the commentators' capacity to comment and the commentators' willingness to risk physical exhaustion and even commercial failure in devotion to *ḥadīth* study.

The *Tanqīḥ*'s content initially received mixed reviews. Ibn Ḥajar penned a corrective gloss on it and the Alexandrian Mālikī judge Badr al-Dīn al-Damāmīnī (d. 827/1424) wrote a commentary on the *Ṣaḥīḥ* that unequivocally criticized it, sometimes unfairly.[25] Al-Damāmīnī drew heavily on the form of the *Tanqīḥ* while claiming to correct its many grammatical, morphological, and linguistic errors. Most damning, for al-Damāmīnī, was al-Zarkashī's errors in the transmission of the *ḥadīth*s. Al-Damāmīnī's work was somewhat longer than al-Zarkashī's and circulated in Egypt, Yemen, and India, where al-Damāmīnī traveled for teaching and study.[26]

Nevertheless, al-Zarkashī's shorter work was more pragmatic, and al-Suyūṭī no doubt recognized its power for reciters and students who, as ample manuscript evidence collected from the period shows, incorporated snippets of it in the margins of their copies of *Ṣaḥīḥ al-Bukhārī*.[27] In spite of its flaws, al-Zarkashī's work was ideal for quick reference, its comments fit comfortably on the periphery of a *ḥadīth* collection's base text, and sought to provide no more and no less than any reciter needed to know, whether sight reading or preparing to recite from memory. The fact that so many eminent scholarly authorities read and responded to the *Tanqīḥ*, including Ibn Ḥajar and al-Damāmīnī, but also Muḥammad al-Birmāwī (d. 831/1428), Zakariyyā' al-Anṣārī (d. 926/1520), and Shihāb al-Dīn al-Qasṭallānī (d. 923/1517), is testament to its popularity and wide-circulation.[28] It was, to the applause of some and the jeers of others, a source for the *ḥadīth* commentarial sound bites of its day.

Suyūṭī wrote, in the introduction to the *Tawshīḥ*:

> [This commentary on *Ṣaḥīḥ al-Bukhārī*] runs along the way of the notes of Imām Badr al-Dīn al-Zarkashī, called *al-Tanqīḥ*. It contains benefits

24 Ibid.

25 Ibn Ḥajar, *Ḥawāshī*; al-Damāmīnī, *Taʿaqqubāt* 150–1; idem, *Maṣābīḥ* i, 54–64.

26 For biographical information on al-Damāmīnī see Ḥasanī, *Itḥāf* 245–6; Ishaq, *India's Contribution* 87–8.

27 Al-Bukhārī, *Ṣaḥīḥ* f. 36b.

28 Al-Damāmīnī, *Taʿaqqubāt* 16–7.

and additions that the reciter (*al-qāriʾ*) and listener (*al-mustamiʿ*) need concerning:

- [the *Ṣaḥīḥ*'s] correct phrasing
- commentary on [the *Ṣaḥīḥ*'s] obscure words (*tafsīr gharībihi*)
- clarification on variants in [the *Ṣaḥīḥ*'s] transmissions (*ikhtilāf riwāyātihi*)
- additions to a *ḥadīth* which was not mentioned in [the *Ṣaḥīḥ*'s narration of a *ḥadīth*'s] path (*ṭarīqihi*)
- a chapter heading (*tarjama*) [in the *Ṣaḥīḥ*] whose phrasing comes from a *ḥadīth* traced [to the Prophet] (*marfūʿ*)
- connecting a chainless (*taʿlīq*) [*ḥadīth*] whose full connection is not given in the *Ṣaḥīḥ*
- identifying unknown persons
- [rectifying] problems of syntax
- reconciling controversies[29]

"In this way," al-Suyūṭī wrote, "nothing is missing from the commentary except legal derivation (*istinbāṭ*). I am determined to compose a book in this fashion on all of the six books [of *ḥadīth*] to gain *usefulness without toil* and reach the end without affliction."[30] The list of nine aspects of the collection to be explained is indeed modeled on al-Zarkashī's. One notable point of confusion that al-Zarkashī explicitly clarified in the text that al-Suyūṭī did not was the esoteric relationship between each *ḥadīth* and the chapter heading under which al-Bukhārī placed it. This technique, developed by traditional commentators on *Ṣaḥīḥ al-Bukhārī*, had grown in popularity throughout the Mamlūk period and even began to generate its own genre.[31] While esoteric commentary on al-Bukhārī's chapter headings is related to legal derivation (*istinbāṭ*), a task al-Suyūṭī perhaps thought was better to leave to the reader, it is not synonymous with it. As we will see, however, al-Suyūṭī does include discussion of both al-Bukhārī's chapter headings and his opinion on the legal derivation of *ḥadīth*, albeit infrequently. In other words, al-Suyūṭī, as al-Zarkashī did before him, left the number of aspects of *ḥadīth* that he believed merited explanation largely in tact, diminishing only the volume and frequency with which he believed they merited it.

29 Al-Suyūṭī, *Tawshīḥ* 41–2.

30 Ibid. 42; Dihlawī, *Garden* 341. Emphasis mine.

31 Ibn Rushayd, *Tarjumān*; Ibn al-Munayyir, *Mutawārī*; al-Bulqīnī, *Tarājim*.

2 Strategies of Exclusion and Inclusion in al-Suyūṭī's *Tawshīḥ*

Although al-Suyūṭī's *Tawshīḥ* was theoretically modeled on the *Tanqīḥ*, it was far from a supercommentary on it. In fact, in order to succeed in his aim of providing the audience with a reading experience that was useful but free from toil, al-Suyūṭī chose to exclude most of the commentary tradition he inherited, including many of al-Zarkashī's clarifications.[32] Ironically, al-Suyūṭī excluded so much that the work's most recent editors can see no other way to maintain the aims al-Suyūṭī promised in the introduction other than by adding a dense layer of footnotes to fill in much of what al-Suyūṭī excluded. While this may help repackage the *Tawshīḥ* for modern audiences, it obscures the fact that al-Suyūṭī's contribution to the commentary tradition was, in some sense, his strategic omissions. The point, for al-Suyūṭī, was not to offer commentary on nine aspects for every *ḥadīth* he commented upon, but only when a problem rose to a level of what al-Suyūṭī perceived to be of practical value.

This is especially clear when discussing issues concerning the interpretation of al-Bukhārī's chapter headings (*tarājim*) under which the *ḥadīth*s were organized and al-Bukhārī's abridgements (*ikhtiṣār*) of select *ḥadīth*s. The technique of disclosing the esoteric meaning of the *Ṣaḥīḥ* through al-Bukhārī's sometimes quizzical chapter headings and abridgements was first brought into the mainstream by Ibn Ḥajar's commentary *Fatḥ al-bārī*.[33] The hermeneutics of chapter headings performed the triple function of maintaining the authority of the *Ṣaḥīḥ*, opening up new aspects of the texts for creative interpretation, but limited the authority to interpret to experts with rarefied knowledge al-Bukhārī's chapter headings. Al-Suyūṭī, however, had little patience for the grander theories proposed by Ibn Ḥajar to harmonize apparent inconsistencies in al-Bukhārī's chapter headings. For instance, in the first *ḥadīth*, "actions are by intentions," in which al-Bukhārī omits a key phrase from the middle of it, al-Suyūṭī excludes Ibn Ḥajar's creative attempts to discern al-Bukhārī's intention in making the apparent abridgement, and instead states that al-Bukhārī conservatively transmitted the *ḥadīth* from his teacher in the way he heard it.[34] Similarly, in the second *ḥadīth*, when al-Suyūṭī quotes *ḥadīth* critic Abū Bakr Aḥmad al-Ismāʿīlī (d. 371/981–2) of Jurjān, who openly wondered what rele-

32 Although there is some overlap between the two works in the *lemmata* upon which they clarify, al-Suyūṭī did not always choose to clarify the same *lemmata* in his *Tawshīḥ*. For example, cp. al-Zarkashī, *Tanqīḥ* iii, 1212; and al-Suyūṭī, *Tawshīḥ* ix, 3982.

33 Ibn Ḥajar, *Hady* 13–4. For an annotated translation of Ibn Ḥajar's section on the *tarājim* and *ikhtiṣār*, consult Fadel, Ibn Ḥajar's *Hady* 180–5.

34 Cp. al-Suyūṭī, *Tawshīḥ* i, 128; and Ibn Ḥajar, *Fatḥ* i, 15–6.

vance the *ḥadīth* could have had to the chapter heading titled "How Revelation Began," al-Suyūṭī omits any mention of Ibn Ḥajar's critical attempt to solve the question.[35] Whether or not one agrees with al-Suyūṭī's approach, these examples illustrate cases in which al-Suyūṭī was not arbitrarily abridging his predecessors, but thought carefully about what his audience practically needed to know, even at the cost of creating an impression of consensus on matters upon which there were on-going debates among scholars.

And yet, at many other moments, the reasoning behind many of the exclusions is not entirely clear. In an unusually extended digression on the history of decorating the Kaʿba with a *kiswa*, al-Suyūṭī borrows heavily from Ibn Ḥajar's *Fatḥ al-bārī* to chronicle the practice since it was first recorded. Strangely, while Ibn Ḥajar tracked the practice up to his present era—the ninth/fifteenth century—al-Suyūṭī quotes a source that halts the narrative a century earlier.[36] Likewise, in a report about "a little stick-legged Ethiopian" who will demolish the Kaʿba at the end of time, al-Suyūṭī indicates to his readers that the *ḥadīth* reported by Aḥmad b. Ḥanbal contained the additional phrase that "no one will live long after that."[37] But this is only a part of what predecessors, such as Ibn Ḥajar, informed their readers that Aḥmad b. Ḥanbal added: "no one will live long after that, and they will be the ones who loot its treasure."[38] In this case, the omission appears arbitrary. Even in the name of maintaining brevity, the erasure only saved a line or a few lines of space on a folio's page.

Al-Suyūṭī sometimes presented a truncated version of a legal debate that would give a far different impression of the field than if one had read al-Suyūṭī's predecessors unmediated. Consider, for example, al-Suyūṭī's comments on the *ḥadīth* of the treaty of Ḥudaybiyya in which the phrasing, taken literally, suggested that Muḥammad wrote the treaty himself by hand. Al-Suyūṭī, characterizing the controversy, wrote, "a group takes this literally, and they allege that [Muḥammad] wrote by hand. Others are of the opinion that he ordered someone to write it."[39] Al-Suyūṭī's characterization opened the door to contemporary debate where none really existed. After all, only a handful of scholars have ever argued the *ḥadīth* should be taken literally. Among them was Abū l-Walīd al-Bājī (d. 474/1081), a Mālikī jurist who preceded al-Suyūṭī by five centuries, and who was taken to task locally and transregionally for appearing to call

35 Cp. al-Suyūṭī, *Tawshīḥ* i 134; and Ibn Ḥajar, *Fatḥ* i, 19–22.

36 Cp. al-Suyūṭī, *Tawshīḥ* iii, 1266; and Ibn Ḥajar, *Fatḥ* iii, 458–60 (*Kitāb al-Ḥajj: bāb kiswat al-Kaʿba*).

37 Al-Suyūṭī, *Tawshīḥ* iii, 1267.

38 Ibn Ḥajar, *Fatḥ* iii, 461 (*Kitāb al-Ḥajj: bāb hadm al-Kaʿba*).

39 Al-Suyūṭī, *Tawshīḥ* vi, 2638.

into question Muḥammad's status as an "unlettered Prophet" (*nabī ummī*).[40] Unlike Ibn Ḥajar, al-Suyūṭī's *Tawshīḥ* gives us no sense of the contemporary proportions or stakes of the debate, and offers no opinion of his own to guide the reader on the more favorable or favored interpretation.[41] Again, it is not clear what exegetical principle is guiding these omissions.

One way of gaining insight into the process by which al-Suyūṭī composed the *Tawshīḥ* is to examine the frequency and diversity of al-Suyūṭī's citations from other sources over the course of the work. While readers find a great number and variety of sources cited in the opening book on "How revelation began," by the middle of the "Book of Faith" (*Kitāb al-Īmān*) and even more so in the "Book of Knowledge" (*Kitāb al-ʿIlm*), the diversity and frequency of sources cited begins to narrow substantially. About a third of the way through his commentary, in the "Book of Festivals" (*Kitāb al-ʿĪdīn*), al-Suyūṭī's citations are spartan by comparison, providing only clarifications on pronunciation and pointing the reader to variant transmissions of the *ḥadīth*.[42] Although it could be a coincidence that the *ḥadīth*s that al-Suyūṭī believed required greater elaboration happened to be near the beginning of the work, it could also be a deliberate technique that al-Suyūṭī employed to demonstrate his authority as a repository of knowledge at the beginning of the work, allowing him to rest on his laurels in the body of the work. Notable exceptions to this trend of narrowing the diversity and frequency of his citations are his commentaries on popular *ḥadīth*s such as the *ḥadīth* of Jibrīl, and the closing *ḥadīth* on glorifying God (*tasbīḥ*).[43] These two *ḥadīth*s have traditionally attracted dense layers of commentary, and this is a small indication that al-Suyūṭī was acutely aware of the interests of his audience and was careful to include greater layers of commentary on more well-known *ḥadīth*s.

Sometimes al-Suyūṭī suggests readers consult his own works for further reading. In his relatively extended commentary on the *ḥadīth* concerning "the seven who will be shaded on the day when there is no shade but his shade," he not only mentions a volume he wrote on this subject, but also suggests that the reader refer to his discussion on the same *ḥadīth* in his commentary on the *Muwaṭṭaʾ*.[44] At another point, he encourages readers to consult his commentary on *Ṣaḥīḥ Muslim*, even though he drafted his commentary on *Ṣaḥīḥ*

40 Al-Bājī, *Taḥqīq* 115–8; Fierro, Local 82.
41 Ibn Ḥajar, *Fatḥ* vii, 504 (*Kitāb al-Maghāzī: bāb ʿumrat al-qaḍāʾ*).
42 Al-Suyūṭī, *Tawshīḥ* iii, 879–902. For a similar trend, see *Kitāb al-Jazāʾ al-ṣayyid* in ibid. iv, 1373–97.
43 Ibid. i, 217–21 and ix, 4361–3.
44 Ibid. ii, 689; Anas and al-Suyūṭī, *Muwaṭṭaʾ* ii, 234–6.

al-Bukhārī prior to his commentary on *Ṣaḥīḥ Muslim*.[45] This important clue tells us that al-Suyūṭī must have gone back and revised his work later, adding notes such as this one. This self-citation goes both ways. When al-Suyūṭī encounters the *ḥadīth* of Jibrīl for a second time in his commentary on *Ṣaḥīḥ Muslim*, rather than repeat himself, he instructs readers to consult his *Tawshīḥ* for more information.[46] In fact, al-Suyūṭī encourages readers to consult the *Tawshīḥ* five times in the first two volumes of his commentary on *Ṣaḥīḥ Muslim*, suggesting that this earlier work was still very much on his mind as he began his commentary on *Ṣaḥīḥ Muslim*. Before one quickly labels this practice as yet another example of al-Suyūṭī's shameless self-promotion[47]—and it may very well be that—in the context of al-Suyūṭī's principle of "usefulness without toil" it is also a subtle acknowledgement that some readers might seek to toil in greater layers of commentary than al-Suyūṭī believed was practically necessary.

3 Balancing Concision and Usefulness: The Case of *taʿzīr* in the *Tawshīḥ*

What did al-Suyūṭī do when faced with a controversial *ḥadīth*, that most of his predecessors believed required more elaborate commentary to be of practical use? In other words, when the toil of excess was useful, how did al-Suyūṭī balance the need for practical value against the goal of exegetical concision? To shed light on this question, I will examine one such controversial *ḥadīth* from al-Bukhārī's heading on the limits of discretionary punishment, or *taʿzīr*:

> ʿAmr b. ʿAlī narrated to us, stating: Fuḍayl b. Sulaymān narrated to us, stating: Muslim b. Abī Maryam narrated to us, stating: it was narrated to me that ʿAbd al-Raḥmān b. Jābir, on the authority of someone who heard the Prophet say:
>
> > There is no punishment (*lā ʿuqūba*) in excess of ten strokes (*ḍarabāt*) except in the case of [violating] a boundary (*ḥadd*) among the boundaries (*ḥudūd*) of God.[48]

45 Al-Suyūṭī, *Tawshīḥ* iv, 1486.

46 Al-Suyūṭī, *Dībāj* i, 6.

47 Ignaz Goldziher once described him as "the talented scholar offended in his vanity who is moved to an extravagant assertion of his own worth." See M. Barry and J.O. Hunwick, Ignaz Goldziher 12.

48 Al-Suyūṭī, *Tawshīḥ* ix, 4016.

Before hearing al-Suyūṭī's opinion on this *ḥadīth*, let us consult, as al-Suyūṭī would have done, the earliest commentary on this section of the *Ṣaḥīḥ*: Ibn Baṭṭāl's, which was composed in eleventh-century Andalusia. When we do, we find this *ḥadīth*'s reliability was called into question for containing an unknown transmitter ("someone who heard the Prophet say…").[49] This allowed Mālikī judges to discard the *ḥadīth* in favor of an opinion attributed to Ibn Mālik that gave judges the fullest discretion possible, even the power to recommend the death penalty.[50] Likewise, Ḥanafīs and Shāfiʿīs ignored the *ḥadīth* but restricted *taʿzīr* to forty and twenty lashes respectively, based on the least amount of lashes stipulated for a free person (forty) or a slave (twenty) who transgressed a *ḥadd* such as drinking wine.[51] Only Aḥmad b. Ḥanbal (d. 241/855) and his colleagues Isḥāq b. Rāhawayh (d. 238/853)[52] and al-Layth b. Saʿd (d. 175/791) read the *ḥadīth* as an unambiguous command not to exceed ten lashes except in case of a *ḥadd*.[53]

If we then move across time, as al-Suyūṭī would have done as well, and consult a more recent commentary, Ibn Ḥajar's *Fatḥ al-bārī*, we find that *Ṣaḥīḥ al-Bukhārī*'s stature in the Mamlūk period left representatives of multiple schools unable to deny, in the final analysis, the *ḥadīth*'s reliability. Mamlūk era jurists thus searched for new ways to justify discretionary punishment broader than ten lashes. Ibn Ḥajar tells us that Ibn Taymiyya (d. 728/1328) and Ibn Qayyim al-Jawziyya (d. 751/1350) argued that judges had mistakenly projected backwards their technical meaning for the term "*ḥadd*" on this *ḥadīth*, which, during the lifetime of the Prophet, they claimed, meant any disobedience (*maʿṣiya*) regarding the law, great or small.[54] On this originalist reading, the ten lashes *ḥadīth* might only apply to a father disciplining his child, otherwise the sentence was up to the judge's full discretion. In this way, even a judge who saw *taʿzīr* as being restricted by the "ten lashes" tradition could, like the Mālikīs, sentence the offender in excess of ten lashes, as long as the act fell broadly in the category of *maʿṣiya*.

49 Ibn Baṭṭāl, *Sharḥ* viii, 485.

50 Ibid.

51 Ibid.

52 In addition to being one of Aḥmad b. Ḥanbal's students, Ibn Rāhawayh was one of al-Bukhārī's teachers.

53 Ibn Baṭṭāl, *Sharḥ* viii, 485.

54 Ibn Ḥajar, *Fatḥ* xii, 178 (*Kitāb al-Ḥudūd: bāb kam al-taʿzīr wa-l-adab*). See also a discussion of *taʿzīr* in a *ḥadīth* commentary composed for an audience of Ḥanbalī jurists in training in eigth/fourteenth-century Damascus: Ibn Rajab, *Jāmiʿ* 62.

Ibn Ḥajar refuted this opinion by arguing that the *ḥadīth*'s meaning rests on an implied understanding that it is possible to distinguish between different kinds of disobedience, greater and lesser.[55] The greater, for Ibn Ḥajar, were the exceptions that can exceed ten as stipulated in the Quran. If the definition of *ḥadd* were extended to include all manner of offenses against God, both greater and lesser, it would make the exception the rule.

As several studies in Mamlūk society point out, *taʿzīr* was an important implement of the sultan's apparatus, especially the *muḥtasib*, a legal official entrusted with wide-ranging powers, including the supervision of moral behavior in the marketplace.[56] Generations of Mamlūk era Shāfiʿī chief justices thus called for limits to *taʿzīr* at the risk of their own obsolescence. After all, the Mamlūk political elite were reported to have "frequently referred cases requiring (*taʿzīr*) to Mālikī" judges, who had greater leeway.[57]

Much, then, was at stake in the interpretation of this *ḥadīth*. In light of this, how did al-Suyūṭī thread the needle within the constraints of his historical context and in light of his exegetical ideal to achieve "usefulness without toil"? Al-Suyūṭī comments in the *Tawshīḥ*:

> Most people [of knowledge are of the opinion that] it is permissible to go beyond [ten strokes]. They respond [to critics] that [say] this [*ḥadīth*] was abrogated by the consensus of the companions.
>
> In my opinion, [the *ḥadīth*] was not abrogated. However, the *ḥadīth* conveys a preference, not a requirement.[58]

First, what has al-Suyūṭī excluded from the commentary tradition? Despite his promise in his introduction, al-Suyūṭī does not make any mention of early debates over the unknown transmitter. This may be tied to al-Suyūṭī's and his audiences' expectations that al-Bukhārī's standards in *ḥadīth* criticism simply guaranteed the authenticity of the *ḥadīth*. Nor does al-Suyūṭī mention either the debates among the classical legal authorities over the acceptable number of lashes nor the more recent debate provoked by Ibn Taymiyya that challenged the juristic discourse, and Ibn Ḥajar's reasoned response to it. This indicates that, at the very least, defending his predecessor or the Shāfiʿī school was

55 Ibn Ḥajar, *Fatḥ* xii, 178 (*Kitāb al-Ḥudūd: bāb kam al-taʿzīr wa-l-adab*).

56 Stilt, *Islamic law* 11–2, 200. A comprehensive study of *taʿzīr* in the larger context of punishment in Islamic thought and practice during the Seljuq dynasty (5th/11th–7th/13th centuries) has been undertaken by Lange, *Justice* 215–43.

57 Rapoport, Legal diversity 221.

58 Al-Suyūṭī, *Tawshīḥ* ix, 4017.

not of primary concern to al-Suyūṭī or his imagined readership, which he may have hoped would be broader than his legal school affiliation. He also left out the only thing al-Zarkashī left in—the correct pronunciation of the Arabic for "lashes."[59]

But what did al-Suyūṭī add to the tradition? While he affirms the authority of the *ḥadīth*, he characterizes the limit of ten lashes as a preference rather than a requirement, which would permit judges, on occasion, to exercise their full discretion.[60] In this way, he offers a new solution, one that allows his multiple audiences to have their cake and eat it too. And yet, al-Suyūṭī remains silent about the basis for which he distinguishes preference from requirement. He offers no grammatical justification, no prooftexts, no traditional opinions to support his own. In other words, this case lays bare a paradox at the heart of al-Suyūṭī's approach: he makes the *ḥadīth* useful to the largest audience while ironically omitting more than might be necessary to justify that use.

Lastly, let us compare this discussion with al-Suyūṭī's commentary on *Ṣaḥīḥ Muslim* that also contains this *ḥadīth*. In this work, we find al-Suyūṭī offer the following comment on the "ten lashes" *ḥadīth*:

> [Aḥmad b. Ḥanbal] and some of our contemporaries take this *ḥadīth* at face value. They say, going beyond ten strokes is not permitted. And those who permit it respond: "The *ḥadīth* is abrogated." The interpretation of some of the Mālikīs is that the *ḥadīth* was specific to its time, because [ten strokes] sufficed the wrongdoers among them.[61]

Here al-Suyūṭī includes additional information on what groups are at the extremes: the Ḥanbalīs were on one side, and the Mālikīs were on the other. But rather than hearing al-Suyūṭī's own opinion at the end, we hear the justification he claimed the Mālikīs used to bolster their position: this *ḥadīth*, he claimed they argued, was specific to an earlier time when ten lashes sufficed. By ending with this Mālikī justification, perhaps al-Suyūṭī was subtly deferring to the Mālikīs to whom the political élite also deferred on this matter. Alternatively, the absence of al-Suyūṭī's opinion in this work could mark a change in al-Suyūṭī's approach. He believed it was now up to the audience, not the commentator, to come up with their own verdict after hearing the opinions of the two extremes.

59 Al-Zarkashī, *Tanqīḥ* iii, 1213.

60 Al-Suyūṭī, *Tawshīḥ* ix, 4017.

61 Al-Suyūṭī, *Dībāj* iv, 308.

In his commentaries on later collections like Abū Dā'ūd and Ibn Māja, al-Suyūṭī skips over this *ḥadīth* entirely. Even if we take these later commentaries to be unfinished drafts, as al-Suyūṭī once described them, it is curious that he would have skipped over this *ḥadīth*, when he had already formulated opinions on it in two of his previous works. His treatment of *ta'zīr*, then, suggests that, at the least, working within the same generic constraints of concision, he never fully settled the question of how much commentary was too much, and how little was too little.

4 Conclusion: Al-Suyūṭī and the Case for Rethinking Knowledge as a Social Practice

In our own scholarly tradition, we often measure ourselves by our claims to interpretive originality and comprehensiveness. We also project those measures into the past, seeking out that which was most original and comprehensive in the work of scholarly traditions of the Middle Ages. To be sure, the appreciation of an original and comprehensive scholarly contribution is one defining feature that we share with al-Suyūṭī's scholarly tradition. After all, in al-Suyūṭī's own estimation of his *oeuvre*, he placed at the top those works that "nothing comparable has been composed in the world, as far as I know," and that his contemporaries could not "produce its like due to what that would require of breadth of vision, abundance of information, effort, and diligence."[62] But even by his own estimation, most of his scholarly output was not included in this category. If not by originality or encyclopedic excess, then, how were the successes of these works measured? Al-Suyūṭī's "usefulness without toil," I have argued, was one such measure. But useful for whom? And did he succeed?

Suyūṭī was neither enamored of the intellectual élites of his day, nor those "common people, rabble, women, and old men" who claimed intellectual or religious authority.[63] Al-Suyūṭī's audience, then, was a group of educated readers—many of whom lived abroad—who were neither aspiring experts nor lay people. This was an audience who had little time to pore over the encyclopedic *ḥadīth* commentaries of the age, but still sought a guide to clarify the canonical *ḥadīth* collections' conspicuous difficulties. For this market of

62 Saleh, al-Suyūṭī 86; al-Suyūṭī, *Taḥadduth* 105. In 1871, Goldziher once wrote that "al-Suyūṭī constantly attaches great importance to blazing new trails in his works, trails never trodden by others." See Barry and Hunwick, Ignaz Goldziher 94.

63 Sartain, *Biography* 31.

readers, practicality and ease of use rather than originality and comprehensiveness was most valued.

By modeling his work on al-Zarkashī's *Tanqīḥ*, al-Suyūṭī hoped that those who consulted the *Tawshīḥ* and his serial commentaries on other key *ḥadīth* collections would come away knowing, among other things, how to pronounce and identify obscure words and names, important variants contained in other collections, and be aware of any major scholarly controversies. In some cases, al-Suyūṭī pared down the commentary tradition he inherited strategically, keeping denser commentary on more popular *ḥadīth*, and excising commentary that served esoteric debates. In other cases, his choices to abridge or omit appeared arbitrary. A close examination of the case of al-Suyūṭī's commentary on *taʿzīr* shows the degree to which al-Suyūṭī himself toiled to strike the right balance between concision and elaboration as he came face to face with a paradox inherent in the task of composing a commentary that was both pragmatic and brief: excess can obscure a useful point, but some points require elaborate explanations to be useful.

To take this insight a step further, I believe that al-Suyūṭī's work helps us begin to rethink knowledge as a *social practice* in the Mamlūk era. Michael Chamberlain was among the first to bring the concept of a "social practice" and "symbolic capital" into common parlance among scholars of Mamlūk history over the past two decades.[64] Informed by Max Weber and Pierre Bourdieu, Chamberlain persuasively documented how representatives of the civilian elite "acquired and used the rare symbolic capital by which they claimed power, resources, and social honor and passed them on within lineages" in his well known monograph on Mamlūk-era Damascus.[65] To frame al-Suyūṭī's contribution to *ḥadīth* commentary as a "social practice" is to suggest we expand our definition of this concept to include exegetical goods and resources, which are defined by and defining of the Islamic intellectual tradition. This expanded usage is in line with the thinking of anthropologist and theorist Talal Asad and moral philosopher Alasdair MacIntyre. MacIntyre, in a quote popularized by Asad, defined a social practice, in part, as a "living tradition ... an historically extended, socially embodied argument, and an argument precisely in part about the goods which constitute that tradition [...]."[66] This definition of a social practice consists of what theorist Alasdair MacIntyre has termed goods

64 Chamberlain, *Knowledge* 22 and *passim*. For a recent example of a scholar influenced by Chamberlain's work, see Sayeed, *Women* 114 fnn. 18, 139 and *passim*.

65 See Chamberlain, *Knowledge* 22.

66 Asad, Idea 14–5; MacIntyre, *After Virtue* 222.

"external" to a social practice—such as material rewards and institutional rewards such as prestige—as well as goods "internal" to it, such as a novel solution to a long-standing interpretive problem.[67]

Since the *ḥadīth* commentary tradition is oriented towards goods that can only be defined by the tradition itself, while also being embedded in larger institutions of power, it would qualify as a "social practice" in MacIntyre's technical sense. Hence, in framing *ḥadīth* commentary as a social practice, it is important for historians of Mamlūk intellectual life to consider the competition for social goods *and* the competition for exegetical goods. This Asadian/MacIntyrean conception of a social practice expands Bourdieu's more limited conception, which analyzed competition for material and symbolic goods, but did not fully consider those goods on offer within an interpretive tradition.[68]

While I have endeavored elsewhere to understand the sense of the aesthetic of excess that was paradigmatic of Mamlūk-era *ḥadīth* commentaries on *Ṣaḥīḥ al-Bukhārī*, al-Suyūṭī's extraordinary concision calls our attention to an alternate trend. In a period of virtuosic comprehensiveness, al-Suyūṭī strived to make a user-friendly *ḥadīth* commentary, one that struck a balance between inclusion and exclusion, between making a point and leaving the reader without one. In doing so, scholars such as al-Suyūṭī were not only competing for social capital, prestige, and commercial success in the book market—although they were indeed doing that—they were simultaneously committed to realizing certain exegetical goods defining of and defined by their tradition. In the case of al-Suyūṭī's commentary on *Ṣaḥīḥ al-Bukhārī*, "usefulness without toil" was the exegetical good he sought and sometimes struggled to achieve.

Bibliography

Primary Sources

Anas b. Mālik and Jalāl al-Dīn al-Suyūṭī, *Muwaṭṭaʾ al-imām Mālik wa-sharḥuhu Tanwīr al-ḥawālik*, 2 vols., Egypt [Cairo] 1951.

al-ʿAydarūs, *Taʾrīkh al-nūr al-sāfir ʿan akhbār al-qarn al-ʿāshir*, Beirut 2001.

al-Bājī, *al-Muntaqā: sharḥ Muwaṭṭaʾ Mālik*, 9 vols., Beirut 1999.

al-Bājī, *Taḥqīq al-madhhab*, ed. A.ʿA.R. Ibn ʿAqīl, Riyadh 1983.

67 Ibid. 175–6.

68 Bourdieu, *Outline*, 171–183. I elaborate on the theoretical underpinnings of this argument further in the introduction to my forthcoming monograph on *ḥadīth* commentary and the politics of interpretation.

al-Bukhārī, *Ṣaḥīḥ al-Bukhārī*, Princeton University Library, Garrett Collection 341 Bq (ca. 14th century).

al-Bulqīnī, *Kitāb Tarājim al-Bukhārī al-musammā Munāsabāt abwāb Ṣaḥīḥ al-Bukhārī li-baʿḍihā baʿḍan*, ed. A. b. F. Sallūm, Riyadh 2010.

al-Damāmīnī, *Maṣābīḥ al-Jāmiʿ*, ed. N.D. Ṭālib, 10 vols., Qatar 2009.

al-Damāmīnī, *Taʿaqqubāt al-ʿallāma Badr al-Dīn al-Damāmīnī fī kitābihi Maṣābīḥ al-Jāmiʿ al-ṣaḥīḥ ʿalā l-imām Badr al-Dīn al-Zarkashī fī kitābihi l-Tanqīḥ li-alfāẓ al-Jāmiʿ al-ṣaḥīḥ fī l-qaḍāyā al-naḥwiyya wa-l-ṣarfiyya wa-l-lughawiyya*, ed. ʿA. b. S. al-Ḥakamī, Medina 1995.

Dihlawī, *The garden of the* hadith *scholars*: Bustān al-muḥaddithīn, trans. M.A. Nadwī and A.A. Bewley, London 2007.

Ibn Baṭṭāl, *Sharḥ Saḥīḥ al-Bukhārī*, 11 vols., Riyadh 2003.

Ibn Ḥajar al-ʿAsqalānī, *Fatḥ al-bārī*, ed. ʿA.ʿA. Ibn Bāz, 13 vols., Beirut 1970.

Ibn Ḥajar al-ʿAsqalānī, *Hady al-sārī*, ed. ʿA.Q. Sh. al-Ḥamad, Riyadh 2000.

Ibn Ḥajar al-ʿAsqalānī, *Ḥawāshī Tanqīḥ al-Zarkashī ʿalā l-Bukhārī*, Beirut 2008.

Ibn al-Munayyir, *al-Mutawārī ʿalā abwāb al-Bukhārī*, Beirut 1990.

Ibn Rajab, *Jāmiʿ al-ʿulūm wa-l-ḥikam: Sharḥ khamsīn ḥadīthan min jawāmiʿ al-kalim*, Damascus 2008.

Ibn Rushayd, *Tarjumān al-tarājim ʿalā abwāb Ṣaḥīḥ al-Bukhārī*, Beirut 2008.

al-Nasāʾī, al-Suyūṭī, and al-Sindī, *Sunan al-Nasāʾī: bi-Sharḥ al-Suyūṭī wa-l-Sindī*, Cairo 1999.

al-Nawawī, *Ṣaḥīḥ Muslim bi-sharḥ al-Nawawī*, 18 vols., Cairo 1969.

al-Qasṭallānī, *Irshād al-sārī*, 10 vols., Bulaq 1905.

al-Safīri, *ʿIddat aḥādīth Ṣaḥīḥ al-Bukhārī*, Mingana IA 938, Cadburry Research Center at Birmingham University Library (18th century).

al-Suyūṭī, *al-Taḥadduth bi-niʿmat Allāh*, in E.M. Sartain (ed.), *Jalāl al-dīn al-Suyūṭī.* ii: *al-Taḥadduth bi-niʿmat Allāh* (University of Cambridge Oriental Publications 24), Cambridge 1975.

al-Suyūṭī, *al-Dībāj ʿalā Ṣaḥīḥ Muslim b. Ḥajjāj*, ed. A.I. al-Ḥawaynī l-Atharī, 6 vols., al-Khabar 1991.

al-Suyūṭī, *Ḥusn al-muḥāḍara fī taʾrikh Miṣr wa-l-Qāhira*, ed. M.A. al-F. Ibrāhīm, 2 vols., Cairo 1967–8.

al-Suyūṭī, *al-Tawshīḥ sharḥ al-Jāmiʿ al-ṣaḥīḥ: Sharḥ Ṣaḥīḥ al-Bukhārī*, ed. R.J. Riḍwān, 9 vols., Riyadh 1998.

al-Suyūṭī and Aḥmad b. Ḥanbal, *ʿUqūd al-zabarjad fī iʿrāb al-ḥadīth al-nabawī*, ed. S. Quḍāh, Beirut 1994.

al-Zarkashī, *al-Tanqīḥ li-alfāẓ al-Jāmiʿ al-Ṣaḥīḥ*, ed. Y. b. M.ʿA. al-Ḥakamī, 3 vols., Riyadh 2003.

Secondary Sources

Asad, T., The idea of an anthropology of Islam, in *Occasional Papers*, Washington DC 1986.

Barry M., Hunwick, J.O., Ignaz Goldziher on al-Suyūṭī, in *MW* 68 (1978), 79–99.

Blecher, J., Ḥadith commentary in the presence of students, patrons, and rivals: Ibn Ḥajar and *Ṣaḥīḥ al-Bukhārī* in Mamlūk Cairo, in *Oriens* 41 (2013), 261–87.

Bourdieu, P., *Outline of a theory of practice,* trans. R. Nice, (Cambridge Studies in Social and Cultural Anthropology 16), Cambridge 1977 [*Esquisse d'une théorie de la pratique*, Geneva 1972].

Brown, J.A.C., *Hadith*, Oxford 2009.

Calder, N., *Islamic jurisprudence in the classical era*, Cambridge 2010.

Chamberlain, M., *Knowledge and social practice in medieval Damascus 1190–1350*, Cambridge 1994.

Davidson, G., Carrying on the tradition: An intellectual and social history of post-canonical hadith transmission, PhD diss., University of Chicago 2014.

Fadel, M., Ibn Ḥajar's *Hady al-Sārī*: A medieval interpretation of the structure of al-Bukhārī's *al-Jāmiʿ al-Ṣaḥīḥ*: Introduction and translation, in *JNES* 54 (1995), 161–95.

Fierro, M., Local and global in *ḥadīth* Literature: The case of al-Andalus, in C.H.M. Versteegh, N. Boekhoff-van der Voort, J. Wagemakers (eds.), *The transmission and dynamics of the textual sources of Islam: Essays in honour of Harald Motzki*, Leiden 2011, 63–90.

Ḥasanī, M.ʿI.ʿA., *Itḥāf al-qārī bi-maʿrifat juhūd wa-aʿmāl al-ʿulamāʾ ʿalā Ṣaḥīḥ al-Bukhārī*, Damascus 1987.

Ishaq, M., *India's contribution to the study of* hadith *literature*, Dacca 1955.

Jaques, R.K., *Ibn Hajar*, New Delhi 2009.

Lange, C., *Justice, punishement and the medieval Muslim imagination*, Cambridge 2008.

MacIntyre, A., *After virtue: A study in moral theory*, Notre Dame, Indiana 1983, [3]2007.

Muhanna, E., Why was the fourteenth century a century of Arabic encyclopaedism?, in J. König and G. Woolf (eds.), *Encyclopaedism from Antiquity to the Renaissance*, Cambridge 2013.

Rapoport, Y., Legal diversity in the age of *Taqlīd*: The four chief *qāḍīs* under the Mamlūks, in *Islamic Law and Society* 10 (2003), 210–28.

Rippin, A., Al-Zarkashī and al-Suyutī [*sic*] on the function of the "occasion of revelation" material, in *IC* 59 (1985), 243–58.

Saleh, M.J., Al-Suyūṭī and his works: Their place in Islamic scholarship from Mamlūk times to the present, in *MSR* 5 (2001), 73–89.

Sartain, E.M., *Jalāl al-Dīn al-Suyūṭī.* i: *Biography and Background,* (University of Cambridge Oriental Publications 23), Cambridge 1975.

Sayeed, A., *Women and the transmission of religious knowledge in Islam,* Cambridge 2013.

Stilt, K., *Islamic law in action: Authority, discretion, and everyday experiences in Mamlūk Egypt,* Oxford 2012.

CHAPTER 10

History, Comparativism, and Morphology: Al-Suyūṭī and Modern Historical Linguistics

Francesco Grande

1 Introduction

This paper investigates several aspects of al-Suyūṭī's linguistic thought and their relationship with modern historical linguistics with a particular regard to morphology. Section 1 illustrates the methodological underpinnings of modern historical linguistics. Section 2 explores a potential parallelism between these and the methods of which al-Suyūṭī avails himself in his description of Arabic. Particular attention is paid to al-Suyūṭī's treatise *al-Muzhir fī ʿulūm al-lugha wa-anwāʿihā* and to the three conceptual elements of history, comparativism and morphology. Finally, section 3 provides the main conclusions, clarifying the extent to which al-Suyūṭī's linguistic thought and modern historical linguistics converge.

2 The Emergence of Modern Historical Linguistics: A Review and Reconsideration

The emergence of modern historical linguistics is traditionally dated back to the nineteenth century when German scholars such as Franz Bopp (1791–1867) and August Schleicher (1821–1868) founded this scientific discipline and established the so-called "comparative method". This was used in the description of mainly—though not exclusively—Indo-European languages.[1]

As terms such as "historical" and "comparative" indicate, the epistemological discourse on modern historical linguistics (MHL henceforth) generally tends to identify its methodological bases by comparing languages within a given language-family. In addition, it includes the study of the history of these languages

1 In a famous work that was published in its definitive form posthumously in 1871, Schleicher actually discussed not only the Indo-European cladistic model (*Stammbaumtheorie*) but also the structure of non-Indo-European languages (cp. Schleicher, *Compendium* 1–9). We will return later on this point.

 | DOI 10.1163/9789004334526_012

and the regularity of phonetic rules that, from this perspective, are responsible for the change from one given language stage to another.[2] Furthermore, the epistemological discourse on MHL also describes history as a methodology underpinning this science, which is deeply rooted in a Darwinian framework: the history of a (given) language(s) is driven by evolution.[3] Continuing in this strain, we should also recognize that the beginnings of MHL, thus characterized, are largely indebted to contemporary sciences such as biology, anatomy, and chemistry—in short, the so-called natural sciences.[4]

It is hardly questionable that it is precisely traceable or measurable methods such as historical investigation and comparativism that have made MHL a scientific discipline. However, it is also true that the epistemological discourse on the emergence of such a science often associates the above methodological underpinnings with some stereotypes. According to textual research carried out in the 1960s, the most notable of these is Schleicher's interpretation of the historical change undergone by (a given) language(s) in terms of Darwin's evolutionism, which in bare bones proceeds from simple to complex. In fact, ascribing to Schleicher such an interpretation is clearly at odds with his well-known view that Greek, Latin and Sanskrit, for instance, are the result of the corruption and decay (*Verfall*) of their perfect, common Indo-European ancestor. This view, which interprets language change as a complex-to-simple process, owes more to the theory of *dégénération* formulated by the French Illuminist Buffon (1707–1788) than to Darwin's evolutionism.[5]

Another interesting stereotype concerning the rise of MHL revolves around the underlying methodology labeled as comparativism. While the claim is often found in the literature that this method brings into comparison the linguistic codes traditionally known as languages (in order to reconstruct a common ancestor),[6] closer scrutiny of the foundation works of this discipline reveals that, in fact, the latter was also concerned with linguistic codes

2 See e.g. Bloomfield, *Language* 3–20, and Lehmann, *Linguistics* 23–46.

3 See e.g. Lehmann, *Linguistics* 31: "In his *Compendium* (1871) Schleicher attempted to apply the procedures of the natural sciences. In this effort he was strongly influenced by the ideas on evolution." Cp. also the references mentioned in Maher, Tradition of Darwinism 9.

4 See e.g. Lehmann, *Linguistics* 27, and the previous fn. Cp. also Salmon, Morphology 16–7.

5 Maher, Tradition of Darwinism 5–7. This study also shows that the Darwinian character of early MHL is a commonplace that arguably arose, among other things, as a consequence of Schleicher's interest for Darwinism, to which he devoted, in effect, the study *Die Darwinsche Theorie und die Sprachwissenschaft.*

6 See e.g. Lehmann, *Linguistics* 8: "after Jones's statement, however, scholars in Europe began systematic comparison of older forms of English and German with Latin, Greek, Sanskrit and other languages."

smaller or greater than languages, the so-called dialects and language-families. Thus, between 1868 and 1872, Schleicher's pupils Johannes Schmidt and Hugo Schuchardt developed a diffusionist theory of linguistic change (*Wellentheorie*) in opposition to their teacher's *Stammbaumtheorie* (published in its definitive form in 1871) also based on the comparison of Romance dialects. In a similar vein, Max Müller (1823–1900), a contemporary of Schleicher that subscribed in full to his doctrine,[7] stressed the point that (Old) German dialects, as are Gothic and Old High German, are the original context that gave rise to the phenomenon of German *Lautverschiebung* (consonantal shift) first observed by Rask and the Grimm brothers.[8] Finally, Schleicher himself drew a typological comparison among Indo-European and other language-families.[9]

A further stereotype associated with MHL revolves around the widespread belief among scholars that, as alluded to above, the regularity of phonetic rules was a methodological basis of this science, as it emerged in the nineteenth century. Yet, after recognizing the "physical" and, that is, the precise nature of phonetic rules in the first scientific treatment of the genetic relationship among Indo-European languages, Franz Bopp did not include them among his interpretive tools.[10] Rather, he considered the comparison of linguistic forms as a merely reliable tool, and morphology—as opposed to phonetics or phonology—as the relevant level of linguistic analysis. In this respect, Bopp was heavily influenced by the science of biology in his time, where the very term "morphology" (*Morphologie, morphologie*) denoted the study of the exterior forms of living beings. This was especially relevant in the French and German scientific milieu as opposed to the German erudite literary milieu which, instead, interpreted the biological term "morphology" in the dynamic sense of "study of transformations," after Goethe's botanic theory.[11]

Such a "static" conception of biological or linguistic morphology is in all likelihood rooted in Aristotle's "visual" definition of form as an "appearance (or

7 Leroy, *Trends* 20–4.

8 Müller, *Stratification* 29–30. In consequence of this focus on the dialectal factors involved in German *Lautverschiebung*, Müller preferred an explanation of this phenomenon in terms of dialectal variation ("développement dialectal") over a more influential explanation in terms of phonetic rules. Such a "dialectal" analysis of *Lautverschiebung* also leads to a better knowledge of the role of phonetic rules within MHL, as will be clarified shortly.

9 Campbell, *Linguistics* 188, and fn. 1 above.

10 Maher, Tradition of Darwinism 7; Lehmann, *Linguistics* 158. Likewise, Müller explained German *Lautverschiebung* in terms of dialectal variation rather than of phonetic rules: cp. fn. 8 above and the end of sect. 2.3, where his statements in this connection are quoted in full.

11 Salmon, Morphology 16–7.

figure) of the idea (τὴν δὲ μορφὴν, τὸ σχῆμα τῆς ἰδέας)."[12] This amounts to saying that in nineteenth-century Europe, scholars viewed a biological or linguistic form as an entity that was discrete and salient enough to be perceived by sight and, by extension, hearing.[13] The Aristotelian definition of form aside, nineteenth-century linguistic morphology shared the method of organizing knowledge with its biologic counterpart. In presenting data or rather forms, both biological and linguistic morphology did not merely rely on a simple relation such as inclusion, examples of which being general classes based on a shared feature, and preferred instead to combine it with other kinds of relations, such as position. Technically speaking, the former organizational criterion can be defined as a classification, and the latter as a system.[14] To understand this distinction, we may contrast a geographical classification, which informs us that cities such as Milan and Venice are both located within the Italian country, thereby subsuming them under the common heading of "Italy" (inclusion), with a geographical map, which also tells us that Milan is west of Venice (inclusion plus position).

Moving to an example closer to linguistic morphology, Schleicher interprets Greek, Latin, and Sankrit as belonging to one and the same class, Indo-European, since, in addition to sharing a set of lexical forms (inclusion), they also manifest common semantic-syntactic behavior (*Bedeutung und Beziehung*) in these forms.[15] The Greek, Latin and Sankrit forms *hippos, equus*, and *aśvaḥ*, for instance, express the meanings of "masculine, singular, subject" by combining them into a single suffix *os/us/aḥ*, according to the semantic-syntactic behavior traditionally known as "inflection," which therefore qualifies as a relation that differs from inclusion. This characterizes Schleicher's description of Indo-European morphology as a system rather than a classification. Similarly, once we realize that phonetic rules are traditionally construed as logical mathematical operations that dynamically process an input into an output (e.g. palatalization: *s* → *š*), they can be easily restated in more static terms—as is generally the case for operations—as relations that tie together a

12 Eco, *Struttura* 257, and references therein.

13 It appears that what makes a biological or linguistic entity discrete and salient to perception is its frequent occurrence or repetition. Such an issue, however, falls beyond the scope of this paper and will not undergo further investigation here.

14 O'Hara, Systematics 82–3. "Relation" has to be understood in the meaning it has in hard sciences, namely as a property that ties together pairs of elements. Cp. also Hockett, Description 394.

15 Salmon, Morphology 18, and references cited therein. Cp. also fn. 1 above.

pair of forms, for instance, *š* = palatalized *s*.[16] Thus, even conceding that phonetic rules played a key role in the emerging MHL, such rules were an essential and integral component of MHL's morphology in the sense that they were among the *non-inclusive* relations that characterized it as a system.

The overall picture that emerges from the discussion of the epistemological stereotypes associated with the emergence of MHL is that its scientific character is the sum of three methodological underpinnings, which converge only in part with those ascribed to it in the literature. These are:

(i) history, as a complex-to-simple process, and tending to corruption in a pre-Darwinian sense;
(ii) comparativism, as applied to linguistic codes smaller or greater than languages;
(iii) morphology, as originally defined in terms of
  a. visual saliency;
  b. systemic relations, notably phonetic rules.[17]

An important implication of a reconceptualization of (the beginnings of) MHL along these lines is that any kind of linguistic investigation that possesses the methodological underpinnings listed in (i–iii) can be plausibly regarded as an instance of historically-oriented scientific linguistics. The remainder of this paper explores this implication, with particular regard to the Arabic linguistic tradition, as exemplified by its late exponent al-Suyūṭī (d. 911/1505).

3 The Linguistic Thought of Al-Suyūṭī: A Review and Reconsideration

3.1 *Epistemological Background*

Al-Suyūṭī's life and works have been studied extensively in the literature,[18] so there hardly needs to be a discussion of them, except in relation to his linguistic production. In fact, despite a revival of interest in the Egyptian polymath in recent times, there is one facet of his linguistic production that still remains underrepresented in modern scholarship, notably his writings on morphology (*ṣarf*). This issue is not trivial, given that morphology forms one of the two

16 Hockett, Description 395–7.

17 I.e., relational properties that encompass, but are not confined to, inclusion.

18 See Geoffroy, al-Suyūṭī; Ḥammūda, *al-Suyūṭī* 15–172; Saleh, al-Suyūṭī 73–5, 83–8; Spevack, al-Suyūṭī; Spevack, *Archetypal*, 71–125.

pillars (the other being syntax/*naḥw*) of the Arabic grammatical tradition (AGT henceforth).[19]

It appears that both Arab and Western scholars condemned this aspect of al-Suyūṭī's thought to oblivion. In the Arab world, the proceedings of the most recent themed international conferences[20] on al-Suyūṭī and the most recent issue of a journal dedicated to him[21] mainly investigate his interests in law and religion, and the sole study that deals with his linguistic thought in these publications gives only a cursory glimpse at morphology.[22] Ḥammūda's monograph,[23] which provides an in-depth illustration of al-Suyūṭī's linguistic thought, represents an important exception to the general lack of interest in the Egyptian polymath's views on Arabic morphology. That said, the author chooses not to dedicate a separate conceptual section to al-Suyūṭī's treatment of Arabic morphology and, instead, merges it with al-Suyūṭī's treatment of Arabic syntax, thereby somewhat obscuring our understanding of his morphological analyses. A further notable exception to this trend is Sulemain's investigation of *taʿlīl*, a methodological principle of AGT that is meant to account for linguistic data that, on first impression, deviates from the rules of Arabic language. Suleiman, in fact, illustrates how in the treatise *al-Iqtirāḥ fī uṣūl al-naḥw* al-Suyūṭī applies the principle of *taʿlīl* to a broad range of Arabic data,[24] among which we find morphological phenomena such as the suffixation of the morphemic material *-mma* to *Allāhu*.[25]

Similarly, Western curriculum scholars briefly touch upon al-Suyūṭī's works on (Arabic) morphology.[26] The notable exceptions are Czapkiewicz and Loucel,[27] who both examine the topic of glottogony at length. Here, however, al-Suyūṭī intermingles linguistic considerations with theological reflection.

It would therefore be desirable to rescue al-Suyūṭī's work on morphology from the oblivion it has been relegated to, and to contribute, by means of this

19 Owens, *Arabic Grammar* 70.

20 These conferences have been held in Egypt, one in 1976 under the title *Jalāl al-Dīn al-Suyūṭī*, and the other in 1993 under the title *Jalāl al-Dīn al-Suyūṭī: al-iḥtifāʾ bi-dhikrā murūr khamsat qurūn ʿalā wafātih*. The proceedings of these conferences have appeared in 1978 and 1995, respectively. See Saleh, al-Suyūṭī 81–2 for further details.

21 The issue 13 of *al-Turāth al-ʿArabī*, which appeared in 1993.

22 Al-Rājiḥī, Dars 386–7.

23 Ḥammūda, *al-Suyūṭī* 11, 177. Cp. also Ikhwan 2009 for a critical edition and translation of ch. twenty of the *Muzhir*.

24 Suleiman, *Taʿlīl* 178–96.

25 Ibid. 185. See also sect. 2.2 below for details and examples.

26 See e.g. Rabin, *West-Arabian* 10; Owens, *History* 75–7; Spevack, al-Suyūṭī 386.

27 See e.g. Czapkiewicz, *Language* 9–40; Loucel, Origine 151–81.

rediscovery, to the ongoing revival of scholarly interest in this figure. In this respect, the rediscovery of al-Suyūṭī's thought on morphology appears to be not only a philological but also an epistemological matter. In fact, consensus has recently been growing among Arabists that, contrary to the received view, al-Suyūṭī's historical and juridical work cannot be easily dismissed as compilatory, and should instead be reassessed as endowed with originality and scientific methods akin to those used in modern fields such as, for instance, historiography and law.[28] This being the case, we may entertain, by extension, the hypothesis that some of the methods MHL avails itself of in the analysis of linguistic phenomena, morphology included, are also found in al-Suyūṭī's work. A first clue to this effect is provided in chapter forty of his treatise *al-Muzhir fī ʿulūm al-lugha wa-anwāʿihā*, entitled *Bāb maʿrifat al-ashbāh wa-l-naẓāʾir*.[29] Here, the Egyptian polymath (i) cites his sources with accuracy, and (ii) offers a critical review of them. In fact, Geoffroy precisely considers such a bipartite procedure—source description plus critical review—as one of the defining characters of the scientific method that underlies al-Suyūṭī's historical and juridical writings.[30] With respect to the passage in question, al-Suyūṭī (i) clarifies the material support of some of the morphological treatises he consulted, such as the *Kitāb Laysa fī kalām al-ʿArab* by Ibn Khālawayh (d. 370/980). This he describes as published in three huge volumes (*fī thalāthati mujalladātin ḍakhmāt*)[31] and then (ii) proceeds to draw a critical distinction between the two different positions that Arab grammarians adopt vis-à-vis the departure point of their morphological descriptions, which consists of a quite simple morphological pattern known in the Western grammar as "geminated" (e.g. *ḥaẓẓ* "fortune"). Some of them isolate (*ifrād*) this pattern as an independent biconsonantal class, by interpreting it as including two Cs, one of which has undergone reduplication (*ḥ ẓ*). Others, instead, interpret the same pattern as including three Cs, two of which are phonologically identical (*ḥ ẓ ẓ*), and therefore regard it as a particular subclass of the triconsonantal class (*wa-aktharu l-naḥwiyyīna lā yufridu hadhā l-nawʿa bi-l-dhikri wa-yudkhiluhu fī muṭlaqi l-thulātiyyi wa-minhum man yusammīhi thunāʾiyyan wa-naḥnu khtarnā ifrādahu bi-l-dhikr*).[32]

However, while certainly indicative of a general "modern scientific" attitude on behalf of al-Suyūṭī, the bipartite procedure under scrutiny is not peculiar to

28 Geoffroy, al-Suyūṭī 914–5; Suleiman, *Taʿlīl* 179.

29 See the end of this section for a translation and explanation of the title in question.

30 Geoffroy, al-Suyūṭī 914–5.

31 Al-Suyūṭī, *Muzhir* ii, 3.

32 Ibid. 5.

the analysis of morphological data he develops in chapter forty of the *Muzhir*. In other words, this procedure seems to be a necessary though not sufficient condition for a "modern scientific" reappraisal of the Egyptian's polymath work on morphology. Accordingly, we should seek in the *Muzhir*, chapter forty included, further methodological underpinnings that are more specifically rooted in al-Suyūṭī's morphological description of Arabic, and that, in the best case, correspond to those used in MHL to a reasonable extent.

The next four sections aim at substantiating such a hypothesis by showing that in the *Muzhir* we can find conceptual equivalents for the methodological underpinnings of MHL defined along the lines detailed in sect. 1, and summarized there under (i–iii). For clarity's sake, each section examines one of these three aspects of MHL, and its potential relation with one of the methodological aspects of al-Suyūṭī's morphological description.

Before proceeding to the next section, a clarification is in order. The following discussion of this hypothesis often assumes the form of a case study in the aforementioned *Bāb maʿrifat al-ashbāh wa-l-naẓāʾir*, as the latter occupies a large portion of the *Muzhir* (about 300 pages in the printed edition consulted[33]) bearing significant witness to al-Suyūṭī's interest in Arabic morphology.[34] A bird's eye view of this chapter reveals that it is, in essence, a glossed and contextualized list of frequent and infrequent morphological patterns.[35] In turn, this chapter can be further divided into three smaller conceptual sections. The first section mentions the Arabic patterns in order of increasing morphological complexity.[36] The second section deals with the phonotactic restrictions that affect them.[37] Finally, the third section addresses the morphological patterns to which some kind of lexical or grammatical peculiarity is attached. Examples of this are rare words, unusual types of affixation, *dualia/pluralia tantum* and cases of mismatch between natural and grammatical gender. The presentation of these peculiarities is achieved by means of a rather predictable technique of analysis, the so-called *al-ashbāh wa-l-naẓāʾir* (lit. "Similitudes and parallels"). Al-Suyūṭī either glosses the patterns in questions or reports the original linguistic context in which they occur and, that is, the word(s) that precede(s) and follow(s) such patterns.[38]

33 Ibid. 3–301.
34 Cp. also Saleh, al-Suyūṭī 76.
35 Ḥammūda, *al-Suyūṭī* 292.
36 Al-Suyūṭī, *Muzhir* ii, 3–41.
37 Ibid. 42–118.
38 Ibid. 119–301.

Upon closer scrutiny, however, the technique of *al-ashbāh wa-l-naẓāʾir*, originating in the field of Quranic exegesis where it effectively denotes the study of synonymy and semantic collocations,[39] cuts across chapter forty entirely, albeit to a lesser degree. For instance, at the outset of the first conceptual section, al-Suyūṭī discusses the pattern *fiʿal*, also manifest in the adjectives, and exemplifies it by means of the adjective *qiyam* as it occurs in the Quranic collocation (Q 6:161) *dīnan qiyaman* "right religion" (*wa-ʿalā fiʿalin-i sman naḥwa ḍilaʿin wa-ṣifatan naḥwa ziyamin fa-ammā qiyamun* [...] *qawluhu taʿālā dīnan qiyaman*).[40] Furthermore, in the same section he glosses the unusual word *yathbira*, which instantiates the pattern *yafʿila*, with the more understandable synonym *māʾ* "water" (*illā annahu* [= Abā Zaydin] *dhakara wazna yafʿilat-in yathbiratan-i sma māʾ*).[41] Given the pervasiveness of the technique of *al-ashbāh wa-l-naẓāʾir* throughout chapter forty, it comes as no surprise that al-Suyūṭī named this chapter after it, that is, *Bāb maʿrifat al-ashbāh wa-l-naẓāʾir*.[42]

3.2 *History*

The main idea that pervades this section is that, for ideological reasons, a historical perspective has nourished AGT since its very beginnings. It is worth considering, in this respect, medieval sources of Arabic grammar and *adab* literature explored by Fück, according to which AGT arose in reaction to the Arabic-Islamic expansion, and related sedentarization, when the non-native speakers of Arabic that inhabited the conquered territories learned the pure Bedouin speech and corrupted it. While Western scholarship has often denied that history is a constitutive element of AGT, a point to which we will return shortly, the view expressed in these sources is in essence historical in that they clearly perceive the Arabic language in relation to a "before" (the pre-Islamic times) and an "after" (the Islamization period).[43]

Furthermore, Fück's research has highlighted that such a historical view is organized in Arabic medieval sources around two major concepts. The first, as

39 See e.g. Abdul-Raof, *Exegesis* 88.

40 Al-Suyūṭī, *Muzhir* ii, 5.

41 Ibid. 11. It should be also noted that Ibn Manẓūr (d. 711/1311–2) provides a different gloss for this word, by explaining it as a toponym ending with a feminine marker (and treating it accordingly as a diptote noun): *wa-yathbiratu smu arḍ* (*Lisān* i, 470).

42 The interpretation offered here for the title of the chapter forty of the *Muzhir* is neither confirmed nor refuted by Ḥammūda, *al-Suyūṭī* 292, who is very concise in his presentation of the contents of this chapter (cp. fn. 35 above) and provides no (alternative) interpretation for its title.

43 Fück, *ʿArabīya* 5–7, in particular the fnn. 4 and 5 therein.

alluded to above, is the corruption of Arabic, a concept that can be regarded in modern terms as sociolinguistic. The other, which in modern terms is purely linguistic and more precisely syntactic, is desinential inflection. The two concepts are deeply interrelated owing to the fact that, according to primary sources, the corruption of Arabic most palpably manifests itself in desinential inflection.[44] Al-Suyūṭī is no exception to this trend: in chapter nine of the *Muzhir* he lists desinential inflection among the features of Arabic for which Bedouins constitute a reference model (*uttukila ʿalayhim*). This is in sharp contrast to either sedentarized or foreign people (*ḥaḍariyyin, ghayrahum mina l-umami*), who are unreliable sources of Arabic (*lam yuʾkhad*), because of their corrupted Arabic varieties (*fasadat alsinatuhum*).[45]

Fück himself, however, warns Western Arabists against a "totalizing" misinterpretation of the salient relation between language corruption and syntax, which simplistically reduces the object of the historical investigation of AGT to such a relation. Indeed, AGT made great efforts to describe corrupted Arabic as manifesting itself at *all* linguistic levels, from writing to morphology,[46] although such levels could have been felt by native speakers of Arabic as less salient than the dropping or inconsistent use of desinential inflection.

The detailed survey of the morphological pattern *fāʿūl* that al-Suyūṭī provides in chapter forty of the *Muzhir* is instructive in exemplifying Fück's consideration. Here, the term *nāṭūr*, based on this pattern, is expounded as follows: "a keeper of palm-trees and vines, after that the Arabs came to use it in their language, even if it was a foreign word" (*wa-l-nāṭūru ḥāfiẓu l-nakhli wa-l-shajari wa-qad takallamat bihi l-ʿArabu wa-in kāna aʿjamiyyan*).[47] In this passage, the subordinate clause describing the foreign nature of *nāṭūr* is opened by the concessive conjunction *wa-in* ("even if") that negatively connotes the introduction of this word into Arabic, as described in the main clause. A corrupted character of Arabic results from the entire sentence that, in turn, enters into a semantic relation with the context in which this sentence occurs, notably al-Suyūṭī's description of Arabic morphology subsuming *nāṭūr* and many other foreign words (*hālūm, jāmūs, qābūs, sābūr, ṭālūt, jālūt, ṣābūn, rāqūd*)[48] under the pattern *fāʿūl*. In short, according to this passage of the *Muzhir*, morphology manifests the corruption of Arabic insofar as the pattern *fāʿūl* is concerned.

---

44 Ibid. 5.

45 Al-Suyūṭī, *Muzhir* i, 121–2. Most of this passage is reproduced in sect. 2.3 below.

46 Fück, *ʿArabīya* 5.

47 Al-Suyūṭī, *Muzhir* ii, 123.

48 Ibid. 122–4. Fleisch, *Philologie* i, 369–70 mentions this passage, and concurs with al-Suyūṭī in regarding *fāʿūl* as a foreign ("syriaque-araméen") pattern.

The discussion so far reveals that beyond the simplistic approach, still frequently adopted in the Western study of AGT, there is some evidence that:

- al-Suyūṭī shared with the sources of AGT explored by Fück a historical conception of the *lughat al-ḍād*, according to which the Arabic language used before Arabic-Islamic expansion changed after that the latter took place;
- the historical conception at issue was not naïve in that it deliberately drew on sociolinguistic reasoning such as religious and political ideology to determine the cause and manner of this change: foreigners and corruption, respectively. It further drew on linguistic reasoning to determine the object of this change, namely the levels of Arabic in which the foreign-induced corruption manifested itself, morphology included, as shown by al-Suyūṭī's treatment of the pattern *fāʿūl*.

To further substantiate the hypothesis that al-Suyūṭī had a historical conception of Arabic along these lines, we need to consider another epistemological problem that, besides the simplistic approach pointed out by Fück, affects the Western study of AGT—the problem of marginalization.[49]

As alluded to at the outset of the present section, the problem of marginalization lies in the fact that the general historical attitude of AGT toward Arabic, as well as Fück's textual research that brought it to light, are not fully integrated within the mainstream disciplines of Arab(ic) linguistics and sociolinguistics. In effect, these disciplines either tend to dismiss AGT as lacking a historical perspective altogether or discuss Fück's historically-oriented theory on the relationship between Arabic and its dialects without acknowledging that the theoretical core of such a theory is already found in Arabic medieval sources studied by the German scholar.[50] This state of affairs gives rise to an

49 In the following, the evidence that we will offer for the hypothesis that al-Suyūṭī had a historical conception of Arabic is directly culled from primary sources. Alternatively, we can also adduce an argument of common sense in support of this hypothesis, based on the fact that, from a socio-cultural standpoint, AGT coalesced with the other Arabic-Islamic sciences into one connected whole (cp. Suleiman, *Taʿlīl* 36 and Ghersetti's review of Suleiman's book in QSA 18 (2000) 250). On these grounds, it seems quite unnatural that al-Suyūṭī, who composed many historical treatises (cp. Saleh, al-Suyūṭī 77, 86), did not avail himself of a historical perspective in his linguistic works.

50 A caveat is in order here. Primary sources plausibly provide a historical conception of Arabic, and especially of the relationship between Arabic and its dialects, which rests on historical materials that cannot always be regarded as reliable. For instance, after mentioning an anecdote about the corruption of Arabic transmitted by Ibn al-Anbārī, in

epistemological paradox which can be exemplified as follows. Despite the fact that Ibn al-Anbārī (d. 577/1181) transmits an anecdote about the emergence of AGT, in which he portrays foreigners as responsible for the corruption of Arabic in time and provides a discussion of their "incorrect" Arabic, which involves a fair amount of technicalities, Fleisch affirms that "on ne pouvait travailler que l'Arabiyya authentique, l'Arabiyya du désert [...] le développement ultérieur de la langue fut exclu de la recherche grammaticale."[51]

In all likelihood, this paradox finds its ground in a sort of methodological overlap that Western Arabists make between the linguistic facts available for (Pre-)Classical Arabic, and their sources, notably native informants. For instance, Owens points out that Late grammarians tended to repeat and take extracts from their predecessors, often citing the very same data, instead of gathering their data from the linguistic community contemporary to them.[52] Yet, a methodological tenet of this sort does not necessarily imply that the Late grammarians projected the old data they availed themselves of forward to their present-day linguistic reality, or vice versa, that they projected back their present-day linguistic reality to their old data, thereby adopting a "flat" and undifferentiated synchronic (or panchronic) approach. Rather, their choice of using old data in the description of Arabic simply means that, for the above ideological reasons, they were not interested in relying on contemporary informants.[53] Al-Suyūṭī, in particular, provides clear evidence for this epistemological attitude, when he explicitly states in chapter ten of the *Muzhir*: *wa-l-matrūku mā kāna qadīman mina l-lughāti thumma turika wa-stuʿmila ghayruhu*

---

which foreigners are blamed for two grammatical mistakes, Versteegh, *Arabic language* 50–1, interestingly points out that one of the two mistakes in question is genuine, whereas the other "may have been fabricated."

51 Fleisch, *Philologie* i, 46. See the previous fn. for details on the anecdote reported by Ibn al-Anbārī. A more elaborate criticism to AGT is advanced by Owens, *History* 76. While recognizing that the Arab "grammarians were certainly aware of the notion of change," and hence of diachrony, Owens remarks that a general diachronic awareness of this sort is not enough to ascribe to them a historical perspective as the latter also implies the systematic application of a comparative method (cp. the methodological underpinning labelled as (ii) at the end of sect. 1), which according to him "did not exist until the nineteenth century." This issue is deferred to the end of sect. 2.3, where we will argue that Owens' criticism can be accepted only in part.

52 Owens, *History* 7. Cp. also fn. 71 below for a definition of *lugha*.

53 But see Alhawary, Elicitation 14–6 and Suleiman, *Taʿlīl* 76–8 for a different attitude of Ibn Jinnī in this regard.

wa-amthilatu dhālika kathīratun fī kutubi l-lugha.[54] This passage can be adduced as *locus probans* that al-Suyūṭī shared with the mainstream lexicographical tradition interest for some (Pre-)Classical words that do not belong to current usage (cp. his technical definition of them as *matrūk* "not normally uttered"),[55] such as *anbadha* in the sense of *nabadha* "to throw dates or raisins into a bag or skin, and pour water on them, so as to obtain a liquor" (*wa-anbadha nabīdhan lughatun ḍaʿīfatun fī nabadha*); and that the lack of usage of these words was due to their archaic (*qadīm*) status, particularly within a scenario of dialectal variation (cp. the key-words *l-lughāti, lughatun ḍaʿīfatun*).

The main lesson that can be learnt from this first reconsideration of the paradoxical lack of diachrony generally ascribed to AGT is that it partially confirms results arrived at through our study of al-Suyūṭī's treatment of the pattern *fāʿūl* in chapter forty of the *Muzhir*, namely that the Egyptian polymath had, generally speaking, a historical approach to Arabic (cp. the said key-word *qadīm*), and that, specifically for the object of linguistic change, he regarded morphology as such (cp. his application of the "diachronic" definition of *matrūk* to the verbal (= morphological) pattern *afʿal*, as opposed to the more common verbal pattern *faʿal* in the case of the root *n b dh*).

Bearing this in mind, let us return to the paradox of the lack of diachrony that informs Western epistemological discourse on AGT and its causes. In addition to the above methodological overlap between linguistic data and sources, such causes include a non-exhaustive interpretation of some interpretive tools of AGT. Thus, in examining the two interlocked notions of *aṣl*/*farʿ* and referring to AGT, Owens maintains "In general a historical perspective is missing in it" since a historically attested and irregular form such as *qāla* "he said" (the so-called *farʿ*) can be derived from an unattested and regular form such as *qawala* (the so-called *aṣl*) which corresponds, in modern linguistic terms, to a synchronic notion such as a phonological representation (as opposed to the *farʿ*/phonetic representation), and therefore cannot be likened to a diachronic notion such as an ancestor form (as opposed to the *farʿ*/offshoot form).[56] Plainly, the burden of proof for Owens' interpretation of *farʿ*, and especially for its synchronic

54 Al-Suyūṭī, *Muzhir* i, 214. In this passage al-Suyūṭī cites the "Second Teacher" al-Fārābī (d. 339/950), who in his work *Dīwān al-adab* reports six instances of allomorphy, in which a given verbal or nominal meaning can be assigned two different morphological patterns. Five instances of allomorphy involve verbs (e.g. *nabadha/anbadha*: see the following discussion), and the remaining instance involves a noun (*lahja/lahaja* "dialect").

55 This translation of the term *matrūk* is based on Baalbaki, *Legacy* 142.

56 Owens, *History* 75.

character, rests on its being an unattested and regular form. However, recent textual research by Baalbaki shows that Arab grammarians also regarded a historically attested and irregular form, as is the apocopate-jussive verb *yakun*, as an instance of *aṣl* as Ibn Jinnī (d. 392/1002) precisely analyzes the form *yakun* in terms of *aṣl*, with respect to the equally attested and irregular form *yaku*, analyzed accordingly as the *farʿ* of *yakun* (cp. the alternation *lam yakun*/*lam yaku* "he was not").[57] In this light, the historically unattested and regular character is no longer a necessary condition of *aṣl* and rather co-exists with its historically attested and irregular character. This, in turn, justifies a diachronic interpretation of the pair *aṣl*/*farʿ*, by virtue of which one is identified with the ancestor form, and the other with its offshoot.[58]

Remarkably, al-Suyūṭī appears to subscribe to a similar interpretation of the alternation (*lam*) *yakun*/*yaku* as illustrated in what follows. In chapter twenty-two of the *Muzhir* (*takhfīfu l-kalimati bi-l-ḥadhfi naḥwa lam yaku*)[59] and in chapter fifty-six of *al-Itqān fī ʿulūm al-Qurʾān* (*al-takhfīfu li-kathrati dawarānihi fī l-kalāmi ka-mā fī ḥadhfi* [...] *nūni lam yaku*),[60] the Egyptian polymath derives the form *yaku* from the form *yakun* by means of a deletion-rule (*ḥadhf*) that targets the sound *n* in *yakun*, and is driven by the need of "lightening" (*takhfīf*) this verb.[61] Al-Suyūṭī further elaborates on this point in the *Iqtirāḥ* to identify "lightening" and the related deletion-rule with a form of rational justification (*ʿilla*) of the (apparent) irregularities of Arabic grammar,[62] such as the word *yaku* in the verbal domain. It is precisely al-Suyūṭī's mention of the notion of *ʿilla* in this context that creates a strong parallel between his analysis and that of Ibn Jinnī regarding the alternation (*lam*) *yakun*/*yaku*. In fact, AGT (al-Suyūṭī included)[63] traditionally construes the *ʿilla* as any linguistic phenomenon that converts a *aṣl* into a *farʿ*, and that can consist of either a (meta)physical explanation or a grammatical (phonetic, morphological etc.) rule.[64] On

57 Baalbaki, *Aṣl* 191–2. The alternation *lam yakun*/*lam yaku* is seemingly a leitmotif of AGT, as Sībawayhi mentions it at the very outset of his famous work (cp. *Kitāb* i, 25).

58 Baalbaki, *Aṣl* 191–2. Cp. also Suleiman, *Taʿlīl* 178–196.

59 Al-Suyūṭī, *Muzhir* i, 324.

60 Al-Suyūṭī, *Itqān* iii, 191.

61 In AGT, this is a concept that denotes the physical condition, on the part of the speaker, of reducing the expenditure of energy in pronunciation, mental processing etc.: cp. Guillaume, Approach 178. This amounts to saying that "lightening" and the related deletion-rule proceed from complex to simple.

62 Al-Suyūṭī, *Iqtirāḥ* 263. Cp. also the previous sect.

63 Suleiman, *Taʿlīl* 180.

64 Guillaume, Approach 179; Suleiman, *Taʿlīl* 31–2. In particular, the fact that the notion of *ʿilla* shares two defining properties with the modern notion of phonetic rule makes it possible to liken one to the other. These properties are the change from sound A to sound B,

these grounds, al-Suyūṭī's definition of "lightening" and deletion in terms of *ʿilla* (with the former corresponding, more accurately, to a physical explanation, and the latter to a phonetic rule) implies that, as suggested above, he concurs with Ibn Jinnī in interpreting the alternation (*lam*) *yakun*/*yaku* as a pair *aṣl*/*farʿ*.

In the same treatise al-Suyūṭī also invokes the *ʿilla* "lightening" or deletion to shed light on the nominal domain, following al-Zamakhsharī's (d. 538/1144) analysis, which reads as follows: *qawlu l-Zamakhsharī fī l-Mufaṣṣali fī lladhī* […] *khaffafūhu min ghayri wajhin fa-qālū lladhi bi-ḥadhfi l-yāʾi thumma lladh bi-ḥadhfi l-ḥarakati thumma ḥadhafūhu raʾsan wa-jtazaʾū bi-lāmi l-taʿrīfi lladhī fī awwalihi wa-kadhā faʿalū fī llatī.*[65] This passage builds on three interesting lines of reasoning. Firstly, the words that undergo "lightening" and deletion are all relativizers (*lladh*/*tī*, *lladh*/*ti*, *lladh*/*t*, *l*-). According to al-Zamakhsharī himself as well as other grammarians and lexicographers[66] these belong to the real usage of (Pre-)Classical Arabic rather than being unuttered representations in the speaker's mind, as shown by the verb *qāla* that is often associated with them (cp. *qālū lladhi* in this passage).

The second line of reasoning of al-Zamakhsharī's/al-Suyūṭī's description is that the *ʿilla* "lightening"/deletion expresses itself through development in time as it proceeds from the relativizer *lladh*/*tī* to the relativizer *l*- passing through the relativizers *lladh*/*ti*, *lladh*/*t*. In particular, the developmental character of this line of reasoning is apparent in the choice of the prepositions of motion *min* "from", *bi* "through" that link the mention of one relativizer to that of another (cp. *khaffafūhu* [= *lladhī*] *min ghayri wajhin fa-qālū lladhi bi-ḥadhfi l-yāʾi*). Moreover, the temporal character of the same line of reasoning is evident in the usage of the connectors *fa*-, *thumma* that accompany each single mention of relativizer, with the caveat that these connectors must receive a temporal (rather than logical) reading, as they co-occur in the text with the verb *qāla* (cp. *fa-qālū*). As we have just pointed out, in fact, this verb of saying refers to a past action in the real world (rather than to a preceding logical step in the speaker's mind).

---

and the presence of a phonetic and/or morphological environment (see e.g. Bloomfield, *Language* 364–5: "change of phonemes … consists of two layers of habit … One layer is phonemic … The other layer consists of … combination of phonemes.") In this respect, the *ʿilla* "lightening"/deletion qualifies as a phonetic rule because of the change from *n* to zero in the morphological environment *yakun*.

65 Al-Suyūṭī, *Iqtirāḥ* 280.

66 See e.g. Rabin, *West-Arabian* 39, 89.

Finally, a third line of reasoning that underlies al-Zamakhsharī's/al-Suyūṭī's description of the relativizers *lladh/tī* etc. is that their development in time proceeds from complex to simple. The manner in which al-Zamakhsharī and al-Suyūṭī mention such relativizers expresses this idea clearly as it follows an order of decreasing length (*lladh/tī, lladh/ti, lladh/t, l-*).

From the association of ideas between the *ʿilla* "lightening"/deletion that operates in the alternation (*lam*) *yakun/yaku*, as described in the *Muzhir*, *Itqān* and the temporal, developmental and "decreasing" nature of this *ʿilla*, as described in the *Iqtirāḥ*, we can infer that al-Suyūṭī, not unlike Ibn Jinnī and al-Zamakhsharī and contrary to standard assumptions, *was indeed aware of a historical approach in his analysis of the alternation in question*. From a broader perspective, the above discussion of the paradoxical lack of diachrony usually ascribed to AGT, with particular reference to the interlocked notions of *aṣl/farʿ/ʿilla*, reveals that al-Suyūṭī actually applied a historical approach to explore morphological facts in this specific domain. What transpires is that al-Suyūṭī's historical approach to such notions regarded morphology as the object of linguistic change, just as his historical approach to the foreign pattern *fāʿūl* (cp. *nāṭūr*) and to the *matrūk* pattern *afʿala* (cp. *anbadha*) did. What is more, al-Suyūṭī's historical approach to the concepts of *aṣl/farʿ/ʿilla* shared the aim of elucidating the manner of linguistic change with his historical approach to the foreign pattern *fāʿūl*. On the one hand, al-Suyūṭī characterized the manner of linguistic change as a complex-to-simple process when he expounded the concepts of *aṣl*, *farʿ*, *ʿilla*[67] while, on the other, he considered the same phenomenon in terms of corruption when examining the foreign pattern *fāʿūl*.[68]

As emerges from a study of the *Muzhir* and, to a lesser extent, of the *Iqtirāḥ* and *Itqān*, al-Suyūṭī's historical approach to Arabic language in this respect is strikingly similar to the methodological underpinning of MHL summarized under (i) in sect. 1. Furthermore, the fact that al-Suyūṭī indicates dialectal variation (cp. the previous discussion on the stereotype of simplification, and on *matrūk* words) and morphology (as stressed throughout this section) as, respectively, the sociolinguistic and linguistic dimensions in which the change undergone by Arabic occurs, also paves the way for establishing a parallel between al-Suyūṭī's historically-oriented approach to Arabic and the methodological underpinnings of MHL summarized as (ii–iii) in sect. 1.[69] This insight is developed in the next two sections.

---

67 Cp. fn. 61 above.

68 Cp. the above translation of al-Suyūṭī's gloss of the word *nāṭūr*.

69 Another aspect of similarity between MHL and al-Suyūṭī's linguistic thought is that both blend the historical approach with the idea that the cause of linguistic change is due

3.3 *Comparativism*

As illustrated at the end of sect. 2.1 al-Suyūṭī classifies Arabic patterns according to a purely morphological criterion of increasing complexity in chapter forty of the *Muzhir*. This criterion, which leads him to list the short vowel pattern *fuʿil* at the very beginning of this classification, is an essential part of a more general morphological reasoning, also apparent from the position that al-Suyūṭī assigns to the same pattern within a subset that only includes nominal patterns. The pattern *fuʿil* is found at the end of the "nominal" subset in question, since it is generally used as a verbal pattern, and only exceptionally "recycled" (*manqūl*), as it were, as a nominal pattern: *wa-ʿalā fuʿilin naḥwa duʾilin ruʾimin wa-wuʿilin lughatun fī l-waʿili wa-duʾilin wa-ruʾimin-ismā jins* […] *manqūlatayni mina l-fiʿl*.[70]

Yet, despite its adherence to the original text, an account of al-Suyūṭī's treatment of the pattern *fuʿil* along these lines is not complete. In fact, in sect. 2.2 the study of the Arabistic stereotype, referred to there as a "simplistic approach", has revealed that the Egyptian polymath regards the purely linguistic level of morphology only as the locus of a given anomaly such as the "unexpected" change of "immutable" Arabic. But, as seen by the socio-cultural factor of foreign influence, he also invokes a sociolinguistic level to determine the cause and manner of this anomaly. The question therefore arises of whether the morphological anomaly represented by *fuʿil* finds its *raison d'être* in a kind of sociolinguistic phenomenon.

To answer this question, it is useful to point out that al-Suyūṭī exemplifies the subset containing the morphological pattern *fuʿil* through the word *wuʿil* "mountain-goat", which he describes in sociolinguistic terms as a "dialectal word", or rather a diatopic variant (*lugha*).[71] This does not seem to be an isolated case. A closer examination of the passage of the *Muzhir* concerning the alternation *anbadha*/*nabadha*, discussed in sect. 2.2 with reference to its diachronic aspect, and especially the loss of *afʿala* to the advantage of *faʿala*,

to foreign influence. For instance, the retroflex Cs that set Sanskrit apart from other Indo-European languages have been interpreted from Schleicher onward as the result of the contact of this language with the neighboring Dravidian languages (Schleicher, *Compendium* 162–3; Lehmann, *Linguistics* 136). This issue will not be further discussed here.

70 Al-Suyūṭī, *Muzhir* ii, 6.

71 On the correspondence between *lugha* and the traditional Western notion of "dialect(al word)", cp. Iványi, Lugha 88. Sociolinguistics reformulates the notion of "dialect(al word)" in a variationist framework, a dialect being defined as "A regionally or socially distinctive variety of language" (Crystal, *Dictionary* 142), whence the current translation of *lugha* as "diatopic variant".

brings to light a sociolinguistic aspect as well. Here, the morphological patterns *afʿala* and *faʿala* are said to be capable, prior to this loss, of conveying the meaning of the root *n b dh* by co-existing as two different diatopic variants within a scenario of dialectal variation (cp. the key-words *l-lughāti, lughatun ḍaʿīfatun*). Similarly, the passage of the *Muzhir* concerning the salient relation between syntax and language corruption, which we have touched upon in sect. 2.2 in dealing with the interplay between the linguistic and sociolinguistic dimensions in al-Suyūṭī's reflection on Arabic, actually portrays a more complex kind of relation which includes morphology and dialectal variation. This state of affairs is evident in two lists found at the beginning of this passage. The first mentions the Arabic tribes and related dialects in decreasing order of linguistic purity, or, in increasing order of linguistic corruption: Qays, Tamīm, Asad, Hudhayl, Kināna, Ṭayyiʾ. The other list mentions the morphological component in addition to the lexical and syntactical components (*gharīb, iʿrāb, taṣrīf*): *wa-min bayna qabāʾili l-ʿArabi wa-hum Qaysun, Tamīmun, wa-Asadun fa-inna hāʾulāʾi hum-u-lladhīna ʿanhum aktharu mā ukhidha wa-muʿẓamuhu wa-ʿalayhim-uttukila fī l-gharībi wa-fī l-iʿrābi wa-l-taṣrīfi thumma Hudhaylun wa-baʿḍu Kinānata wa-baʿdu l-Ṭayyiʾīna wa-lam yuʾkhadh ʿan ghayrihim min sāʾiri qabāʾilihim wa-bi-l-jumlati fa-innahu lam yuʾkhadh ʿan ḥaḍariyyin qaṭṭu.*[72]

Taken as a whole, all the above passages of the *Muzhir* testify to a specific kind of interplay between the linguistic and sociolinguistic levels. According to this kind of interplay, the anomaly observed in the linguistic level, especially in its morphological sub-level (the verbal pattern *fuʿil* "recycled" for the nominal domain; the verbal pattern *afʿala* that unexpectedly co-exists with *faʿala*; the speech corruption in *taṣrīf*), is explained by having recourse to the sociolinguistic level, which always includes, *inter alia*, the sub-level of dialectal variation.

This kind of interplay, furthermore, appears to consist of at least two conceptual elements that are particularly relevant for our discussion. First, the fact that in the *Muzhir* al-Suyūṭī lists the tribes/dialects, i.e., the sociolinguistic level, with respect to morphology, i.e., the linguistic level, is tantamount to saying that he compares linguistic codes "smaller" than languages against morphological features. This procedure can be certainly likened to the methodological underpinning summarized as (ii) in sect. 1. The more so, if we consider

72 Al-Suyūṭī, *Muzhir* i, 121–2. Space limitations prevent us from including the original passage in full, but the interested reader is referred to Larcher, Langue Arabe 125–7, who reproduces the complete text, and translates it in French. Suleiman, *Taʿlīl* 23, offers an English translation of a portion of the same passage.

that al-Suyūṭī corroborates the status of linguistic codes of the PCA dialects by carrying out an in-depth investigation of their *ʿillas*, which re-conceptualizes all dialects, irrespective of their degree of corruption (cp. the aforementioned passage of the *Muzhir*) "as linguistic codes in their own right."[73] This re-conceptualization is achieved in the *Iqtirāḥ* by means of a "relativistic" shift of perspective. In fact, Suleiman's textual research on the *Khaṣāʾiṣ* and the *Iqtirāḥ* shows that by virtue of this epistemological shift Ibn Jinnī, and al-Suyūṭī after him, conceive linguistic facts, such as the said dialectal word *wuʿil*, as anomalous with respect to the more pure dialects that exhibit the variant *waʿil*,[74] but as "totally regular in their respective dialects."[75] In modern terms, deviations from a monolithic grammar of Arabic are better seen as the regularities of many "mini-grammars" of this language. Thus, what makes it possible for Ibn Jinnī and al-Suyūṭī to compare PCA dialects, in striking resemblance to (ii), is the rejection of an esocentric model, which regards the features of such dialects as anomalies, in favor of an endocentric model, where these features are recognized rather as instances of inner self-consistency. In turn, a "relativistic" shift of perspective of this sort effectively renders the PCA dialects real linguistic codes, or systems and therefore objects pertaining to the sphere of linguistic analysis proper, comparison included.

Concretely, the same "relativistic" shift impacts the interpretive tools al-Suyūṭī employs in his description of the PCA dialects. To account for their differences in terms of inner regularity and, at once, of phonetic rules, he assumes that these kinds of rules apply optionally rather than systematically, depending on this or that dialect, and construes this assumption as a *ʿilla*. By way of illustration, given a constant phonetic environment, the so-called *imāla*-rule ($a \rightarrow i$)[76] is said in the *Iqtirāḥ* to apply in the Hijazi dialect, but not in other PCA dialects.[77]

A second aspect of the relation that al-Suyūṭī posits between morphology and dialectal variation, which further enhances the parallelism between his reflection on Arabic and MHL requires highlighting. This is the "ontological continuum", so to speak, that ties the sociolinguistic and historical approaches to Arabic language. On the one hand, in chapter ten of the *Muzhir* (cp. sect. 2.2)

73 Suleiman, *Taʿlīl* 181.

74 Cp. fn. 70 above and the related passage.

75 Suleiman, *Taʿlīl* 75.

76 This is admittedly a simplified account of the *imāla*-rule. See Owens, *History* 195–229, for extensive discussion. Cp. also fn. 64 above.

77 Suleiman, *Taʿlīl* 188–9.

and in the *Iqtirāḥ* (a) al-Suyūṭī characterizes the diachronic change that favors *nabadha* over *anbadha* (cp. the key-words *thumma turika* in his statement: *thumma turika wa-stuʿmila ghayruhu*) as originating in a context of synchronic variation in which *nabadha* and *anbadha* co-exist as diatopic variants (cp. the key-word *lughatun* in his statement: *wa-anbadha nabīdhan lughatun ḍaʿīfatun fī nabadha* and fn. 71 above). (b) Moreover, he characterizes the diatopic variants *nabadha* and *anbadha* observed in such a context as two linguistic items belonging to two different linguistic systems (cp. again the key-word *lughatun*, and the aforementioned "endocentric" model of description).

On the other hand, Ratcliffe[78] remarks that in both MHL and modern sociolinguistics (cp. Labov's work) (a) "a variety of linguists with a variety of interests and concerns have made the point that synchronic variation is a necessary condition for change." Ratcliffe also remarks that (b) "variation is defined [...] in sociolinguistic terms not as variation in a system but variation among the systems of different members of the speech community."

What transpires from these statements is that al-Suyūṭī's views on the "sociolinguistic-historical" continuum, as expressed in the *Muzhir*, find interesting parallels in MHL and modern sociolinguistics (cp. (a) above), as does the "endocentric" model of description that he devises in the *Iqtirāḥ* (cp. (b) above).

In short, the main achievement of this section is that al-Suyūṭī and, more generally, AGT were cognizant of what is termed as "comparative method" in MHL to a significant extent. It is hardly deniable that al-Suyūṭī's comparativist techniques lacked any reference to core constituents of the comparative method used by the proponents of the *Stammbaumtheorie*, such as the comparison among the linguistic codes traditionally referred to as "languages", as are Akkadian, Arabic, Aramaic and Hebrew, or the systematic application of phonetic rules, as Owens rightly observes.[79] These same techniques, nonetheless, dovetail with the comparative method adopted by the advocates of the *Wellentheorie* in two aspects. Indeed, this kind of comparative method shares with al-Suyūṭī's, and AGT's, comparativist techniques the focus on the comparison among linguistic codes smaller than languages and the explanation of change as the diachronic consequence of variegated conditions of synchronic/sociolinguistic variation, rather than of a systematic application

78 Ratcliffe, *Plural* 20.

79 Cp. fn. 51 above.

of phonetic rules.[80] To this, we could add that even in the formative phases of *Stammbaumtheorie* itself the systematic application of phonetic rules had a limited role. As reported in sect. 1, Bopp did not use these rules in the first scientific description of the genetic relationship among Indo-European languages. Moreover, the idea that German *Lautverschiebung* takes place in a context of dialectal variation (cp. sect. 1) entails, in Müller's formulation, that this instance of consonantal shift cannot be interpreted in terms of the systematic application of phonetic rules, but in terms of dialectal variation: "jusqu'à ce qu'on rend compte rationnellement de cet échange, qu'on appelle *Lautverschiebung*, je contribuerai de l'attribuer non à l'altération phonétique, mais au développement dialectal."[81]

3.4 *Morphology*

The discussion so far has assumed a certain amount of linguistic common sense when dealing with morphology and al-Suyūṭī's attitude toward it: this level of linguistic analysis has been basically intended as involving words, and the similarities and differences that they exhibit. However, it seems desirable to provide a less naïve definition of morphology, especially in light of the accurate parallelism between al-Suyūṭī's linguistic thought and the methodological underpinnings of MHL referred to as (i, ii) in sect. 1. On the basis of a parallelism of this sort, we may also wonder whether al-Suyūṭī had a non-ingenuous conception of morphology, and to what extent this conception dovetails with the methodological underpinning of MHL referred to as (iii) in sect. 1. To answer this question, it is important to bear in mind that (iii) is itself made up of two conceptual elements: a notion of physical discreteness or saliency that is construed metaphorically in visual terms (cp. (iii.a) in sect. 1.1); and, the notion that morphological units are linked to each other as a system by means of non-inclusive relations, which can manifest themselves as phonetic rules (cp. (iii.b) in sect. 1.1). Starting with the first conceptual element, we would

80 On the non-systematic application of phonetic rules in al-Suyūṭī's comparative method, cp. the notion of *jawāz* discussed in this section in connection with his "endocentric" model of description. The systematic application of phonetic rules played a rather peripheral role also in the comparative method applied in the *Wellentheorie*, as shown by the (perhaps somewhat pretentious) motto "chaque mot a son histoire", which is often mistakenly attributed to the Swiss dialectologist Gilliéron, but was actually first formulated by Schuchardt, one of the two founders of the *Wellentheorie* (Campbell, *Linguistics* 188).

81 Müller, *Stratification* 29. Cp. also fnn. 8, 10 above.

like to stress the point that in the *Muzhir* al-Suyūṭī makes use of expressions such as *ṣūrat al-iʿlāl, ṣūrat al-jamʿ, fī l-lafẓ fī ṣūrat* X in which the "visual" term *ṣūra* "image, appearance, form" is combined on the syntagmatic axis with the morphological terms *iʿlāl* "glide status of a C in the root", *jamʿ* "plural", *lafẓ* "sound-side, *signans*, signifiant", a distributional behavior which clearly indicates that *ṣūra* has a technical morphological sense like *iʿlāl, jamʿ, lafẓ*. We find these expressions in the following passages, which heavily draw on Ibn Jinnī's *al-Khaṣāʾiṣ* and deal with origin of language, dialectal variation, and solecisms (*aghlāṭ*), respectively: *anna fī naqli l-aṣli ilā aṣlin ākhara naḥwa ṣabara wa-baṣura wa-ḍaraba wa-rabaḍa ṣūrata l-iʿlāli naḥwa qawlihim mā aṭyabahu wa-ayṭabahu* [...];[82] *wa-minhā l-ikhtilāfu fī ṣūrati l-jamʿi naḥwa asrā wa-asārā;*[83] *li-anna malakan fī l-lafẓi fī ṣūrati falakin wa-ḥalak.*[84]

These passages therefore can serve as *loci probantes* for the hypothesis that al-Suyūṭī's conception of morphology included a notion that corresponds to (iii.a) to a great extent. More generally, the same consideration carries over to AGT, which extensively uses the notion of *ṣūra* in its descriptions of morphology.[85]

Regarding the second conceptual element, (iii.b), it appears to find a counterpart in al-Suyūṭī's resort to *ʿilla* to explain morphological alternations such as *yakun*/*yaku*. A crucial clue in this respect lies in the paradigmatic axis, where the term *ʿilla* has the distributional property of being interchangeable with or, in more traditional terms, is synonymous with the terms *sabab* and *jāmiʿ*. These terms both belong to the semantic field of "linking", based on textual research by Carter and Hasan, who accordingly translate *sabab* as "semantic link" and *jāmiʿ* as "link".[86] In this interpretive scenario, the *ʿilla* can be identified with some sort of linguistic relation. Insofar as al-Suyūṭī's analysis of Arabic is concerned, especially as carried out in the *Muzhir* and the *Iqtirāḥ*, the *ʿilla*/relation doesn't manifest itself in the form of inclusion but rather

82 "Permutation from one root into another (e.g., from *ṣabara* into *baṣura*, or from *ḍaraba* into *rabaḍa*) includes the form of a weak root, as when they say: *mā aṭyabahu and mā ayṭabahu* 'How good is it!'" (al-Suyūṭī, *Muzhir* i, 246).

83 "Among these [phenomena, we mention] difference in the form of the plural, e.g., *asrā* 'captives' and *asārā* 'id.'" (ibid. 257).

84 "Because on the sound side *malak* 'property' is modeled after the form of *falak* 'celestial body' and *ḥalak* 'intense blackness'" [i.e., CaCaC] (ibid. 495).

85 Cp. al-Ḥadīthī, *Ṣarf* 86. Whether the philosophical/morphological notion of *ṣūra* is due to Greek influence or not (cp. sect. 1), is a complex issue that falls outside the scope of this study.

86 Cp. Suleiman, *Taʿlīl* 2, 106 and references therein. Cp. also Guillaume, Approach 180: "explaining a fact in this framework [= *ʿilla*] usually consists in relating it to another, supposedly more basic.".

takes the form of a systemic and, that is, non-inclusive relation such as deletion which is capable of tying together a pair of morphological units (cp. the phenomenon of *ḥadhf* in sect. 2.2). For instance, the alternation *yakun*/*yaku* can be "statically" represented as a relation: *yaku* = (partially) deleted *yakun* (cp. also the relation: *ś̌* = palatalized *s* at the end of sect. 1). Furthermore, as discussed at length in sect. 2.2,[87] the notion of *ʿilla* can be also described in more traditional and "dynamic" terms as a phonetic rule, since it involves a change from sound A to sound B and the morphological context in which this change occurs, just as a phonetic rule does. For instance, the *ʿilla* "lightening"/deletion discussed by al-Suyūṭī involves the change of *n* into zero in the morphological environment *yakun*.

Credibility is thus lent to the hypothesis that al-Suyūṭī's conception of morphology included, *inter alia*, the conceptual element (iii.b). On these grounds, it seems safe to maintain that al-Suyūṭī's conception of morphology is highly reminiscent of the methodological underpinning of MHL labeled as (iii) in sect. 1.

4 Conclusions

In sections 2.2, 2.3, 2.4 significant textual evidence has been examined that highlights a striking similarity between al-Suyūṭī's methods of linguistic analysis, as applied especially to the morphological domain, and three defining characters of MHL: history, comparativism, and morphology. We have achieved this result, which can contribute to reconsidering the rather stereotyped skepticism toward the diachronic attitude of AGT, both by reviewing the epistemological literature that investigates the methodological underpinnings of MHL, and by performing a close reading of some passages of al-Suyūṭī's linguistic works such as the *Muzhir*.

Establishing a parallelism of this sort between al-Suyūṭī's methodology of linguistic analysis and MHL's implies that the Egyptian polymath shared with the proponents of the *Stammbaumtheorie* the idea of developing a non-ingenuous historical approach to language, which took into due consideration the change undergone by it, and which can be therefore defined as a diachronic attitude *stricto sensu*. The same parallelism also implies that this historical approach was accompanied by a comparative approach to language. Such a bipartite approach can be defined as a diachronic approach *lato sensu*, and constitutes the real aspect of modernity of al-Suyūṭī's treatment of Arabic morphology.

87 See in particular fn. 64 above.

In this respect it is worth observing that the widespread criticism that al-Suyūṭī and, more generally, AGT had no clear perception of a comparative approach to the Arabic language as they never drew a comparison between Arabic and other languages, loses most of its force as soon as we realize that the observational process of linguistic comparison in and of itself certainly presupposes a linguistic object independently of the size of the object, as shown by the capability of linguistic comparison to target any kind of linguistic unit, from phonemes—if not even phonological features—to syntactic constructions. This being the case, the linguistic comparison that al-Suyūṭī and AGT applied to Arabic dialects, or intralinguistic comparison, is not ontologically different from the linguistic comparison that Schleicher, Bopp and others applied to Indo-European languages which is interlinguistic comparison.

Finally, the parallelism between al-Suyūṭī's methodology of linguistic analysis and MHL's, as established in this study, has considerable implications for our comprehension of the very notion of diachrony regardless of whether linguistic analysis combines it with a comparative approach or not. This parallelism, in fact, supports the view, usually ascribed to Jakobson[88] and sociolinguists,[89] that the Saussurean dichotomy between diachrony and synchrony should be abandoned in favor of a unified treatment of these linguistic dimensions, in the sense that a given instance of diachronic change in time is an instance of synchronic variation in space.

Bibliography

Primary Sources

Ibn Manẓūr, *Lisān al-ʿArab*, ed. ʿA.ʿA. al-Kabīr, M.A. Ḥasaballāh and H.M. al-Shādhilī, 9 vols., Cairo 1980.

Sībawayhi, *al-Kitāb*, ed. ʿA. al-S.M. Hārūn, 5 vols., Cairo 1982.

al-Suyūṭī, *al-Muzhir fī ʿulūm al-lugha wa-anwāʿihā*, ed. M.A. Jār al-Mawlā, M.A. al-F. Ibrāhīm and ʿA.M. al-Bijāwī, 2 vols., Cairo n.d.

al-Suyūṭī, *al-Iqtirāḥ fī uṣūl al-nawḥ*, ed. M.S. Yāqūt, Alexandria 2006.

al-Suyūṭī, *al-Itqān fī ʿulūm al-Qurʾān*, ed. M.A. al-F. Ibrāhīm, 4 vols., Cairo 1974.

---

88 Jakobson, Contribution 529–30. However, the statement of Max Müller quoted at the end of sect. 2.3 arguably shows that this scholar foreshadowed a unified conception of diachrony and synchrony, when he reduced the "altération phonétique" (cp. a diachronic phonetic rule) to "développement dialectal" (cp. dialectal variation in synchrony).

89 Cp. the end of sect. 2.3, and especially Ratcliffe's considerations cited there.

Secondary Sources

Abdul-Raof, H., *Theological approaches to Qur'anic exegesis: A practical comparative-contrastive analysis*, New York 2012.

Alhawary, M.T., Elicitation techniques and considerations in data collection in early Arabic grammatical tradition, in *Journal of Arabic Linguistic Tradition* 1 (2003), 1–24.

Baalbaki, R., Aṣl, in *EALL*, i, 191–5.

Baalbaki, R., *The legacy of the Kitāb: Sībawayhi's analytical methods within the context of the Arabic grammatical theory*, Leiden 2008.

Bloomfield, L., *Language*, New York 1933.

Campbell, L., *Historical linguistics: An introduction*, Edinburgh 1998.

Crystal, D., *A dictionary of linguistics and phonetics*, Malden, MA 2008.

Czapkiewicz, A., *The views of the medieval Arab philologists on language and its origin in the light of 'as-Suyūṭī's "al-Muzhir"*, Kraków 1988.

Eco, U., *La struttura assente*, Milano 1968.

Fleisch, H., *Traité de philologie arabe*, 2 vols., Beirut 1961–79.

Fück, J.W., *'Arabīya: Untersuchungen zur arabischen Sprach- und Stilgeschichte*, Berlin 1950.

Jakobson, R., Typological studies and their contribution to historical comparative linguistics, in R. Jakobson, *Selected writings*, i, The Hague 1962, 523–32.

Geoffroy, É., al-Suyūṭī, in *EI*², ix, 913–6.

Guillaume, J.-P., Grammatical tradition: Approach, in *EALL*, ii, 175–82.

al-Hadīthī, Kh., *Abniyat al-ṣarf fī Kitāb Sībawayhi*, Baghdad 1965.

Ḥammūda, Ṭ.S., *Jalāl al-Dīn al-Suyūṭī: 'Aṣruhu wa-ḥayātuhu wa-āthāruhu wa-juhūduhu fī l-dars al-lughawī*, Beirut 1989.

Hockett, Ch., Two models of grammatical description, in M. Joos (ed.), *Readings in linguistics*, New York 1958, 386–99.

Ikhwan, M., *Kitāb al-Muzhir of Jalāl al-Dīn al-Suyūṭī*: A critical edition and translation of section twenty on Islamic terms, in *Al-Jāmi'a* 47 (2009), 377–410.

Iványi, T., Lugha, in *EALL*, iii, 88–95.

Larcher, P., Un texte d'al-Fārābī sur la « langue arabe » réécrit?, in L. Edzard and J. Watson (eds.), *Grammar as a window onto Arabic humanism*, Wiesbaden 2006, 108–29.

Lehmann, Ch., *Historical linguistics: An introduction*, London 1962.

Leroy, M., *Main trends in modern linguistics*, Berkeley 1967.

Loucel, H., L'origine du langage d'après les grammairiens arabes: iv, in *Arabica* 11 (1964), 151–87.

Maher, J.P., More on the history of the comparative method: The tradition of Darwinism in August Schleicher's Work, in *Anthropological linguistics* 8 (1966), 1–12.

Müller, F.M., *La stratification du langage*, Paris 1869.

O'Hara, R.J., Trees of History in Systematics and Philology, in *Memorie della Società Italiana di Scienze Naturali e del Museo Civico di Storia Naturale di Milano* 27 (1996), 81–8.

Owens, J., Traditional Arabic grammar, in G.E. Booij, Ch. Lehmann and J. Mugdan (eds.), *Morphologie: Ein internationales Handbuch zur Flexion und Wortbildung*, i, Berlin 2000, 67–75.

Owens, J., *A linguistic history of Arabic*, New York 2006.

Rabin, Ch., *Ancient West-Arabian*, London 1951.

al-Rājiḥī, I., al-Suyūṭī wa-l-dars al-lughawī, in High Council of Literature, Arts and Social Sciences (ed.), *Jalāl al-Dīn al-Suyūṭī: al-Iḥtifāʾ bi-dhikrā murūr khamsat qurūn ʿalā wafātih*, Cairo 1978, 378–88.

Ratcliffe, R.R., *The broken plural problem in Arabic and comparative Semitic: Allomorphy and analogy in non-concatenative morphology*, Amsterdam 1998.

Saleh, M.J., Al-Suyūṭī and his works: Their place in Islamic scholarship from Mamlūk times to the present, in *MSR* 5 (2001), 73–89.

Salmon, P., The term morphology, in G.E. Booij, Ch. Lehmann and J. Mugdan (eds.), *Morphologie: Ein internationales Handbuch zur Flexion und Wortbildung*, i, Berlin 2000, 15–22.

Schleicher, A., *Compendium der vergleichenden Grammatik der indogermanischen Sprachen*, Weimar 1871.

Spevack, A., Jalāl al-Dīn al-Suyūṭī, in J.E. Lowry and D.J. Stewart (eds.), *Essays in Arabic literary biography* 1350–1850 (Mîzân. Studien zur Literatur in der islamischen Welt 17: Essays in Arabic literary biography), Wiesbaden 2009, 386–409.

Spevack, A., *The archetypal sunnī scholar: Law, theology, and mysticism in the synthesis of al-Bājūrī*, New York 2014.

Suleiman, Y., *The Arabic grammatical tradition: A study in taʿlīl*, Edinburgh 1999.

Versteegh, K., *The Arabic language*, Edinburgh 1997.

Versteegh, K. et al. (eds.), in *EALL*, 5 vols., Leiden and Boston, 2006–9.

CHAPTER 11

Al-Suyūṭī and Erotic Literature

Jaakko Hämeen-Anttila

Erotica form an important part of Classical Arabic literature, but they have received rather scarce scholarly attention. In the West, al-Nafzāwī's *al-Rawḍ al-ʿāṭir* remains the rare exception, commonly known even to the general audience. In the late Mamlūk and Early Ottoman East al-Tījānī's *Tuḥfat al-ʿarūs* and Ibn Kamāl-Pāshā's *Kitāb Rujūʿ al-shaykh ilā ṣibāhu fī l-quwwa ʿalā l-bāh* enjoyed a similar position as *the* erotic books. In the earlier Mamlūk period, the *Jawāmiʿ* (or *Jāmiʿ*) *al-ladhdha* played the same role.[1]

Arabic erotica, however, compose a much wider genre than this small selection would lead one to think. Most pieces of Arabic erotic literature, with the above exceptions, remained unpublished for centuries, but especially since the 1990s the situation has improved, and today we have a wider selection of works available to us, even though still usually and unfortunately in inferior editions.

The proliferation of editions has also brought al-Suyūṭī to the limelight as an author of erotica. His production in this field has been known to the academic world since, at least, Brockelmann, but the majority of his works remained for a long time unpublished and inaccessible.[2] The definition of what belongs to erotica is, of course, vague, as the Arabs themselves did not have a clearly defined and distinct genre for erotic writings.[3] Al-Suyūṭī's oeuvre contains at least two works that, by any definition, belong to the genre, viz. *al-Wishāḥ fī fawāʾid al-nikāḥ* and *Nawādir al-ayk fī maʿrifat al-nayk*.[4] In addition, al-Suyūṭī wrote several works that deal with erotica from a lexicographical, literary, legal

1 Probably written by ʿAlī b. Naṣr al-Kātib; see Myrne, Discussing *Ghayra*, 48.

2 For surveys of erotic texts written by or attributed to al-Suyūṭī, see *GAL* ii, 153–4, *GAL S* ii, 191–2, nos. 207–15, and Declich, Erotologia/as-Suyûṭî. For al-Suyūṭī in general, see also Spevack, al-Suyūṭī.

3 Even in poetry, the situation is far from clear. While the genre of *mujūn* does provide plenty of erotic material, it also contains parodies, satires and, e.g., blasphemous poems without any erotic elements. Moreover, *ghazals*, especially *mudhakkarāt*, often contain openly sexual materials (cp. Hämeen-Anttila, Abū Nuwās). For *mujūn*, see, e.g., van Gelder, *Bad*; Rowson, Mujūn and Szombathy, Mujūn. For erotic literature in Classical Arabic literature in general, see Hämeen-Anttila, Obscene.

4 Declich, Erotologia/as-Suyûṭî 137, also lists his *Mabāsim al-milāḥ*, but this work was never completed, cp. below.

 | DOI 10.1163/9789004334526_013

or medical point of view and could also be discussed as erotica in a wider sense.[5]

In surveying the published Arabic erotica, or works still remaining unpublished in manuscript form, one finds several other works attributed to the Egyptian polygraph. Many of these are, however, pseudepigrapha, as al-Suyūṭī seems to have received a certain reputation, or even notoriety, as a writer of erotica. Erotic literature belongs to genres ridden with various pseudepigrapha. These, with one exception, will not be discussed in this paper.

In assessing the authorship of erotic works, we err on the safe side by beginning with what al-Suyūṭī himself says in the Preface to the *Wishāḥ*, which, though not listed in his autobibliography, is without the slightest doubt his.

In the *Wishāḥ* (34), al-Suyūṭī gives a brief list of his works concerned with *nikāḥ*, as the author himself understands it. This list, it should be emphasized, is not a list of completed works but of drafts. Al-Suyūṭī himself writes: *wa-qad sawwadtu fī dhālika* (i.e., *nikāḥ*) *musawwadāt muta'addida* ("I have prepared many drafts on this subject," i.e. erotica). The works he considers to belong to *nikāḥ*, to avoid using any modern term, are the following (adding here the *Wishāḥ* itself):

1. *al-Ifṣāḥ fī asmā' al-nikāḥ*
2. *al-Yawāqīt al-thamīna fī ṣifāt al-samīna*
3. *Mabāsim al-milāḥ wa-mabāsim al-ṣibāḥ fī mawāsim al-nikāḥ*
4. *al-Wishāḥ fī fawā'id al-nikāḥ*

Al-ifṣāḥ fī asmā' al-nikāḥ, concerned with lexicography and containing material that was also included in the *Wishāḥ* (*Wishāḥ* 91–196 *al-Bāb al-thānī: Fann al-lugha*), is a dry list of words used for intercourse and sexual organs.[6] The second work on the list, *al-Yawāqīt al-thamīna fī ṣifāt al-samīna*, is a lexicographically oriented *adab* work. Even though concerned with *nikāḥ* in the sense al-Suyūṭī gives it, these two works are somewhat marginal from the point of view of my definition of erotics.

5 Declich, Erotologia and Erotologia/as-Suyûṭî, understands the genre very catholically and includes a wide variety of texts under the category of "erotologia". I restrict my discussion here by excluding texts that are oriented towards lexicography, medicine, law, and romantic literature, although all these contain erotic elements among other materials. The *sine qua non* of erotica is, in my understanding, the inclusion of openly sexual material meant to titillate or to provoke reactions.

6 It is probable that *al-Ifṣāḥ bi-fawā'id al-nikāḥ*, mentioned in al-Suyūṭī's *Taḥadduth* (114 and fn. 99) is the same as this.

After this, al-Suyūṭī mentions his *Mabāsim al-milāḥ* and finally his present work, the *Wishāḥ*. The *Mabāsim* he introduces as his magnum opus on erotica, but it is clear that it was never finished. Its materials were used for the *Wishāḥ*, which contains exactly the same chapters as the *Mabāsim*, the contents of which are listed in *Wishāḥ* 34–5, and also his other erotica mined the same source for materials. Of the *Mabāsim*, al-Suyūṭī writes: *thumma sawwadtu musawwadatan kubrā sammaytuhā Mabāsim al-milāḥ wa-mabāsim al-ṣibāḥ fī mawāsim al-nikāḥ… ghayra annahā balaghat naḥwa khamsīna kurrāsan fa-staṭaltuhā wa-sa'imtu min ṭūlihā wa-maliltuhā fa-ṣana'tu minhā hādhā l-mukhtaṣar fī naḥwi 'ushrihā* ("then I prepared a great draft, which I called *Mabāsim al-milāḥ wa-mabāsim al-ṣibāḥ fī mawāsim al-nikāḥ*… It grew up to 50 *kurrās* and I felt it to be excessively long and became weary and tired of it, so I made this abbreviated version of it, about a tenth part of the original"). This leaves little doubt that the *Mabāsim* was never finished. The author, in fact, uses three different expressions to say that he himself became weary and considered it of excessive length.

The *Wishāḥ* is a well-organized book, a typical *adab* collection. It gives the material in strict order (1. *al-Ḥadīth wa-l-āthār*; 2. *al-Lugha*; 3. *al-Nawādir wa-l-akhbār*; 4. *al-Asjā' wa-l-ash'ār*; 5. *al-Tashrīḥ*—meaning here anatomy in general; 6. *al-Ṭibb*; and 7. *al-Bāh*). In contrast to the *Nawāḍir*, to be discussed below, this book also refers to religious authority at the end of the Preface (*Wishāḥ* 35) by quoting from Abū Dā'ūd al-Sijistānī's *Kitāb al-Maṣāḥif* how Zayd b. Thābit had told that the Prophet spoke with him of all possible things, thus giving implicit authority for including all possible things, erotica among them, as topics suitable for discussion.

The outspoken material in the work is preceded by a long and exhaustive—one could even say exhausting—second chapter, which contains detailed lists of names and expressions for sexual parts, coition, and the noises made during it (*Wishāḥ* 91–196). The material in this chapter is mainly taken from lexicographical and grammatical works, presumably through the *Mabāsim*.[7] Only the end of the book is clearly erotic, al-Suyūṭī referring to and excerpting the lists of sexual positions[8] in the *Jawāmi' al-ladhdha* (about 20 positions, *Wishāḥ* 392–7) and the *Rujū' al-shaykh ilā ṣibāhu* (45 positions, *Wishāḥ* 393), and other books, totaling over 100 different positions, adding that these are listed in full

7 Ibn al-Qūṭiyya, *Af'āl*; al-Fīrūzābādī, *Qāmūs*; al-Tha'ālibī, *Fiqh al-lugha*; Abū Ḥayyān, *Sharḥ al-Tashīl*; Ibn al-Qaṭṭā', [(*Abniyat*) *al-af'āl*] (cp. GAL i, 308, GAL s i, 540); al-Zajjāj, *Khalq al-insān*; Ibn Durayd, *Jamhara*; Ibn Sīda, *Muḥkam* (quoted respectively in *Wishāḥ* 98, 100, 106, 117; 98, 108, 155; 101; 123; 143–53; 157; 157; 158); etc.

8 Some have already been given (*Wishāḥ* 361–2), and in some of the anecdotes.

in his *al-musawwada al-kubrā*, i.e., the unpublished *Mabāsim* (*Wishāḥ* 393). Of other erotic works, al-Suyūṭī quotes al-Tījānī's *Tuḥfat al-ʿarūs* (*Wishāḥ* 214, 231, 245), al-Tīfāshī's *Qādimat al-janāḥ* (*Wishāḥ* 223), and the anonymous *Rawḍat al-azhār* (*Wishāḥ* 255),[9] thus excerpting several of the main works of Arabic erotica in addition to a large number of other *adab* works. The long list of sources, here only selectively mentioned, gives the work an extremely erudite character.

Al-Suyūṭī tackled erotic topics in two further works:

5. *Shaqāʾiq al-utrunj fī raqāʾiq al-ghunj*[10]
6. *Nawāḍir al-ayk fī maʿrifat al-nayk*

The latter was only written after the *Wishāḥ* and, hence, does not figure on the list in its preface. The dating of the former is unclear, but al-Suyūṭī seems deliberately to have excluded it from the list in the *Wishāḥ* as it is mentioned by him in his *al-Taḥadduth bi-niʿmat Allāh* (123, no. 24). The latter, on the other hand, does not mention the *Wishāḥ*, which implies that the *Wishāḥ* was written after it. Al-Suyūṭī seems to have conceived of the work in terms of a legal treatise (whether it is permissible to make noises during coition or not), rather than *nikāḥ*. In *al-Taḥadduth* 123, the work is listed under the heading *Mā ullifa fī wāqiʿāt al-fatāwā min kurrās wa-fawqahu wa-dūnahu*.

The *Shaqāʾiq* resembles the *Wishāḥ*, but is considerably shorter, covering less than 50 pages in the lavishly printed edition, and its theme is restricted to noises made during coition. The author himself calls it a *juzʾ* (*Shaqāʾiq* 63, at the beginning of the text) and it is, thus, not considered by him a fully-fledged finalized work. The work is lexically inspired and learned and the material is mainly culled from lexicographical and religious sources.

The *Shaqāʾiq* contains only a limited number of verses and anecdotes. It quotes, though less extensively, many of the same sources as the *Wishāḥ*—al-Suyūṭī worked in his erotic works in the same fashion as he did in many of his other works, excerpting a set of earlier works and composing several works out of the material used in these sources. The sources quoted in the *Shaqāʾiq* include, among many others, Ibn Durayd, *Jamhara*; Ibn al-Qūṭiyya, *Afʿāl* and al-Fīrūzābādī, *Qāmūs*.[11] Of the erotic works, he quotes al-Tījānī, *Tuḥfat*

9 This may refer to the similarly titled work by al-Qurṭubī, for which see GAL S i, 596.

10 [Editor's note] On this see Daniela Rodica Firanescu, Revisiting love and coquetry, (241–59).

11 Respectively quoted in *Shaqāʾiq* 63, 64.

al-ʿarūs, al-Tīfāshī, *Qādimat al-janāḥ*, and the anonymous *Murshid al-labīb ilā muʿāsharat al-ḥabīb*.[12]

At the end of the book (*Shaqāʾiq* 108), the author quotes a saying by al-Qāsim b. Muḥammad b. Abī Bakr, an authoritative early Muslim, to the effect that—in modern terms—whatever happens between two consenting adults is their own concern (*idh khalawtum fa-fʿalū mā shiʾtum*).[13] This also seems to be al-Suyūṭī's position on the question of erotica. At least he, a polymath and religious scholar, seems to have written freely on the topic.[14]

The *Nawāḍir al-ayk* is more explicit. In the preface (*Nawāḍir* 31), al-Suyūṭī refers to the book as a *dhayl* to his *Wishāḥ*. The stylistic difference between the more respectable *nikāḥ* in the full title of the *Wishāḥ* versus *nayk* in the full title of this book seems deliberate. At the beginning of the book (*Nawāḍir* 31–5), al-Suyūṭī quotes different kinds of authoritative texts, even though as a whole the *Nawāḍir* is much less academic than the *Wishāḥ*: He begins with a line of poetry, quotes what in modern terms would be archaeological evidence (a stone from Ḥulwān—cp. also the variant of this story *Nawāḍir* 37–8), provides a maxim, involves both Hippocrates and Galen, and finally gives a specimen of Indian wisdom. Each type of evidence is represented by one, and only one, example (with the exception of medicine), as if introducing various sources of authority for discussing *nikāḥ* in terms not always decent and getting done with it as soon as possible. The religious aspect is somewhat surprisingly lacking in the Preface of this particular book.

In the *Nawāḍir*, al-Suyūṭi uses the same sources as in his other erotic books, though quoting them more sparingly. They, however, include his usual selection of erotica, especially *Jawāmiʿ* (or *Jāmiʿ*) *al-ladhdha* and *Rujūʿ al-shaykh ilā ṣibāhu*. From the latter he quotes a long list of sexual positions (*Nawāḍir* 129–42), obviously excerpting here from his own *Mabāsim*.[15] From the former

12 Respectively quoted in *Shaqāʾiq* 68, 91, 99, 100; 90; 96, 97. This may be the same as Aḥmad b. Muḥammad Ibn Falīta (al-Yamanī), *Rushd al-labīb ilā muʿāsharat al-ḥabīb*, which I have not been able to peruse. [Editor's note: on this see Firanescu, Revisiting love and coquetry, (248)]. I thank Antonella Ghersetti for drawing my attention to this book.

13 For a similar saying, see al-Jāḥiẓ, *Mufākhara* ii, 94.

14 That he freely quotes in this serious work, as also in his other works on *nikāḥ*, from various erotic manuals shows that works of explicitly erotic content were considered by him and his readers to be authoritative mainstream works, suitable to be quoted side by side with lexicographical authorities such as Ibn Durayd.

15 There is much uncertainty as to the real author of this book and whether there were two books of this title or only one. Both al-Tīfāshī (for whom, see *GAL* i, 495) and Ibn Kamāl-pāshā (see *GAL* ii, 452, no. 103) are credited with a book of this title. The latter author died in 941/1535, so either al-Suyūṭī is extensively using a younger contemporary's book

he gives quotations on pp. 113, 116, 123–128,[16] and 128. Other erotic works are not explicitly quoted in the *Nawāḍir*.[17] In comparison to the *Wishāḥ* and the *Shaqāʾiq*, the *Nawāḍir* is marked by a less extensive use of explicit quotations, both from erotic and other works.

It is extremely probable that al-Suyūṭī has written these three works (*Wishāḥ*, *Shaqāʾiq*, *Nawāḍir*) by excerpting the very same sources[18] and dividing the material into three different works, most probably first collecting a huge mass of materials in his *Mabāsim* and then, after giving up the idea of composing one comprehensive encyclopedia on *nikāḥ*, publishing this material in a series of shorter, and less exhaustive, monographs.

In *Nawāḍir* (159–62), al-Suyūṭī gives in excerpts 55 verses of an outspokenly erotic *qaṣīda*, which is anonymous and popular and, according to him, originally contained 105 verses and was written in poor language which he himself polished before including the excerpts in his book (*Nawāḍir* 163). It should be emphasized that al-Suyūṭī did not edit the *contents* of the poem, but only its substandard *language*: as it stands, the poem gives graphical descriptions of sexual positions, which, moreover, come from the mouth of a girl who wishes a man to do this and that to her, which must have made it sound even less decent in late Mamlūk ears. However, al-Suyūṭī did not find this reprehensible. He also responded to this poem by writing a similar poem of his own (*Nawāḍir* 163–6), 60 verses long,[19] to show the superiority of his poetic talent—and, again, refraining from censoring the contents in any way and publishing the

---

or quoting from a book by al-Tīfāshī. It is also possible that Ibn Kamāl-pāshā's book is an elaboration of al-Tīfāshī's. A comparison of *Nawāḍir* 129–52, with the book attributed in the edition to Ibn Kamāl-pāshā, *Rujūʿ* 100–10 (ed. al-Jamal) = 64–8 (ed. 1309) shows strong similarities but also obvious differences. As he is very free when quoting from erotic manuals, the changes may be due to al-Suyūṭī.

16 A comparison of this passage with the *Jawāmiʿ al-ladhdha* 150–1, shows that al-Suyūṭī is quoting very freely, although one has to keep in mind that the manuscripts of the erotic works tend to differ greatly from each other. Lacking a critical edition, we cannot be sure whether al-Suyūṭī had the same text in front of him as we have in the edition. However, the changes are so considerable that it is improbable that al-Suyūṭī endeavoured to quote his source verbatim.

17 Ibn Abī Ḥajala's *Nayyirāt* (read: *Dīwān*) *al-ṣabāba* is quoted (*Nawāḍir* 41). The text is correctly quoted as *Dīwān al-ṣabāba* on p. 70.

18 In addition to those already discussed, one may mention al-Wadāʿī's *Tadhkira*, quoted both in the *Shaqāʾiq* 96 and the *Nawāḍir* 65 (here written al-Wādiʿī); for the author, see GAL ii, 9.

19 It may be that the length of his own poem has induced him to quote the anonymous poem in excerpts only, not to show that his was the shorter of the two poems.

poem under his own name. These two poems are followed by another anonymous poem (*Nawādir* 166–68) of an even more outspoken nature, beginning: *khudh rijlahā wa-rmi ʿalā ẓahrihā / wa-ḥakkiki l-zubba ʿalā shufrihā* ("take her legs and throw her on her back / and then rub your penis against her cunt"), and continuing on similar lines.[20]

This openness shows that al-Suyūṭī was not disturbed by the material and was prepared to quote explicit material in a book circulating under his own name, even quoting his very outspoken poem in it, seemingly without scruples.

What perhaps distinguishes this work from any other pieces of Arabic erotica is the preponderance of openly sexually-oriented verses in the collection, covering the middle part of the text. Mildly erotic verses of the *ghazal* type abound, of course, in any anthology, as do various *mujūn* poems, but the material al-Suyūṭī presents is mostly very graphic and the number of poets he quotes is considerable, so that the *Nawādir* should be closely perused by anyone wishing to write on erotic verse in Arabic literature. Along with later poets, he gives a good selection of, e.g., Abū Ḥukayma's verses (*Nawādir* 82–3, 92). Anecdotal material and maxims are only marginally present, which, in an erotic anthology, is anomalous and is probably to be explained with reference to the preponderance of this material in the *Wishāḥ*, which was to be supplemented, not duplicated, by the *Nawādir*.

From a structural point of view, the work seems only half finished. It amasses materials in a rather haphazard way and it is not easy to see any logic behind the organization—most probably there wasn't one. This, together with the fact that the *Nawādir* is explicitly stated to be a *dhayl* to the *Wishāḥ*, shows that we are dealing with one of the final works by al-Suyūṭī, which he obviously did not have time or energy to polish but gave out more or less as a collection of materials, an afterthougth to the *Wishāḥ*, as it were.

In connection with al-Suyūṭī's erotica, one should also mention:

7. *Rashf al-zulāl min al-siḥr al-ḥalāl*

This book, also known as *Maqāmat al-nisāʾ*, belongs to the genre of *maqāma*, with a connection to the "*adab* of professions".[21] The work consists of a set of twenty very short *maqāma*s, rather simple for the genre. In the Preface some

20 This poem opens a series of half a dozen poems at the end of the book (*Nawādir* 166–70), which are attributed to a person, or persons, whose identity al-Suyūṭī conceals, using expressions such as *wa-qāla man lā yusammā sāmaḥahu llāh*.

21 Cp., e.g., Sadan, Kings, and, for a case of profession *maqāma* Hämeen-Anttila, *Maqama* 337.

young men listen to a preacher who condemns illicit, and especially homosexual, sex. Convinced by his words, the young men decide instantly to get married. This is no sooner suggested than done, and the next morning they reconvene to inform each other of their experiences in the nuptial chamber. Each tells an outspoken story of the night with his newly wedded spouse, using the specialized vocabulary of their respective professions. Thus, e.g., in the 7th *maqāma* the Lexicographer (al-Lughawī) manages to squeeze into a few lines (*Rashf* 447) several allusions to well-known lexicographical works, partly in uncouth connections.[22] The last speaker, the Sufi, relates for his part what happened *lammā ḥaṣala l-tajallī wa-l-kashf* ("when it was time to unveil and strip her"), thus using two technical terms of mysticism for the unveiling of the bride (*Rashf* 466). There are few narrative elements in this descriptive work.

Al-Suyūṭī himself mentions few of these pieces of erotica on the list of his works. It is not that he would have endeavoured to hide them, as they circulated openly under his own name; likewise, his later fame shows that his name was soon attached to the genre of erotica, so his achievements in this field, too, must have been well known—one usually attributes works to people who have become well known in a particular genre. It seems that many of these works were written by him late in life, after he had compiled his *Taḥadduth*.

Of the works wrongly attributed to al-Suyūṭī one deserves special attention, namely:

8. *al-Īḍāḥ fī ʿilm al-nikāḥ*

Who the author of the text is, is not clear. Brockelmann accepts it as a genuine work by al-Suyūṭī,[23] but the attribution is, to say the least, dubious and some manuscripts give ʿAbd al-Raḥmān b. Naṣr al-Shīrāzī as the author, and Abū l-Faraj ʿAbd al-Raḥmān b. Naṣr al-Shayzarī (physician, 6th/12th c.), the author of *Rawḍat al-qulūb wa-nuzhat al-muḥibb wa-l-maḥbūb*, may also be its real author.[24]

The style of the book differs from that of genuine erotic works by al-Suyūṭī. It uses none of the sources excerpted for his other works and, moreover, gives few explicit quotations from any learned sources, contrary to al-Suyūṭī's usual habit. The only work explicitly quoted is al-Masʿūdī's *Murūj al-dhahab*

22 E.g., *kuss muḥkam al-asās* alludes to two venerable dictionaries, Ibn Sīda's *al-Muḥkam wa-l-muḥīṭ al-aʿẓam* and al-Zamakhsharī's *Asās al-balāgha*.

23 *GAL S* ii, 191–2, no. 210.

24 I thank Antonella Ghersetti for suggesting the identification with al-Shayzarī.

(*Īḍāḥ* 126).[25] In addition, *Dīwān al-ṣabāba* is referred to (*Īḍāḥ* 128). The text uses colloquial expressions,[26] and, what is perhaps the strongest argument against al-Suyūṭī's authorship, quotes popular narratives known from the *Alf layla wa-layla*, something he does not seem to have done in any of his other works.[27] The explicit contents themselves would not necessitate excluding al-Suyūṭī from the authorship, but it seems very improbable that the work could be by him. In the improbable case that the book was, after all, by al-Suyūṭī, it would probably have been written only after the *Nawāḍir*.[28] The author seems to be Egyptian, as several Egyptian elements would suggest.[29]

The work is a random collection of material ranging from the explicitly erotic to stories where this element is negligible. It quotes pseudo-scientific material attributed to Avicenna (*Īḍāḥ* 130, 138), Galen, Plato and Aristotle (*Īḍāḥ* 137), as well as to some unnamed philosophers (*baʿḍ al-ḥukamāʾ*, *Īḍāḥ* 131; *al-ḥakīm*, ibid. 146). It conspicuously often uses pseudo-*isnād*s, often parodically (*Īḍāḥ* 122, 123, 124—*ruwiya ʿan Iblīs*!—ibid. 145).[30] Another distinguishing feature of the work is the openly parodic use of Quranic and religious vocabulary (*Īḍāḥ* 123, 124, 125), which does not easily fit the authorial profile of al-Suyūṭī. As in most erotic works, those of al-Suyūṭī as well as of others, the material is heterosexual.

25 The passage is found in *Murūj* §2053 (where we have the correct reading al-Ḥārith b. Kalada for the edition's al-Ḥārith b. Kinda). The quotation, not necessarily and even not probably coming directly from the *Murūj*, which was a rare book by this time, is again rather free. It would seem that the anecdotes on al-Ḥajjāj in the *Īḍāḥ* were lifted as a block from one unidentified source, as some of them have nothing to do with the erotic subject matter of the *Īḍāḥ*.

26 *Rāyiḥ yaqtulnī*; *fard zubb*; *ʿād yasmaʿ* and *jāb*; *kamān shwayyah* (*Īḍāḥ* 122, 124, 125, 134).

27 The three wishes (*Īḍāḥ* 133 = Lyons *Arabian Nights* ii, 587; Littmann, *Erzählungen* iv, 329–31); The Jewish judge and his virtuous wife (*Īḍāḥ* 139–42 = Lyons *Arabian Nights* ii, 327–30; Littmann, *Erzählungen* iii, 708–12); and The pious Israelite and his wife (*Īḍāḥ* 142–4 = Lyons *Arabian Nights* ii, 335–8; Littmann *Erzählungen* iii, 720–5). As these stories are not restricted to the *Arabian Nights*' tradition and could have been taken from some other source, they cannot be used for dating either of the works. For the interrelatedness of the *Arabian Nights* and post-Mongol literature, see most recently Marzolph, Studio.

28 As a potential argument in favour of al-Suyūṭī's authorship one might, though, mention that the temporal sequence of his two genuine works, *Wishāḥ* and *Nawāḍir*, shows a lessening of explicitly quoted sources and an increase in popular material, as well as a development towards less structural cohesion. Against this background, one could speculate on the *Īḍāḥ* merely being the peak of this development.

29 Cp., e.g., the preponderance of Egyptian place names (*Īḍāḥ* 125, 145).

30 A pseudo-*isnād* is also used in the beginning of the *Rashf*, but there it is short and the stylistic device is conventional in the *maqāma* genre, cp. Hämeen-Anttila, *Maqama* 46–8.

Whoever its author, the work contains material aimed at shocking the reader, both by its explicitness and, even more so, by mixing almost pornographic elements with religion. As an example of this, one might quote the beginning of the book (*Īḍāḥ* 122), which reads: "Praise be to Him who has embellished the chests of virgins with breasts and has set women's thighs as benches for the wild asses of pricks and who has made the prick-spears stand erect, ready to push in cunts, not chests," etc. This passage, in fact, may have caused the misattribution—if such it is—to al-Suyūṭī, as the *khuṭba* may have been lifted from his *Nawāḍir* (106), where it is attributed to an anonymous author (*li-baʿḍihim*). Whether the *Nawāḍir* or some earlier book is the source of the *khuṭba*, it most probably is not by al-Suyūṭī, as this section of the *Nawāḍir* consists exclusively of quotations and he does not otherwise conceal his authorship when quoting explicit material.

A comparison of the two texts again shows differences between them, as if one, or both, of the versions had been freely modified. It is slightly difficult to understand why al-Suyūṭī should have modified a text he himself had quoted in another of his works to this extent, so the comparison favours the supposition that the *Īḍāḥ* is by a different author.[31]

As I have drawn attention to,[32] there follows after this an imaginary and hilarious discussion preceded by an openly fictitious *isnād*, narrated by an anonymous friend, who has sex with his neighbours through a breach in the wall (*ḥukiya ʿan baʿḍ al-aṣdiqāʾ wa-l-khullān wa-nayyākī l-jīrān min shuqūq al-ḥīṭān*). The story involves, among other characters, Cunt, Cock and Reverend (literally *ḥājj*) Balls (*Īḍāḥ* 122–3).[33] Instead of a fully-fledged Cock and Bull story, though, we only have a brief Cock and Balls dialogue.

To make sure the reader understands we are treading in dangerous territory, the author defines, using Quranic terms, all girls over fourteen as old hags (*ʿajūz fī l-*ghābirīn*)[34] that should be avoided. Both ideas—the preference for young girls and the avoidance of old women—are present in many respectable books that discuss whom a man should marry, but the outrageous way of defining who is an old hag must have provoked even the pre-modern reader, especially as Quranic terms were borrowed for this purpose. Even more outrageous are

31 The *Īḍāḥ* is definitely the later of the two, but it cannot be excluded that both works derive the *khuṭba* from a third source. As al-Suyūṭī is very free in his quotations, the version of the *Īḍāḥ* may well be truer to the original.

32 Hämeen-Anttila, Obscene.

33 Translated as Madame Slit, Mr. Tool and Al Hajj Eggs in ps.-al-Suyūṭī, *Secrets*, 33–4.

34 The text reads *fī l-ʿābirīn*, failing to recognize an allusion to Q 26: 171; 37: 135.

the mock *ḥadīths* narrated on the authority of Iblīs (*Īḍāḥ* 124) and the listing (*Īḍāḥ* 125) of whores bearing names that make Rushdie's *Satanic Verses* sound innocent: Umm al-Khayr, Khadīja, Ḥalīma, Fāṭima, and Bilqīs.

To conclude, it remains to say some words on al-Suyūṭī's relation to erotica in general. Why did he write works belonging to this genre? The first part of the answer is a counter-question: why should he not have done so? It is obvious that the relation to erotic literature was more relaxed in Mediaeval Arabic culture—both Mamlūk and otherwise—than in the Victorian and perhaps even the modern world.[35] Not that the topic was completely unproblematic, as we see from the explanations often given in the preface (of the type: "I would not have written this, had not my patron pressed me to") and the religious arguments used to defend the selection of the topic, the two favourites being that a) God has created the language, or at least the nouns, as testified by the famous scene with Adam in Q 2:31–33 and hence words are not impure or sinful in themselves, without actions, and b) the *ḥadīth* defending comic relief in the middle of a serious work, here "comic" being often subtly and on purpose confused with "pornographic".

The second part of the answer is somewhat more specific. As we can easily see from the list of al-Suyūṭī's publications, he aimed at being a polymath and set about proving it by profuse publications that more or less cover the whole range of Mediaeval Arabic learned literature. Erotica was also a subject that was considered a separate science (*ʿilm*), though only a minor one, and a true polymath should be able to prove himself also in this field.

The erotic works of al-Suyūṭī contain little homosexual material. This has been seen by Aaron Spevack as programmatic,[36] but this need not be the case. Although homosexuality is common in comic anecdotes and *ghazals*, erotic manuals are in general mainly heterosexual, and al-Suyūṭī may just have been following the tradition.[37] On the other hand, he did have a reputation to defend and probably was himself somewhat on the conservative side, so that not advertising overtly illicit sex goes well with what one might expect of him.

35 Cp. Hämeen-Anttila, Obscene.

36 Spevack, al-Suyūṭī 401; Spevack speaks of the licit character of sex in al-Suyūṭī's works and bases himself mainly on the *khuṭba* that forms the starting point of the *Rashf al-zulāl*.

37 A similar, well-known case of the genre defining whether the author takes a homosexual or a heterosexual stance comes from Persian literature, where the same authors used to write mainly homosexual *ghazals* but almost without exception heterosexual romantic *masnavis*.

Lorenzo Declich[38] has seen al-Suyūṭī's erotic works of strictly heterosexual content as a programmatic response to what he may have seen as the loosening morals of the late Mamlūk society. This may, perhaps, be overdoing the case and gives more serious attention to these works than they deserve. It is obvious that al-Suyūṭī liked to see himself as a polymath, so, basically, one might expect him to write on every conceivable topic, erotica among them. His occasional references to the legitimacy and preferability of matrimonial sex are to be seen as a topos in erotic literature, and also authors who are very outspoken in their writings often pay lip service to Islamic morals. Had he wished to attack homosexuality in Mamlūk society, he would have had much more powerful means to do so than compiling collections of erotica.

When it comes to specifically homosexual love, al-Suyūṭī is perhaps not quite as strict as Declich and Spevack would have it. In a dialogue on homosexuality in Paradise between ʿAlī b. al-Walīd al-Muʿtazilī and Abū Yūsuf al-Qazwīnī, which al-Suyūṭī relates on the authority of Ibn ʿAqīl al-Ḥanbalī (*Nawāḍir* 64), the last word is given to Ibn al-Walīd, who is of the opinion that homosexual love, as well as wine, exist in Paradise, despite the two being prohibited on earth, thus giving an implicit approval to homosexuality as such when considered outside of the sphere of the *sharīʿa*.

Al-Suyūṭī's wish to appear as a polymath may well have been one of the main causes why he also delved into the field of erotica. A further cause may simply have been his joie-de-vivre: although now and then falling into dry, antiquarian learnedness, he is also able to show himself to be a man who enjoys life in all its variety.

Bibliography

Primary Sources

Ibn Kamāl-pāshā, *Kitāb Rujūʿ al-shaykh ilā ṣibāhu*, in *al-Jins ʿinda l-ʿarab. Nuṣūṣ mukhtāra*, Köln 1997, ii, 7–182.

Ibn Kamāl-pāshā, *Kitāb Rujūʿ al-shaykh ilā ṣibāhu*, [Bulaq] 1309 AH.

al-Jāḥiẓ, *Mufākharat al-jawārī wa-l-ghilmān*, in al-Jāḥiẓ, *Rasāʾil* ed. ʿA. al-S.M. Hārūn, ii, Cairo 1384/1964, 91–137.

38 Erotologia/as-Suyûṭî 143–6.

al-Masʿūdī, *Murūj al-dhahab*, ed. B. de Meynard and P. de Courteille, rev. C. Pellat, 7 vols. (Publications de l'Université Libanaise. Section des études historiques 11), Beyrut 1966–79.
al-Suyūṭī, *al-Taḥadduth bi-niʿmat Allāh*, in E.M. Sartain (ed.), *Jalāl al-dīn al-Suyūṭī.* ii: *al-Taḥadduth bi-niʿmat Allāh* (University of Cambridge Oriental Publications 24), Cambridge 1975.
al-Suyūṭī, *Nawāḍir al-ayk fī maʿrifat al-nayk*, ed. Ṭ.Ḥ. ʿAbd al-Qawī, Syria n.d.
al-Suyūṭī, *Rashf al-zulāl*, in A. ʿImrān (ed.), al-Suyūṭī, *Faḍāʾil al-nikāḥ*, Damascus 2013, 432–67.
al-Suyūṭī, *Shaqāʾiq al-utrunj fī raqāʾiq al-ghunj*, ed. M.S. al-Rifāʿī, Syria n.d.
al-Suyūṭī, *al-Wishāḥ fī fawāʾid al-nikāḥ*, ed. Ṭ.Ḥ. ʿAbd al-Qawī, Syria n.d.
Ps.-al-Suyūṭī, *al-Īḍāḥ fī ʿilm al-nikāḥ*, in *al-Jins ʿinda l-ʿarab. Nuṣūṣ mukhtāra*, Köln 1997, i, 121–146; *The secrets of oriental sexuology. The book of exposition (Kitab al-Izah fi'Ilm al-Nikah b-it-Tamam w-al-Kamal)*, literally translated from the Arabic by an English Bohemian, Paris 1896, repr. London 1987.

Secondary Sources

Brockelmann, C., *Geschichte der arabischen Literatur* [GAL], 2 vols. and *Supplementbände* [GAL S], 3 vols., Leiden 1937–49.
Declich, L., L'erotologia araba: profilo bibliografico, in RSO 68 (1994), 249–65.
Declich, L., L'erotologia di Galâl ad-Dîn as-Suyûṭî, in *Alifbâ* 17 (1995), 125–46.
van Gelder, G.J., *The bad and the ugly. Attitudes towards invective poetry* (hijāʾ) *in Classical Arabic literature* (Publication of the "De Goeje Fund" 26), Leiden, New York, Koebenhavn and Köln 1988.
Hämeen-Anttila, J., *MAQAMA. A history of a genre* (DA 5), Wiesbaden 2002.
Hämeen-Anttila, J., Abu Nuwās and *ghazal* as a genre, in T. Bauer and A. Neuwirth (eds.), *Ghazal as world literature I: Transformations of a literary genre* (BTS 89), 2005, 87–105.
Hämeen-Anttila, J., What is obscene? Obscenity in Classical Arabic literature, in A. Talib, M. Hammond and A. Schippers (eds.), *The rude, the bad and the bawdy: Essays in honour of Professor Geert Jan van Gelder*, [Warminster] 2014, 13–23.
Littmann, E., *Die Erzählungen aus den Tausendundein Nächten*, 6 vols., Wiesbaden 1953.
Lyons, M.C., *The Arabian nights. Tales of 1001 nights*, 3 vols., London 2008.
Marzolph, U., In the studio of the Nights, in MEL 17 (2014), 43–57.
Myrne, P., Discussing *Ghayra* in Abbasid Literature: Jealousy as a Manly Virtue or Sign of Mutual Affection, in *Journal of Abbasid Studies* 1 (2014), 46–65.
Rowson, E.K., Mujūn, in J. Scott Meisami and P. Starkey (eds.), EAL, ii, London and New York 1998, 546–8.

Sadan, J., Kings and craftsmen—a pattern of contrasts: On the history of a Mediaeval Arabic humoristic form, 2 parts, *SI* 56 (1982), 5–49; 62 (1985), 89–120.

Spevack, A., Jalāl al-Dīn al-Suyūṭī, in J.E. Lowry and D.J. Stewart (eds.), *Essays in Arabic literary biography 1350–1850* (Mîzân. Studien zur Literatur in der islamischen Welt 17,2: Essays in Arabic literary biography), Wiesbaden 2009, 386–409.

Szombathy, Z., Mujūn. *Libertinism in Medieval Muslim society and literature*, [Cambridge], 2013.

CHAPTER 12

Revisiting Love and Coquetry in Medieval Arabic Islam: Al-Suyūṭī's Perspective

Daniela Rodica Firanescu

1 Introduction

The last few decades have witnessed a vivid interest in the Arabic heritage works devoted to eroticism and sexuality, generically designated as *kutub al-bāh*[1] (books on sexual intercourse); a peculiar interest has been attached to a specific area, apparently subjacent to the larger concept of sexuality (*bāh*), namely to *adab al-nikāḥ*, a syntagm translatable by "literature on matrimonial sexual intercourse". Numerous such heritage books on *adab al-nikāḥ* have been (re-)edited and published in modern editions, the editors indicating in their introductions, almost invariably, that this specific type of Arabic medieval literary heritage did not receive the deserved attention in the past, that the manuscripts were neglected, their publication was censored by the institutions responsible with the preservation of a suitably impeccable Islamic morality, and the published texts were truncated, purged from passages considered as using an exceedingly explicit sexual terminology (*ṣarāḥa*) or indecent, impudent expressions (*taʿābīr fāḥisha*).[2] The revival of the interest in *adab al-nikāḥ* is viewed by the Arab editors as a reparatory act, as well as a work of recuperation of this type of texts that are now considered valuable since they complete the image of "the wideness of the Islamic civilisation and its concern with all the human material and spiritual necessities."[3]

As illustrated by Rowson,[4] the erotic literature in Arabic was represented by early writings, from the ninth and tenth century, many of them lost without a trace. Here comes the role of later authors—some of them influential theologians such as Jalāl al-Dīn al-Suyūṭī (d. 911/1505), an emblematic figure of the

1 In our view, *bāh* (coitus, cohabitation with a woman) is the larger term, while *nikāḥ* refers more specifically to the sexual behavior within the conjugal couple, a hypothesis that still has to be examined. Generally, the two terms are parallel (synonyms: *jimāʿ*, *waṭʾ*).

2 Cp. al-ʿĀmil, Turāth; ʿUmrān, Īrūtīkiyya, etc.

3 ʿUmrān, Īrūtīkiyya 7.

4 Rowson, Arabic: Middle Ages 48, referring to the books of al-Namlī.

 | DOI 10.1163/9789004334526_014

Mamlūk period—who have preserved, at least partly, through quotations and compilation work, the contributions of early authors in the field.

1.2 *The Citrons' Sisters*

The list of books on matrimonial sexuality authored by (or ascribed to) al-Suyūṭī, provided by Kadar,[5] comprises (without being complete) nine titles; among them, a small treatise of eroticism that interests us here, composed, probably, in the late fifteenth century CE, entitled *Shaqā'iq al-utrunj fī raqā'iq al-ghunuj*[6]—that we translate *The citrons' sisters: On women of sensitive coquetry*, abbreviated *CS*. Our translation of the title takes into consideration the spirit of the treatise: women must be "sensitive" to men's needs and the whole arsenal of feminine coquetry must be orientated towards men's satisfaction. The treatise is devoted to the complex notion of *ghunj* that we translate by "sensitive feminine coquetry", a syntagm encompassing a complex semantic area, approached in detail in this paper.

We use, preponderantly, the text edited and published by ʿĀdil al-ʿĀmil (Damascus, 1988), abbreviated *Sh1*; exceptionally, we use as well the text edited by Q.K. al-Janābī, revised and introduced by Anwar ʿUmrān (Damascus, 2013), abbreviated *Sh2*. The book contains four chapters devoted to the study of the women's sensitive coquetry as reflected in: 1. language (*al-lugha*); 2. religious patrimonial texts (*al-āthār*): the Quran and the prophetical traditions (*aḥādīth nabawiyya*); 3. anecdotal literature (*al-akhbār*); 4. poetry (*al-ashʿār*).

As we have dealt with the first two chapters of the book in a previous article,[7] the present paper has two main purposes: 1. to complete the image of the notion of "sensitive feminine coquetry" (*ghunj*) as reflected within the "patrimonial narratives" (or "anecdotic literature", *akhbār*), approached in chapter 3 of the treatise; 2. to take an attentive look at the shaping of the "culture of gender" and its system of values (still current, to a large extent) in the Arab Islamic medieval civilisation. The translation of the excerpts from *CS* is ours.

---

5 Kadar, before Introduction to *Fann al-nikāḥ* i.

6 The form *ghunuj* (parallel to the more frequently used *ghunj*) creates prosodic (rhythmic) symmetry. [Editor's note] On *Shaqā'iq al-utrunj* see also Jaakko Hämeen-Anttila, Al-Suyūṭī and erotic literature, (230–1).

7 Firanescu, Amour.

2 The Title's Translation and Interpretation

The title *Shaqā'iq al-utrunj fī raqā'iq al-ghunuj* has been translated into English, in various writings, as: *The citron halves or the delicacy of women*; *The citron halves or the daintiness of women*; *The citron halves: on elegant lusty mannerisms*, etc. If there is variation in the translation of the second part of the title, the first part has constantly been translated *The citron halves*, understanding *shaqā'iq* as "halves" (i.e. as plural of *shaqq* or *shiqq*); however, the substantive *shaqā'iq* could be considered in the context the plural of *shaqīqa* (full sister, sister on paternal and maternal side) rather than plural of *shiqq* (half). At least three arguments make possible to accept *shaqā'iq* as meaning "sisters": 1. *shiqq* (half, side, part) has the commonly used plural (built on the morphological pattern *af'āl*) *ashqāq*; 2. the morpho-syntactic and semantic symmetry in the title is expected: if the adjective *raqā'iq* clearly refers to "gentle/sensitive women", we might suppose that the noun *shaqā'iq*, built on the same pattern—*fa'ā'il*—also refers to women; 3. *utrunj* is in fact a (collective) plural. Considering also that there are two types of "construct state" (*iḍāfa*) associated in the Arabic title—a possession construction, "the sisters of the citrons" (*shaqā'iq al-utrunj*), and the qualification annexation "the women of (or having, manifesting) sensitive coquetry" (*raqā'iq al-ghunuj*), we are inclined to translate the title *The citrons' sisters: On women of sensitive coquetry*.

The simile contained in the title is quite transparent: women of sensitive coquetry are similar to (or the sisters of) citrons, equal or equivalent to citrons. Yet, a further step towards the disambiguation of the title raises the question: why the citron, precisely? Could the citron evoke the prophetical *ḥadīth* (commonly known as *ḥadīth al-utrujja* "the *ḥadīth* of the citron") below?

> *Qāla rasūlu llāh: mathalu l-mu'mini llādhī yaqra'u l-Qur'āna ka-mathali l-utrujjati: rīḥuhā ṭayyib^{un} wa-ṭa'muhā ṭayyib^{un}*... (Allah's Messenger said: The example of a believer who recites the Qur'an [and acts on its orders], is that of a citron which smells good and tastes good...)[8]

The form *utrujja* is a variant used in parallel with *utrunja*. We tend to believe that the title given to this treatise by the theologian al-Suyūṭī echoes the aforementioned *ḥadīth*. Accordingly, we infer—a suggestion contained from the start, in the title—that the most appreciable or laudable women are those who display "sensitive" (to men's needs and pleasure) coquetry, in a similar way in which the most appreciable among the believers are those who read the

8 Khan, Translation vii, 211 (*ḥadīth* 5427).

Quran. Thus, the syntagm *shaqāʾiq al-utrunj* is a metaphorical way of designating the most appreciated women, who are like the citron among other kinds of fruits. Significantly, the association between woman and food appears as well in the same chapter seven of "The Book of Foods (Meals)" of *Ṣaḥīḥ al-Bukhārī*, in a *ḥadīth* that follows immediately the one of the citron:

> Qāla rasūlu llāh: *faḍlu ʿĀʾishata ʿalā l-nisāʾi ka-faḍli l-tharīdi ʿalā sāʾiri l-ṭaʿām.*" ("Allah's Messenger said: *The superiority of ʿĀʾisha to other ladies is like the superiority of al-tharīd to other kinds of food.*)[9]

3 Revisiting "De L'amour et la Coquetterie en Islam Arabe Médiéval: La Perspective d'as-Suyūṭī"[10]

In order to relate the first two chapters to the third, a short revisitation of our above-mentioned article imposes itself. We need to reiterate that al-Suyūṭī's discourse on feminine coquetry situates in the background the idea of "conjugal couple" in the sense of Chebel's remark: "… en Islam, seule la coquetterie destinée à satisfaire les époux est encouragée, ce qui rend toute autre flatterie douteuse aux yeux du *fiqh*."[11] The conjugal couple constitutes the frame within which a woman/wife is supposed to use her seductive arsenal; however, the text refers as well to slave concubines (*jawārī*) and slaves trained in the art of dancing and singing (*qiyān*), professional providers of fleshly pleasure.

The semantic core of the complex term *ghunj* is represented by women's verbal expression of sensuality: addressing exciting, stimulant speech (allusive, frank, or even obscene, *kalām fāḥish*) in the prelude of the fleshly encounter or during it. Beyond the verbalized expression, this recommended feminine form of sensuality also includes: the tone of the voice (the babied, pampered, coddled, rhythmic way of speaking—*takassur*); the voice inflexions: waiving in speaking, modulating the voice with grace/harmoniously, undulating the voice—*tarkhīm al-kalām*; and the vocalizations: murmurs, whispering (*hams*); snoring (*shakhīr*) during the intercourse, raising the voice through the nose or snorting (*nakhīr*), etc. (the translation of the words *shakhīr* and *nakhīr* by "snoring" and, respectively, "snorting", is both literal and contextually appropriate; in our view, the author effectively means these types of sounds produced

9 Ibid. (*ḥadīth* 5428).

10 Firanescu, Amour.

11 Chebel, *Encyclopédie* 166.

by raising the voice through the nose). This type of erotic behavior is characterized as purely feminine.

We have indicated[12] that *ghunj* was used by al-Suyūṭī as a generic term (having, in the text, a whole series of synonyms, from the same root or different roots: *taghannuj, tabaghnuj, ghināj*; *dall, dalāl*; *shikl, shakl*) encompassing the three following main components:

a) *Al-ʿirāba* (with the variants *iʿrāba, iʿrāb, istiʿrāb, taʿrīb, ʿirab*) that designates a wife's tender, courtly, flirtatious conduct towards her husband; *ʿurub* (sing. *ʿariba*; also *ʿarūb*) are the women/wives who love, cherish, and desire their husbands, adopting towards them flirtatious and seductive manners; *ʿarūb* is defined as a woman who behaves like a libertine coquette, a courtesan, a prostitute with her husband (*al-mutabadhdhila li-zawjihā*).

b) *Al-rafath*—a complex notion related to provocative sensuality and sexual exhortation, that has two manifestations: verbal/vocal, and motional. To the verbal expression of sensuality is associated a motional sub-type of *rafath*, described as a purely feminine feature: the sensuality of a woman's gestures (*īmāʾ*) and movements, the provocative way of walking (sway, swing, shake the body in walking, undulate the hips/haunch/waist or move with a smooth wave-like motion) and, during the fleshly union, making welcoming corporal movements (*rahz*) in accordance with the man's sexual penchants. Finally, the sublimation of *rafath* by a woman is expressing the ardent desire—verbally, vocally, and through gestures and motion—during the intercourse, along with expressing (or faking) languor, fatigue, and exhaustion (*tahāluk*). The purpose of the feminine *rafath* in all its forms is to please the man, to create for him the sensation of *rifq* (kindness, gentleness) from the woman's part, the sensation that she is his partner, accomplice, and gentle companion through the sexual intercourse.

c) *Al-ḥaṣāna wa-l-ʿiffa*: the woman's inaccessibility and fight against any seductive attempt coming from any man other than her husband, and her chastity/integrity/virtuousness in front of the illicit fleshly temptation (*ghulma*), in all circumstances other than the "conjugal" intercourse.

4 In Completion to Chapter Two, *Fī l-āthār* (in the Patrimonial Religious Texts): *Ghunj* as "A Woman's Erotic Vocalization"

A few pages at the end of the second chapter of *CS* (*Sh1* 39–40; *Sh2* 415–6)—that we did not approach in "De l'amour et la coquetterie..."—deal with

12 Firanescu, Amour 56–61.

a specific sector of the extended semantic area covered by the term *ghunj*: "a woman's vocal erotic behavior" or "copulatory vocalization". As described in the text, this appears to be an important part of a woman's sexually stimulating arsenal, instrumental in facilitating the water/sweat emergence from the ears, thus completing the participation of all the parts of the body and sense organs to the love making; once the sense of hearing "takes its share of lust", the state of "total impurity caused by the sexual intercourse" (*janāba*) is achieved (as illustrated by the metonymic sense of the saying "there is major impurity under every hair"—seemingly a weak *ḥadīth*) (*Sh2* 414–5):

قال بعض الأطباء: الحكمة في الغنج أن يأخذ السمع حظه من الجماع فيسهل خروج الماء من جارحة السمع فإن الماء يخرج من تحت كل جزء من البدن، ولهذا ورد تحت كل شعرة جنابة، وكل جزء له نصيب من اللذة فنصيب العينين النظر ونصيب الفخذين وبقايا أسفال البدن المُماسة، ونصيب سائر أعلى البدن الضم والمعانقة، ولم يبق إلا حاسة السمع فنصيبها سماع الغنج.

> Some physicians said: the underlying reason of the [woman's] erotic vocalization is to allow the sense of hearing to take its share in the sexual intercourse and thus to facilitate the emergence/effusion of the water from the ears, since the water emerges from every part of the body, the reason for which it was said "there is impurity beneath every single hair". Every part [of the body] takes its share of lust: the eyes' share is the gaze; the thighs' share and that of the rest of the lower parts of the body is the touching; the share of most of the upper parts [of the body] are the hug and embrace; there is only the sense of hearing left: so, its share is to listen to the "[woman's] erotic vocalization".

We have translated the word *ghunj*, in the above paragraph, by including the specification "woman's" (erotic vocalization) because this activity or behavior is ascribed in the text exclusively to women; it is presented as a purely feminine trait and practice, never associated with the masculine behavior. The man participating in the sexual intercourse is presented as the beneficiary of this facility or tenderness services offered by the female partner.

Al-Suyūṭī reinforces the usefulness of the erotic vocalization to the man that listens to it with a proverb (reported after al-Wadāʿī) or a popular saying (marked by the colloquial question word *ēysh*) stating that he who is "deaf" (physically or possibly figuratively, in the sense of "the one who doesn't listen") to a woman's erotic vocalization doesn't take benefit of it; by extension, in other possible contexts than erotic: the one who doesn't listen to what could be beneficial to him misses a benefit or an advantage (*Sh2* 415):

إيش ينفع الغنج في أذن الأطرش.

Literally: What is the benefit of tender words [whispered] in the years of the deaf?

4.1 *The Components of the Feminine Copulatory Vocalization and Verbalization and their Role* (*Chapter Two*)

a) Modulating the voice graciously/sensitively and producing pain vocalizations (*Sh2* 415)

... ترخيم الكلام عند مخاطبة الرجل ما يحب وتارة تتألم وتارة تستزيده بشجي صوتها وإرقاق نغمها...

Modulating the voice graciously when addressing the man the words that please him; at times, she expresses/produces pain vocalizations, at other times she asks for more, through the moving/touching inflexions of her voice and the softening of her melodic voice tone.

A poetic (the poet is not specified) illustration of the suitability of this erotic tool:

ويعجبني منك عند الجماع / حياة الكلام وموت النظر.

Literally: I like at you during the encounter / the life of the speech and the death of the gaze.

b) The erotic breathing tools and artifices (snoring, sighing) (*Sh2* 415)

ولا بد في أثناء ذلك من شخير دقيق وتنهد رقيق...

During the intercourse, delicate/relentless snoring and sensitive sighing are required...

The erotic breathing tools, along with other strategic vocalizations from the feminine arsenal—like kisses and bites, named "the fruit of love" (*thamar al-hawā*), that may be used as well by men—are meant "to reinforce the man's sexual appetite and to incite him to resume his performance."

c) Keeping away from shyness while speaking during the intercourse (*ijtināb al-ḥayāʾ*)

It is recommended that the woman throws off the shyness/shame (*ḥayāʾ*) and adopts sexual licentiousness (*khalāʿa*), a feature illustrated by a prophetic *ḥadīth* (*Sh2* 415):

وقد روي عن النبي، صلى الله عليه وسلم إنه قال: خير نسائكم التي إذا خلعت خلعت معه الحياء، وإذا لبسته لبست معه الحياء. يعني مع زوجها.

> It was narrated about the Prophet—Allah's blessings and peace be upon him—that he said : The best of your women is the one who, if she takes it[13] off, takes off with it the shyness, and when she puts it on, she puts on/wears with it the shyness. I mean with her husband.

One will note the implicit recommendation that such behavior should be displayed by a woman exclusively "with her husband."

An anecdote excerpt from Aḥmad b. Muḥammad al-Yamanī's [Ibn Falīta] *Rushd al-labīb*, inserted by al-Suyūṭī in the text, reinforces the suitability of this behavioral trait: a magistrate's wife used to display, by her very nature, shameless verbal behavior during intercourse (*kānat maṭbūʿa ʿalā l-khalāʿa ʿinda l-jimāʿ*); when he heard from her what he had not heard before, he kept her at distance from him, but when he came to her a second time, and did not hear anything from what she used to say before, he found himself deprived from his capacity to perform and the lust he had felt the first time, so he asked her to go back to the way she used to talk, and keep away from shyness, as far as she could … This paragraph implies dirty talk, though there is no example given.

d) the role of rhythm-keeper played by vocalization (related to the previous component) (*Sh2 41*)

ومن دقيق هذه الصفة أن يكون غنج المرأة ورهز الرجل متطابقين كالإيقاع على الغناء ولا يخرج أحدهما عن الآخر.

13 The clothing (*jilbāb*, as it appears explicitly in a related *ḥadīth*, commented upon immediately after, by al-Suyūṭī, *Sh2*. 416).

A subtle aspect of this quality is that the woman's copulatory vocalization and the man's motion must be in mutual agreement, like the rhythm and the singing; never should one of them deviate from the other.

4.2 *Some Peculiar Varieties of Vocal Artifices and Related Types of Women*

Most of the following illustrations of feminine vocal strategies, inserted at the end of chapter two, are excerpt from *Dalā'il al-nubuwwa* by al-Bayhaqī (as indicated by the editor of *Sh1*); al-Suyūṭī does almost exclusively compilation work:

a) the snorting, moaning/sobbing woman (*Sh1 41*)

وقيل: منهن النهاقة وهي التي تعلي صوتها في الغنج بالنخير والشهيق.

It was said: among them there is the one who sobs, which is the one whose copulatory vocalization consists in the nasal rising of her voice/snorting and moaning/groaning/sobbing/braying.

b) the acceptable silence and the silent woman (*Sh1* 41)

وكثير من النساء من تستعمل السكوت عند الجماع ولكن مع رشاقة الحركة وإظهار القبول للوطء وضم الرجل إليها وتقبيله مرة بعد مرة ومساعدته بالرهز، وهذه صفة محمودة غير مكروهة.

Numerous are the women who use the silence during the intercourse, but along with the gracefulness of the movements, with showing their assent to the riding/intercourse, embracing the man and kissing him over and over again, and helping him with the bodily motion; this is a laudable characteristic, not disagreeable/reprehensible.

c) the cursing/swearing woman and the one who invokes evil (*Sh1* 41)

وفيهن من يكون غنجها كله سبا للرجل ودعاء عليه، وهذه عادةُ صنعاء وما يليها.

There are among them those whose copulatory vocalization consists entirely in cursing the man and invoking the evil upon him; this is the practice in Sanaa and the surrounding regions.

d) the desiring woman who does not master the art of seduction (*Sh1* 41)

ومنهن المشتهية التي لا تحسن التغنج ولا التكسر وهذا عام في نساء الجبل وما والاها من بلاد المشرق ونساء العجم.

> There is among them the desiring woman who masters neither the art of seduction nor the coddling way of speaking and this is a general feature of the women from the mountain [could be the Mount Sinai also called in Arabic Jabal Mūsā?] and its neighboring Eastern regions, and the Persians' [or the non-Arabs'?] women.

5 The Notion of *ghunj* in the Patrimonial Narratives (Chapter Three)

The third chapter of *CS* (43–46 in *Sh1* that we use here) includes a number of reported anecdotes meant to represent pieces of evidence or reference points that support and illustrate the views (some belonging to al-Suyūṭī, some others to the authors he quotes) related to *ghunj*, exposed in the previous chapters.

The anecdotes are excerpt from books that, in al-Suyūṭī's time, were already important pieces of the literary heritage, such as *Kitāb al-Aghānī* by Abū l-Faraj al-Iṣfahānī, *Tuḥfat al-ʿarūs* by al-Tījānī, *Kitāb Jāmiʿ al-ladhdha* by ʿAlī b. Naṣr al-Kātib, *Dalāʾil al-nubuwwa* by al-Bayhaqī and others. The anecdotes' contents are meant to assess the validity of the descriptions and prescriptions relative to women's erotic behavior, formulated by the authors of the discourse, all of them men.

Technically, the anecdotic type of discourse produced in chapter three uses classical narrative artifices. In most of the anecdotes, *ghunj* refers to auditory effects (various noises and vocalizations) produced by women during intercourse that are heard by involuntary ear-witnesses, who relate the story in details, describing the noises. The witnesses are considered reliable by the principal narrator—al-Suyūṭī or another author quoted by him—their reports being reproduced in the text.

The use of the narrative technique of witnesses' testimonies is meant to increase the degree of persuasiveness and pretended authenticity of the anecdotes' content. Thus, the author creates a complex type of macro-discourse that uses testimonies as arguments in support of his thesis or views (as well as others' views, promoted by him) on women's erotic behavior. This becomes particularly relevant from the perspective of the institution of the "culture of gender" through the matrimonial literature.

5.1 *Vocalizations and Auditory Effects Produced by Women*

a) snorting and sobbing/moaning/sighing (*Sh1* 43; *Kitāb al-Aghānī*)

فشخرت ونخرت وأتت بالعجائب من الرهز وأنا أسمع.

> She snorted/snored and sobbed/moaned, and performed astonishing ways of *rahz* while I was hearing.

Context: a woman hears the noises accompanying the conjugal couple's intercourse; when the husband leaves the wife, the female involuntary witness addresses her disapproval with respect to the noise the wife had made.

Note: in the context, *rahz*—that usually refers to the man's or the couple's motion during intercourse (but can signify as well the woman's welcoming motion/undulation)—is used with reference to auditory effects; this could be either a secondary meaning or a metonymic (effect replacing cause) use in the sense of "woman's rhythmic sounds/vocalizations facilitating the man's movements".[14]

The wife replies to her female friend:

إنّا نستهبّ هذه الفحول بكل ما نقدر عليه وكل ما يحركها فما الذي أنكرت من ذلك؟

> We strive to awake these male organs in every way we can and by all means that set them in motion: so, what did you disapprove in this?

b) snorting and snoring heavily (*Sh1*43; *Tuḥfat al-ʿarūs*)

لما زُفّت عائشة بنت طلحة إلى زوجها مصعب بن الزبير سمعت إمرأة بينهما، وهو يجامعها، شخيرا وغطيطا في الجماع لم يسمع مثله. فقالت لها ذلك فقالت لها عائشة: إن الخيل لا تشرب إلا بالصفير.

> When ʿĀʾisha bint Ṭalḥa was given in marriage to her husband Muṣʿab b. al-Zubayr, a women heard between the two of them, while he was making love to her, noises of snorting and heavy snoring never heard before. She told her this, and ʿĀʾisha answered: truly, horses don't drink water without snoring/whinnying.

14 Cp. Firanescu, Amour 60.

c) complaining/reproaching (as a way of hyperbolizing the man's performance) (*Sh1* 44; *Sharḥ al-Maqāmāt*)

أقبل رجل على علي بن أبي طالب – رضي الله تعالى عنه—فقال : يا أمير المؤمنين إنّ لي إمرأة كلما غشيتها تقول : قتلتني قتلتني، فقال له علي رضي الله تعالى عنه : أُقتُلْها وعليّ اثمُها.

> A man came to ʿAlī b. Abī Ṭālib—may Allah be pleased with him—and told him: O, commander of the faithful, I got a woman who, at any time I sleep with her, says *you are killing me, you are killing me*; at this, ʿAlī—may Allah be pleased with him—replied: *kill her then, and I shall assume the sin*.

d) snorting/snoring like crazy (*Sh1* 45; *al-Qāmūs al-muḥīṭ*)

إمرأة منخار، تنخر عند الجماع كأنها مجنونة.

> A snorting woman is the one who snorts during the intercourse as if she were possessed/insane/crazy.

e) talking nonsense and obscenities (*Sh1* 45; *Kitāb Jāmiʿ al-ladhdha*)

تزوج قاض إمرأة من أهل المدينة فكان إذا غشِيَها أهجرت في القول وأفحشت، فاشتد ذلك على القاضي ونهاها عنه، ولما عاد إليها صمتت عن ذلك القول، ففتُرَ نشاطه، فلما رأى ذلك قال لها: عودي إلى عملك الأول.

> A judge married a woman from Medina. Every time he was sleeping with her, she was talking nonsense and saying obscenities, which became unbearable for the judge, so he took distance from her. When he returned to her, she abstained from saying what she used to say, so his vigor weakened, and when he saw this, told her: go back to what you used to do!

f) snorting and moaning/groaning/sighing/braying to bring out the water (*Sh1* 46; unspecified source)

قيل لامرأة : أي شيء أوقع في القلوب وقت النكاح، قالت: موضعٌ لا يسمع فيه إلا النخير والشهيق يجلب الماء من غشاء الدماغ ومخارج العظام.

A woman was asked: what is the most pleasurable thing during the intercourse? She said: a position in which one doesn't hear but snorting and moaning/groaning/sighing that brings the water out from the brain's membrane and the bones' articulations.

g) snoring, snorting, neighing, mumbling/growling/snarling, and whinnying (*Sh1* 46; unspecified source)

قال بعضهم : إنما يطيّب الن. . .ك شدة الرهز (. . .) والشخير والنخير والصهيل والهمهمة والحمحمة.

Some of them said: among the things that make f... ing enjoyable are snoring, snorting, neighing, mumbling/growling/snarling, and whinnying.

h) the silence of the fainting woman (*Sh1* 45; *Nasīb al-gharīb*)

قال : (. . .) زوجتي مجنونة (. . .) إذا جامعتها غُشي عليها. فقال: تلك الربوخ، لست لها بأهل، طلِّقها فطلّقَها، فتزوجها القاضي. قال ابن الدهان : أراد أن ذلك يحمد منها.

He said: (...) *my wife is insane (...), if I sleep with her, she loses consciousness. The other said: this is the fainting woman, and you are not to be married with her: repudiate her!* So he did, and the judge married her. Ibn al-Dahhān meant that this trait of her was laudable/praiseworthy.

The adjective (used as substantive) *rubūkh* designates the woman who faints during the intercourse because of the ardent desire (*min shiddat al-shahwa*—as stated in the foot note of *Sh1*); there is no effective characterization of the vocal/auditory effect accompanying this type of behavior, which may imply that the reaction of fainting is accompanied, at the acoustic level, by silence (fainting noiselessness, as extreme form of feminine erotic reaction).

5.2 *The Role of Copulatory Verbalization and Vocalizations*

They influence sexual activity by preventing the man's loss of vigor and virile performance. Their role is compared to various auditory stimuli in other human activities requiring hard work and effort; thus, they range among natural, stimulant effects accompanying natural occupations exerted in the ancient Arabs' environment. The following passage supports the idea that "*naturalia non sunt turpia*", implying that the human copulatory vocalization is an organic reaction that produces an acoustic effect stimulating sexual activity (*Shı* 46; *Nuzhat al-mudhākara*):

سماع ما يُلذّ له تأثير في النشاط. ألا ترى أن أهل الصناعات الذين يكدّون برا وبحرا اذا خافوا الملالة والفتورَ ترنموا وشغِلوا أنفسهم عن ألم التعب، وترى الشجعان وأبناء الحروب قد احتالوا بنفخ أصناف اليراعات وقرعوا الطبول لتهون عليهم الشدائد، وترى الإبل حين يحدولها الحادي فتُمعن في سيرها، ويُصْفَر للدواب فتردَ الماء وتشرب على الصفير.

> Hearing what produces pleasure has effect on sexual activity. Don't you see that those who work hard, by land and sea, when they fear getting bored and weak, they intone/chant/sing to distract themselves from [feeling] the pain of drudgery? You see that the braves and those who go to war resort to blowing various kinds of nays [shepherd flutes] and beat the drums in order to belittle the hardship; as you see that camels, when the caravan leader urges them forward by chanting, put all their efforts into the motion; [as you see that] riding animals are whistled at, so that they head towards the water source and drink, urged by the whistle.

5.3 *The Notion of* ghunj *in the Corpus* (*Chapters One-Three*)

Meanings:

- Extended/comprehensive meaning: "sensitive coquetry" in the sense of feminine flirtatious, seductive, and erotic behavior directed towards man/husband's pleasure and satisfaction. In this extended meaning, *ghunj* is the sexual component of the more encompassing notion of *ḥusn al-tabaʿʿul lil-baʿl/zawj* that accepts, depending on the context, two translations: "mastering the art of being a good wife to her husband", in a larger, more moral and ethical sense, and "behaving, sexually, in such a way to make the man/husband happy by granting him full satisfaction", in a more restrained, sex-centred context. In the latter sense, a synonym of *tabaʿʿul* (verbal noun of the denominative verb *tabaʿʿala,* built on the substantive *baʿl,* man/husband, with the feminine form *baʿla,* wife), used in the text, is *taṣannuʿ*, translatable, in the context of occurrence, by "affected/stilted/faking manner of talking" and interpretable as "talking in a manner that observes man's needs, sensitive to his needs".

- Restrained meaning: feminine copulatory verbalizations and vocalizations (auditory effects); synonym (sometimes encompassing additional, motional aspects): *rafath*.
- Peculiar meaning: the beauty/gracefulness/friendliness of the eyes. In *Shı* 42, the word *ghunj* appears with this meaning in the interpretation of the word *maḥabba* from Q 20:39 (Sura Ṭā-hā) *wa-alqaytu ʿalayka maḥabbatan minnī*... (And I endued thee with love from Me..., in Pickthall's translation)—that refers to Allah's gift to Moses—through *ghunj fī ʿaynayhi* (*ghunj* in his eyes). This interpretation or paraphrase is attributed to a certain al-Zahrī (the editor of *Shı* doesn't give details on him). Al-Suyūṭī extracts the paraphrase (and the whole chain of *isnād* that situates al-Zahrī as author of the above interpretation) from *Musnad al-Ṣūfiyya* by Ḥafṣ al-Mālīnī. *Lisān al-ʿArab* explains the meaning of *ghunj* in relation to eyes: *ghunj* is/signifies the beauty of [one's] eyes (*al-ghunju malāḥatu l-ʿaynayn*).

6 Final Remarks: Characterisation of the Discourse; Macro-Illocutionary Speech Acts;[15] Institution of the "Culture of Gender"

a. Al-Suyūṭī's discourse in the *CS* is not that of a theological work, although the author's theological background is apparent from some formulations and present in sub-text; it is rather meant to be entertaining, with a penchant to the spirit of *mujūn*[16] (libertinage, indulgence in pleasure) literature, a trend already consecrated in medieval Arabic literature, long before the fourteenth century. It represents a melange between the type of discourse produced in early (from eleventh-twelfth centuries CE), more conservative, religion-centred or purely theological texts on "rules/manners of the conjugal erotic behaviour" (*ādāb al-nikāḥ*)—such as al-Ghazālī's *Kitāb Ādāb al-nikāḥ*—in which the moral-ethical code of Islamic piety and sense of sexual modesty are preached, and the type of discourse produced in newer (thirteenth–fifteenth centuries CE), almost purely anecdotic texts, focusing on entertainment or vulgarizing fleshly desire for impudence and licentiousness. The resulting amalgam does not lack a touch of licentious humor that recalls the "fabliau" genre in French literature (dating from the twelfth century, with the apogee in the thirteenth-fourteenth centuries, a chronology reminding that of *adab al-nikāḥ* works, in Arabic literature).

15 The pragmatic notions related to discourse analysis and speech acts are borrowed from: Austin, *How to do*; Searle, Taxonomy; Searle & Vanderveken, *Foundations*.

16 Cp. definition by Rowson, Mujūn 546.

b. *The citrons' sisters* constitutes a relevant example of transgression of the religious, ethical, and legal treatment of *nikāḥ*—in the sense of "conjugal sexuality"—towards a treatment that privileges the pure erotic, performance-related view of sexuality, which is secular, worldly, in its essence. Indeed, al-Suyūṭī added other contributions to the literature on *nikāḥ* that, at his time, in the fifteenth century, was not anymore the field of "*ādāb*" (plural!) *al-nikāḥ* or rules/manners of the conjugal erotic behavior, but had become the domain of *adab* (singular, in the sense of belles-lettres) *al-nikāḥ* or purely erotic-sexist, anecdotic and entertainment literature. A particularly illustrative example is his *Nawāḍir al-ayk fī maʿrifat al-nayk* (The thicket's blooms of gracefulness: on the art of the fleshly embrace),[17] abundant in excerpts from erotic poetry, anecdotes, and descriptions of physical details related to the sexual organs, positions, etc.

c. The *CS* type of discourse is only partly "constative" or descriptive; it is largely "performative", with a strong directive/declarative component, aiming at creating a model of the ideal feminine erotic behavior and instituting it, through strong recommendations addressed to women, to conform to the instituted model.

The notion of "mastering the art of being a good wife" (*ḥusnu t-tabaʿʿul li-zawjihā*) is a good example of such aim at instituting a model: recurrent in the text (*Sh1* 34; 35 twice; other occurrences, in slightly different formulations), it is introduced in an authoritative manner, through excerpts from prophetical traditions, stating that the art of being a good wife is a woman's *jihād* and even more than that: it compensates for (or is the equivalent of) all that a Muslim man accomplishes through the duties ascribed to him as a man: the Friday prayer, the visit of the ill, the participation to funerals, the pilgrimage, the *jihād* on Allah's path (*Sh1* 35). The same notion is discussed, immediately after the illustrations through prophetical traditions, this time at the purely sexual level and under the authority of "the Persian scholars and Indian wise men, experts in sexuality." Performing declarative illocutionary acts, and placing itself under various authorities, this type of discourse not only institutes a model, but has the force emanating from an institution,[18] that of an "Islamic moral law of conduct imposed to women", a law that, ultimately, al-Suyūṭī represents, serves, and promotes through this text (and similar ones).

17 Our translation.

18 "Institutions characteristically require illocutionary acts to be issued by authorities of various kinds which have the force of declarations" (Searle, Taxonomy 360).

d. In the light of the above-mentioned considerations and from the perspective of the culture of gender, the discourse of *CS* is:

- man-centred: produced mainly by men; the author of the text and the cited authors are exclusively males. The text reflects men's position, interests, and authority; it explicitly or implicitly aims at women's conformation to men's prescriptions. The macro-illocutionary speech act, at the entire text's level, has the main components: "assertive" and "directive".
- man-oriented: women's behavior is described in evaluative terms, some echoing those used in the Islamic law: praiseworthy/laudable (*yuḥmadu* [*minhā*]), not disgusting/non-reprehensible (*ghayr makrūh*), disgusting/reprehensible (*makrūh*). The macro-illocutionary speech act performed through this type of recurrent utterances is "comissive" (with variations on the scale accept/consent→refuse/reject) and "declarative" (trying to "change the world by saying so," in Searle & Vanderveken's terms).[19]

e. Al-Suyūṭī selects from a vast matrimonial literature examples and anecdotes that compose a model of the ideal, recommended behavior of women/wives in the matrimonial love and sex relation, which is—according to the Islamic prescriptions and men's affirmed preferences—to please their husbands.

In Europe, during the same or almost same period—twelfth-thirteenth centuries—the discourse on sexuality was as well man-centred. Referring to "the articulation of sexuality in northern France around 1200," Baldwin[20] analyzes five discourses produced by men, to which he adds two feminine discourses from the same period, belonging to Marie de France and Marie d'Oignies; he notes that the discourse of the two women "did not differ markedly from their male contemporaries in their approach of sexuality." He states:

> Like previous studies, this present work is therefore subject to the overwhelming masculine bias of the surviving source materials. The male spokesmen constructed paradigms of gender relations in accordance with their underlying interests. As feminist critics have detected from traditional patriarchal discourse, their language was pervasively phalologocentric, and their presumptions were heterosexual. Male-female relations were translated into formulations that were both binary and reifications of foundational categories. According to R. Howard Bloch, they voiced the traditional misogynistic speech act in which woman is

19 Searle and Vanderveken, *Foundations* 37.

20 *Language*, Introduction xx.

the subject, and the predicate is a more general term (either negative or positive) that essentializes or abstracts the feminine condition.

The *CS* falls, under all the above-mentioned aspects, within the general frame of the Medieval, man-oriented erotic perspective.

f. The feminine figures in *CS*—protagonists of the anecdotes or participants to the dialogues inserted in the religious patrimonial texts—are presented either as "agents" perpetrating the acts described or prescribed by men, or as "witnesses" certifying the men's claims, serving as good illustrations of their ideas. The women's figures and discourse detectable in *CS* (as in other similar works by al-Suyūṭī) deserve to be the object of further examination resulting in a more comprehensible and revealing study of the "culture of gender" in the Mamlūk period and medieval Islam in general.

Bibliography

Primary Sources

al-Bukhārī, *Ṣaḥīḥ*, in M.M. Khan (ed. and trans.), *The translation of the meanings of* Ṣaḥīḥ al-Bukhārī, vii, Riadh 1997.
al-Ghazālī, Kitāb Ādāb al-nikāḥ, in *Iḥyā' 'ulūm al-dīn*, ii, Cairo n.d., 32–89.
Ibn Falīta (al-Yamanī), *Rushd al-labīb ilā mu'āsharat al-ḥabīb*, n. ed., al-Māya 2002.
Ibn Manẓūr, *Lisān al-'Arab*, 6 vols., Cairo n.d.
al-Nafzāwī, M., *al-Rawḍ al-'āṭir fī nuzhat al-khāṭir. Shahādāt wa-mukhtārāt*, ed. H. al-Khayyir, Damascus 1990.
al-Suyūṭī, [*Sh1*] *Shaqā'iq al-utrunj fī raqā'iq al-ghunuj* ed. 'Ā. al-'Āmil. Damascus 1988.
al-Suyūṭī, [*Sh2*] ed. Q.K. al-Janābī in *al-Imām Jalāl al-Dīn al-Suyūṭī: Faḍā'il al-nikāḥ*, Damascus 2013, 399–417.
al-Suyūṭī, *al-Wishāḥ fī fawā'id al-nikāḥ*, in Q.K. al-Janābī (ed.), *al-Imām Jalāl al-Dīn al-Suyūṭī: Faḍā'il al-nikāḥ*, rev. and intr. A. 'Umrān, Damascus 2013.

Secondary Sources

al-'Āmil, 'Ā. al-Turāth wa-l-jins, in 'Ā. al-'Āmil (ed.), *Shaqā'iq al-utrunj fī raqā'iq al-ghunj li-Jalāl al-Dīn al-Suyūṭī*, Damascus 1988.
Austin, J.L., *How to do things with words*, London 1962.
Baldwin, J.W., *The language of sex: Five voices from Northern France around 1200*, Chicago and London 1994.
Bloch, R.H., Introduction, in *The fabliaux*, trans. N.E. Dubin, New York 2013.
Bouhdiba, A., *La sexualité en Islam*, Paris 1975.

Chebel, M., *Encyclopédie de l'amour en Islam. Erotisme, beauté et sexualité dans le Monde Arabe, en Perse et en Turquie*, Paris 1995.

Firanescu, R., De l'amour et la coquetterie en islam arabe médiéval: la perspective d'as-Suyūṭī, in N. Anghelescu and G. Grigore (eds.), *Romano-Arabica* n.s. 2 (2002) (Discourses on Love in the Orient), 55–62.

al-Janābī, Q.K., Introduction, in Q.K. al-Janābī (ed.), *al-Imām Jalāl al-Dīn al-Suyūṭī: Faḍā'il al-nikāḥ*, Damascus 2013, 8–19.

Jumʿa, J., Muqaddima: al-Īrūtīkiyya al-ʿarabiyya, in J. Jumʿa (ed. and comp.), *al-Rawḍ al-ʿāṭir fī nuzhat al-khāṭir. The Perfumed Garden by Shaikh Nefzawi*, London 1989, ²1993, 11–7.

Kadar, G., Introductions, in G. Kadar (ed.), *Fann al-nikāḥ: Fī turāth shaykh al-islām Jalāl al-Dīn al-Suyūṭī* (Maktabat al-jins fī ḥayāt al-ʿArab), 3 vols., Beirut 2011, i, 9–49; ii, 9–11.

Kadar, G., Introduction, in *Nuzhat al-muta'ammil wa-murshid al-muta'ahhil fī Faḍā'il al-nikāḥ li-shaykh al-islām Jalāl al-Dīn al-Suyūṭī wa-l-shaykh Muḥammad Quṭb al-Dīn al-Aznīqī* (Maktabat al-jins fī ḥayāt al-ʿArab), Beirut 2012, 7–30.

Kazimirski Biberstein, A. de, *Dictionnaire Arabe-Francais*, 2 vols., Paris 1860.

Lacy, N.J., *Reading fabliaux*, New York and London 1993.

Rowson, E.K., Arabic [erotic literature]: Middle Ages to Nineteenth century, in G. Brulotte and J. Phillips (eds.), *Encyclopedia of erotic literature*, i, New York 2006, 41–61.

Rowson, E.K., Mujūn, in J. Scott Meisami and P. Starkey (eds.), *EAL*, ii, London and New York 1998, 546–8.

Searle, J.R., A taxonomy of illocutionary acts, in K. Gunderson (ed.), *Language, mind and knowledge* (Minnesota Studies in the Philosophy of Science 7) Minneapolis 1975, 334–9.

Searle, J.R. and D. Vanderveken, *Foundations of illocutionary logic*, Cambridge 1985.

ʿUmrān, A., al-Īrūtīkiyya: Ṭarīq al-madīna, in Q.K. al-Janābī (ed.), *al-Imām Jalāl al-Dīn al-Suyūṭī: Faḍā'il al-nikāḥ*, Damascus 2013, 5–7.

Index of Names*

(Persons; people, tribes, ethnic groups; juridical and theological schools; places)

Persons: Premodern

ʿAbd al-Bāsiṭ 106n35
ʿAbd al-Malik b. Marwān 98, 108
ʿAbd al-Raḥmān b. Jābir 191
ʿAbd al-Raḥmān b. Naṣr al-Shīrāzī *see* al-Shayzarī
Abū Bakr 52, 103, 150, 151nb
Abū Bakr al-Ismāʿīlī 188
Abū Dāʾūd al-Sijistānī 195, 229
Abū Dulāma 137
Abū l-Faraj ʿAbd al-Raḥmān b. Naṣr al-Shayzarī *see* al-Shayzarī
Abū l-Fatḥ al-Adīb 68n27
Abū Ḥāmid al-Qudsī 103n23
Abū Ḥanīfa 65, 185
Abū Ḥilāl al-ʿAskarī 74
Abū Ḥukayma 233
Abū Hurayra 148, 153
Abū l-Khayr al-Tinānī 137
Abū Muslim 74
Abū Shāma, ʿAbd al-Raḥmān 103, 104n24
Abū l-Shaykh 163n61
Abū Ṭālib al-Makkī 21, 22, 23, 36
Abū Yūsuf al-Qazwīnī 238
Adam 101, 237
ʿAḍud al-Dawla 108n42
Aḥmad (ʿAlī Bāy's brother) 52
Aḥmad al-Ḥākim bi-amr Allāh II 100, 101, 106, 106n33
Aḥmad b. Ḥanbal *see* Ibn Ḥanbal
Aḥmad al-Qaramānī 113
ʿĀʾisha 147, 150, 152, 154, 244
ʿĀʾisha bint Ṭalḥa 251
ʿAlī b. Abī Ṭālib 18, 52, 252
ʿAlī b. al-Midyānī 156
ʿAlī b. Naṣr al-Kātib 227n1
ʿAlī b. al-Walīd al-Muʿtazilī 238
ʿAlī Bāy 52
al-Āmidī 25, 33n50, 34
ʿAmr b. ʿAlī 191
Anas b. Mālik 65, 67, 184, 192
al-Anṣārī, Zakariyyāʾ 31, 32, 186
al-Āqṣarāʾī, Yaḥyā b. Muḥammad 56
Aristotle 203, 235
al-Ashʿarī 36, 37, 44
al-Ashraf Khalīl 104
ʿĀṣim b. ʿUmar b. Qatāda 149
Āsiya 56
Askiya al-Ḥājj Muḥammad 92, 92n60, 93, 93n62, 94
al-Asyūṭī, Abū l-Ṭayyib 48
al-Asyūtī, Kamāl al-Dīn 102n19, 156n38
ʿAṭāʾ b. Abī Rabāḥ 137
Avicenna 235
al-ʿAynī, Badr al-Dīn 182, 184
al-Azharī, Abū Manṣūr 74

al-Bājī, Abū l-Walīd 189
al-Bājūrī 26, 27n29, 29, 29n38, 30, 30n38, 31, 31n42, 32, 32n45, 33, 33n50, 34, 35, 36
al-Baqillānī 38
Barqūq, al-Nāṣirī al-Ẓāhirī 48, 48n10, 52
Barqūq, al-Ẓāhirī 56, 82
Bāyazīd II 112n63
Baybars I 75, 98, 103, 104, 104n26, 106, 109, 111, 111n57
Baybars II 105n29
al-Bayhaqī 76, 149, 151, 249
Bilāl 130, 132, 136
al-Biqāʿī 11
al-Birmāwī, Ibrāhīm b. Muḥammad 26, 29, 30, 30n39, 31, 33, 34, 35, 36
al-Birmāwī, Muḥammad 186
Bopp, F. 201, 203, 221, 224
Buffon, G.L. 202

* The article al-, l- is not considered for the alphabetical order.

al-Bukhārī 74, 150, 154, 156, 182, 187, 188, 191, 192n52, 193
al-Bulqīnī, ʿAlam al-Dīn 49, 128, 144n5, 185
al-Bulqīnī, Jalāl al-Dīn 144, 144n5, 148, 150, 152, 154, 156, 164, 165

al-Dhahabī 36, 128
al-Damāmīnī, Badr al-Dīn 186
al-Damīrī, Kamāl al-Dīn 60
al-Duwayhī 73

al-Fārābī 213n54
al-Fāsī 132
Fāṭima (niece of Shaqrā') 56
Fuḍayl b. Sulaymān 191

Galen 231, 235
al-Ghayṭī, Najm al-Dīn 12
al-Ghazālī 8, 12, 24, 28, 33, 34, 37, 38, 41, 43, 44, 84, 124, 255
Gilliéron, J. 221n80
Goethe, J.W. 203
Grimm (brothers) 203

Ḥafṣ al-Mālīnī 255
al-Ḥajjāj 235n25
al-Ḥākim al-Nīsābūrī 148, 149, 153
al-Ḥalabī, Abū ʿAbdallāh 130
Ḥām 120, 131, 132
al-Ḥārith b. Kalada 235n25
Hārūn al-Rashīd 108, 111n59
Ḥasan al-Baṣrī 18
Hippocrates 231
Ḥudhayfa 151

Iblīs 235, 237
Ibn ʿAbbās 22, 130
Ibn Abī Ḥajala 232n17
Ibn Abī Yaʿlā 74
Ibn al-Anbārī 211n50, 212, 212n51
Ibn ʿAqīl al-Ḥanbalī 238
Ibn al-ʿArabī 10, 11, 13n23, 16, 42, 44, 160, 161
Ibn ʿAsākir 129
Ibn al-ʿAṭṭār 64, 71, 72
Ibn Baṭṭāl 192
Ibn Baṭṭūṭa 72
Ibn Bint al-Aʿazz, Tāj al-Dīn 111, 111n59
Ibn al-Dahhān 253
Ibn Daqīq al-ʿĪd 33, 33n50, 34, 35
Ibn Durayd 231n14
Ibn Faḍl Allāh al-ʿUmarī 100, 101, 103n23, 105, 106
Ibn al-Fāriḍ 42, 161
Ibn Falīta al-Yamanī, Aḥmad b. Muḥammad 231n12, 248
Ibn Ḥajar al-ʿAsqalānī 8, 25, 26, 29, 31, 32, 32n43, 33, 33n48, 34, 60, 65, 73, 74, 156, 156n38, 157, 160, 182, 184, 185, 186, 188, 189, 190, 192, 193
Ibn Ḥajar al-Haytamī 12, 70, 76
Ibn al-Ḥājj 68, 75, 76
Ibn Ḥanbal 41, 65, 184, 189, 192, 192n52, 194
Ibn Ḥazm, ʿAbd Allāh b. Abī Bakr 149
Ibn Imām al-Kāmiliyya 9
Ibn al-ʿIrāqī, Walī l-Dīn Aḥmad b. ʿAbd al-Raḥīm 56
Ibn Isḥāq 149
Ibn Iyās 81, 107n38, 109, 111n59, 113
Ibn al-Jawzī 120, 129, 131, 131n70 and 77, 132, 135, 138, 139, 153
Ibn Jinnī 212n53, 214, 215, 216, 219, 222
Ibn Kamāl-Pāshā 227, 231n15
Ibn al-Karakī, Burhān al-Dīn Ibrāhīm b. ʿAbd al-Raḥmān 52, 53, 59
Ibn Khālawayh 207
Ibn Khaldūn 48n11
Ibn Māja 183, 195
Ibn Manẓūr 209n41
Ibn Masʿūd 160
Ibn Muzhir, Badr al-Dīn Muḥammad b. Abī Bakr 58
Ibn Qayyim al-Jawziyya 67, 69, 76, 192
Ibn Sabʿīn 11
Ibn al-Ṣalāḥ 25, 27, 29, 31n42, 34, 35
Ibn al-Shiḥna 56
Ibn Sīrīn 73
Ibn Taghrī Birdī 106n34
Ibn Taymiyya 8, 16, 38, 41, 41n79, 42, 44, 74, 76, 192, 193
Ibn al-ʿUqāb, ʿAbd al-Khāliq b. Muḥammad 59n62
Ibn al-Yamanī 151
Ibrāhīm (ʿAbbasid prince) 100–101
ʿIkrima 157
Īnāl al-Ashqar 48
ʿĪsā 131

Isḥāq b. Rāhawayh 192
al-Isnāwī 76
al-ʿIzz b. ʿAbd al-Salām 19, 33

al-Jabarī 156
al-Jadd b. Qays 149
al-Jāḥiẓ 119
Jalāl al-Dīn Maḥmūd b. ʿAlī b. Aṣfar 49n16
Japheth 131
al-Jawjarī, Muḥammad b. ʿAbd al-Munʿim 50, 51, 52
Jibrīl 190, 191
al-Jīlānī, ʿAbd al-Qādir 72n49
Jones 202n6
al-Junayd 8, 10, 11
al-Juwaynī 33

Kāfūr al-Ikhshīdī 137, 138
al-Kāfiyajī, Muḥyī l-Dīn 37n63, 48, 185
al-Kalābādhī, Abū Bakr 39, 44
al-Kalāʿī 70
al-Khaṭīb al-Baghdādī 76
Khunjī-Iṣfahānī, Faḍl Allāh b. Rūzbihān 103n23
al-Kurdī, Muḥammad b. Sulaymān 29, 34
al-Kutubī 68n27

al-Layth b. Saʿd 111n59, 192
Luqmān 130, 136

al-Malik al-Nāṣir 72
al-Manṣūr (Abū Bakr) 105
al-Maqrīzī 58, 60, 72, 105n31, 163, 163n65
Marie de France 258
Marie d'Oignies 258
Marʿī b. Yūsuf Karmī 113
Mary 154n28
al-Masʿūdī 234
al-Māwardī 76
al-Mīqātī, ʿAbd al-Khāliq 59
Misṭaḥ b. Uthātha 150, 151nb
al-Mu'ayyad Shaykh 55, 56, 184
Muḥammad Bābā al-Tinbuktī 92, 93
Muḥammad Ḥayāt al-Sindī 183
Muḥammad al-Maghribī 9
Mujāhid 157
Müller, M. 203, 203n8 and 10, 221, 224n88
al-Munāwī, Yaḥyā 49
Muṣʿab b. al-Zubayr 251
Muslim 148, 149, 153, 160
Muslim b. Abī Maryam 191
al-Mustaʿīn 112n62
al-Mustakfī bi-llāh I 100, 101, 105, 106
al-Mustakfī bi-llāh II 102n19
al-Mustanṣir bi-llāh 103, 106
al-Mutanabbī 137
al-Mutawakkil I 111n59, 112n62
al-Mutawakkil II 102, 102n19 and 20, 107, 107n38, 109, 109n49, 111n56, 112n63
al-Mutawakkil III 113
al-Muzanī 30, 31, 31n42, 33

al-Nābulusī 70
al-Nafzāwī 227
al-Nahrawālī, Quṭb al-Dīn 113
Najāshī 130, 131, 132, 136
al-Nasā'ī 183
al-Nāṣir Faraj 56
al-Nāṣir Muḥammad 100, 101, 105, 105n30, 106
al-Nāṣir Muḥammad IV 109
al-Nawawī, Muḥyī l-Dīn 25, 27, 30, 31, 31n42, 32, 32n43 and 45, 33, 33n48, 34, 35, 37, 76, 185
Noah 131, 132
Nūr al-Dīn Zengī 110n57

Plato 235

Qalāwūn 104, 104n27
al-Qalqashandī 72, 103n23
Qānṣawh al-Ghawrī 59, 82, 94
al-Qāsim b. Muḥammad b. Abī Bakr 231
al-Qasṭallānī, Shihāb al-Dīn 184, 186
Qāytbāy 48, 51, 52, 53, 53n32, 56, 57n50, 58n59, 75, 81, 82, 84, 86, 87, 94, 106, 107, 107n37, 109, 110, 112, 112n63

al-Rāfiʿī 30, 31, 32, 32n43, 33, 33n48
al-Ramlī, Shihāb al-Dīn 12, 25, 26, 29, 31, 32, 32n43 and 45, 33, 33n48
Rask, R. 203
al-Rāzī 36, 37

al-Sābūnī 76
al-Ṣafadī 76
Saʿīd b. Jubayr 157

al-Sakhāwī 48, 49, 106n35, 125n42, 146, 163, 163n65, 184
Ṣalāḥ al-Dīn 16, 54n34
al-Sanūsī 38
Sayyida Nafīsa 112n63
Schleicher, A. 201, 201n1, 202, 202n3 and 5, 203, 204, 217n69, 224
Schmidt, J. 203
Schuchardt, H. 203, 221n80
Selim 10n15
al-Shabrāmallisī 31, 32, 32n45
al-Shādhilī, ʿAbd al-Qādir 10, 17, 17n9, 43, 53n32, 59, 91, 109n49, 123, 124
al-Shāfiʿī 18, 24, 30, 31, 31n42, 33, 34, 43, 65
Shāh Suwār 56
Shaqrāʾ 56
al-Shaʿrānī, ʿAbd al-Wahhāb 10
al-Shayzarī, Abū l-Faraj ʿAbd al-Raḥmān b. Naṣr 234
Shaykh Sharmant 60
Shem 131
al-Shīrāzī 33
al-Shīrāzī, ʿAbd al-Raḥmān b. Naṣr *see* al-Shayzarī
al-Shirbīnī 31
al-Shumunnī 128
Shuqrān al-Ḥabashī 136
Sībawayhi 214n57
al-Sīrāmī, Shams al-Dīn Muḥammad b. Mūsā 185
al-Subkī, Tāj al-Dīn 18, 43
al-Subkī, Taqī l-Dīn 56, 61, 65, 69, 76, 76n70
Suḥaym 137
al-Sulamī, Ṣafwān b. al-Muʿaṭṭal 154
al-Suyūṭī *also see* al-Asyūṭī

al-Ṭabarānī 128, 130
al-Ṭabarī 128
al-Ṭahāwī 38
al-Ṭāʾiʿ 108n42
Tamīm al-Dārī 60
al-Thaʿālibī 66, 67, 76
al-Tīfāshī 231n15
al-Tirmidhī 128
Ṭumānbāy 53, 59, 81, 82
al-Turkumānī 65, 66, 71

Ubayy b. Kaʿb 22
ʿUmar 148
pact of 67, 73
Umm Ayman 136

al-Wadāʿī 246
al-Wāḥidī 148, 150, 151, 152, 153, 156, 157, 158, 166
al-Wansharīsī 12n19
al-Washshāʾ, Abū l-Ṭayyib 68n26
al-Wāthiq bi-llāh 101, 105, 106, 106n34 and 35

Yasār al-Ḥabashī 136

al-Zamakhsharī 215, 216
al-Zarkashī, Badr al-Dīn 60, 146, 155, 164, 165, 185, 186, 187, 188, 194
Zayd b. Thābit 22, 229

Persons: Modern

ʿAbd al-Ḥalīm Maḥmūd 12
Abū Isḥāq al-Ḥawaynī 183n6
al-Albānī 183n6
ʿAlī Jumuʿa 12
Arazi, A. 57n52, 58, 65
Asad, T. 196

Baalbaki, R. 214
Baldwin, J.W. 257
Bauer, T. 121
Berkey, J. 100n9
Blake, W. 182
Bloch, R.H. 257
Bloomfield, L. 215n64
Bourdieu, P. 196, 197
Brustad, K. 125

Calder, N. 24n24
Carter, M. 222
Chamberlain, M. 196
Chebel, M. 244
Cooperson, M. 134
Cragg, K. 147

Darwin, C. 201
Declich, L. 227n4, 228n5, 238
Donner, F. 129

Fattal, A. 67
Fernandes, L. 58n54
Fleisch, H. 210n48, 212
Fück, J. 209, 210, 211

Garcin, J.-C. 83, 98n2, 100, 100n9, 104, 110, 112
Genette, G. 128
Geoffroy, É. 83, 126, 207
Gibb, H.A.R. 133
Gilliot, C. 143, 145, 145n11, 165, 172n
Goldziher, I. 191n47, 195n62

Hallaq, W. 24, 28
Ḥammūda, T.S. 206, 209n42
Hasan, A. 222
Hassan, M. 99n5, 112
Hernandez, R.S. 47n1, 51n25
Hunwick, J. 92
Hurgronje, S. 30n38

Ikhwan, M. 163
Irwin, R. 163

Krawulsky, D. 172n

Lambton, A.K.S. 90
Lange, C. 193n56
Leder, S. 126
Lehmann 202n6
Lewis, B. 119, 120

MacIntyre, A. 196, 197
Maher, J.P. 202n5

Nemoy, L. 163
Newhall, A.W. 83
Nolin, K. 145, 159, 164, 165

Owens, J. 212, 212n51, 213, 220

Ratcliffe, R.R. 220
Rippin, A. 145n11, 154, 155
Rotter, G. 118, 119, 121, 138
Rowson, E.K. 241

Saleh, M. 110
Sartain, E.M. 47, 48, 49n12, 53, 58, 59, 86, 123, 185
Schacht, J. 30n38
Schimmel, A. 110
Shoshan, B. 146n17
Spevack, A. 237, 238
Suleiman, Y. 206, 219

Tritton, A.S. 67

Versteegh, K. 212n50
Voll, J. 157

Wansbrough, J. 148n20, 172n
Wasserstein, D. J. 70n41
Weber, M. 196
Winters, M. 90

Zuhayr ʿUthmān ʿAlī Nūr 143, 145

People, Tribes, Ethnic Groups

Abyssinians (*also see* Ḥabash) 118–142
Anṣār 132
Arabs 64, 66, 69n32, 74, 131, 210, 227, 253
Asad 218

Christians 37, 69, 73

Ḥabash/Ḥabasha/Ḥubshān 118n3, 122, 127, 129, 130, 131
Hudhayl 218

Jews 64, 69, 73, 74, 82

Kināna 218

Mongols 106

Persians 131, 250

Qays 218
Quraysh 91, 130, 132

Sūdān 119, 120, 129, 130, 131, 135

Tamīm 218
Ṭayyi' 218

Juridical and Theological Schools, Sufi orders

Aḥmadiyya 9
Ashʿarī 8, 15, 16, 18, 36–39, 41, 42, 43, 44
Atharī 16, 37, 38, 41, 42, 44

Ḥanafī 42, 56, 59, 65, 66, 75, 192
Ḥanbalī 16, 41, 43, 65, 72n49, 74, 192n54, 194

Mālikī 43, 65, 74, 82, 110n57, 186, 189, 192, 193, 194
Māturīdī 16, 18, 39, 42, 43, 44

Qādirī 16
Qādiriyya 9

Shādhilī 9, 10, 15, 16, 17, 37, 43, 161
Shāfiʿī 8, 15, 15n1, 16, 17, 17n9, 18, 19, 24, 25, 26, 29, 30, 31, 32, 36, 42, 43, 44, 47, 65, 66, 69, 72, 73, 74, 75, 76, 77, 110n57, 124, 185, 192, 193
Suhrawardiyya 9

Places

Abyssinia 118n3, 119n7, 120, 131n70, 136
Africa
  North Africa 125, 156n39
  North-West Africa 17, 38, 42
  West Africa 93n65, 183
Aleppo 55
Alexandria 124n40,
Algeria 12n19
Andalusia 192
Asyūṭ 48, 60n68
Azhar (mosque) 60

Badr (battle of) 136
Baghdad 10, 99, 103, 103n23, 104, 104n24, 113, 120
Barqūq al-Nāṣirī l-Ẓāhirī (tomb/mausoleum of) 48, 49, 52, 53, 53n32, 59, 82, 106, 124
Baybars II (mosque complex) 102n19
Baybarsiyya (khānqāh/madrasa) 48, 49, 51n25, 52, 53, 56, 57, 58, 59, 124
Bejaya 12n19
Byzantium 149

Cairo 10, 10n15, 47, 49, 50, 51, 52, 59, 92, 93, 98, 100, 101, 102n19, 103, 103n23, 106, 106n35, 107, 107n38, 108, 108n42, 110, 110n57, 113, 124, 146, 182, 183, 184
Citadel 52, 53, 52n32, 82, 107, 184

Damascus 103n23, 192n54, 196
Damietta 124n40
Dawrakī 55

Egypt 10n15, 12, 16, 17, 29, 39, 42, 57, 60, 64, 66n13, 92, 98, 99n5, 103, 103n23, 104, 104n24, 106, 106n35, 123, 124, 137, 163, 184, 186, 206n20
Ethiopia 125

France 257

Gao 92

Ḥabasha (land of) 118n3, 120, 130, 131
Hijaz 124, 125, 183
Holy Station 72
Ḥudaybiyya (treaty of) 189
al-Ḥujra (Medina) 51
Ḥunayn (battle of) 153, 153n23

Ibn Ṭūlūn (mosque) 47, 59, 145, 146
India 8, 125, 156n39, 186
Iraq 106, 119
Isfahan 64, 74
Istanbul 42, 113

Jakarta 42
Jawjar 50

Jenne 92
Jurjān 188

Kaʿba 72, 189
Khashshābiyya (zāwiya) 57n52
Khaybar 74

Maghrib 183
Maḥmūdiyya (madrasa/library) 49, 49n16
Mali 92
al-Masjid al-Ḥarām 51
Mecca 10, 51, 92, 153, 153n23, 160
Medina 51, 51n26, 52n28, 53, 103n23, 136, 160, 252
Muʾayyadiyya (madrasa) 50

Persia 74, 125
Prophet's mosque 51, 52

al-Qarāfa 48
  Bāb al-Qarāfa 60
Qāytbāy (madrasa) 51, 52n28, 53
Qijmāsiyya (madrasa) 50
Qūṣ 100, 105
Quṭbiyya (madrasa) 50

Rabat 92
Rawḍa 49
Rūm 125

Sahel 92
Ṣalāḥiyya (khānqāh) 57n52
Sayyida Nafīsa (shrine) 107
Shaykhū (mosque) 47, 48, 49n12, 59, 124
Shaykhūniyya (khānqāh/madrasa) 48, 49n12, 57n52, 59, 124, 184
Songhay Empire 92
al-Suyūṭī (zāwiya) 60
Syria 57, 92, 110n54, 123, 125, 184

Tabūk 149
Takrūr 8, 92, 93, 125
Timbuktu 92

Umm al-Sulṭān Shaʿbān (madrasa) 50

Yemen 125, 184, 186

Index of Titles*

Kitāb Adab al-khaṭīb 64
Kitāb al-Aghānī 250, 251
Af'āl (Kitāb Taṣārīf al-af'āl) 230
al-Aḥadīth al-ḥisān fī faḍl al-ṭaylasān 64, 75
al-Aḥādīth al-munīfa fī faḍl al-salṭana al-sharīfa 83, 88–94
al-Aḥādīth al-mutqana fī faḍl al-salṭana al-sharīfa (recte al-Aḥādīth al-munīfa fī faḍl al-salṭana al-sharīfa *see above*) 92, 93
Alf layla wa-layla 235
al-Asās fī faḍl Banī l-'Abbās 102
Azhār al-'urūsh fī akhbār al-Ḥubūsh 119

Badhl al-majhūd fī khizānat Maḥmūd 49
al-Bāhir fī ḥukm al-nabī bi-l-bāṭin wa-l-ẓāhir 9
Bahjat al-'ābidīn bi-tarjamat Jalāl al-Dīn 91, 123
Bulūgh al-umniyya *see* Ḥusn al-niyya wa-bulūgh al-umniyya fī l-Khānqāh al-Rukniyya
Kitāb al-Burhān fī 'ulūm al-Qur'ān 143, 144, 145, 146, 159, 164, 165, 173–5, 185

Dalā'il al-nubuwwa 149, 151, 249, 250
Darr al-ghamāma fī dharr al-ṭaylasān wa-l-'adhaba wa-l-'imāma 76
al-Dībāj 'alā Ṣaḥīḥ Muslim b. Ḥajjāj 183n6
Dīwān al-adab 213n54
Dīwān al-ṣabāba 232n17, 235
al-Durr al-manthūr fī l-tafsīr bi-l-ma'thūr 144n8, 153, 161, 163

al-Faḍl al-'amīm fī iqṭā' Tamīm 60
Kitāb Fakhr al-Sūdān 'alā l-Biḍān 119
al-Farīda fī l-naḥw wa-l-taṣrīf wa-l-khaṭṭ 92
Fatāwā (Taqī l-Dīn al-Subkī) 69
Fatḥ al-barī 66, 188, 189, 192
Fayṣal al-tafriqa bayna al-īmān wa-l-zandaqa 38
al-Fulk al-mashḥūn 75n67

Genesis (Book of) 132

al-Ḥabā'ik fī akhbār al-malā'ik 162–3
al-Ḥāwī lil-fatāwī 12, 50, 51, 53, 54, 55, 56, 61
al-Hay'a al-saniyya fī l-hay'a al-sunniyya 163
Ḥusn al-muḥāḍara fī ta'rīkh Miṣr wa-l-Qāhira (*also* Ḥusn al-muḥāḍara fī akhbār Miṣr wa-l-Qāhira) 98, 100, 102, 103, 163
Ḥusn al-niyya wa-bulūgh al-umniyya fī l-Khānqāh al-Rukniyya (also Juz' fī l-Khānqāh al-Baybarsiyya) 57n52

al-Īḍāḥ fī 'ilm al-nikāḥ 234–237
al-Ifṣāḥ fī asmā' al-nikāḥ 228
Iḥyā' 'ulūm al-dīn 38, 41
al-Ilmām bi-akhbār man bi-arḍ al-Ḥabasha min mulūk al-Islām 119n7
al-Ināfa fī rutbat al-khilāfa 84, 91
al-Inṣāf fī tamyīz al-awqāf 47n1, 50, 53, 54, 56, 60, 61n74
al-Iqtirāḥ fī uṣūl al-naḥw 206, 214, 216, 219, 220, 222
al-Iqtiṣād fī l-i'tiqād 38
Kitāb al-Itqān fī 'ulūm al-Qur'ān 41, 44, 143–181, 185, 214, 216

Jamhara (al-Jamhara fī l-lugha) 230
Jāmi' al-ladhdha (*also* Jawāmi' al-ladhdha) 227, 229, 231, 232n16, 250, 252
Juz' fī l-Khānqāh al-Baybarsiyya *see* Ḥusn al-niyya wa-bulūgh al-umniyya fī l-Khānqāh al-Rukniyya

Kashf al-ḍabāba fī mas'alat al-istināba 54, 59, 60
al-Khaṣā'iṣ 219, 222

Kitāb Laysa fī kalām al-'Arab 207
Lubāb al-nuqūl fī asbāb al-nuzūl 144, 156, 159

Mā rawāhu l-asāṭīn fī 'adam al-majī' ilā l-salāṭīn 83–87, 94
al-Mabāḥith al-zakiyya fī l-mas'alat al-Dawrakiyya 55

* The article *al-* and the word *Kitāb* are not considered for the alphabetical order.

Mabāsim al-milāḥ wa-mabāsim al-ṣibāḥ fī mawāsim al-nikāḥ 227n4, 228, 229, 230, 231, 232
Maqāmat al-nisāʾ *see* Rashf al-zulāl
Kitāb al-Maṣāḥif 229
Mawāqiʿ al-ʿulūm fī mawāqiʿ al-nujūm 144, 144n5, 165
al-Minaḥ al-ḥamīda fī Sharḥ al-Farīda 92
Murshid al-labīb ilā muʿāsharat al-ḥabīb 231
Murūj al-dhahab 234, 235n25
Musnad (Abū Ḥanīfa) 185
Musnad (Ibn Ḥanbal) 184
Musnad (al-Shāfiʿī) 185
Musnad al-Ṣūfiyya 255
Muʿtarak al-aqrān fī iʿjāz al-Qurʾān 145, 165
al-Mutawakkilī fī mā warada fī l-Qurʾān bi-l-lugha al-Ḥabashiyya ... 102
Muwashshā *see* al-Ẓarf wa-l-ẓurafāʾ
al-Muwaṭṭaʾ 184, 190
al-Muzhir fī ʿulūm al-lugha wa-anwāʿihā 163, 201, 207, 208, 209n42, 210, 212–4, 216–20, 222–3

al-Naql al-mastūr fī jawāz qabḍ al-maʿlūm min ghayr ḥuḍūr 54
Nasīb al-gharīb 253
Nawāḍir al-ayk fī maʿrifat al-nayk 227, 229, 230, 231–3, 235, 235n28, 236, 238, 256
Nuzhat al-ʿumr fī tafḍīl bayna al-Bīḍ wa-l-Sūd wa-l-Sumr 119

Qādimat al-janāḥ 230, 231
al-Qāmūs al-muḥīṭ 230, 252
al-Qawl al-mushayyad fī waqf al-Muʾayyad 55
Qūt al-qulūb 21

al-Radd ʿalā man akhlada ilā l-arḍ wa-jahila anna l-ijtihād fī kull ʿasr farḍ 18, 24, 29, 33n50, 43
Rafʿ al-bās ʿan Banī l-ʿAbbās 102
Rafʿ shaʾn al-Ḥubshān 118–42
Rashf al-zulāl min al-siḥr al-ḥalāl 233–4, 235n30, 237n36
al-Rawḍ al-ʿāṭir 227
Rawḍat al-azhār 230
Rawḍat al-qulūb wa-nuzhat al-muḥibb wa-l-maḥbūb 234

al-Risāla al-Baybarsiyya (*also see* al-Ṭalʿa al-shamsiyya fī tabyīn al-jinsiyya min sharṭ al-Baybarsiyya) 47n1, 57
al-Risāla al-Qudsiyya 38
al-Risāla al-Sulṭāniyya 83–87, 94
Kitāb Rujūʿ al-shaykh ilā ṣibāhu fī l-quwwa ʿalā l-bāh 227, 229, 231
Rushd al-labīb ilā muʿāsharat al-ḥabīb 231n12, 248

Ṣaḥīḥ (al-Bukhārī) 66, 154, 182, 183, 184, 186, 187, 188, 190, 192, 197, 244
Ṣaḥīḥ (Muslim) 148, 150, 183, 185, 190, 191, 194
Satanic Verses 237
Ṣawn al-manṭiq wa-l-kalām ʿan fann al-manṭiq wa-l-kalām 18, 37, 38, 41, 44
Shadd al-athwāb fī sadd al-abwāb 51, 61n75
Shaqāʾiq al-utrunj fī raqāʾiq al-ghunj 230–1, 232, 242–258
Sharḥ al-Maqāmāt 252
Ṣubḥ al-aʿshā 72
Sunan (Abū Dāʾūd al-Sijistānī) 66
Sunan (al-Nasāʾī) 183

al-Taʿarruf li-madhhab ahl al-taṣawwuf 39
Tadhkira (al-Wadāʿī) 232n18
al-Taḥadduth bi-niʿmat Allāh 123, 126, 230, 234
Kitāb al-Taḥbīr fī ʿilm al-tafsīr 143–181
al-Ṭalʿa al-shamsiyya fī tabyīn al-jinsiyya min sharṭ al-Baybarsiyya (*also see* al-Risāla al-Baybarsiyya) 57
Tanbīh al-ghabī bi tabriʾat Ibn ʿArabī 11
Tanbīh al-ghabī ilā takfīr Ibn ʿArabī 11
Tanbīh al-wāqif ʿalā sharṭ al-wāqif 56
al-Tanqīḥ li-alfāẓ al-Jāmiʿ al-Ṣaḥīḥ 185, 186, 188, 196
Tanwīr al-ghabash fī faḍl al-Sūdān wa-l-Ḥabash 119
Taʾrīkh al-khulafāʾ 98, 100, 102, 107
Taʾrīkh madīnat Dimashq 129
al-Tawshīḥ sharḥ al-Jāmiʿ al-ṣaḥiḥ 182, 185, 186, 188–96
Taʾyīd al-ḥaqīqa al-ʿaliyya wa-tashyīd al-ṭarīqa al-Shādhiliyya 10, 11, 15–46
Tuḥfat al-ʿarūs 227, 230–231, 250, 251
Tuḥfat al-kirām fī khabar al-ahrām 163

al-Wajh al-nāḍir fī mā yaqbiḍuhu al-nāẓir (*also* al-Wajh al-nāẓir fī mā yaqtaḍīhi al-nāẓir) 58, 110
al-Wishāḥ fī fawāʾid al-nikāḥ 227, 228–30, 231, 232, 233, 235n28

al-Yawāqīt al-thamīna fī ṣifāt al-samīna 228

al-Ẓarf wa-l-ẓurafāʾ 68n26

Printed in the United States
By Bookmasters